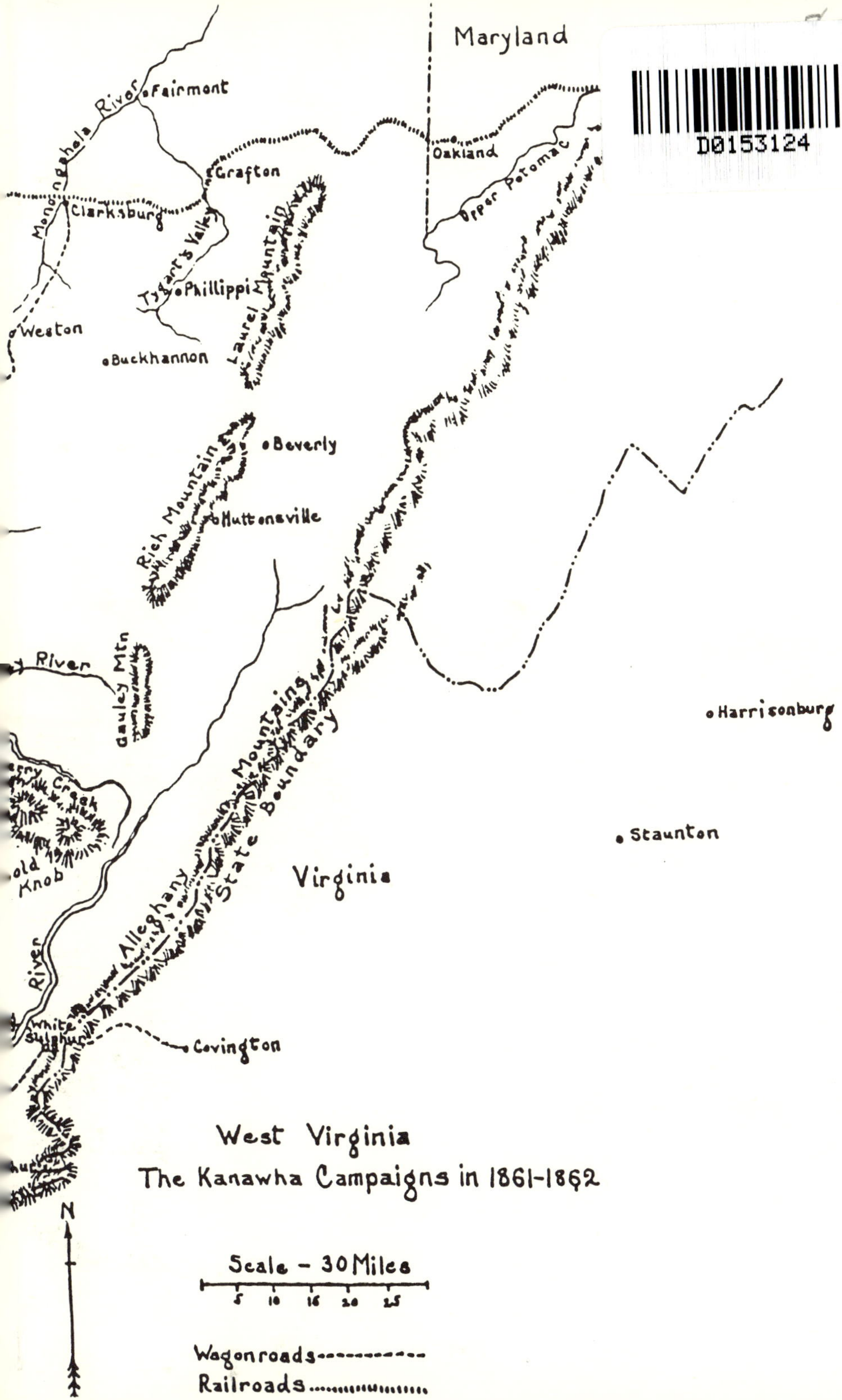


West Virginia
The Kanawha Campaigns in 1861-1862

# War Diaries:

## The 1861 Kanawha Valley Campaigns

By

David L. Phillips

and

Rebecca L. Hill, Chief Researcher

---

Leesburg, Virginia

1990

Published in Leesburg, Virginia, by Gauley Mount Press, 313 Lounsbury Court, NE, Leesburg, Virginia 22075.

LIBRARY OF CONGRESS
CATALOG CARD NO. 90- 85172

ISBN 0-9628218-0-2

Printed in the United States of America

# Preface

My purpose in this book has been to reconstruct some of the long-forgotten events that occurred in the southern portion of the state of West Virginia during the early days of the Civil War. There are many local stories in the area regarding the Confederate occupation of the area early in the war and the Union invasion that eventually secured the region from the Rebels to permit the Union loyalists to form a new state that would actively oppose the Confederacy.

Stories were told of a bridge that was burned at Gauley Bridge, of the destruction of the "ammunition dump" at Glen Ferris, and of the cannon which was lost on the summit of Cotton Hill, but few details were ever available to those interested in pursuing the story.

This study began as a research project designed to gather material for a historical novel on the area during that war, but as the true stories were located, I soon realized that the truth was far more fascinating than any fiction I would ever be able to construct. The central figures in the story were able to record their emotions and observations in such a way that I felt that many others would want to discover them.

They have told the story and their words were left intact as far as possible. Their misspellings and errors in grammar are left as in the original. Where previous editors corrected their mistakes in extremely distracting brackets, I have chosen to leave these errors in place. Each shows the rush or pressure the writer must have been under as he or she wrote while waiting on the initiation of combat or the landing of shells on a home.

My contribution was limited to the placing of events they were describing into historical perspective. There were events going on around them -- primarily on the other side -- about which they were unaware. I have tried to connect the events as far possible as seen from both sides of the story. This gives a fairly unique view of the war that was fought in the Kanawha Valley in 1861 and 1862.

What is shown in the story are the emotions of very

real people caught up in the first war where civilians became legitimate targets of the opposing forces and the wanton destruction of civilian property was a goal.

One of the reasons for continuing with this long-term effort involved the need to correct some of the misconceptions held in "legend" regarding Ellen Tompins. Some of the previous articles about the Civil War in the area didn't go as far as they should have in explaining her role. Many people felt that she was simply interested in saving her property and would "collaborate" with the Union forces in order to accomplish her goal. The actual story shows a very courageous woman who frequently defied her "captors" and may have been very active in supporting the Southern cause.

If there appears to be a Confederate bias in the development to the story, it is unintentional. If this is actually present, it is probably due to the surprise associated with the discovery of several unsuspected Rebels in the family tree. One was in the Confederate Artillery battalion which supplied guns and crews to fire on the Federal camp at Gauley Bridge in 1862.

If a dedication is necessary, this should be for the veterans of the war who took the time to write about their experiences in order to tell the story of this conflict to future generations. Their purpose was frequently obvious. Beuhring Jones, the commander of the 60th Virginia and a resident of Fayetteville, said:

***"... It is a duty we owe to ourselves and to posterity, to preserve a faithful record of the events that occurred during that fearful period, and thereby to warn all future generations to avoid the fatal whirlpool of civil contention."***

David L. Phillips
Gauley Bridge, West Virginia
Thanksgiving, 1989

Contents

Introduction
*Balance of Power Begins to Tilt* ................................1

Cast ......................................................................8

Section one
*So Excellent a Colonel*................................................17
The story of Christopher Quarles Tompkins, Captain, U.S. Army; Colonel, Confederate States Army; and the men of the 22nd Virginia Volunteer Infantry Regiment during the Kanawha Valley Campaigns of 1861 and 1862.

Section two
*Gentleman General*.....................................................80
The story of Brigadier General Joseph Dolson Cox, member of the Ohio Legislature, State Militia officer, and commander of the Federal forces that fought in the Kanawha Valley.

Section three
*Conflicting Duties*....................................................190
The story of Isaac Noyes Smith, attorney, member of the Virginia legislature, private in the Kanawha Riflemen, and Major, Confederate States Army.

Section four
*Mistress of the Mansion*...........................................289
The story of Ellen Wilkins Tompkins, wife of Christopher Tompkins, captive of General Cox, and friend to many sick men on both sides.

Section five
*The Rest of the War*..................................................378
The story of the activities and problems of the primary participants during the remainder of the war.

Section six
*Epilog*.......................................................................463

Index.........................................................................465

## *BALANCE OF POWER BEGINS TO TILT*

*Amalgamation is ther theme*
*And that will never do*
*Come lets go down to the Battle ground*
*And Whip the Nothern Crue*[1]

*Politically, the United States had been relatively stable until the middle of the 1840's. A balance of power had developed within the Congress over the issue of slavery and the dominant Democratic party was fairly well-controlled by Southern interests. The Democrats had developed the concept of "Manifest Destiny" and were willing to use force to spread their enlightened institutions throughout the continent. Manifest Destiny became a campaign issue in the election that brought President Polk into office and the campaign slogan "54-40 or Fight" left little doubt in the minds of Canadians regarding the territorial goals of the Democrats. Their party platform also demanded a southern border for Texas on the Rio Grande River. Polk later compromised with Great Britain in the north, but was soon to send American troops against Mexico. The Democrats, however, weren't the only political party in the Congress. The opposition Whigs were against the war from the start, but the Democratic majority controlled the issue when it was put to a vote. The Whigs were able to make a political issue of the war by criticizing its conduct and they also opposed any territorial gains made at the expense of Mexico through conquest -- a primary goal of the Democrats.*

*The Whigs were later able to gain control of the House of Representatives and continue their attack on the Democrat administration. A new Whig Congressman from Illinois, Abraham Lincoln, was quite active in the House debates. The Whigs were soon able to pass a resolution that*

1 Howe, Henry. *The Times of the Rebellion in the West;* Cincinnati: 1867. This set of verses was captured at Camp Gauley after the battle of Carnifex Ferry in 1861

*declared the war was unconstitutionally started by President Polk.*

*When the fighting was over, the treaty with Mexico resulted in the acquisition of more territory for Texas, portions of Oklahoma, Colorado, and Wyoming, and added totally new areas that were to become New Mexico, Arizona, Nevada, Utah, and California. The young country had more than doubled the amount of territory under its control and now serious questions began to develop that would eventually result in Civil War.*

*The central issue involved the institution of slavery -- would the Southerners be permitted to take their slaves into the newly-obtained territories? This basic question became one of the largest problems the Congress was ever to face and the debates eventually changed the political complexion of the nation.*

*Two very different sections had developed in the young country -- free and slave -- but the differences went beyond the single issue of slavery. These two groupings of states were different economically, educationally, socially, and practically the only major institution that was in common were the two political parties -- Democrats and Whigs. There were Northern Whigs and Southern Whigs and Democrats were spread throughout both regions where they normally voted along party lines. The war with Mexico would change all of this and the Wilmot Priviso --an amendment to a war appropriations bill -- was the legislative catalyst which started the changes. This amendment simply stated that slavery would not be permitted in any territory gained from Mexico. Wilmot, a Pennsylvania Democrat, proposed the legislation for Northern Democrats trying to regain control of their party from their Southern counterparts and a Northern coalition, composed of the Northern Democrats and Whigs, were able to pass the Proviso over the objecting votes of the Southern Democrats and Whigs in the House of Representatives. This was a new development in American politics -- the party unity that had been common on previous issues was now in the past as the country's political affairs began to reflect regional views.*

*Wilmot came back to the House floor the following Congressional session to defend his Proviso which was under serious attack from Southern interests. His speech is interesting:*

*"Sir, It will be recollected by all present, that, at the last session of Congress, an amendment was moved by me to a bill of the same character as this, in the form of a proviso, by which slavery should be excluded from any territory that might subsequently be acquired by the United States from the Republic of Mexico.*

*"Sir, on that occasion, that proviso was sustained by a very decided majority of this house. Nay, sir, more, it was sustained by a majority of the Republican party on this floor. I am prepared, I think, to show that the entire South were then willing to acquiensce in what appeared to be, and, in so far as the action of this house was concerned, what was the legislative will and declaration of the Union on this subject. It passed this House. Sir, there were no threats of disunion sounded in our ears. It passed here and went to the Senate, and it was the judgement of the public, and of men well informed, that, had it not been defeated there for want of time, it would have passed that body and become the established law of the land....*

*"...There was then no cry that the Union was to be severed in consequence. The South, like brave men defeated, bowed to the voice and judgement of the nation. No, sir, no cry of disunion then. Why now? The hesitation and the wavering of the northern men on this question has encouraged the South to assume a bolder attitude. This cry of disunion proceeds from no resolve of the South. It comes, sir, from the cowardice of the North....*

*"But, sir, the issue now presented is not whether slavery shall exist unmolested where it now is, but whether it shall be carried to new and distant regions, now free, where the footprint of the slave cannot be found. This, sir, is the issue. Upon it I take my stand, and from it I cannot be frightened or driven by idle charges of abolitionism. I ask not that slavery be abolished. I demand that this Government preserve the integrity of free territory against*

*the aggressions of slavery -- against its wrongful usurpations. Sir, I was in favor of the annexation of Texas....The Democracy of the North, almost to a man, went for annexation. Yes, sir, here was an empire larger than France given up to slavery. Shall further concessions be made by the North? Shall we give up free territory, the inheritance of free labor? Must we yield this also? Never, sir, never, until we ourselves are fit to be slaves. The North may be betrayed by her Representatives, but upon this great question she will be true to herself -- true to posterity. Defeat! Sir, there can be no defeat. Defeat to-day will but arouse the teeming millions of the North, and lead to a more decisive and triumphant victory to-morrow.*

*"But, sir, we are told, that the joint blood and treasure of the whole country being expended in this acquisition, therefore it should be divided, and slavery allowed to take its share. Sir, the South has her share already; the instalment for slavery was paid in advance. We were fighting this war for Texas and for the South. I affirm it -- every intelligent man knows it -- Texas is the primary cause of this war. For this, sir, northern treasure is being exhausted, and northern blood poured out upon the plains of Mexico. We are fighting this war cheerfully, not reluctantly -- cheerfully fighting this war for Texas; and yet we seek not to change the character of her institutions. Slavery is there: there let it remain....*

*"Now, sir, we are told that California is ours; that New Mexico is ours -- won by the valor of our arms. They are free. Shall they remain free? Shall these fair provinces be the inheritance and homes of the white labor of freemen or the black labor of slaves? This, sir, is the issue -- this is the question. The North has the right, and her representatives here have the power.... But the South contend, that in their emigration to this free territory, they have the right to take and hold slaves, the same as other property. Unless the amendment I have offered be adopted, or other early legislation is had upon this subject, they will do so. Indeed, they unitedly, as one man, have declared their right and purpose to do so, and the work had already begun. Slavery follows in the rear of our armies. Shall the war power of*

*our Government be exerted to produce such a result? Shall this Government depart from its neutrality on this question, and lend its power and influence to plant slavery in these territories? There is no question of abolition here, sir. Shall the South be permitted, by aggression, by invasion of the right, by subduing free territory, and planting slavery upon it, to wrest these provinces from northern freemen, and turn them to the accomplishment of their own sectional purposes and schemes? This is the question. Men of the North answer. Shall it be so? Shall we of the North submit to it? If we do, we are coward slaves, and deserve to have the manacles fastened upon our own limbs."*[2]

*Wilmot was prophetic in one way. His statement "Defeat to-day will but arouse the teeming millions of the North, and lead to a more decisive and triumphant victory to-morrow" was, unfortunately, accurate. The fear that one section would become more politically powerful than the other fueled the fires of these arguments and the spiral toward violence continued.*

*The fear that developed as the uncertain shifting of this balance of power continued was also an important political as well as a psychological factor as previously unheard of political alliances and coalitions began to form. Northern politicians from both parties feared any additional Southern control within the Congress. Few non-slave states had been admitted to the Union since the Revolution, but five additional slave states had been admitted along with ten extra slavery votes in the Senate and the potential for many more votes in the House. Most Northern political leaders were concerned that most of the newly acquired territory would also be admitted as slave states and they would find themselves totally controlled by a Congress dominated by Southern interests. This political fear -- not some moral superiority regarding human rights for the slaves -- began to split the nation into two hostile*

[2] *Wilmot, David; "Wilmot Defends His Proviso", America, Great Crises in Our History as Told by its Makers,* Vol. III, 1925, pg. 81-84

*sections. Political domination of one group by the other was the central issue. Slavery was one of the symptoms of the problem, but not because a majority of those who opposed it did so for moral purposes.*

*Most Americans who opposed the spread of slavery did so because they felt that free labor resulted in more rapid economic development. They believed that ambition for a better life resulted in upward mobility of the individual and that this would lead to increased prosperity for everyone. They felt that slavery reduced opportunities for poor whites to adequately develop themselves and that large areas would remain in poverty -- except for the slave-owning aristocrats who also controlled the region's political infrastructure.*

*While Northern Democrats and Whigs feared Southern domination, Southerners were also afraid that the potential addition of ten new free states would leave them firmly in the control of the Northern wings of their political parties. Southerners felt they had a legitimate claim to settling the new land since most of the territory gained from Mexico was below the old Missouri Compromise line of 36 degrees - 30 minutes where slavery* **was** *permitted. Southern politicians also felt they had earned special priviledges in the region since they had furnished most of the soldiers who fought in the Mexican War. The fear on both sides began to cause a hardening of opposing positions.*

*The debates on the subject of slavery in the new territories began to include the words Civil War and Secession -- primarily as Southern politicians worked these words into their speeches to sway the votes of moderate Congressmen in key roll calls. The moderates generally voted the Southern way rather than risk a confrontation that could lead to a disintegration of the Union.*

*Compromise after compromise held the two sides together, but the gulf that was beginning to split them gradually began to widen. The constant barrage of rhetoric from both sides for over a decade resulted in hardened attitudes in the general population in both regions of the country. This was one of the major reasons that the war to come was fought with such intensity -- constant political propaganda from the leadership of both sides convinced the ordinary citizens in each region that their way of life was threatened by the other side and after hearing this for fourteen or fifteen years,* ***everyone was quite willing to fight.***

## CAST

*(In order of appearance)*

**Henry A. Wise:**

Confederate brigadier-general, commander of Wise's Legion and former governor of Virginia who signed the death warrant of John Brown. Wise was the initial Rebel commander in the Kanawha valley campaigns.

**Jacob D. Cox:**

Federal brigadier-general in command of the Union troops from Ohio when these were ordered into the Kanawha valley to confront those forces under Wise. Later occupied the area for the Union and was a Corps commander in the battles at Atlanta.

**George McClellan:**

Federal major-general in command of all of the volunteer forces from Ohio. Crossed into northwestern Virginia and his troops fought the first land battle of the war at Philippi. He was soon ordered to take command of the Army of the Potomac and served in that capacity until relieved by Lincoln.

**Christopher Tompkins:**

Confederate colonel in initial command of the Virginia volunteers recruited in the Kanawha valley for the Confederacy. He participated in most of the early fighting, but left the service and worked for the remainder of the war at the Tredegar Works in Richmond.

**John B. Floyd:**

Confederate brigadier-general in command of a brigade and the forces under the command of Wise in the Kanawha valley fighting. He had been both a governor of Virginia and the Secretary of War in the Federal government. Floyd was under indictment in Federal court for acts alleged to have been committed while in office and greatly feared capture by the Union army which would deliver him to trial.

**William Walker:**

A former physician from Tennessee who was a major leader of the "filibusters", a group of southerners who attempted to conquer territory for southern interests in Latin America where slavery could be extended. Walker was able to capture and hold Nicargua for a few years before being forced from power. He was later captured and executed in a similar attempt. Several veterans of Walker's expeditions were serving as officers in Wise's Legion.

**Ellen W. Tompkins:**

The wife of Christopher Tompkins. She was from Baltimore and lived at Gauley Mount, their farm which was located on a mountain top a few miles to the east of Gauley Bridge, Virginia. She and her children were held by the Union garrison which occupied the area in the summer of 1861 and the surrounding region was the scene of numerous small battles and skirmishes during the early part of the war.

**William S. Rosecrans:**

A Federal major-general who assumed command of all the Union forces in western Virginia after General McClellan left for Washington. Rosecrans was commander of the Federals in the area of Gauley Bridge when the majority of the fighting occurred. He was to continue to have a distinguished military career during the early phases of the war.

**James H. Miller:**

He was the postmaster at Gauley Bridge and owned the town's inn and stage stop. He was apparently a Confederate sympathizer and his son accompanied Ellen Tompkins to Richmond when she was first permitted to leave the farm.

**John McCausland:**

He was a colonel in the Confederate army during the initial stages of the war and was involved in mobilizing the volunteers in the Kanawha valley for the Confederacy. He commanded the 36th Virginia Volunteer Infantry Regiment and was later to gain noterity when he ordered the burning of Chambersburg, Pennsylvania.

**George S. Patton:**

Initially, he was the commander of a Confederate company, the Kanawha Riflemen and served in the 22nd Virginia under Christopher Tompkins. He was later killed in the third battle of Winchester, Virginia. Patton was the grandfather of George Patton of World War II.

**John K. Thompson:**

He was a VMI cadet sent into the Kanawha valley with John McCausland to drill troops rallying to the Confederacy. He was wounded in several battles and lost an eye, but remained in Confederate service. He was the son of a western Virginia physician and was familar with both the area and its' inhabitants.

**William F. Bahlmann:**

Bahlmann was a member of the "Fayetteville Rifles", a volunteer company that was incorporated into the 22nd Virginia.

**Beuhring H. Jones:**

Initially, Jones was a Confederate captain who participated in the early fighting in the Kanawha valley. He was later to become the commander of the 60th Virginia Infantry and was captured during the battle of Piedmont. He wrote and edited a book of stories and poetry while held as a prisoner of war called *The Sunny Land.*

**James M. Corns:**

Corns was a Mexican War veteran who organized a cavalry company for Confederate service which was incorporated into the 8th Virginia Cavalry.

**Issac N. Smith:**

He had a diverse background: an attorney, a member of

the Virginia legislature, a private in the "Kanawha Riflemen", and later a major in the 22nd Virginia Infantry. He served under and was the close friend of Christopher Tompkins. He left Confederate service after the winter campaign at Cotton Hill. His father, Benjamin Smith, was a leading Unionist in the valley and was a organizer of the state of West Virgina.

**Robert E. Lee:**

Lee was the commander of the Virginia state forces at the time of the opening battles of the war. He was new to command at this level and was unable or unwilling to manage the constantly bickering generals serving under him, Wise and Floyd. He had served under Floyd while the latter was Secretary of War and had been involved in capturing John Brown -- in Virgina -- while Wise was the state governor. Lee later discovered his ability in leading men in war and became a legendary figure in American history.

**O. Jennings Wise:**

He was the commander of the premier pre-war militia company in Virginia, the Richmond Light Infantry Blues. and accompanied his father, Henry Wise, into the Kanawha valley. Captain Wise provided guards for Ellen Tompkins' property at Gauley Mount and was later killed at Roanoke Island while attempting to hold off an amphibious assault under Federal General Burnside.

**Charles F. Henningsen:**

He was an englishman who had served as a soldier of fortune in several of the world's conflicts, including the filibuster invasions of Latin America. He served as a colonel in Wise's Legion.

**Henry Heth:**

Heth served as a Confederate colonel in Floyd's brigade, but later became a general and served with distinction.

**William W. Loring:**

He was a Confederate brigadier-general serving under Lee in the Cheat Mountain area of western Virginia. Loring was a veteran of the Mexican war where he served as a major. His prestige in the early phases of the war was great. He had distinguished himself as a major in a war where Lee had been a captain and Stonewall Jackson had served as a lieutenant. He was relieved after misinterpreting, misunderstanding, or disregarding his orders to hold the Kanawha valley following the successful 1862 invasion.

**William C. Reynolds:**

Confederate private from the "Kanawha Riflemen" who served with the 22nd Virginia in the Kanawha valley fighting.

**James Sedinger:**

He was a member of the "Border Rangers", a volunteer cavalry company which later was incorporated into the 8th Virginia Cavalry.

**Albert G. Jenkins:**

Initially a captain in command of the "Border Rangers", but later colonel of the 8th Virginia cavalry. Jenkins became one of the best cavalry commanders in the Confederate army, but was mortally wounded in the battle of Cloyd's Mountain in southwestern Virginia.

**Lieutenant-Colonel Frizell:**

He was an excellent combat commander of the 11th Ohio Volunteer Infantry during the Kanawha valley fighting. He assumed command after DeVilliers was captured. He later resigned his commission from the Union army.

**Philander P. Lane:**

A company commander in the 11th Ohio, Lane was the engineer who rebuilt all of the bridges which were destroyed during Wise's retreat from the Kanawha valley. Lane was able to re-build the bridges nearly as fast as the Confederates were able to burn them and the Federal pursuit was always close to the retreating Rebels. He later forced the dual court martial of both himself and Colonel DeVilliers in order to remove the unjust and unskilled colonel from command.

**General Benham:**

Initially, he was an engineer captain in the Federal army, but was appointed a brigadier-general. He participated in the Kanawha campaigns until his slowness to manuever permitted the escape of the entire Confederate army under Floyd. He was dismissed by Rosecrans and recommended for court martial.

**E. B. Tyler:**

He was a Federal colonel in command of the Seventh Ohio Volunteer Infantry Regiment. This unit was surprised at breakfast by the attacking Confederates at the battle of Cross Lanes and nearly destroyed.

**St. George Croghan:**

Croghan was the cavalry commander in Floyd's small army. He was killed at the skirmish at McCoy's Mill during the retreat of the Rebel army from Cotton Hill in late 1861.

**Joel H. Abbott:**

He was a Confederate cavalryman assigned to the 8th Virginia cavalry. He was from the Fayetteville, Virginia, area and was a guide who lead the Confederate artillerymen to positions on Cotton Hill above the town of Gauley Bridge. The Federal camp was shelled over a period of nearly two weeks and when this tactic was repeated in 1862, Abbott later reported that a cannon was left in a concealed location on the mountain.

**Colonel DeVilliers:**

A Frenchman, he claimed to be a veteran of the French

army who had served in Algiers. He was a drillmaster in the Ohio regiments and was later elected colonel of the 11th Ohio. He served in this capacity until he mistakenly rode up to Confederate officers following the battle of Scary Creek and was captured. He was later able to rejoin the regiment, a fact regretted by all, and he remained in command until cashiered from the service after a court martial.

**"Plus":**

The nickname of Noyes Rand, a member of the "Kanawha Riflemen" and later adjutant of the 22nd Virginia. He was a close associate of Issac Smith.

**Joab Smith:**

He was a school teacher who enlisted into the Confederate regiments being organized in the Kanawha valley. He was the cousin of Isaac Smith, but hated his Unionist uncle, Benjamin -- Isaac's father. Joab Smith was later to die of disease contracted on Sewell Mountain.

**Sarah Cooch:**

She was the sister of Ellen Tompkins who lived in Delaware. Ellen frequently wrote to her sister, Sarah, and the letters were preserved.

**Rutherford B. Hayes:**

He served as an officer in the 23rd Ohio Volunteer Infantry Regiment and was later appointed to serve as the Judge Advocate of Cox's small Union army. He later was to distinguish himself in the war and was elected President of the United States.

**Milton W. Humphries:**

A young student at Washington College when the war erupted, Humphries enlisted in a Confederate artillery battery and became a sergeant before the end of the war. He participated in most of the fighting in the Kanawha valley and served in Early's Shenandoah valley campaign. He is credited with the development of indirect artillery firing which he used in the battle of Fayetteville, Virginia, in 1862.

**John A. J. Lightburn:**

A veteran of the Mexican War, this boyhood friend of Stonewall Jackson was the commander of Federal forces in the Kanawha valley during the 1862 invasion of Confederates under W.W. Loring.

**Donald McDonald:**

This Federal sergeant is credited with destroying the new suspension bridge over Gauley River just prior to its capture by Loring's forces in 1862. McDonald was captured the following day by Confederate sergeant Andrew Summers and sent to prison.

**Andrew Summers:**

He was a Confederate sergeant who captured Union sergeant McDonald after the latter had managed to destroy the strategic bridge over Gauley River in 1862. Summers was a member of the 60th Virginia and was himself captured after the Rebel defeat at Piedmont in 1864 -- by Sergeant McDonald, the man he had captured at Gauley Bridge.

## *Christopher Quarles Tompkins*

*Christopher Tompkins is the single figure who links the stories of the others in this study together. He was the enemy of General Cox, the commander and friend of Isaac Smith, and the husband of Ellen Tompkins. He is the central figure in the study, but unfortunately, there is little in the written record which was done personally by him. His few letters and his 1863 diary have been examined, but most of the material on Tompkins was developed from the writings of others.*

*He was a professional soldier in an army managed by amateurs -- and even worse, politicians. This habit of placing political appointees in command of military units was a long-standing practice in the National government and was a practice which was greatly disliked by the professional officers in service at the time. Tompkins was to experience several of these "political Generals" during the course of his career and eventually left the Army.*

*Christopher Tompkins was a man of honor who was living at a time when the previously-held romantic notions regarding warfare were about to be sorely tested as modern warfare tactics were evolving. He held strongly to his principles and eventually left Confederate service because of his concern for his family's safety, worries about Isaac Smith and the men of his 22nd Virginia, and his desire to "mitigate atrocities" as the level of combat began to escalate.*

## So Excellent A Colonel

*Be brave and Bold you Valiant boys*
*and keep your Armors Bright*
*For Sothern boys Wonts nothing else*
*But just the things that right*[1]

The eagle flew high in the overcast sky, but was still able to see what the small figures were doing on the mountain top. There appeared to be two separate groups of men and each side wore distinctive clothing. Those occupying the eastern summit had coats that were either grey or brown while the men on the smaller, western mountain top wore dark blue clothing.

There was a greater difference between the two sides than the type and color of their garments. The sharp-eyed eagle watched as the men wearing grey moved out of their fortifications in a long, open line and began to move toward the opposite camp. The soldiers in blue responded with both noise and smoke without leaving the security of their camp as the others began to slow their advance as a few fell to the ground. Those who fell frequently cried out in pain as their clothing slowly became stained with red.

The eagle was confused by all of this. He had an instinctive fear of the smoke and noise and he began to circle higher into the stormy sky. These people were crazy! There was no reason to remain to watch all of this and there was no obvious reason for all of the violence that it had witnessed. The grey and brown men had made several attempts to get into the entrenchments of the blue men and after each run forward, they would withdraw, pick up their injured friends, and return to their camp. There was so little in all of this to be gained. The single thing that the grey men had to show for their repeated efforts was several additional injured men.

The eagle had seen enough of this. He could spend his

[1] Howe, Henry; *The Times of the Rebellion in the West*; Cincinnati: 1867, pg. 48. This set of verses was captured at Camp Gauley following the battle of Carnifex Ferry.

time more productively soaring along the high cliffs adjacent to New River. He could always count on a fish meal easily taken from one of the osprey -- a better fisherman than the eagle. Fighting for food was something that the eagle could comprehend, but the fighting for the hilltops which was going on below was impossible to understand. Maybe by watching for a little longer he would be able to figure out this stupidity, but the weather was getting worse and there was a good chance that the osprey was out catching an evening meal for the both of them.

One of the men dressed in grey watched the eagle as it circled high above the rain-drenched hillside. He sat inside the front opening of a slab-camp, a three-sided structure that had been recently constructed to keep some of the officers dry. The men from his Twenty-second Virginia Infantry Regiment had volunteered to build this crude structure for a special few of their officers -- even before they had managed to get themselves out of the elements. They were good, brave men and didn't deserve the stupidity which had lead them into all of this.

The weather was terrible. Cold and constant rain had been their continuous companions since the Confederate troops had first arrived here, but the weather was not the cause of the depression that the Rebel Colonel was experiencing. He had been in cold, wet weather before and would never think of sparing himself or the men any necessary hardships, if the performance of duty required that everyone become wet and uncomfortable. The present military situation had no great effect on him. He was a brave man who had experienced combat in far more difficult circumstances than this mountaintop war's setting. He had been responsible for the safety and the conduct of those placed under his command since the day he graduated from West Point. The military career he had chosen for himself so long ago would have been exactly as he had imagined it in his youth, if his superior officers had been selected with only half the thought that had gone into his training. The political appointees posing as generals had been a serious problem for his career in the past and he had left the regular army because of them and the rediculous practice of placing militarily-illiterate appointees in command of troops in combat. This practice wasn't a dangerous problem as long as the political commander remained satisfied to simply wear the stars of command, but when he felt that he should actually be the "general", problems normally became overwhelming. The politician's normal habit of assuming command had driven him from the old army in 1846 and why he thought things would be different this time was as unclear to him as it would be to the eagle circling above. Even some of the incompetents from his first war were busy fouling up this one. He had about as many worries as one man could be expected to manage. The political generals had caused his earlier resignation and the same type of individual could leave him with little other choice than a second resignation this time around.

Not the least of his concerns involved his family. They were on his farm located above Gauley Bridge and were probably interned or held captive by the Federal troops who had occupied the area. Ellen and the children had remained there after the Confederate regiments under the command of Virginia's former governor, Henry A. Wise, had withdrawn from the upper Kanawha valley in order to avoid being trapped between two Federal armies from Ohio. One small army, under the command of General Cox, had been steadily moving up the valley while a second, larger force under General McClellan manuevered in the northwestern regions of the state and could have easily slipped behind the poorly prepared Confederate force by moving down roads that ran parallel to Gauley River. The poorly-trained and under-equipped Rebel troops would have been unable to withstand a simultaneous assault by both of these armies and the Confederate column abandoned Charleston, retreated to the vicinity of Gauley Bridge where they spent a few days before crossing the river and burning the strategic bridge behind them. That was the last that he had seen of Ellen and the children.

What a curious turn of events. Here he was, a Confederate Colonel, serving under the command of a man he had once despised. Brigadier-General Henry Wise had been a member of Congress long before he had become Virginia's governor. He could easily recall their first association -- painful, even though it was an old memory in both time and distance. While serving in the Third Artillery Regiment during the Florida wars against the Seminoles as a Second-Lieutenant, the Colonel had participated in a serious battle against a large indian force on January 24, 1838. At the same time, Congressman Henry Wise was belittling the dangerous missions of the soldiers by standing in the House of Representatives and declaring that the war was a disgrace. He said that the army couldn't defeat one thousand indians and that he would rather pay to secure the indians in their hammocks than fight them.[2]

That had been quite a day for the young officer. The indians were reported to be hiding in a hammock, prepared to fight. His commander, General Jesup, ordered an immediate attack across a cypress swamp where the soldier's horses floundered until the dragoons were forced to dismount to charge on foot as the supporting artillerymen also charged. The artillery had been deployed into the swamps as infantry during this savage war. A single six-pounder cannon blasted into the hammock which concealed the indians while Congreve rockets hissed off into the thick vegetation.

The indians had quickly retreated to new positions behind a stream about thirty yards wide and built up sustained gunfire that halted the combined dragoon and artillerymen's attack. General Jesup bravely rode up to the edge of the stream to rally the soldiers and was wounded in the face, but waved the men on. The attack continued as indian resistance began to melt away under the constant pressure of the army. The young officer's first experience with combat had been the "Action of Locha-Hatchee" and seven soldiers and volunteers were dead and thirty-one others were wounded.

[2] Mahone, John K.; *History of the Second Seminole War: 1835-1842*, University of Florida Press, 1967, pg. 234

He and his soldiers had been doing their duty under difficult and dangerous circumstances while his current "general" was standing in Congress condemning the actions of brave, dying men. Colonel Christopher Quarles Tompkins certainly had reason to be preoccupied as he sat there in the opening of the crude log hut.

Even becoming a soldier was not easy. He had to struggle to collect enough endorsements and recommendations in order to receive an appointment from Virginia to West Point. Letters were sent to the War Department from professors, ministers, and even from one of Virginia's most prominent politicians, John Tyler -- later to become President.

The letters from Tyler were probably instrumental in securing the appointment. Tyler wrote in one letter:

"Washington Dec 24, 1831

" I had the honor of adressing to your predecessor in the War Department a letter of recommendation of M. Christopher Tompkins of the county of Matthews State of Virginia for a cadet's appointment in the military academy.
"May I invite your attention to the claims of this young gentleman as manifested by testimonials doubtlessly on file in your office and to add that my own convictions of his suitability are confirmed by a longer and more intimate acquaintance with him.

With Sentiments of Great Respect
I am Sir Yr Most Obt Srvt
John Tyler"[3]

Tyler was sufficiently well-known to become a national figure when he became President in 1841 and his endorsement was obviously sufficient to assure an appointment to the Military Academy at West Point for the young man from Matthews County. A new cadet from Virginia began military training with forty-eight other

3 Tompkins' Military Academy application papers are in the National Archives, Record Group No. 94, Records of the Adjutant General's Office, 1870's - 1917.

young men in 1832.[4]

The Confederate Colonel could remember the graduation day on July 1, 1836 and his arrival at his regiment's headquarters in Florida that September. Men like Wise and that other "general" in his present chain-of-command, Floyd, would never understand what it was like to be an officer in the old army. He had been assigned to the Third Artillery and had remained with it for the duration of his military career. He had lived and worked with men who could be trusted in any situation. The other officers assigned to the regiment were like his brothers and they knew from long association the various strengths and weaknesses of one another. They worked as a team and regardless of the situation, the honor of the regiment was their constant responsibility and was taken seriously. It was difficult to know who could be trusted in this current rabble of volunteers, militia, and scoundrels. The early days were formative ones and he relished the memories.

The duty in Florida was dangerous and difficult. Six months prior to Tompkins' arrival, the Seminoles and their Negro allies had massacred Company B of the Third Artillery. A detachment of eight officers, including a surgeon, and one hundred enlisted men was ambushed. The artillerymen had been deployed as "redlegged infantrymen" by the War Department because of the limited availability of infantry in the army at the time and the fact that artillery had little value in the swamps. The indians seldom massed in a target of suitable size for the effective use of cannon. The army equipped the artillerymen and their officers with small arms and sent them out as infantry. While these men were soldiers, they were not adequately trained in basic infantry tactics and when the indians under the chief, Osceola, discovered that the column of soldiers was moving without placing any security teams along its flanks, they attacked.

The commander, Major Dade, and half of his command dropped with the first volley. The survivors were able to

4 *Register of Graduates*, West Point Library

withdraw to construct a triangular breastwork while the indians were reorganizing for their final attack. The soldiers from Company B were able to hold off the warriors until their single cannon ran out of ammunition and then the position was overrun. The indians didn't scalp or loot the surviving wounded, but a group of their negro allies swarmed in to kill the injured and loot the dead.One wounded survivor was left to die in pain, but was able to survive to tell the details of the attack.

Tompkins and his "redlegged infantry" learned a lot about swamp warfare and there were no additional massacres of this magnitude for the remainder of the war. The soldiers who emerged from the Florida Wars were not the typical veterans that the nation had become familar with following her earlier wars. These veterans had several years of small unit patrolling experience in difficult terrain and they were prepared to go after the indians on their own terms. This was the most difficult theater of operations yet encountered by the young country and the tactics of the Seminoles were frustrating to the conventional commanders of the army who were responsible for the conduct of the war.

The terrain through which operations were conducted was made up primarily of swamps and small hammocks which were used as camps and areas of cultivation by the indians. The underbrush was nearly impenetrable and a member of the Eighth Infantry Regiment later described it:

"The undergrowth...consisting of scrub-oak, palmetto,and grapevines; so thick that a passage can only be made with the assistance of an axe, cutting a foot-path as through a wall. At a distance of ten feet an individual is totally obscured.... The thick saw-palmetto made it almost impossible for the troops to get from lake to lake. Their clothes were torn to pieces, and their feet, legs, and hands lacerated as cut by a knife. The execution of the hazardous duties committed to the younger officers, many of them

[5] Mahone, John K., *History of the Second Seminole War: 1835-1842*, University of Florida Press, 1967, pg. 104-105

volunteers, elicited the praise of the commander of the army, as well as the commendation of their respective commanders."[6]

This was a very difficult first assignment for a new officer and the combination of rough terrain and skilled enemy warriors provided lessons that were not soon forgotten. The junior officers were expected to take their troops into the swamps for prolonged periods and conduct scouting operations against the indians. The Seminoles were capable of gathering sufficient forces to ambush the small patrols, if the officers leading the patrols were careless. This experience made the survivors into excellent officers and this was the tour of duty where Colonel Tompkins developed his leadership skills. The duty for the junior officers -- Tompkins was a Second-Lieutenant at the time -- was unusual for that period. Seldom in the past had young officers had to lead small patrols into enemy territory for such long periods. An average patrol was described by an officer who served in the Florida Wars:

"The particular service devolving upon the officer in the scouts through the country, was quite debilitating in professional exertions as the climate upon his constitution.... The officer with his command of thirty or forty men, resembled more a banditti than a body of soldiers in the service of their country. He, at the head of his little band, without shoes or stockings, his pantaloons sustained by a belt, in which were thrust a brace of pistols, without vest or coat, his cap with a leathern flap behind, to divert the rain from coursing down his back; in this manner he lead his detachment through bog and water, day after day; dependent for food upon the contents of his haversack strapped to his back."[7]

[6] Sprague, John T., *The Origin, Progress, and Conclusion of the Florida War*, University of Florida Press, 1964, pg. 285

[7] *Ibid*, pg. 287

This was the career for a new army officer in the late 1830's and Christopher Tompkins served in this capacity as long as any of the other officers in the army during that period. He wrote about his early career in a letter to George Cullum from Paint Creek, Virginia, in 1856. Cullum was involved in preparing a "Biographical Register" of West Point graduates. In response to Cullum's inquiry, Tompkins wrote:

"...as to your inquiries I was in Florida from the time I joined my regiment in September 1836 until the middle of 1838 when we were out to Cherokee country.

"The fall of 1838 returned to Florida and remained until March 1840, when I was ordered north on recruiting service -- again rejoined my regiment in Florida in the fall of 1841 and remained until the coming spring when we were ordered out and distributed to different posts..."[8]

The Confederate Colonel had served through most of the Second Seminole War and had learned military lessons that most of the other officers assigned to Wise's command couldn't guess. Tompkins was an experienced, professional officer with combat experience which was quite a different type from that gained by several of the others who served in the Mexican War. The lessons that Tompkins had learned were different even from the experience gained from the few veterans of William Walker's expeditions against Nicargua who were also serving under Wise. The long, uncomfortable, dangerous, and politically unpopular duty in Florida was unique in the army's experience.

Officers and soldiers serving in the Florida regiments were quite aware of the general attitude in Congress regarding their activities against the indians. Debates about the Florida War were common as military budgets were considered or reports on the conduct of the war were

8 Personal letter from Christopher Tompkins to George W. Cullum dated 25 October 1855. A copy of this letter is in the library at West Point.

reviewed by special investigating committees. Congressman Wise was making a political issue out of the army's conduct in the protracted war and a Pennsylvania Representative declared that he would not vote for any of the army budget until he learned better how the military's money was being used. There was a great deal of concern over the welfare of the indians and this also became a minor political issue. A Florida delegate who was far more familar with the actual situation in Florida told his co-workers that their concerns for the indians were misplaced and "while they were butchering white men, the indians and negroes received the white's sympathy."[9]

Many of the soldiers serving in Florida actually did sympathize with the plight of the indians and felt that the entire war was unnecessary. One of the commanding generals in Florida (there were several as unsuccessful generals were rotated to other duties), General Jesup, wrote an interesting letter to the Secretary of War, Joel Poinsett, in which he attempted to explain that there had never been a case in America in which the indians had been pushed out before the white men actually needed the land. He felt that the Seminoles were not in the way of the white advance in Florida and he advised Poinsett that if the policy of forcing the indians out was not reversed, the war could rage on for many years. Jesup asked that the Seminoles be allowed to remain on a special reservation and felt so strongly about the case he was attempting to make, he had an aide handcarry the letter to Washington. The request was denied and soon fighting again broke out.[10] The war continued until May 10, 1842, when the government notified the army that they should halt hostilities as soon as possible. The war was soon over, but it had been a painful experience for the Third Artillery Regiment. It had been a very costly war -- the regiment's average strength was normally less than 400 men, but the Third Artillery lost eight officers to disease, three in battle, 125 enlisted men to disease and 133 in combat. Tompkins and several of the

---

9 Mahone, *Second Seminole War*, pg. 235
10 *Ibid*, pg. 235-236

other officers would not forget their experiences in the Florida War.[11] They were fighting an enemy that they did not hate and they fought for a nation that didn't appreciate the sacrifice that the soldiers were making. This was Tompkins' introduction to politicians and the effect they can have on the army's ability to conduct combat operations. The dislike that developed was to remain with him for a long time and have a substantial effect on his second attempt at a military career.

Even the short break the Regiment had from the Florida campaigning in 1838 involved equally distasteful duty forced on them by politicians in Washington. They were ordered into Georgia to assist in the forced removal of the Cherokee indians from their homes -- which had been secured by treaty rights with the Federal government -- to new areas west of the Mississippi River. After long periods of negotiation, the Cherokee leadership had signed a treaty in 1835 in which they agreed to relocate, but there was a great deal of opposition within the tribe to this re-written treaty. There was also much white resistance to the government plan to forcibly relocate these civilized, Christian indians who had been allies of General Jackson in the war against the Creeks. The relocation was finally ordered by President Van Buren and the army started the move during the winter months and nearly one-quarter of the indians died of exposure and disease before reaching their new territory.

This was not a pleasant experience for the soldiers ordered to uproot the civilized indians from their homes in the middle of winter and escort them across half of the continent. This, of course, had been ordered by the politicians in Washington who generally interfered in the army's business.

This first six years of Tompkins' career set the tone for the remainder. He had served in the worst and most politically unpopular conflict that the young nation had yet to endure and obeyed orders of politicians that resulted in

---

11 Mahone, *Second Seminole War*, provides casualty figures on pg. 309; Sprague, *Origin*, gives unit strength on pg. 105-106

the deaths of many of the Cherokees his regiment were escorting. He became suspicious of both politicians and political appointees in his chain-of command and both were to make frequent appearances.

As Colonel Tompkins sat by the smouldering fire placed in front of the open log hut, the weather was still bad and the news was even worse. The other "political" general in the area, General Floyd, was due to arrive shortly and his presence would greatly complicate the current situation on Sewell Mountain. General Wise, the current commander at "Camp Defiance" on Sewell Mountain -- the same Congressman who had expressed outrage at the army's conduct of the Florida War -- had later become governor of Virginia. He was the bitter enemy of General Floyd, also a former governor of Virginia and the two had never expressed a kind word between themselves. Unfortunately for Tompkins, Wise, and the volunteers from the western region of Virginia, Floyd's commission was granted a few days prior to that of Wise and when he arrived on Sewell Mountain, Floyd would be in command.

Tompkins had serious doubts about Floyd's honesty. Floyd had been the Secretary of War under President Buchannan and had been accused of misuse of government funds and property. The crisis that came with the election of Abraham Lincoln and the attack on Fort Sumpter provided Floyd with the excuse to resign from the Buchannan Cabinet and flee from Washington just before an investigation was initiated by a Congressional Committee. Even without considering the accusations regarding his basic honesty, Tompkins was sure of two things about his soon-to-arrive commander: Floyd was not a soldier and he was not an honorable man.

All of this made Tompkins think of another, similar incident involving political appointees during the Mexican War while he was assigned to the garrison at Monterey, California. He wrote about his California duty in a letter to George Cullum:

"In 1846 July 14th I sailed from New York in the

Transport Sloop of War Lexington and after a voyage of six months ... was landed at Monterey California -- remained there until a short while before the acceptance of my resignation -- never having seen a hostile Mexican in that territory, for the American flag was flying over every post where I worked the coast and the quarrelling pretty much confined to our own officers Genl Kearney and Fremont and Stockton."[12]

Tompkins had decided to leave the army and his latest experience with bickering, politically-appointed generals did little to convince him to reverse his decision. He was a professional officer trained for and experienced in war and he had chosen to remain in the army during a period when many of his friends were leaving to enter careers as engineers with new private enterprises that were developing rapidly in the new country. There were few other schools in the country at the time other than West Point where engineers were trained. A West Point graduate could get a salary several times that which was paid in the army. Officers were not well-paid in the 1840's - a Lieutenant-Colonel was paid $1328 and a Major received $1,038. The pay of a Lieutenant who had graduated from West Point was several times less than that available in the commercial world. This resulted in a continual drain on the Officer Corps of the army. They simply could not compete with the commercial establishments for well-trained men.

He had remained in the army during that difficult period -- probably out of a sense of duty to a combination of loyalties: his country, his regiment, and his friends who were relying on him. But he was missing the combat of the Mexican War where many of his friends and classmates were fighting. They were winning brevet promotions that would help their post-war army careers immensely while he was sitting in California watching several generals bicker among themselves.

He submitted his resignation from the army while in

[12] Tompkins' letter to George Cullum, 25 October 1855.

California and this was accepted on September 22, 1847.[13]

There were simply too many factors in operation against the military career that he had chosen as a young man. The early experiences in the Florida Wars, the incompetence of the generals with whom he served in California, being unable to share the risks and glory of his classmates fighting the Mexicans -- all combined with long periods of absence from the young wife he had married while on recruiting duty in Baltimore -- lead to the decision to leave the army. But the character of the young man had been permanently molded by the hard experiences he faced during his early army duty. Faced with the frequent threat of death or permanent disability from combat with Seminole warriors or from contracting a tropical disease, the young Tompkins matured and the ideals of honor and duty came to mean more to him than many of his contemporaries.

He returned to Virginia and settled in the Richmond area. Tompkins described his occupation during this period as a "manufacturer of iron and steel"until 1855.[14]

A second key event in his life is also recorded briefly in his letters to the West Point biographer, George Cullum. Tompkins simply joined the Virginia militia. Taken in isolation, this is not a major, significant factor, but it was to be quite important in 1861. He served as a Captain in the Virginia Volunteers until 1849 and was appointed a Lieutenant-Colonel when the incumbent Colonel resigned.[15]

His military relationship with the state of Virginia continued during a period of history when being a Virginian meant something special. There were powerful and emotional ties to this special state that were widely held by most of the population. Virginia was seen as the "Mother of States" as immigrants from Virginia had settled

13 Cullum, George W.; *Biographical Register of Officers and Graduates of the U.S. Military Academy at West Point, N.Y.*, Vol. 1, (1802-1840), D. Van Nostrand, pg. 408

14 Tompkins letter to Cullum, 25 October 1855

15 *Ibid*

in other areas that later were admitted to the Union. She was also called "Mother of Presidents" because of the number of Virginian's who held that particular office. The state capital, Richmond, was one of the cultural centers of the young country. Christopher Tompkins was a member of that special group of people, the Virginia elite, which had provided presidents and culture to the rest of the country. A Tompkins had been Vice-President under James Monroe and the family was sufficiently well-connected politically to have secured an endorsement from John Tyler, a future president, that helped young Christopher enter West Point.

Most Virginians of the time felt an intense loyalty to the state and Christopher Tompkins was no exception. Later, when war had produced a split in the state and the western regions were forming a separate state, the name "Kanawha" was rejected in favor of "West Virginia" out of pride in what the "Old Dominion" had been to the delegates at the statehood convention. Even as Tompkins was sitting beside that smouldering fire on the top of Sewell Mountain reviewing his past and his probable future, there was no doubt about his loyalty to Virginia.

As he sat thinking, his wife wrote a letter from Gauley Mount to her sister in Delaware. Ellen Tompkins obviously knew her husband better than anyone else and she described his probable course of action :"...but as the authorities wish him to be a General, I can't say what he will do except one thing is certain, he will do all he can for his state."[16]

This was the political, cultural, and emotional environment surrounding Tompkins after he left the army. He was working in a company that was involved in the manufacturing of iron and steel and this employment was probably in association with a former West Point classmate, Joseph R. Anderson. Anderson resigned from the army in 1837 -- shortly after graduation -- and worked

[16] Tompkins, Ellen W., "The Colonel's Lady,", *The Virginia Magazine of History and Biography*, edited by Ellen Wilkins Tompkins, October 1961, pg. 415

in a Richmond cannon foundry.[17]

Later, after sustaining a serious wound, Confederate General Joseph R. Anderson left active service and managed the South's major armaments factory, the Tredegar Works.[18] West Point classmates are normally quite close and the association begun by these two that began as cadets was to endure a civil war.

Tompkins remained in Richmond until April, 1855, when he relocated to Western Virginia. He wrote to George Cullum that "...since then I have been superintendent of the Paint Creek Coal and Iron Mining and Manufacturing Company, Kanawha County, Va."[19] He had also purchased 820 acres on the top of Gauley Mountain, near both New and Gauley Rivers where he began to develop a farm.

The farm was located in a remote location in Fayette County and the area was quite different from the surroundings to which the Tompkins' family were accustomed. The region was located in the rough terrain in the middle of the Trans-Allegheny section of the state and politically as well as culturally, the area was unlike the eastern section of the state. The region was primarily rural and the population was not normally well- educated. Tompkins soon became one of the leading citizens in the area and his duty with the Virginia Militia also probably continued. He continued to work in the coal business and made some interesting acquaintences. One of these was the President of the Cannel Coal Company, William S. Rosecrans, another West Point graduate.

Rosecrans graduated from the Military Academy in 1842 and served in the army's Engineer Corps at Fortress Monroe, at West Point as an instructor, and at the Washington Naval Yard. Promotion in the peacetime army was slow and when Lieutenant Rosecrans was thirty-four

17 *Register of Graduates*, West Point Library

18 Tompkins' letter to Cullum, 25 October, 1855

19 *Ibid*

years old, he resigned because of poor health.[20]

The coal business was opening up areas that needed development in western Virginia and Rosecrans worked as an engineer to develop methods for shipping the oil refined from cannel coal to markets along the Ohio and Mississippi Rivers.

Tompkins sent a very personal letter to Rosecrans shortly after the war had started and it referred to a previous association between the two, but they didn't serve together while they were on active duty in the army. Comparing their duty assignments doesn't reveal any in the same location. The only obvious time there could have been a relationship between the two was during the pre-war period when both were actively involved in the business of transporting both coal and coal oil to market. Both had attended West Point and with that in common, a firm friendship would have developed. This friendship would play a part in more serious matters later in 1861.

Christopher Tompkins was a proud, honest man who had regrets that he had left the army after so many years of hardship, sacrifice, and service with the men of his regiment. He had been in uniform since 1832 when he became a cadet. There obviously were some good times during those fifteen years or he would have resigned earlier. Eighteen of his classmates had yielded their military careers to the well-paid private sector economy by either declining their commissions at graduation or had resigned early in their service. Tompkins had remained in uniform when it was obviously quite easy the depart for a larger salary. His duty in the Virginia Militia later in his life was a natural outlet for the frustration that he must have felt by not being able to utilize the military skills and experience that he had worked so hard to attain. He alluded to his frustration when he wrote to George Cullum:

"...On the whole I regret that my autobiography is so

[20] Reid, Whitelaw; *Ohio in the War: Her Statesmen, Her Generals and Soldiers*, Moore, Wilstach, and Baldwin: 1868, pg. 313

[21] Tompkins" letter to Cullum, 25 October, 1855

meagre and unimportant, but I do not know that I can mend it...."[22]

The most significant event, however, was a very simple, but binding act taken by Tompkins when he was administered the oath of office that assured his allegiance to the state of Virginia as a state officer. An oath was not taken lightly by gentlemen such as Tompkins and once taken, these were firm and could not be shed easily. He was now sworn to defend the state of Virginia from both internal and external enemies and was required to obey the orders of the Governor of the state as well as the officers placed in positions superior to himself. This oath was to prove important in 1861.

In addition to his part-time military responsibilities, Tompkins worked on the farm that he was developing and he retained a residence in Richmond for family use during the severe winter months. By 1861, the farm, Gauley Mount, had a large house, an overseer's house, a barn, and numerous small houses on the property.[23]

The house was reported to be the most beautiful residence west of the Alleghenies. Tompkins was able to live the life of a country gentleman while he was on the farm. It was reported that he had a fine library, rare paintings on the walls, and that he owned some of the finest guns and fishing tackle made. He even had a tutor for his children who resided on the farm.[24] Christopher Tompkins had done well for himself and his family since he left the army.

## The Departure

The newly commissioned Confederate Colonel had walked to his horse after a sad farewell with his pretty wife.

22 Tompkins' letter to Cullum, 25 October, 1855

23 Tompkins. "Colonel's Lady", pg. 387

24 Hull, Forrest, "Gauley Mount, The Story of an Old House of the Civil War Days", *The West Virginia Review*, October, 1926. Pg. 142-143

His daughter had looked on and had cried gently for a few minutes, but the three sons were proud and excited. They, like the rest of the area's population believed that the war would be over in two months and wasn't it true that a Southerner could whip ten Yankees, anyway?

The Colonel knew better. Tough training at West Point, bitter experiences in the Seminole wars, and the loss of classmates in the Mexican War had taught him some severe lessons that he feared many others would also have to learn the hard way. Many of his classmates and fellow soldiers in the regular army had been from the North and had shown that they were just as capable as anyone else when it came to the practice of warfare.

The timing for all of this couldn't have been worse. Everything had been going well for him since he left the army in 1847. His lovely wife from Baltimore and their four children had joined him on their eight hundred-twenty acre farm which was located on a mountain overlooking the beautiful valleys containing both Gauley and New Rivers. He had moved into the upper Kanawha Valley in 1855 and had become one of the foremost citizens of the area. He had no doubt that his popularity with the local population was a major factor considered in Richmond when Robert Garnett sent him his new commission.[25]

The politicians were sure he would be able to rally many of these western Virginians to the newly-forming Confederacy. The timing of this war wasn't the best, but perhaps open hostilities could still be avoided. Virginia had not yet seceded from the Union to join the Southern states and maybe war could be prevented. He would have chosen a different path for the country, if he had been able.

He mounted his horse, rode down the steep James River and Kanawha Turnpike, and crossed the covered bridge into the hamlet of Gauley Bridge. The small town consisted only of a cluster of two or three houses, a country store, a small tavern, and a church. All were scattered along the base of the mountain beside the road which

[25] Hotchkiss, Jed., "Virginia," *Confederate Military History*, Vol. III, edited by Clement A. Evans, pg. 59

turned from the Gauley River valley to follow the broad Kanawha to the west.[26]

This would be the last opportunity to send letters to Richmond before moving down the Kanawha River to begin recruiting troops for Virginia. The area's postmaster, James Miller,[27] was well known to everyone and was a man to be trusted. A short conversation would ensure that any letters received from the field would be carried to his wife on the mountain.

There was time for one last glance across the river toward the home and family at Gauley Mount, the farm he had worked so hard to build. He turned the horse on the turnpike to continue the long ride to the new recruiting and training camp. He would work hard to do his duty for Virginia. There would be a short, patriotic speech in Charleston, and then the work of training soldiers would begin.

Young John McCausland had been sent to the valley from the Virginia Military Institute[28], but the actual training for combat would have to be organized by an experienced, professional officer. The long days spent at West Point and drilling troops in the regular army would now prove to be valuable.

The western counties of the Commonwealth were very important to the planners for the new Confederacy. The bottom land was rich and would provide large quantities of both food and forage for the Southern troops. The sons of the farmers were expected to volunteer in droves for Confederate military service and when properly trained, they would be in a position to defend the western frontier from invasion by pro-Union forces gathering in Ohio. The Kanawha Valley also produced large amounts of a commodity that most of the South was lacking -- salt. This item was necessary for far more than simply flavoring food.

---

[26] Cox, Jacob D., *Military Reminiscences of the Civil War*, Vol. I, pg. 83

[27] Blackwell, Lyle M., *Gauley Bridge: The Town and Its First Church*, McClain Printing, Parsons: 1980, pg. 79

[28] Hotchkiss, "Virginia", pg. 59

It was an essential ingredient used in the preservation of meat and the South had little of it. The Kanawha salines would be an excellent source of a constant supply of salt for the South and they had only to hold the Kanawha Valley and prevent Union forces from pushing them out to have a moderate source of this item. Everyone was confident that the Rebels would be able organize forces in the Kanawha Valley area and defend the western approaches to Richmond, gather additional recruits, and possibly begin offensive operations against Federal forces as they tried to cross over the Ohio River. The Colonel was aware that there was much in war that cannot be controlled, much less planned. He knew that if the initial defensive campaigns which would be fought on Virginia's soil did not develop well, all of them would have to abandon the Kanawha Valley, their homes and families, and move into better defensive terrain in the mountains to the east. With their families living in areas under the control of the invading enemy forces, it would be impossible to predict how many of the untrained, undisciplined recruits would remain with their regiments if the South were to experience defeats in any of the initial fighting. Most of the young farmers who were rallying to the Southern cause were lukewarm to the idea of a new nation as they had lived all of their lives far from the influence of the mainstream South. Most of these poor, small farmers had no interest in slavery and there was a historical greviance over the economic control of the western counties by the politicians in eastern Virginia. The Westerners had few reasons to rally to the support of Virginia and generally had better relations with their natural trading partners across and down the Ohio River rather than over the rugged Allegheny Mountains.

If it came to fighting, the best chance for Southern victory was in defeating invading the Federal forces as quickly as possible. If many of the early fights were lost only those soldiers with very strong reasons would remain

[29] Ambler, Charles H., *West Virginia: Stories and Biographies*, Rand-McNally, Chicago: 1942, pg. 190-196

to continue the fight. Defeat would be one thing, but being forced to retreat from their families would require levels of dedication possessed by only a few.

Lingering doubts remained as the new Colonel rode further down the road. A long ride remained before he arrived at the recruiting and training camp located downstream from Charleston to the west of Coal River on the farm of William and Beverly Tompkins. The local militia units entering on duty with Virginia's state forces used the Tompkins' mansion, Valcoulon, as their headquarters and the new base of operations was named Camp Tompkins in honor of both the new commander and their hosts.[30]

## An Approaching Storm

The differences in the eastern and western sections of Virginia were both social and economic. There were nearly as many slaves as whites in the east and many of the whites could afford to spend some of their time engaged in social activities. The Trans-Allegheny Virginians were entirely different. As a group, they owned fewer slaves and spent most of their time working to earn a living. They had little leisure time to spend on anything other than their churches.

There was a substantial difference in the politics of the two regions. The Virginia Constitution of 1776, which governed both areas, allowed for two representatives from each county regardless of population. The east had more counties and the westerners complained that representation in Richmond should be proportional to the number of white inhabitants and they felt that the western counties were not represented equally. The western Virginians claimed that they had been denied state-chartered banks and other internal improvements because they did not have a fair share of the government in Richmond. There were also complaints about the rules regarding the right to vote. The State Constitution permitted only those with twenty-five

30 Cohen, Stan, ***Kanawha County Images: A Bicentennial History 1788-1988***, Pictorial Histories, Charleston, pg. 89; Reynolds, William C., *Diary*, 3 June 1861 entry mentions the christening of the camp.

acres of improved or fifty acres of unimproved land to vote. The voting population of Virginia in 1830 was less than fifty thousand out of a population of about six hundred thousand. Most of these voters were living in the eastern counties and they had sufficient political influence in the state legislature to give them control over the western region. Because of this, there was a long-standing resentment because of the lack of control the westerners had over their own affairs.[31]

In spite of the arguments of the western politicians, no changes were made until the Virginia Constitutional Convention of 1829-1830 convened. The new Constitution that resulted allowed for changes in the voting practices and reformed the selection process for people serving in state and county governments, but the arrangements for assembly representation so offended the westerners that there was open discussion of secession from Virginia to form another state. The formation of a separate state wasn't a new concept when it finally happened in 1863. The Civil War was simply the catalyst that caused the westerners to separate from Virginia -- there were serious differences between the two regions long before the outbreak of the war.

The differences weren't limited to only politics. There were differences in the style of religion practiced between tne two sides. The well-established Baptists, Methodists, Prsebyterians, and Episcopalians in the eastern counties had a long association with the practice of slavery and fully accepted it as an institution. The western areas were populated with more recent immigrants from Europe and while they were associated with the same churches, they also attended services in Quaker, Mennonite, and Dunkard congregations which had more limited experience with slaves. Differences over the slavery question were found between the two regional church groupings and some differences could not be reconciled. The Methodists actually divided their church into two groups in 1846 over the slavery problem and the geographic line separating the

31 Ambler, *West Virginia: Stories*, pg. 190-200

western branch from the parent church closely parallels the present boundary of West Virginia.[32]

Westerners were generally opposed to slavery. This belief was not necessarily due to excessive humanitarian principles -- they felt that slavery was responsible for keeping additional immigrants out of western Virginia and that the lack of population slowed the general development of the region. With the eastern counties controlling the legislature, tax laws beneficial to the east were passed over the objections of the westerners. For example, a provision in a law prevented taxation of slaves under the age of twelve and taxes on slaves over that age were not permitted to exceed those on an assessed value of $300.00 each. The western farmer, however, had to pay full taxes on his calves, colts, lambs, and pigs while Negro boys and girl slaves -- property -- went untaxed. The westerners also saw that the revenue from these taxes was used to support public works east of the mountains while roads and banks in the western areas were scarce.[33]

Given the great differences between the two sections, it is surprising that there had not been a division of the state of Virginia prior to the Civil War. It is equally surprising that so many westerners joined the Confederate forces and remained for the duration of the war. The long-standing differences between the two regions may help explain the high desertion rates from the Confederate regiments raised in the western counties at the onset of the war. When these men realized that they would be forced by the invading Union armies to retreat from their homes -- leaving their families and property to the mercies of their Unionist neighbors -- they found few binding ties to hold them to the Rebel cause. The state of Virginia had always managed to over-tax them to the benefit of the easterners without proper representation. These men found few reasons to risk their lives for their home state and most saw that they had much to gain by attempting to form a new state where they

32 Ambler, *West Virginia: Stories*, pg. 197-198

33 *Ibid*, pg. 199

could manage their own affairs. At best, they felt they would do well by trying to remain neutral and wait out the war.

## Assembling Forces

Lieutenant-Colonel John McCausland was authorized on April 29, 1861 to muster into state service as many as ten companies of volunteers and direct military operations in the western regions of the state. He was informed that Captain Patton's Kanawha Riflemen, Captain Swann's company, and two companies from Putnam county would be willing to offer their services and that his small force would be provided 500 muskets and four field pieces. McCausland was assisted by a Virginia Military Institute cadet, John K. Thompson, the son of a phsician living near Poca.[34]

Colonel Christopher Q. Tompkins received his commission on May 3 and was directed to take command of all the troops in the Kanawha valley.

It became difficult to recruit large numbers of soldiers in the area and Tompkins sent McCausland to Richmond to discuss the problem directly with Governor Letcher. The message was plain:

"He will inform you of the disaffection of this population and the difficulty of obtaining reliable troops for the emergency...I have now under my command here 340 men, and when the companies now in process of formation in this valley have been completed it is probable that their number will not exceed 1,000 men. It is doubtful, in my mind, whether the militia will obey a call to the field."[35]

Tompkins was determined to complete his assignment and issued a proclamation in Charleston which was designed to attract more recruits:

---

34 White, *Confederate Military History*, Vol. II, pg. 26

35 Stutler, Boyd B., *West Virginia in the Civil War*, pg. 51

**"Men of Virginia! Men of Kanawha! To Arms!**

"The enemy has invaded your soil and threatens to overrun your country under the pretext of protection. You cannot serve two masters. You have not the right to repudiate allegiance to your state. Be not seduced by his sophistry or intimidated by his threats. Rise and strike for your firesides and altars. Repel the aggressors and preserve your honor and your rights. Rally in every neighborhood with or without arms. Organize and unite with sons of the soil to defend it. Report yourselves without delay to those nearest to you in military position. Come to the aid of your mothers, wives and sisters. Let every man who would uphold his rights turn out with such arms as he may get and drive the invader back."[36]

Units from the mountain counties began to assemble and march to Camp Tompkins for six weeks of military instruction. During the first week of June, the Fayetteville Rifles and the Mountain Cove Guards moved down the Kanawha valley to join the regiments forming under the command of Colonel Tompkins.

The companies assigned to the First Kanawha Regiment were from several different counties and were designated by letters as well as their colorful nicknames:

| | | |
|---|---|---|
| Company A.... | Border Riflemen......... | Putnam County |
| Company C.... | Mountain Cove Guards..... | Fayette COunty |
| Company D.... | Nicholas Blues........... | Nicholas County |
| Company E.... | Elk River Tigers......... | Clay County |
| Company F.... | Rocky Point Greys........ | Monroe County |
| Company G... | Wyoming Riflemen......... | Wyoming County |
| Company H.... | Kanawha Riflemen......... | Kanawha County |
| Company I.... | Boone Company............ | Fayette County |
| Company K.... | Kanawha Rangers.......... | Boone County[37] |
| Company K.... | Fayetteville Rifles...... | Fayette County |

Fayette County provided three companies for the early

36 White, *Confederate Military History*, Vol. II, pg. 27

37 Husley, Val; "Men of Virginia - Men of Kanawha - To Arms", *West Virginia History*, Vol. XXXV, No. 3, pg 222

regiments which were forming for Confederate service. Most of the citizens of Fayette county were in sympathy with the Southern cause, the county representative voted for the Ordinance of Secession, and the people of the county sent no delegates to either of the conventions which met at Wheeling to take steps to form an independent state so that they might remain in the Union. The local government officials in the county, the Justices of the Peace, met at Fayetteville in June, 1861, and adopted the following resolutions unanimously:

"Whereas, our state has been invaded by a hostile army of northern fanatics and we feel bound to resist said invasion to the last extremity resolved therefore,

"First: That we feel it to be our duty in accordance with an act of the legislature passed January 19th, 1861, to levy on the people of the county from time to time as may be necessary to enable us to resist said invasion successfully such amount of money as we shall think practicable and expedient.

"Second: That we will then, after money and property are exhausted, feel it to be our duty to levy for said purpose on the credit of the county and when that also is gone, we will eat roots, and drink water and still fight for our liberty unto death.

"Third: That should any of the members of this court feel friendly to the North, we invite them or him to peacefully and civilly resign their or his commission."[38]

The generally pro-Southern feeling of the local magistrates may not have been as unamious as the proclamation may have indicated or there would not have been any need for the third paragraph. While the citizens of Fayette County were sympathetic toward the Confederate cause, there was less than total agreement among the population and a full company from the county also enlisted into the Federal army. The county was to

38 Peters, J.T. and Carden, H.B., *History of Fayette County, West Virginia*; Charleston, Jarrett Printing: 1926, pg. 213-214

experience a great deal of conflict during 1861-1862 as both sides quickly recognized the strategic value of the positions in the area around Gauley Bridge.

Colonel Tompkins had excellent raw material with which to work. The Kanawha Riflemen had been organized in 1856 by Captain George S. Patton and was patterned after the well-known Richmond Light Infantry Blues. The company was originally called the Kanawha Minutemen, but in 1859 the name was changed. The company was composed of young aristocrats and men of high standing from Charleston and was thought to be the best drilled company in the Confederate army.[39]

When the war began, the Kanawha Riflemen issued a statement that declared their intentions:

> "We, the Kanawha Riflemen, hereby declare it to be our fixed purpose never to use arms against the state of Virginia, or any other southern state, in any attempt to coerce or subjugate them. That we hereby tender our services to the authorities of the state, to be used in the emergency contemplated."[40]

They were quite serious about resisting any effort of the national government in recruiting them to help punish the seceding states. President Lincoln had recently called for 75,000 state troops to force the southern states back into the Union and this was the catalyst that forced several of the undecided border states to also leave the Union. It is unlikely that the Confederacy would have been able to defend itself against the forces of the central government without the assistance of Virginia. The smaller southern states simply did not have the population, industrial base, or sufficient agricultural resources to be able to confront the diversified and industrial North. The small skirmishes that had been fought prior to Virginia's

[39] Cohen, Stan, "Colonel George S. Patton and the 22nd Virginia Infantry Regiment", *West Virginia History*, Vol. XXVI, No. 3, April, 1965, pg. 178

40 *Ibid*, pg. 178-179

secession would have been the likely limit of military activity which would have lead to a long period of negotiations until some sort of common ground would have been found. The secession of Virginia made it possible for the South to attempt a military solution... Virginia gave them a chance to win![41]

Tompkins and others had very difficult decisions to make when they chose to join the Confederate military. They had invested their fortunes in farms and businesses in the western counties and had enormous financial losses to consider, if Virginia were to lose control of the Trans-Allegheny area.

The new Confederate Colonel was obviously uncomfortable in his present position. Previously-formed volunteer companies were slowly rallying to the training base at Camp Tompkins, but other forces were also gathering which would have a profound effect on the outcome of the war in the Kanawha valley. His area of operations was far from Confederate supply bases which were to the east of the mountainous zone and were connected only with poor roads which were nearly

---

41 A copy of Lincoln's proclamation is in *Harper's History of the Great Rebellion*, New York: 1866, pg. 65

The critical portion of the text required the states to activate their militia units for Federal Service:

*"Whereas the laws of the United States have for some time past and now are opposed, and the execution therefore obstructed in the states of South Carolina, Georgia, Alabama, Florida, Mississippi, Louisana, and Texas, by combinations too powerful to be supressed by the ordinary course of judicial procedings or by the powers vested in the marshalls by law: now, therefore, I, ABRAHAM LINCOLN, President of the United States, in virtue of the power in me vested by the Constitution and the laws, have thought fit to call forth, and hereby do call forth, the militia of the several states of the Union to the aggregate number of 75,000, in order to supress said combinations and to cause the laws to be duly executed..."*

impassable during poor weather -- and the Confederate training base was perilously close to Union forces being organized in Ohio.

By the end of May, 1861, Colonel Tompkins was in command of seven companies of infantry, three of cavalry, and had an artillery element with two field pieces. Additional recruits were being assimilated within the previously organized companies and by the end of June, Tomokins was able to form the companies of recruits into two regiments, the First and Second Kanawha Volunteer Infantry Regiments. Later, these two regiments would be reorganized and be re-designated the 22nd and 36th Virginia Infantry Regiments, respectively.[42]

The recruits were required to furnish their own arms as the Confederate states were not prepared to properly equip the volunteers. Many types of weapons were seen at Camp Tompkins: flintlocks, squirrel guns, and a miscellaneous assortment of pistols. Few of the units had any type of uniform. The Sandy Rangers were dressed in red hunting shirts.

The Fayetteville Rifles and the Mountain Cove Guards were especially grand by comparison. The Fayette County Court had appropriated $5000 to clothe the two companies and the ladies of the area met at the Methodist Church in Fayetteville to sew uniforms for the men.[43]

Captain William F. Bahlmann of the 22nd Virginia wrote after the war:

"Our uniforms were a thing of beauty and a joy forever. They consisted of light blue flannel jackets and dark grey pants. Although we were infantry they put cavalry trimmings on us. The jackets had yellow stripes on the breasts and the pants had yellow stripes down the legs. They put sergeant chevrons on the officers and original markings on the sergeants. Nobody knew anything about the matter and those who thought they knew the most were mistaken... we had no knapsacks but long narrow sacks

42 Scott, J.L., *36th Virginia Infantry*, H.E. Howard: 1987, pg. 3
43 Peters and Carden, *History of Fayette County*, pg. 214

called pokes..."[44]

There was a great deal of confusion regarding uniforms during the early days of the war. Colonel Beuhring Jones recruited a company in Fayette county which was later mustered into Confederate service at Kanawha Falls and became part of the 60th Virginia, but he was initially the commander of the "Dixie Rifles" and later wrote about his experience with his tailor:

"I had just returned from Lewisburg, and sported a grey jacket, gotten up by a tailor of that place, who, by the way of securing the job, had assured me that he was perfectly *Au fait* in all the minutiae pertaining to the decoration of military rank.

"I was quite proud of my up-buttoned, close-fitting 'jacket of grey' and felt all the importance of the commander, until I was startled from my dream of consequentiality by being adressed by an old soldier as 'Corporal Jones'. My 'Knight of the Shears', equally ignorant with myself had braided me as a corporal. My mortification was excessive, nor did I recover my composure until spasmodically I tore off the libelous braid, and cast it disdainfully upon the ground."[45]

These amateur soldiers from all over the western counties were quickly moving toward the Confederate camps in the lower Kanawha valley to learn the arts of war. There was a great deal to be learned from the experienced soldiers from the previously existing volunteer units and from the small number of veterans of service in the Mexican War who were volunteering for their second conflict. The well-drilled Kanawha Riflemen probably

44 Bahlmann, William E., "Down in the Ranks", *The Journal of the Greenbrier Historical Society*, Vol. II, No. 1, October, 1969, pg. 43

45 Jones, Beuhring H., *The Sunny Land*, Inness Co., Baltimore: 1868, pg. 501-527. This story is titled "My First Ninety Days" and is re-printed in Peters and Carden's *History of Fayette County* as "The Dixie Rifles", pg. 229-242.

provided instructors for the training companies and several others were experienced trainers.

The commander of the Kanawha Riflemen. George Patton, had graduated from the Virginia Military Institute in 1852 and was certainly able to drill troops. Captain James M. Corns, a veteran of the Mexican War, had assisted in the formation of novice cavalry companies and veterans like him quickly passed their experience to the new soldiers.[46]

Several VMI cadets were sent into the Kanawha valley to serve as drillmasters for the new troops and all of these new officers assisted Colonel Tompkins in the work of forming the new Confederate regiments that were needed to defend the western counties of Virginia from invasion from Ohio.

Many of the former privates in the volunteer units were soon elected or ordered into positions as officers in their companies. Rapid expansion of the "Army of the Kanawha" required the commissioning of many new officers to supervise the newly mustered units. One relatively young man, Isaac Noyes Smith, had served as a private in the original Kanawha Riflemen, but he was soon commissioned a Major in the new 22nd Virginia Infantry Regiment and would command the regiment in the absence of Colonel Tompkins. As a private, however, Isaac Smith was slightly unusual -- he was a graduate of Washington College in Lexington, had become an attorney, and served a term as a state legislator in Richmond where he represented the people of a portion of the Kanawha valley.[47] Many of the original privates of the Kanawha Riflemen were well-educated and several were lawyers and some were physicians.

Worries for the new Confederate Colonel continued to grow as rumors of Federal troops movements in the Galliopolis, Ohio, area began to reach Camp Tompkins.

46 Dickinson, Jack L., *8th Virginia Cavalry*, H. Howard: 1986, pg. 2

47 Laidley, W. S., *History of Charleston and Kanawha County and Representative Citizens*, Richmond-Arnold Publishing, Chicago, pg. 937; *Bench and Bar of West Virginia*, edited by George W. Atkinson, Virginia Law Book Co., Charleston: 1919, pg. 47

There was a wide stretch of territory to defend and he had only limited numbers of troops available. Fortunately, (and unfortunately) help was on the way. The former governor of Virginia, Henry Wise, had been commissioned a Brigadier-General and had been authorized to recruit troops to form "Wise's Legion".

During his term in the statehouse, Wise had shown favoritism to the westerner's interests and the Confederate authorities expected that he would be popular in the Kanawha valley and he was assigned there -- arriving in Gauley Bridge on June 23 and continuing on to Charleston where he reported on July 6 that he had 2075 men in his command.[48] He had absolutely no formal military training and had received his commission solely because of his previous political position in the state government.

The political and military situation in the region was rapidly changing. Colonel G.A. Porterfield's Confederate volunteers were defeated at Philippi in Virginia's northwestern region on June 3 in the first land battle of the war[49] and civil warfare in western Virginia became a reality. Virginia was firmly in the Confederacy and the new nation's capital was relocated to Richmond from Montgomery, Alabama.

The battle at Philippi was fought over one of the more significant military targets in the area, the Baltimore and Ohio Railroad. This strategic target connected the Union eastern states with pro-Union western states. The early military actions in western Virginia were generally related to attempts by one side or the other to gain control over the railroad or the few other transportation routes passing through the mountainous terrain. These initial campaigns were significant because they brought to national prominence several major officers who would manage the early stages of the war. Generals McClellan, Rosecrans, and even General Lee were involved in their first combat of the Civil War in western Virginia.

[48] Hotchkiss, *Confederate Military History*, Vol. III, pg. 60

[49] Ambler, Charles H., *West Virginia: The Mountain State*, Prentice-Hall, New York: 1946, pg. 351

Union victories and the subsequent consolidation of power by General McClellan in the north-central sections of the region had a major impact on the development of operations which were beginning in the Kanawha valley. The mountainous nature of the terrain in the western counties were obstacles to the movement of large bodies of troops and more significantly, the transport of a sufficient quantity of supplies needed to support military units in the field. Transporation routes in the southwestern counties were generally limited to the James River and Kanawha Turnpike which ran east-west approximately parallel to the New-Kanawha Rivers axis. The north-south routes were even more limited. The major road into the area from the north, the Gauley Bridge -Weston Turnpike, joined the James River and Kanawha Turnpike at Gauley Bridge, but roads into areas farther south than Gauley Bridge were even more limited.[50]

Much of the Confederate planning for military operations in the southern counties had to take into consideration the presence of large numbers of Union troops in the northern part of the state and the relatively rapid movements they could make into the south along the Gauley Bridge - Weston Turnpike. The possibility of being cut off from their depots and line of retreat into eastern Virginia was a possibility that constantly plagued the Rebel planners.

General Wise had little knowledge of military planning and as a "political general", he was only as effective as the professional members of his staff. He had been ordered to move his legion into the Kanawha valley before the recruiting and training of the new recruits to the Confederate army was completed, but they were selected for western duty when the size of his total force was considered by the senior Confederate planners. The slight military ability that he possessed was a good understanding of maps, terrain, and few doubted that he had courage. He was, however, described as erratic, impulsive, explosive, and thoroughly unpredictable. His autocratic manner and

[50] Cox, *Military Reminiscences*, pg. 80-81

rough-shod methods, after taking command in the valley, were resented even by those who were inclined to favor the Confederacy.

Wise was escorted into the western counties by the Richmond Light Infantry Blues, Virginia's oldest militia company. It was commanded by Captain O. Jennings Wise, the general's son and this was the same unit that the Kanawha Riflemen had patterned themselves after when formed in Charleston by Captain Patton. Two other prominent Confederates were on Wise's staff: Colonels Charles Frederick Henningsen and Frank Anderson were soldiers of fortune who had joined the "filibuster army" of William Walker when it invaded Nicargua a few years earlier. Their nickname came from the Spanish word *filibustero* which meant freebooter or pirate and these men attempted to conquer the vast Spanish-speaking territory of Latin America into the United States -- as slave states. Limited by the Missouri Compromise to the north, slavery could reasonably expand as far south as the continental limits, if the territories could be captured. This was the goal of the filibusters, but they succeeded only in capturing and holding Nicargua for a short time before losing to the local, popular forces. Henningsen had been the commander of the small force which had ruthlessly destroyed the city of Grenada.

Wise's staff was relatively experienced and they gradually prepared for combat with the Union forces which were assembling beyond the Ohio River. The area's difficult terrain was still the major obstacle for making successful plans for what would generally be defensive operations. The Allegheny mountains were fairly high and the roads in the region were unpaved and in a poor state of repair. Rains and poor weather could be expected to render the roads and turnpikes unpassable. Eastern Virginia would now pay a major price for all of the years of official neglect

[51] Estvan, Bela, *War Pictures From the South*, pg. 342-344; McPherson, James M., *Battle Cry of Freedom*, Oxford University Press: 1988, pg. 105-116 provides an excellent overview of the "filibusters".

of the western counties. If the legislature had approved funding for road construction prior to the war, the problems associated with moving vast amounts of military supplies would not have been as severe as they became.

The Union forces had an obvious advantage in supplying and moving its forces to conduct what would generally be offensive operations. They could move over relatively level land initially while additional troops and supplies could be transported in substantial quantities aboard riverboats which were plentiful at the time. The Ohio river was the first obstacle to be crossed by the Union soldiers and since downriver commerce had been interrupted by the war, there was an abundance of boats available for military charter. The rivers in the region were excellent transportation routes from the Ohio valley eastward toward Charleston, the major population center in Virginia's western counties.

## Command Changes

The new Colonel from Gauley Bridge obviously knew that the newly arrived general was going to be a problem. Since he had absolutely no military training and was dangerously overconfident, his political experience would be useful only when it came time to blame both the area's population and the new officers for failing to adequately support the Confederacy. While the newly-commissioned Colonel had litttle respect for that type of general, he was a trained, loyal officer who understood what was required in their official relationship. He would do everything that was required to help hold the small command together.

Not only was he stuck with a commander who knew little about military affairs, Tompkins had an assistant who was rapidly becoming a serious irritation. It would take more than a commisssion from Governor Letcher, a few semesters as an artillery instructor at VMI, and a great deal of nerve to make a Lieutenant-Colonel in a combat command. It was indeed unfortunate that John McCausland had been sent into the valley a few days prior to Tompkins receiving his commission. He was now senior to McCausland and now there definitely was some resentment present. The work of training had been going well, but there would be some personality problems in the future. It was difficult to pair up with a twenty-four year old without occasionally stepping on some very sensitive toes. It was equally hard for an experienced professional officer to work with an amateur without occasionally giving guidance and no matter how much it is solicited, this generally produces a slowly building resentment. This was the type of relationship which was evolving between Colonel Tompkins and John McCausland. A naturally-occurring antagonism between the experienced, mature military pragmatist and the young, unforgiving, and invincible firebrand was inevitable. It was indeed a mistake to have sent McCausland into the Kanawha valley as commander prior to the commissioning of Christopher Tompkins for the same duties. This was not, however, the only organizational error for which the Confederacy was going to suffer in the very near future as the poor relations between these two officers began to have an effect on others.

The new general, Henry Wise, was also an unusual politician -- an excellent speaker, but "remarkably profane"[52] -- and he was an ardent secessionist. He had been governor of Virginia at the time of the John Brown raid at Harpers Ferry and had been accused of making that issue into a national affair by consistently accusing the free states of being involved in a conspiracy of plotting to cause slave uprisings in the southern states. His politicizing of the raid caused much of the emotional outbursts on both sides of the issue which began to split the country into irreconcilable sections. He was an experienced, ambitious politician who had served in several different capacities. He served ten years in Congress, was appointed minister to Brazil by President Tyler (a fellow Virginian), and in 1855 he was elected Governor of Virginia. He was a southern activist who had threatened the peace and security of the

52 Hull, "Gauley Mount", pg. 142

nation in the past.[53]

Just prior to the 1856 election, he organized a meeting of southern governors at Raleigh, North Carolina, and after the votes had been counted, he declared that if the Republican, Fremont, had been elected he would have raised an army of twenty thousand men and taken Washington. His antics had a dramatic effect on later developments between North and South.[54]

James Seddon, a prominent Virginian who later became Confederate Secretary of War wrote in December, 1859, about Wise and the John Brown raid:

"In short; with his favorite policy of swaggering and bullying, Wise has exploited this whole affair to his own selfish aggrandizement, to aid his vain hopes for the Presidency, and to strengthen the fragment of a southern part he heads. And as a result has conjured a devil neither he nor perhaps any other can lay, and, arraying the roused pride and animosities of both sections against each other, has brought on a real crisis of imminent peril to both."[55]

This letter was written to R.M.T.Hunter, another leading Virginian. In December, 1859, Hunter was the leading candidate for the Democratic nomination for President in the 1860 election. Seddon recognized at an early date the danger Wise and a few others like him were presenting to the stability of the country. His combative attitude, as well as his "swaggering and bullying", would cause serious problems for the Confederacy in the Kanawha valley as the 1861 military campaigns began to unfold. He was, however, in charge and Colonel Tompkins was a trained officer who would respect the officers placed in positions superior to his own.

Wise was a hard man. In his capacity as governor, he

---

53 Hodges, M.S., *West Virginia Legislative Handbook and Manual and Official Register*, 1929, pg. 881

54 *Ibid*, pg. 881

55 *Ibid*, pg. 882

signed the death warrants of John Brown and his fellow conspirator with a firm hand...even though his own daughter was on her knees before him with tears in her eyes begging him to pardon the two convicted criminals. Wise offered a visitor a good cigar, "these are good Havana's" and said in a stern voice "This man has forfeited his life to the law, and the law must have its course."[54]

He was to pay a severe price for his ambitions that helped to start the war. During the battle for control of Roanoke Island, he was to lose a son, O. Jennings Wise, to a bullet. As he took the dead son's hand in his own, he was heard to say "You have died for me; you have died for your father!" An observer reported that large tears rolled down his cheeks as he repeated "He died for me! He died for me!" as he fell unconscious to the ground.[55]

He was, however, blisslully unaware of the future as he moved confidently to take control of the military situation in the Kanawha valley.

The Confederacy did not fully appreciate the political and military value of the western counties of Virginia. The area was looked on as a sort of Siberia and the generals sent there were regarded as exiles as the primary focus of the war began to center on the area between Washington and Richmond. Wise had been recruiting troops for his "legion" when orders were received to begin conducting operations in the trans-Allegheny region.

The Confederacy formed ten of these "legions" during the war. These were "combined arms teams" similar to regimental combat teams or modern task forces. The legions were composed of infantry, cavalry, and artillery elements under a unified command which was generally well-suited for independent operations. Wise's Legion was composed of three infantry regiments, a cavalry regiment, and a smaller artillery unit.[56]

He and his legion were given a large task. He was

---

54 Estvan, *War Pictures*, pg. 248

55 *Ibid*, pg. 248

56 Wallace, Lee A., Jr., *A Guide to Virginia Military Organizations: 1861-1865*; Lynchburg: 1986, pg. 150

ordered to establish his headquarters in western Virginia and hold back the Federal troops who had already crossed the Ohio. He was also told to move in the direction of Wheeling, where there were conventions being held by Virginia's Unionists to discuss the formation of a new, Union state from Virginia's western counties. If he were able to disrupt these sessions, the Unionists in the area would be dealt a serious reversal from which it would be difficult to recover.

Planning these campaigns were always easier than actually conducting them. No one was more aware of this basic fact of life in the military than was Christopher Tompkins. The problems of terrain alone were quite obvious to him as he sat in the middle of the mountainous region of the state during extremely poor weather as he wondered if the Confederate campaign could be sustained much longer because of the poor roads which were nearly impassable due to their muddy conditions. The lack of forage possibilities for the men as well as their animals in this underpopulated area made military campaigns in the area nearly impossible for either side. Ammunition supplies sufficient to conduct a battle or two were carried by the men, but food had to be hauled in wagons and animal forage had to be hauled to feed the teams for the return trip. This mandatory practice didn't permit the hauling of the amount of rations and general supplies needed to provision the two armies for operations in the mountains.[57]

Tompkins and his staff would not be cold, wet, and hungry in their log camp, if their wagon had been able to reach them. Their food had been consisting of undercooked dough and a piece of nearly raw meat which had been cooked on the hot coals of a campfire.[58]

It hadn't always been this way. The area was having its worst weather in history and the roads, while normally poor, were generally impassable for the supply wagons

[57] Cox, *Military Reminiscences*, pg. 80-81

[58] Childers, William, "A Virginian's Dilemma," *West Virginia History*, Vol. XXVII, No. 3, April, 1966, pg. 185

from either side. The primary road in the area was the turnpike which connected the Kanawha valley with Lewisburg before continuing to the east to connect with highways that lead to Richmond. Tompkins and his family had traveled along the turnpike many times since moving into the mountains to make their new home. The stops at the inns and taverns in the days before the war were only pleasant memories, now. With Ellen and the children held in the middle of the Union camp on Gauley Mountain, pleasant thoughts didn't last long in the consciousness of Colonel Tompkins.

He obviously felt that the war could have been avoided if the extremists in either political party hadn't gained control of the political process. It was men like his "general", Wise, who caused much of the political squabbling and unrest which broke into open warfare. The other "general" in his life at the time, John B. Floyd, was equally bad. Floyd had helped to supply the South with arms from Federal armories while he had served as the Secretary of War in the Buchannan administration and this helped to give the southern radicals the means to consider fighting to ensure that their lifestyle and political system would be continued. If these two "generals" had not been involved in the secession movement, the chances for an open outbreak of hostilities would have been less likely.

Tompkins and many of the other Virginia volunteers were aware of the antics of their respective commanders -- both before and after they had become "generals". Wise was well-known from his days as governor when John Brown was captured, but his antics during the Secession Convention where he reinforced his speech with threatening gestures made with a horse pistol which was waved around at the crowd![59]

If there was an actual villain in Tompkins' reminiscences beside the soaked campfire, this would have probably been the other former governor of Virginia who was in charge of both his brigade as well as Wise's Legion and the Kanawha volunteers facing General Rosecrans'

59 Hodges, *Legislative Handbook*, pg. 882

Federal army on Sewell Mountain. Neither of the two governors stood very high in Tompkins' estimation, but at least Wise was a brave, if reckless, officer. He had personally lead assaults on the Union pickets on several occasions and if he lacked both knowledge of military affairs and leadership ability, Wise was able to compensate for his defiencies in these areas with nerve and loyalty to the officers and men under his command.

Floyd, on the other hand, had left the Buchannan administration under a cloud. He had served as Secretary of War and had managed to transfer substantial quantities of arms and supplies from Federal depots in the North to the southern states. A serious effort was underway in modernizing the large stocks of flintlock muskets into weapons fired by percussion caps, the latest military invention. Floyd was instrumental in having 115,000 of these muskets declared surplus and he allowed these to be sold to the states at the low cost of $2.50 each. He permitted seasoned musket stocks to be traded for green stocks located at the Harpers Ferry arsenal and Floyd was attempting to transfer 124 cannon from Pittsburg to a location in the south when he had to leave office.[60] All of this was done under the nose of President Buchannan, a Pennsylvanian.

Floyd had two other political problems that were awaiting resolution in northern Federal courts, if he were ever to be captured. He had secretly sold the Fort Snelling reservation to a New York syndicate and he had been accused of mishandling $870,000 in indian trust bonds. All of this came to the attention of the government as the Federal garrison at Fort Sumpter was being fired upon and the disagreement within the cabinet about reinforcing the fort gave Floyd an opportunity to resign and leave Washington. Indictments against Floyd were issued and dual investigations were launched in the House of Representatives as the northern press had a field day with the scandal.[61]

60 Hodges, *Legislative Manual*, pg. 881
61 *Ibid*, pg. 881

Floyd feared that he would have to face his accusers in the courts if he were ever captured and this made him cautious. Tompkins, while reflecting beside the campfire, would have recalled that Floyd's entire command moved into their fortifications at Carnifex Ferry rather than march against the small Federal garrison at Gauley Bridge or the even smaller post at Charleston before Union reinforcements from Rosecrans' army then conducting operations in the area of the Baltimore and Ohio railroad could arrive. Tompkins would have remembered that after the fighting at Carnifex Ferry had died down that Floyd and his staff had already planned their retreat before Tompkins had been consulted. He was the most experienced officer in the group, but because of the continuing animosity between Wise and Floyd, Tompkins -- seen as Wise's man by Floyd -- was not even asked for his opinion.[62]

Floyd definitely wasn't a risk-taker. Tompkins greatest point of contention with Floyd was the total lack of respect that he had shown for the Virginia volunteers who had served under Wise before Floyd had arrived in western Virginia to take command. While it was true that the volunteers were little more than rabble at this point in the war, they deserved to be treated as the other soldiers in the small Confederate army that operated in the Kanawha valley. The fact that the slightly more than two regiments recruited from the counties of western Virginia had not been formally assigned to either Wise's or Floyd's commands left them in a precarious position. As they belonged to neither unit, the volunteers were frequently marched back and forth between the two commanders. They were poorly equipped and Tompkins frequently complained over their misuse to General Wise. He wrote:

"Brig. Gen. Henry A. Wise, *Commanding &c.:*

SIR: I have the honor to acknowledge your orders of this date. directing the movement of troops from this camp, and I feel impelled, most respectfully, to enter my protest against its immediate application to the volunteer forces

62 Childers, "Virginian's Dilemma", pg. 179

under my command. I beg you to remember that these troops are now decimated by disease and casualties incurred by weeks of exposure; that they have never been furnished with tents, or even equipments regarded as essential to the ordinary requirements of service, and above all, that they are actually destutute of clothing, except such as they bore upon their persons in the hurried march from Kanawha. The Twenty-second Regiment especially may be mentioned as having incurred losses by the destruction of the steamer Maffet, and their inability to communicate with Charleston, which should be remembered by you as worthy of immediate consideration. I cannot, therefore, under the circumstances report any companies of the volunteer regiments as fit for the field, and believe that their removal from quarters at present would be attended with detrimental consequences in every respect.

"I am, sir, very respectfully, your obedient servant,

C.Q.Tompkins

*Commanding Volunteer Brigade*"[63]

Wise had arrived in the Kanawha valley prior to Floyd, but since Floyd had been assigned his rank prior to Wise being appointed a general, Floyd was the ranking officer, Both were organizing their forces to conduct a campaign in western Virginia, but Wise completed his preparations first and began to move his troops west. Wise was born along the Atlantic shore, but Floyd was from the western area and obviously felt this should have been his exclusive area to defend. He was furious when Wise moved out first.

Henry Heth, one of Floyd's regimental commanders wrote:

"When General Floyd heard this he was simply furious, and cursed Wise a hundred times a day: 'God damn him, why does he come to my country? Why does he not stay in the east and defend his own country, Accomac and Southampton; there is where he belongs. I don't want the

63 *Official Records*, Vol. V, Series I, pg. 786-787

damned rascal here. I will not stand it."[64]

Heth claimed that his ability at "word painting" was inadequate to describe what happened, but he said that the campaign conducted by Floyd and Wise was "one of the most farcical and rediculous campaigns that occurred in our Civil War, or in any war, I believe..."[65] Christopher Tompkins would have agreed with Heth on this!

Wise attempted to recruit more troops as he marched his legion into the mountains. He was fairly popular with the western Virginians as he had attempted to get some western issues passed through the 1850-1851 Virginia Constitutional Convention. He had handled patronage carefully in the western counties while he was Virginia's governor and he had some political support from that part of the state. Jefferson Davis had probably hoped that as a military commander in the area, Wise would be able to rally some of that political support as military allies.

Wise attempted to attract more support as he continued into the mountains. Henry Heth wrote:

> "Wise, when enroute to Western Virginia, I was told, stopped at every crossroad and made a speech, saying: 'Come and join me; bring a musket; if you have no musket bring a rifle; if no rifle, a shotgun; if no shotgun, a pistol; no pistol, a gate hinge; no gate hinge, by God bring an India rubber shoe, but come!"[66]

During better times, Tompkins would probably have smiled as he remembered how quickly the firey political general had pulled stakes and started a forced march back out of the Kanawha valley just ahead of his Federal tormentors. He would have had even less fond memories of the first meeting between the two political generals when they met after Wise's retreat. Henry Heth was at the

---

64 Heth, Henry, "The Memoirs of Henry Heth", edited by James L. Morrison, Jr., *Civil War History*, Vol. VIII, 1962, pg. 13

65 *Ibid*, pg. 12

66 *Ibid*, pg. 13

meeting and wrote about it:

"After the usual formalities had been observed, General Wise stood up, placed his hands on the back of his chair and made a speech. I think he spoke a couple of hours. He reviewed the history of the United States from its discovery, the Revolutionary War, the Mexican War, the causes of the present troubles, his march down the Kanawha River, the affair at Scary Creek, and his retreat to White Sulphur. Floyd listened patiently, General Wise, before taking his seat, asked General Floyd where he was going. Floyd replied, 'Down that road,' pointing to the road on which Wise had retreated. Said Wise, 'What are you going to do, Floyd?' 'Fight,' answered Floyd, intimating that was what Wise had failed to do. If a look could kill,, Floyd would have been annihilated, for I never saw greater hatred condensed in a look before or since."[67]

That meeting set the tone for the military relationship for the the remainder of the campaign between those two. They had a well-developed dislike for one another and had taken their political rivalry much farther than most people would have ever considered. These two politicians were not normal people and their political ambitions -- the desire to be significant leaders in the post-war Confederacy -- were identical. Their goals lead to this intense personal competition that cost the South a major defeat at this early stage of the war. These two spent so much time in conflict with one another that they had little opportunity to be serious about the secondary enemy facing each of their small Rebel armies -- General Rosecrans' Federal army that was slowly gaining control over the western portion of the state of Virginia.

Union General Cox had been confused by the lack of agressive action on the part of the Confederate forces facing him while he was at Gauley Bridge. He was aware that both Wise and Floyd were in the vicinity and that their combined troops outnumbered the Union forces under his

[67] Heth, "Memoirs", pg. 131

command. If attacked, the Federal garrison would probably not have done well against it. The lack of attack mystified Cox. After the war, he discovered the reason why there was no attack:

"I was puzzled at Floyd's inaction at Carnifex Ferry, but the mystery is partly solved by the publication of the Confederate records. There was no cooperation between the commanders, and Wise refused the assistance Floyd demanded, nor could even the authority of Lee reduce the ex-governor to real subordination. The letters of Wise show a capacity for keeping a command in hot water which was unique. If he had been half as troublesome to me as he was to Floyd, I should, indeed, have had a hot time of it. But he did me royal service by preventing anything approaching unity of action between the two principal Confederate columns."[68]

Wise, alone, wasn't the only command problem in that small Confederate army, he was simply the problem that Cox was able to isolate from the confusion of the early stages of the war. His rival, Floyd, certainly earned a great deal of the blame for the errors made by the Rebel forces.

Because of the legal cloud that the former Secretary of War had over his head from his activities during his period of service in the Buchannan administration, Floyd was afraid of facing northern justice. When Henry Heth advised him on Cotton Hill that Rosecrans could possibly capture the entire Confederate command, Floyd responded:

"No sir, I will die before I am captured. Do you know what they say they will do with me if captured? They say they will put me in an iron cage, haul me around their damned country and exhibit me as if I were a wild beast."[69]

This fear of capture was constantly with Floyd and

68 Cox, *Military Reminiscences*, pg. 97

69 Heth, "Memoirs", pg. 17

eventually cost him his commission after he managed to escape from Fort Donelson -- leaving another to surrender in his place to General Grant.[70]

Another problem with Floyd became obvious as the operations continued in the mountainous region of the state -- he obviously wasn't suited to command troops in combat. Many of his supporters felt that since he had been Secretary of War that he had some special and exclusive knowledge of military arts. The editor of the Richmond *Examiner* was a member of Floyd's staff (the ex-governor wanted favorable press reports) and the editor was upset when General Lee was assigned to the senior position in the state's military command structure -- over Floyd. He later discussed this with Henry Heth, claiming that Floyd had forgotten more on the subject of war than Lee would ever know. Heth asked where Floyd had gained this military knowledge and the editor replied:

"Has he not been Secretary of War, and a great military student? It would have done very well to have sent Lee to report to Floyd to dig ditches where Floyd wanted them."[71]

At one time, Heth, like many others in the South may have believed Floyd possessed this ability. Heth wrote after the war:

"I had conceived an idea that a man who had been Secretary of War knew everything pertaining to military matters." Heth soon realized that his assumption was incorrect and he continued his memoirs with this statement: "I soon discovered that my chief was as incapacated for the work he had undertaken as I would have been to lead an Italian opera."[72]

70 Brown, James B., "Life of Brigadier-General John McCausland", *West Virginia History*, Vol. IV, No. 4, July, 1943, pg. 248

71 Heth, "Memoirs", pg. 16

72 *Ibid*, pg. 12

If Tompkins had had been able to read minds, he would have probably have agreed with Heth's assessment. Once again, he was under the control of a political appointee who knew little about military strategy. The situation was worsened by the fact that that his immediate commander was that same type of individual and that there was no one who could intervene in the political squabbling which was continuing. The arrival of General Lee at Sewell Mountain had left many with the hope that the situation would soon be corrected, but Lee's management style at this early stage of the war was not confrontational and there were no sudden changes in the constant bickering between these political generals. Tompkins and several of the other western volunteer officers began to lose hope in the eventual success of their cause.

The military situation in the Sewell Mountain area favored neither side and both were aware of this. The Confederate forces outnumbered the Federals in the area, but there was a larger conflict going on in the region which obviously was to have an effect on the Kanawha theater of operations. Lee and his Confederates were sitting on the summit of Sewell mountain, hoping that Rosecrans would make the mistake of attacking the Rebels in their fortifications. If this were to occur, the Union army would lose large numbers of troops after which the Confederates would probably go on the offensive. The Confederate pickets observed increased activity in the Federal camp on October 4 and they began to prepare for an attack.

Isaac Smith, a Major in Lee's command, wrote of the expected fighting:

"At quarter past three o'clock we were all up, and ready very shortly after to receive the enemy. Every moment we awaited the opening of the enemys guns, and so continued until late in the day. At twelve oclock I thought it more probable no attack would be made during the day. You have no idea of the excitement such a state of things produces..."[73]

[73] Childers, "Virginian's Dilemma", pg. 188-189

As it became obvious that Rosecrans wasn't stupid enough to make this sort of move, Lee began to shift his thinking to an attack of his own. He had received reinforcements from the regiments he had left in position near Cheat Mountain, but the difficult terrain on Sewell Mountain made receiving an attack much preferable to delivering one. The attacking force would sustain serious numbers of casualties and both of the opposing generals knew it!

The increased activity in the Federal camp was the result of a decision recently made by General Rosecrans -- the Union regiments were to pull back to more easily supplied positions near Gauley Bridge. This, however, was a quite dangerous manuever to attempt while under the guns of the enemy. They would be vulnerable to attack and probable defeat to the point of a rout if they were caught outside of their fortifications. The danger of rout was greater if the Confederates were to attack while the Union regiments were strung out along the turnpike like so many plums to be picked by the assaulting Rebel brigades. Most of the Federal troops had been campaigning long enough to be aware of this and they couldn't have been very happy to be put in that predicament. It was simply a very difficult manuever to accomplish under the noses of the enemy pickets.

The Confederate pickets were aware of some movement and noise within the Federal camp during the night and reported this to the officer of the day, Major Isaac Smith. Smith was immediately suspicious and reported the news to his superior officer, Colonel Tompkins. Smith wrote of the outcome:

"...found that one of the pickets had heard great rumblings of wagons but thought nothing unusual as they had heard them every night. The camp was surprised next morning when daylight showed the opposite hill perfectly bare which had been filled with tents and moving men the day before. Colonel Tompkins regretted not having permittted me to report and said he would tell General Lee about it. The General afterwards said I should have advanced the pickets and felt the enemy; just think if I had known that was the way to manage the matter, I should have been the first man to occupy the enemy's camp..."[74]

Colonel Tompkins was a trained military officer, as mentioned previously he had more experience than most of the men in Lee's small army. He advised Smith not to report the noise in the Federal camp, an action that he probably knew was not the best to take. He and Smith had recently been in charge of Floyd's rearguard during the retreat from Carnifex Ferry and he was fully aware of the outcome when a force was caught outside of their fortifications by a superior force. The obvious question arises: Did Tompkins make a mistake that night in October or did he consciously allow the Union regiments to escape down the turnpike to safety?

Tompkins had many reasons to allow them to slip away and only his duty which required the report be made. First, and of real importance, he was under a great obligation to both Rosecrans and Cox for ensuring the safety of his family back at Gauley Mount. This obligation extended to many of the officers he was now facing across the lines and being forced to kill the men who helped his family was probably more than the man could force himself to do. Second, there was some sort of personal relationship between Rosecrans and the Confederate Colonel from their post-army commercial days. They were probably good friends and this would certainly have affected Tompkins' decision to report the noise in the night to General Lee. Third, any running battle with the retreating Union force moving from Sewell Mountain would lead to a strongpoint where the Federals would obviously rally for a last stand. This would have been done in the fortifications previously erected on his farm and his family would have been placed in great danger, if a battle developed around them. These three factors combined with Tompkins' obvious dislike for the political appointees placed in his chain-of-command probably resulted in his "mistake" that allowed the Federal

[74] Childers, "Virginian's Dilemma", pg. 190

regiments to escape from General Lee.

This decision, if it was a conscious decision to give Rosecrans a chance to get out of danger, was to have a great long-term impact on the outcome of the war. The Union armies weren't doing well as a whole at the time. There had been a series of morale-sapping defeats at the hands of the agressive Confederates and one additional defeat of a Union army would have done much to push the Federal government toward negotiations. If Rosecrans had been trapped along the turnpike as his regiments were defeated piecemeal, they would have been out of action and unable to defend the fledgling government forming in the Union areas of western Virginia which was loyal to the Union. By surviving, Rosecrans and his Ohio and Kentucky regiments ensured that the new government would survive to put additional troops into the field against the Rebels and produce a decisive split in the state of Virginia, a political victory which weakened the southern efforts toward victory. The sons of the farmers would now be more likely to enter Federal service rather than follow their state and the blow to the Confederacy as part of their new country seceded to join the Union was as serious as anything up to that point. The escape of Rosecrans had a greater effect than Colonel Tompkins had ever imagined. If Tompkins had been under any sort of self-imposed obligation to General Rosecrans for the protection offered to the Tompkins family, it was now repaid with interest! While there is only circumstantial evidence of this, the character of the Rebel Colonel, if under an obligation, could have allowed the escape to happen.

Tompkins wrote to Rosecrans soon after the retreat to thank him for allowing his wife and daughter to travel to Richmond to get winter clothing. He referred to the problems of the country:

"...I shall continue in all sincerity to refer briefly to the unfortunate condition of our divided country.

"It has been a source of great and momentous concern to myself and whilst I have no idea that either of us will live to see the end of the evils that now exist, I do cherish the hope that we may in our respective spheres accomplish much to mitigate their atrocities.

"I wish I could talk with you and many of my old friends and comrades on your side of the question. I believe we could manage affairs better than the politicians ao at least honestly differ in our respective views.

"But this may never be..."[75]

Mitigating atrocities may have been the intent when Tompkins made the sudden decision to permit the Federal retreat to continue unmolested. The Colonel was beginning to show symptoms that his interest in the war had nearly run its' course. He became a soldier to fight the nation's enemies -- not the men of his own country. The feeling of country, even though it was divided by the radicals of the two political parties, was still strong in the men in both armies. The pickets traded food for salt and tobacco and the officers seemed to genuinely enjoy the brief periods of truce when they could visit and talk.[76] Two others were also feeling the emotions of Christopher Tompkins. General Cox wrote that "I went about my duties with a half choking sense of a grief I dared not think of..."[77] because of the condition of the unfortunate, divided country. Isaac Smith wrote of similar touching emotions from his position on Sewell Mountain. He wrote that "...From this point there is a fine view of the enemy's camp because so near -- can see men and horses plainly and the 'Star spangled

75 Tompkins, "Colonel's Lady", pg. 411-412

76 Hull, Forrest, "The Death of Colonel Croghan", *The West Virginia Review*, Vol. XXVI, No. 1, pg. 22. The article mentions a diary entry by Major Rutherford B. Hayes relating the return of Croghan's body. Hayes says: "A party of Rebels from Floyd's army met us here today with a flag of truce. They had come for the body of Colonel Croghan. We had a good, friendly chat. It seems absurd to be fighting such friendly and civil fellows!"

77 Bailes, Clarice L., "Jacob Dolson Cox in West Virginia", *West Virginia History*, Vol. VI, October, 1944, pg. 8

banner' (in spite of my position I love it yet) waving in the breeze -- ..."[78]

Both Cox and Smith were relatively new soldiers with few ties to the previously-existing National Army. They both, however, were feeling the pressure of this "unnatural" and "fratricidal" war, as they described it. Tompkins was an old soldier and had felt the pressures of long campaigns before. There is a point where everyone has had enough and Christopher Tompkins was rapidly getting there. He had witnessed enough stupidity from political-appointees serving as general officers in previous wars and was rapidly getting his fill of the same type of individual in this one. The arrogance of Floyd and his evil intent toward the volunteers who had served under the command of Tompkins was apparent to everyone, but they were helpless to prevent it. General Lee was the last hope for an actual unified command against the Federal invaders and he was failing to bring Wise and Floyd under his control. Officers began to consider resignation as an option while many of the enlisted men considered the risks of desertion to get away from these idiots who were running the army. For the officer, there had to be an opportunity connected with a chance to maintain his honor when he chose to announce his resignation -- it simply had to be done the proper way. For the private, the risks were greater -- deserters were frequently shot as object lessons to others in the ranks who considering the same option.

"...manage the affairs better than the politicians..." had to be a common thought in the ranks of the cold, hungry, and exhausted Confederate army on Sewell Mountain as they discovered that their prey had escaped to fight again another day. Sickness had reduced their numbers as measles and other childhood diseases begain to affect the previously unexposed farm boys in both armies. Those still capable remained on duty and while the Rebels considered pursuit, the Federals probably congradulated themselves on their luck in escaping from the risks they had taken when

[78] Childers, "Virginian's Dilemma", pg. 187

they slipped out of their fortifications on Sewell Mountain. They were all aware of the risks involved, especially the Federal rearguard which would have to be sacrificed if the Confederate pickets discovered their nightime manuevering.

General Cox wrote of the retreat:

"...Tents were struck at ten o'clock in the evening, and the trains sent on their way under escort at eleven. The column moved as soon as the trains were out of the way, except my own brigade,to which was assigned the duty of rear guard. We remained upon the crest of the hill till half past one, the men formed in line of battle and directed to lie down until time for them to march...It was interesting to observe the effect of this night movement upon the men. Their imagination was excited by the novelty of the situation, and they furnished abundant evidence that the unknown is always, in such cases, the wonderful. The night had cleared off and the stars were out. The Confederate position was eastward from us, and as a bright star rose above the ridge on which the enemy was, we could hear soldiers saying in a low tone to each other, 'there goes a fire ballon, it must be a signal, they must have discovered what we are doing.' The troops had marched but a mile or two when they overtook part of the wagon train toiling slowly over the steep and slippery hills. Here and there a team would be stalled in the mud, and it looked as if daylight would overtake us before even a tolerably defensible position would be reached.... When at last day broke, we had reached a position which was easily defensible, and I could halt the brigade and wait for the others to get entirely out of the way..."[79]

When Lee discovered the deserted Union camp, he ordered a pursuit, but this was small and cautious. The Federal column had managed to put several miles between themselves and the Confederate army as they moved back to the previously prepared positions at Gauley Mount and at

79 Cox, *Military Reminiscences*, pg. 122-123

Gauley Bridge. The small town at the junction of the New, Kanawha, and Gauley Rivers was filled with rations, ammunition, and military stores for use by the troops. They would shorten their supply line considerably by moving back with the knowledge that every mile of advance through the mountains by Lee's forces would stretch their own supply system to its' limits. The roads on Sewell and Gauley Mountain were completely unforgiving and wagon wheel traffic served to make the roads even more impassable. The Union troops prepared to move into their winter quarters in the town and on Gauley Mount as the Confederates planned one last attempt to force the Federal soldiers out of Virginia's territory.

Lee quickly developed a plan which, if successful, would drive the Federals from the Kanawha valley. This new approach was simple to implement, but involved dividing the Confederate force into two parts. Lee would soon send Floyd to the south of New River to make an approach on the Union camps in the area of Gauley Bridge while Lee personally lead the remainder of the Rebel army which had been reinforced by troops under General Loring. Lee and Loring would move down the turnpike toward Gauley Bridge as Floyd manuevered in the same direction, but from the opposite side of New River. Pressed in front by Lee while being shelled by Floyd as their river traffic was threatened, the Federal forces in the upper valley would soon be forced to retreat to positions where they could make a stand. Unfortunately for the Union army, this would have involved a march to near the Ohio River where they would be reinforced quickly by riverboat.

The plan was well-conceived, but circumstances prevented the full deployment of troops against the Federals. There was a serious need for reinforcements in the area to the east of the mountains as the Federals began to threaten vital railroad junctions. Requests for help caused Lee to detatch much of his army for service east of the mountains and Floyd was allowed to continue with his operation against the camps at Gauley Bridge.

This decision of Lee's was far from unanamious. Many officers had doubts as to Floyd's ability and judgement to manage an independent command in combat. Henry Heth was one of Floyd's colonels at the time and he later wrote that he discussed his misgivings with General Lee. He wrote:

"I had a long talk with General Lee and expressed to him my views as to Floyd's ability to excercise an independent command. I told him if Floyd was given an independent command it would be merely a question of time when it would be captured; that I did not think the Confederacy could afford to lose three or four thousand men, simply to gratify the ambition of a politician who was as incapable of fighting then, as a baby. When I had this conversation with the General, it was raining; the next morning it was a bright, beautiful day. I met the General at breakfast.

"He said, 'Well, Colonel, I hope as this is a bright day you take a less gloomy view of matters that you did last night when we parted.'

"I replied, 'No, General, I am much of the same opinion still. I have seen too much incompetency in General Floyd during the past four months to cause me to change my views."[80]

The independent command crossed New River and moved through the sparsely populated area. Several observers were there to record the events as they unfolded, but soldiers such as Colonel Tompkins wouldn't have been very happy with Floyd's plans. They were too far from any type of support and were greatly out-numbered by the Federal forces in the area. Tompkins left no written record of his feelings at this time, but they must have closely paralleled those of Henry Heth. Heth wrote:

"Floyd crossed New River and camped at the base of Cotton Hill. From Cotton Hill, extending along New River, there is a precipitious range of mountains. The distance betwen the base of the mountain and the river is from a half

80 Heth, "Memoirs", pg. 16-17

to a quarter of a mile. The banks of the river are perpendicular and from 80 to 100 feet high, and the river runs like a mountain torrent. The mountain I have mentioned, almost five or six miles from Cotton Hill, slopes down to almost nothing, and is here only two or three hundred yards from the river bank. If I have made myself clear as to the situation of the mountain and the river, it will be seen with a force in Floyd's front marching over Cotton Hill and another marching behind the mountain to where it slopes down into the river, Floyd would be caught in as complete a *cul-de-sac* as man or nature could have constructed.

"I told General Floyd that his position was faulty, that he could not subsist his command where he was, that the roads were becoming worse and worse each day, that he was hauling his provisions 100 miles. I could see that he was not gaining anything by remaining where he was, that General Rosecrans could drive him away whenever he chose to do so. "Let him dare cross the river,' Floyd said, 'and not a damned Yankee will ever recross it, I will never yield a foot of *my country* to the rascals.'

I then added, 'General Rosecrans will capture you and your entire command."[81]

This difficult position of the entire Confederate command under the incompetent Floyd was so obvious to Heth that it would not have escaped the attention of Colonel Tompkins. It certainly didn't go unnoticed by General Rosecrans.

Rosecrans sent orders to General Schenck at Townsend's Ferry which is located about twenty miles upriver from Gauley Bridge to convert his wagons into a ferry and be prepared to cross New River to move into Floyd's rear. Rosecrans also ordered General Benham to march his brigade down the river to a point about six miles below Gauley Bridge, cross the river, and hold his position until orders were received to move into Floyd's rear from

81 Heth, "Memoirs", pg. 17

the opposite direction as that taken by Schenck. General Cox was to hold his position at Gauley Bridge until an opportunity to cross the river came and at that time, he should cross to begin pressing the Confederate pickets.

It was a good plan and would have resulted in the capture of the entire Confederate force with Floyd. The fear of the iron cage reserved for him in the North was coming closer to Floyd as the Federal forces manuevered nearby. Floyd had moved his cannon by hand up Cotton Hill and had quite a surprise for General Rosecrans on November 1, 1861, but he only annoyed the Federal garrison. He was safe from the planned coordinated attack as long as the rivers were at flood stage and too dangerous to cross. When the water began to subside, Floyd began to feel the fear of that cold cage as Rosecrans and Cox began to cross troops over the rivers which had previously shielded him. Cox's regiments were pressing into his front as Benham's brigade began to move into positions from which it would have been possible to cut off the Confederate retreat.

Henry Heth was with Floyd's advance forces and observed everything first hand:

"I was skirmishing with Rosecrans' advance when Floyd, much excited, rode up to me and said a country girl had just ridden in and informed him of the approach of Benham's force. 'By God, they wil get in my rear; I shall be attacked in front and rear; what must I do?'

I think the visions of the iron cage were very vivid then. I said, 'General, leave me with one regiment, a battery of artillery, and a dozen cavalry. Take the rest of your command and, if the mouth of the sac is occupied, cut your way through. Let me take care of myself; I will delay Rosecrans every way I can by causing him to form a line of battle. You may thus save a portion of your command, and yourself, from being caged.'

"Floyd followed my advice. Benham, I was informed, came within a quarter of a mile, or half mile, of the mouth of the *cul-de-sac*, and for reasons best known to himself, came no farther. Rosecrans, we understood, preferred charges against him. Floyd was thus enabled to escape without receiving a shot. As soon as he was safe, he sent word to me of his escape and directed me to follow, which I was not slow to do. I got through all right with the loss of only a few men when skirmishing with Rosecrans."[82]

Colonel Tompkins missed much of the fighting on Cotton Hill. He requested and was granted leave to visit his wife and daughter who had recently been allowed to leave the family farm at Gauley Mount by General Rosecrans. Tompkins rode fast to Lewisburg where his family was waiting and together they went to Richmond for some well-deserved rest. Tompkins turned over his regiment to his second-in-command, Major Isaac Smith, for the period he was to be away.

At about the same time, the Confederates in Floyd's small command became aware that Isaac Smith's father, a prominent Unionist livng in Charleston, was the democratic candidate for governor of the Unionist portion of Virginia. This did little to endear Smith to the erratic, impulsive, vindictive, and probably insane General Floyd. During the campaign of Cotton Hill, Smith felt that he was so grossly insulted by Floyd that he must resign from the Confederate service. He waited to do so until the return of Colonel Tompkins out of loyalty to the regiment under his command and concern for the men in his regiment.[83]

Tompkins returned from leave toward the end of the fighting -- just prior to the actual retreat and encouraged Smith to seek a court of inquiry over the insult of Floyd, but Smith simply wanted to get away from his problem and refused. Tompkins' problems increased shortly afterward when Floyd ordered his artillery to begin firing on the Federal camp at Gauley Mount. The camp was a legitimate target for the cannon, but Tompkins asked Floyd to order a halt in the shelling -- his wife and family were in the house

82 Heth, "Memoirs", pg. 17-18

83 Childers, "Virginian's Dilemma", pg. 194

in the center of the Federal camp.

There had been bad blood between the two since Floyd first moved into the Kanawha valley to take command and Floyd refused to halt the shelling. Tompkins immediately resigned from the Confederate army and left the camp.[84]

The Confederacy lost an excellent officer who would have probably become a general because of the incompetent and irrational behavior of General John B. Floyd.

Floyd cared for little other than his image and felt that leading men in combat was the same as campaigning for votes in an election. This pathetic figure had lead his regiments to a near-disaster on the south side of New River and ran off more men than only Colonel Tompkins and Major Smith. Colonel Heth remained with his regiment; he was fortunate to have served from the onset of the war in Floyd's brigade and wasn't tarnished by service with any of Floyd's rivals, such as Wise.

Heth went on to explain how mistaken Floyd actually was in his leadership techniques by illustrating his actions during one of the worst winter retreats of the war:

"About twelve o'clock at night I reached Floyd's camp. It was raining hard. Floyd had burnt his tents in order to lighten his wagons. Rosecrans was in pursuit. I reported to Floyd; we had a conversation about the condition of affairs.

"He said, 'This is fast becoming a rout. I tell you what I will do; I will have the command assembled and make them a speech and tell them that reinforcements are coming to join me.'

"General,' I answered, 'I would not disturb the men. They have had a hard day's march. Let them sleep. And especially I would not tell them that reinforcements are coming to assist you. They would soon find that it was

[84] Childers, "Virginian's Dilemma", pg. 419

not true, and their confidence in you would be destroyed.'

"But,' said Floyd, "they like to hear me speak.'

"Yes, but now I think they would prefer sleeping. Give orders for the command to move at three o'clock. It is now twelve -- make your speech when the men are assembled, or when on the march tomorrow. Leave me here and I will do all in my power to detain Rosecrans, who is pushing on after you.'

"This he agreed to do. Rosecrans continued the pursuit two days and then gave it up. Floyd's command became badly scattered, and men leaving and going to their homes."[85]

Who could blame them for leaving for home? It was obvious that they were going to be forced to retreat into southwest Virginia, probably over New River again, near Narrows, Virginia. The men from the Kanawha valley and the western counties had enlisted to defend their homes and families from the Union invaders from beyond the Ohio River. They didn't join the Rebel army to be marched about, misused by incompetent politicians posing as generals, and be lead into exile while their homes and families were to be controlled by their enemies.

The men remembered the statements of some of their officers shortly after the fighting at Scary Creek was over and while they had been the victors, they were ordered to retreat from the valley without losing a fight to the enemy. The statements were quite short, but the words had a strong effect on the tired, sick, and cold soldiers as they waded through the thick mud of the roads as they retreated:

***West Virginia had been sold out!***

A great deal of credit must be given to the men who chose to remain with their regiments for the remainder of the war.

---

[85] Heth, "Memoirs", pg. 18

*Jacob Dolson Cox*

*General Jacob Dolson Cox was an officer in the Federal army from Ohio that invaded western Virginia in 1861. He was a brave, scholarly, and honorable officer who had suddenly left from his home to fight for a cause in which he believed.*

*Cox was a careful observer and honest recorder of events which were affecting everyone as the war developed into reality. He was a commander of a major portion of the Union forces that operated in the Kanawha valley of western Virginia prior to that region becoming a state and was the primary opponent of Generals Wise and Floyd of the Confederacy.*

*While he was also the enemy of Christopher Tompkins, he accepted responsibility for the safety of the Tompkins family after the Rebels had retreated past the Confederate Colonel's farm near Gauley Bridge. Once this responsibility had been accepted, it was not taken lightly and strenuous efforts were made in their behalf.*

*Cox was also involved in the affairs of Tompkins' second-in- command, Isaac Smith. Smith sent a diary through the lines for his family and this was captured by Union troops under Cox and was later returned to the Smith family. That diary is the foundation of one of the sections in this study.*

*Jacob Cox was an unusual man who became caught up in unusual times. He was an excellent officer and became a capable leader of soldiers in combat. He had no previous military training, but he was later to command very large Union Corps in some of the largest battles of the war.*

*He was an unusually capable man.*

## Gentleman General

*Come all you brave Virginia boys*
*With hearts both stout and true*
*Come let us go down to the mason line*
*and Whip the Nothern crue*[1]

General Jacob D. Cox commanded the Ohio troops in the Union army during the early campaigns fought in the Kanawha valley. Cox was a lawyer by profession and had been active in the organization of the Republican party in Ohio and with his friends, James A. Garfield, governor-elect Denison, and Samuel P. Chase, they formed the nucleus of a "radical anti-slavery group".[2]

When the Civil War had actually started, Cox held a commission as a Brigadier-General in the Ohio militia and he was soon called to active duty by his friend, Governor Denison. Since Cox had actively supported the Republican Party, he felt he should participate in the conflict militarily, but he described his attitude toward the war in these words:

"I went about my duties with a half-choking sense of grief I dared not think of."[3]

Cox, like most of the men on both sides, was a reluctant soldier. These men would fight if they must, but they all hoped for a short war. Cox went on to express his sentiments about the coming war:

"...I believe that three-fourths of us still cherished the belief that a single campaign would end the war."[4]

His Ohio troops were soon to begin that first campaign and it would begin on the enemy's home ground, western

1 Howe, *Rebellion in the West*, pg. 48
2 Bailes, "Cox in West Virginia", pg. 6
3 Cox, *Military Reminiscences*, pg. 34
4 *Ibid*, pg. 34

Virginia. The inhabitants of the western counties of Virginia had strong Union sentiments and a majority of them had voted against Virginia's Secession Ordinance.[4] These western Virginians had been partially isolated from the eastern regions of the state by the rugged Allegheny mountains and these equally rugged people had developed commercial ties with their more easily reached neighbors in Pennsylvania and Ohio rather than go to the expense of trading with their eastern relations. Transportation along the rivers and valleys pointing to the west provided relatively easy access to markets while the routes to the east were effectively blocked by the mountain barriers to the east. Roads were expensive to build and maintain on the steep hillsides and the state authorities seldom gave the transportation needs of the westerners the amount of attention that they felt was necessary. Westerners complained loudly and often about the lack of attention their public works requirements received from the eastern-dominated government in Richmond.

A difference as significant as the mountains also separated the two segments of the Virginia population -- slavery. There was a difference in the type of agriculture practiced in the two sections. The farms that were developed in the western counties were generally small in size -- restricted by the lack of available flat land. The people who lived in the narrow valleys were a tough, self-reliant folk who raised crops other than than the labor-intensive crops of the east, cotton and tobacco. Slavery was simply not an economically feasible option for the small farmers to consider. Few had sufficient income to even dream about owning servants for their homes.

The slavery issue was a point of contention between the two sections, but it was not because of anti-slavery sentiment. The westerners felt that the eastern-dominated legislature had different rules for taxation -- one for small farmers without slaves and another for eastern slave owners. The small farmers were taxed fully on the assessed value of their property while slaves had a taxation limit

[4] Bailes, "Cox in West Virginia", pg. 9

which was imposed far below their true market value. This and a historical domination of western economic affairs by the east developed into powerful resentment which had threatened to split the state on more than on occasion in the past.[5] The Virginia General Assembly was controlled by the eastern aristocracy and this was deeply resented by the fiercely independent residents of the western counties.

Soon after President Abraham Lincoln called for 75,000 volunteers to "supress combinations too powerful for courts", Virginia's Secession Convention passed the Ordinance of Secession and the split between the two sections began to grow rapidly. A movement began among Unionist Virginians to form a loyal Virginia government and nearby Governor Denison of Ohio ordered General McClellan to deploy troops across the Ohio River to protect these Unionists from Confederate reprisals.

In late May, 1861, the Confederates burned bridges on the Baltimore and Ohio Railroad near the town of Grafton. Since the railroad was a major communication link connecting Washington and the Union states to the west, General Winfield Scott, the commander of the Federal army, ordered McClellan to move troops to contest the Rebel moves and protect the railroad.

Union troops from Ohio moved into western Virginia along the route of the railroad and defeated a Confederate force under Colonel George A. Porterfield at Philipi on June 3, 1861. This was the first land battle of the Civil War and the Confederates came off a poor second in what the Union newspapers fondly called "the Philipi races" since the Rebels were routed from the town.

McClellan continued to move into the region with his Ohio regiments, but also planned to secure the Kanawha valley by ordering a brigade to move across the Ohio River to conduct what were essentially defensive operations. He telegraphed the following orders to General Cox at Camp Denison, named for the incumbent governor, on July 3:

[5] Ambler, Charles H., *West Virginia: The Mountain State*, Prentice-Hall, New York: 1946, pg. 342

"Pursuant to instructions which have been received from the General-in-Chief, Brigadier-General J.D. Cox, Volunteer Services, will immediately repair to Point Pleasant and take command of operations on the Kanawha River."[6]

Cox moved quickly to comply with the order. Troops at his disposal included the Eleventh and Twelfth Ohio Volunteer Infantry Regiments and two Kentucky regiments recruited from steamboat crews and longshoremen and organized in Cincinnati. He reported back to General McClellan on July 11:

"Sir: On Sunday night the 7th instant at about 10 o'clock, I left Camp Denison with seven companies of the Eleventh Regiment Ohio Volunteers (having been preceded the night before by the Twelfth Ohio) and reached Gallipolis with the Eleventh on the 9th instant. The Twelfth arrived there yesterday, and last evening I brought both regiments to this point."[7]

Cox and his small Union force soon crossed the Ohio River and began to move up the Kanawha River valley. Scouts were sent upstream on either side of the river while the main force of Federal infantry was transported on riverboats to keep the troops fresh, rested, and capable of reacting to the enemy's presence on either bank. This was a very relaxed way to begin what was to become a long war.

Cox described a portion of the river voyage:

"Summer clouds lazily drifted across the sky, the boats were dressed in their colors and swarmed with men like bees. The bands played national tunes and as we passed the houses of Union citizens, the inmates would wave their handkerchiefs to us, and were answered by cheers from the troops."[8]

6 Bailes, "Cox in West Virginia", pg. 11

7 *Ibid*, pg. 12

8 *Ibid*, pg. 12

This style of traveling was easy, but the military situation was beginning to heat up as the Ohio soldiers moved deeper into Virginia's territory. Confederate General Wise was preparing to meet Cox's soldiers at a point west of Charleston, the major city in town in the area. The Confederates had positioned 900 men at Coal River, 1600 at two Mile Creek, and an additional 1000 men were scattered to the rear from Gauley Bridge past Summersville to Birch River toward the Confederate positions at Rich Mountain.[9]

Cox's Second Kentucky Regiment first encountered the Confederates at Barboursville near Mud Bridge. James Sedinger, a Confederate cavalryman, gave a brief account of the fight which developed:

"During our first encampment at Coalmouth on the 11th day of July, we were ordered to Barboursville in Cabell County. We had made the march in ten hours. On the morning of the 12th, the Second Kentucky advanced to Barboursville and charged the militia that was posted on the hill in front of the town. The militia, after delivering one fire, broke and left the field. The company marched off the hill in order, without firing a gun and marched back to Coalmouth without the loss of a man or horse. We took the first of the regiment, but no man was hurt of the company. A Mr. Reynotch was killed by the fire and three others slightly wounded of the militia. The loss to the 2nd Kentucky, was four killed and twenty wounded."[10]

Cox had divided his troops into several columns as they moved east into Confederate territory and they were beginning to encounter resistance. Rebel units from Wise's small army were marching to meet them. One young Confederate, William Clark Reynolds, recorded this in his diary on July 12:

---

[9] White, Robert, "West Virginia", *Confederate Military History*, pg. 28.

[10] Sedinger, James, *Border Rangers*, An unpublished manuscript is located in the West Virginia Archives.

"The enemy is said to be advancing on us from different ways. We packed up our kits and prepared to meet them but as the alarms received were not confirmed we rested in place another night."[11]

Cox united his columns to meet the looming Confederate threat and on July 17, he sent Colonel Lowe with the twelfth Ohio and two companies of the Twenty-First Ohio to make a landing at the mouth of Scary Creek. Troops under the command of Albert Gallatin Jenkins discovered the Ohio soldiers as they made their approach to Scary Creek.[12] James Sedinger wrote about the discovery of the Federal troops and the battle that developed:

"... On the 17th, John Thompson and another member of the company on picket duty on the Bill Creek Road, discovered the Yanks moving by skirmish line through a cornfield, about three hundred yards away. They sat on their horses until the lines came within one hundred yards of them -- the Yanks opened fire on them, Both succeeded in getting away without getting hurt. Thompson lost his hat and his false teeth. This was at nine o'clock in the morning. The two men fell back on the infantry at the mouth of Scary. One of them was sent to Camp Tompkins after the rest of the infantry and the Border Rangers at the mouth of Coal ... The enemy drove in our skirmishers about eleven o'clock in the day and the fight opened in earnest. Our company took position with our artillery. Capt. Welch was killed while sighting his guns."[13]

A cannonball from a Union gun struck one of Captain George S. Patton's six-pounder guns killing Welch instantly by decapitating him. A nearby Confederate private was fatally wounded by the explosion. This same

[11] Reynolds, William C., *Diary of William Clark Reynolds*, pg. 14. An unpublished manuscript is located in the West Virginia Archives.

[12] White, "West Virginia", pg. 28

[13] Sedinger, *Border Rangers*, pg. 3-4

gun was removed by the Confederates following the battle and was left at a shop to be repaired where it was captured by the advancing Federal troops.[14] It was taken with the Union soldiers to the upper Kanawha valley where an accidental misfire later maimed two Union soldiers.

Sedinger continued to explain the battle:

"About this time the right flank was turned and the Yanks were firing at us from the front, flank and rear. Capt. Patton ordered the Kanawha Rifles to follow him in a charge and he fell badly wounded. We now received some fresh troops from Coal Mountain who charged the flanking party and drove them back. This charge was successful in turning the left flank of the enemy, who now broke leaving their Lieut.Col. Neff on the field and eighteen men killed, who we buried the next day."[15]

The battle at Scary Creek was won as the Confederates were able to defeat the Federal troops when fresh Rebel soldiers in Captain Coons' company arrived from Coal Moumtain to rout the Union unit that was attacking the Rebel flank. Albert Gallatin Jenkins attacked with his Border Rangers and the Union soldiers retreated from the field.

Sedinger went on to record some interesting events that occurred at the end of the battle:

"Our company mounted their horses and rode over to where the Yankee line of battle was on the top of the hill near Mrs. Simms house. While sitting there a Col. Woodruff, Col. Devillius, and their staff rode up to Captain Jenkins and said to him, 'Well, you have given the Rebels a good sound thrashing today,' when he ordered them to surrender which they did with considerable grumbling. It was twilight and they could not distinguish our uniforms from theirs."[16]

14 White, "West Virginia", pg. 29
15 Sedinger, *Border Rangers*, pg. 5
16 *Ibid*, pg. 5

Reports of the fighting were soon sent to the War Department in Richmond. Confederate General Wise reported that his troops had captured Federal colonels Norton, Woodruff, and DeVilliers, Lieutenant-Colonel Neff, Captains Austin and Ward, and some 10-20 privates. He reported that about 30 of the enemy were killed.[17]

The battle at Scary Creek was seen as a victory in the South. It was the first Confederate victory in an open fight since the war began and did much to restore shaken Rebel confidence.[18] Unfortunately for the South, Wise was not able to take advantage of this small victory as he was concerned that Union troops operating in northwestern Virginia under General McClellan could potentially get in his rear by marching south to Gauley Bridge. He ordered a "retrograde movement" to the east along the James River and Kanawha Turnpike, burning bridges as his troops crossed. The fight at Scary Creek did little to delay the Federal advance. General Cox waited a few days until sufficient wagons had arrived to permit operations to be conducted independently of the riverboats before ordering a general advance. On July 23, he began to maneuver his regiments toward General Wise's stronghold on Tyler Mountain.

William Clark Reynolds and the Kanawha Riflemen had been assigned to the 22nd Virginia Volunteer Infantry and were in the Tyler Mountain camp. Reynolds wrote in his diary on July 23:

"Left the steamer and marched down to Hunter's Stretch where we worked hard all day throwing up breastworks and slept in the trenches at night. Over the mountain and obstructed a road in the afternoon."[19]

He continued with his entry on July 24:

17 White, "West Virginia", pg. 5

18 *Ibid*, pg. 29

19 Reynolds, *Diary of William Clark Reynolds*, pg. 15

"Worked in the trenches again in the morning, deployed as skirmishers in the afternoon but the enemy not coming nearer than three miles we vacated our post according to orders..."[20]

The men of the western regiments were being ordered to fall back, but they knew they were abandoning their homes and families to the control of the Union army. Most were quite unhappy about the retreat -- no matter what General Wise called it. James Sedinger wrote:

"We mounted our horses and rode down to the Captain's house. When we were about one hundred yards, Mrs. Jenkins met us and the Captain proposed three cheers for his little wife. The boys responded quite nobly to the call and made the welcome ring. The family was placed in carriages and all the baggage in wagons and we started for the Kanawha Valley. Upon reaching our old camp, we found that General Wise had ordered a retreat from the valley. We boys felt pretty blue over the matter, as we had just given the Yanks a thrashing on our side of the river, and Gen. Wise with three times the force we had, leaving without firing a gun, heard officers proclaiming that West Virginia was sold out, but the old company stuck to their colors, and started up the Kanawha."[21]

There had always been a general distrust of anyone from east of the mountains among the westerners. With the history of eastern political domination, it is not surprising to read that many of the western Rebels felt they had been "sold out" when General Wise ordered the retreat without bringing the Federal army under fire. As soon as the Confederate pickets on Tyler Mountain were driven back to the main camp, Wise felt that the retreat was fully necessary. The Union commanders brought up their artillery to begin shelling the camp and the advancing Federals nearly cut off the retreat of Colonel Tompkins'

20 Reynolds, *Diary of William Clark Reynolds*, pg. 15
21 Sedinger, *Border Rangers*, pg. 6-7

regiment, the 22nd Virginia. The 22nd withdrew upstream on the steamer, the Julia Maffett, but their dangers were far from over.

William Reynolds wrote about the voyage:

"Went aboard Steamer Moffett and were beautifully entrapped by the Federals but escaped by a miracle to Brownstown."[22]

Sedinger observed the "entrapment" from the shore and described it:

"At two mile creek below Charleston, the enemy had possession of the river bank and planted a battery to try to cut us off. We had two steamboats with us, carrying commisssary stores, and the infantry, who had to leave their boats and come ashore, after setting them on fire and destroying them, we then ran the gauntlet of the infantry and artillery fire and continued our march up the Kanawha, leaving almost everything we held dear behind us, in possession of the enemy."[23]

Union observers also later wrote about the "Julia Maffett incident":

"It had been well known for some time that Wise's forces were at or near Charleston, and that they occupied a most commanding position at 'Tyler Shoals'. Their pickets were encountered near the latter place on the afternoon of the 24th, who retreated on the approach of our advance guard. Soon a burning bridge was encountered, then another, and Col. Frizell knew the enemy were near and possibly retreating. The order to 'double quick' was given, and a request sent back to the General to hurry forward the artillery. On turning a bend in the road a steamboat loaded with troops was discovered crossing the river, and as the breastworks on the hills and across the road were

22 Reynolds, *Diary of William Clark Reynolds*, pg. 15
23 Sedinger, *Border Rangers*, pg. 7

discovered to be tenantless, Col. Frizell quickly surmised that the boat contained the retreating enemy. Hailing the boat the Colonel asked what troops they were, and being answered by the interrogatory if 'you'uns' were rebels the Colonel responded 'ALL RIGHT -- RUN 'ER UP!' and had not the hoisting of the Union flag been too hastily ordered by some officer on the hill adjoining, a valuable lot of ammunition, stores and prisoners would have been most easily captured. The rebel commander saw the flag, and the boat was put across to the opposite shore with all possible speed. Capt. Cotter soon succeeded in getting his six pounders in position, and a shell sent through the steamer not only hastened the disembarkation of the rebels but set fire to the boat, the charred and blackened timbers of the hull of which may yet be seen at low water at the foot of the shoals." [24]

Ohioan Colonel Frizell had replaced DeVilliers after he was captured due to his ignorance following the battle at Scary Creek. Frizell was capable of quick thought. When the voice from the boat had inquired if the new arrivals on the shore were rebels, Frizell's request to the boat captain to "run 'er up" was heard by a Union officer on a nearby hill and was misunderstood to be an order to raise their flag. Undoubtedly, this was the "miracle" referred to by William Reynolds that permitted Colonel Tompkins' 22nd Virginia to escape certain destruction or capture.

The Confederate retreat continued up the Kanawha River and they burned every bridge after they crossed them. Wise's troops passed through Gauley Bridge on July 27 and burned the large bridge over Gauley River as the retreating Rebels moved out of the valley and into mountainous terrain on Gauley Mountain.

Cox moved to occupy Charleston after the suspension bridge across Elk River was repaired. Many bridges were destroyed after the Confederates crossed, but this did little to delay the pursuit of the Union forces. Each major

---

24 Horton and Teverbaugh, *A History of the Eleventh Regiment, Ohio Volunteer Infantry*, W.J. Shuey, Dayton: 1866, pg. 30-31

stream crossing would have been an excellent location for Wise to dig in his heels and resist any further Federal advance, but nothing could halt his "retrograde movement" until his forces were well out of danger.

A Union observer wrote:

"Wise merited the scornful comments of his rival, General Floyd, upon this retreat. He could have held back such a force as Cox's almost indefinitely if he had been a soldier and of cool judgement. Half a dozen streams falling into the Kanawha and passable only by bridges offered fine positions for defense, his left flank always protected by the Kanawha and his right by continuous rocky hills. As Cox had not enough men for safe flanking operations, he could only drive ahead on the one narrow road to the front.

"This road lay close to the river, crossing a number of streams at their mouths, the smaller ones fordable, but seven or eight requiring bridges to replace those Wise had destroyed. Captain Lane's success with the Pocataligo bridge threw all of this work upon him; and he won the respect and admiration of the whole command by his ingenious devices and the zeal, energy and untiring labors of himself and his men. Within ten days he built five important bridges and many lesser ones ... except for Elk River bridge near Charleston ... Wise's men had got only one span (about forty feet) effectively destroyed. Captain Lane put a span of timber in its place and made the other repairs required, all between four o'clock P.M. and two A.M. On the 28th, between Charleston and Gauley, the zealous engineer noted, 'Built four bridges within the last three days.'"[25]

With the bridge-building ability of Captain Lane, Wise had difficulty in putting any significant distance between himself and the pursuing Federal army. He was able to gain some time when he ordered the bridge over

25 Scott, William F., *Philander P. Lane: Colonel of Volunteers in the Civil War*, privately printed, 1920, pg. 40

Gauley River burned. The bridge was burned on the evening of July 27 and the Union soldiers moved, into the town of Gauley Bridge on the morning of July 29.[26] Lane's ability at field construction had eliminated any advantages Wise hoped for by ordering the valley's bridges destroyed.

Cox now held Gauley Bridge and he began to fortify and consolidate his position there. Cox describes the area and its importance best:

"The position at Gauley Bridge was an important one from the military point of veiw. It was where the James River and Kanawha Turnpike, after following the highlands along the course of the New River as it comes from the east, drops into a defile with cliffs on one side and a swift and unfordable torrent upon the other, and then crosses the Gauley River, which is a stream of very similar character. The two rivers, meeting at a right angle, there unite to form the Great Kanawha, which plunges over a ledge of rocks a mile below and winds its way among the hills, some thirty miles, before it becomes a navigable stream even for the lightest class of steamboats. From Gauley Bridge a road runs up the Gauley River to Cross Lanes and Carnifex Ferry, something over twenty miles, and continuing northward reaches Summersville, Sutton, and Weston, making almost the only line of communication between the posts then occupied by our troops in northwestern Virginia and the head of the Kanawha valley."[27]

The road running northward from Gauley Bridge was the route that so worried General Wise and hastened his departure from the Kanawha valley. General McClellan had fought a battle at Rich Mountain successfully in mid-July and was positioned to the north of Wise's area of operations with 20,000 troops and 34 guns.[28]

26 Bailes, "Cox in West Virginia", pg. 19
27 Cox, *Military Reminiscences*, pg. 80-81
28 Scott, *Philander P. Lane*, pg. 28

These troops were far superior in numbers to anything the Confederates could place in the field against them and they had recently been victors in battle, a fact, which would have made them confident of additional success. Little effort would be required on the part of the Federal commander to march the entire army south through Weston, Sutton, and Summersville to Gauley Bridge to get into Wise's rear. If this had happened, Wise's entire command would have probably been put out of the war. Rather than scout up the road and place a regiment in a blocking postion in some easily defended location, Wise chose to make a rapid "retrograde movement" until past the danger in his rear -- the road leading southward into Gauley Bridge.

Cox described the area:

"Southward the country was extremely wild and broken, with few and small settlements and no roads worthy of the name. The crossing of the Gauley was therefore the gate through which all important movements from eastern into southwestern Virginia must necessarily come, and it formed an important link in any chain of posts designed to cover the Ohio valley from invasion. It was also the most advanced single post which could protect the Kanawha valley. Further to the southeast on Flat-top Mountain, was another very strong position, but a post could not be safely maintained there without still holding Gauley Bridge in considerable force, or establishing another post on the bank of New River twenty miles further up. All of these streams flow in rocky beds seamed and fissured to so great a degree that they had no practicable fords. You might go forty miles up New River and at least twenty up the Gauley before you could find a place where either could be passed by infantry or wagons. The little ferries which had been made in a few eddies of the rivers were destroyed in the first campaign, and the post at Gauley became nearly impregnable in front, and could only be turned by long and difficult detours."[29]

The defensive value for the Union force defending the Kanawha valley was immediately obvious to the Federal commander. While Cox had no formal military training prior to the outbreak of the war, he had studied tactics, strategy, and military history in all of the books he could find in both english and french. He had read all of Jomini's works including his *Napoleon and Grandes Operations Militaires.*[30] He was also learning quickly through practical experiences which combined with his natural ability to allow careful planning to help make him an excellent field commander.

Early in the war, General McClellan had developed a plan by which offensive operations against the Confederate Virginia and Tennessee Railroad, and even Richmond, could be routed through the Kanawha valley. It was one thing to look at a map in Colombus and measure an inch or two of terrain containing few roads and overlook the obstacles found there. It was entirely another matter to be at the end of those roads and try to move troops over what was actually one hundred miles of very difficult terrain. Cox explained some of the problems he saw with McClellan's plans:

"An interval of about one hundred miles separated this mountain fastness from the similar passes which guarded eastern Virginia along the line of the Blue Ridge. This debatable ground was sparsely settled and very poor in agricultural resources, so that it could furnish nothing for subsistence of man or beast. The necessity of transporting forage as well as subsistence and ammunition through this mountainous belt forbade any extended operations there; for actual computation showed that the wagon trains could carry no more than the food for the mule teams on the double trip, going and returning, from Gauley Bridge to the Narrows of New River where the Virginia and Tennessee

29 Cox, *Military Reminiscences*, pg. 81

30 Bailes, "Cox in West Virginia", pg. 9

Railroad crossed upon an important bridge .."[31]

Gauley Bridge was the key to the defense of the Kanawha valley and Cox was well aware of its importance, but he had learned that any defense of a fixed position requires vigorous offensive action by small patrols to keep the enemy off balance and prevent any counter-attacks. Before he could get active patrolling missions into enemy-contested areas he had to develop a means to resupply the patrols and this required a method of crossing the Gauley River -- no easy task!

The historian of the 11th Ohio Infantry wrote about the problem of crossing the Gauley River:

"The bridge was five hunded feet long, the abutments one-hundred and fifty feet apart. The stream was three hundred feet wide at ordinary water, swift and turbulent, interspersed with large rocks which rose above the water at a low stage and were buried at a high stage, and there were deep holes between them. To build on the old abutments would certainly take too much time. To build a lower, and therefore shorter, bridge would probably take no less time, and its approaches would be steep and difficult for wheels. The currents and the rocks made a floating bridge impossible.

"Captain Lane decided a ferry as the only means practicable under the circumstances; but the swift and irregular currents presented special difficulties and compelled great caution. There were some flat-boats below the falls in the Kanawha, but they could not be got up. The Gauley above the bridge was so shallow and so filled with rocks that timber could not be floated down. He sent back for a steamboat hawser, to be used as a cable, and set about building a boat sixty feet long, eighteen feet wide, with a capacity of two hundred men or four loaded army wagons and their animals, or two guns and their caissons. Of course it had to be built and caulked bottom up and on the shore, and its great weight made it very difficult to turn

[31] Cox, *Military Reminiscences*, pg. 81-82

over and into the water safely without a derrick, but this was accomplished successfully by simple mechanical means. The hawser was dragged across and secured at both ends, and a 'walk' was built along the outer side of it, on which the men could pass to work the boat, which was secured to the cable by guide-ropes at stem and stern. Six men on the 'walk', pulling on the cable, could easily propel the boat with full loads. On the 4th of August, the fifth day after beginning, the ferry was in regular operation, carrying over the troops and trains."[32]

Once the ferry was complete and put into operation, Cox was able to push supplies across the river for his forward detatchments which were skirmishing eastward along the turnpike. He also began to prepare to meet any counter-attack by the Confederates by preparing defenses in the small town of Gauley Bridge where he set up his base of operations. He wrote:

"Nothing could be more romantically beautiful than the situation of the post at Gauley Bridge. The hamlet had, before our arrival there, consisted of a cluster of two or three dwellings, a country store, a little tavern, and a church, irregularly scattered along the base of the mountain and facing the road which turns from the Gauley valley into that of the Kanawha. The lower slope of the hillside behind the houses was cultivated, and a hedgerow separated the lower fields from the upper pasturage. Above this gentler slope the wooded steeps rose more precipitately, the sandstone rock jutting out into crags and walls, the sharp ridge above having scarcely soil enough to nourish the chestnut trees...

"In the angle between the Gauley and New rivers rose Gauley Mount, the base a perpendicular wall of rocks of varying height, with high wooded slopes above. There was scarcely room for the road between the wall of rocks and the water on the New River side, but after going some

32 Scott, *Philander P. Lane*, pg. 41-42

distance up the valley the highway gradually ascended the hillside, reaching some rolling uplands at a distance of a couple of miles. Here was Gauley Mount, the country house of Colonel C.Q. Tompkins, formerly of the Army of the United States, but now the commandant of a Confederate regiment raised in the Kanawha valley. Across New River the heavy masses of Cotton Mountain rose rough and almost inaccessible from the very water's edge. The western side of Cotton Mountain was less steep, and butresses formed a bench about its base, so that in looking across the Kanawha a mile below the junction of the rivers, one saw some rounded foothills which had been cleared on the top and tilled, and a gap in the mountainous wall made room on that side for a small creek which descended to the Kanawha and whose bed served for a rude country road leading to Fayette C.H. At the base of Cotton Mountain the Kanawha equals the united width of the two tributaries, and flows foaming over broken rocks with treacherous channels between, till it dashes over the horseshoe ledge below, known far and wide as the Kanawha Falls. On either bank near the falls a small mill had been built, that on the right bank a saw-mill and the one on the left for grinding grain.

"Our encampment necessarily included the saw-mill below the falls, where the First Kentucky Regiment was placed to guard the road coming from Fayette C.H. Two regiments were encamped at the bridge upon the hillside above the hedgerow, having an advanced post of half a regiment on the Lewisburg road beyond the Tompkins farm, and scouting the country to Sewell Mountain. Small outposts were stationed some distance up the valley of the Gauley."[33]

Cox took advantage of the period of relative inactivity while Captain Lane completed the ferry by providing for training and mountain warfare experience for the men in his command. His soldiers spent a week exploring and learning how to conduct combat operations in the broken,

[33] Cox, *Military Reminiscences*, pg. 83-84

mountainous terrain. Once the ferry was completed, most of Cox's "Kanawha Brigade" crossed the river and started scouting operations towards the east along the turnpike. These troops reached and established "Camp Lookout",about fifteen miles, and Big Sewell Mountain, thirty miles, from Gauley Bridge.[34] These scouting trips were conducted cautiously as the Federal commander thought that Wise and his army were directly in his front and contact between the two hostile armies would bring on a general engagement, but Wise had retreated "beyond Lewisburg and gone into camp at White Sulphur Springs."[35]

William Clark Reynolds wrote several entries in his diary during the rapid Confederate retreat. He arrived in Lewisburg on August 1, 1861 and wrote:

"Reached Lewisburg in a soaking rain and was quartered in the fair grounds.

"August 2, 1861:

Lewisburg, Greenbrier County, Virginia

"Our quarters were very disagreeable having no convenience of wood or water and nothing but stalls, recently occupied by horses, to sleep in.

"August 3, 1861:

"Left Lewisburg in the morning, resting an hour or two at Greenbrier Bridge and reached the White Sulphur Springs early in the afternoon. Quartered in the Carolina Row. I have walked the whole distance -- 113 miles."[36]

Wise's "retrograde movement" -- actually a full-fledged retreat -- left an indelible mark on all of the participants. They were ordered to abandon their homes and families to Union army control, had to march on foot through terrain -- 113 miles -- where the Union advance could have been halted with miminal effort, and the

---

34 Scott, *Philander P. Lane*, pg. 45

35 *Ibid*, pg. 45

36 Reynolds, *Diary of Willaim Clark Reynolds*, pg. 16

weather was miserable. Large numbers of the Kanawha valley volunteers deserted during the march and went home. Beuhring Jones, later to become the commander of the 60th Virginia Infantry Regiment, was a participant in the retreat who later wrote that he saw a company commander continue to march while his troops dropped off from the rear until none remained. The officer then broke his sword over his knee and went home in disgust.[37] Many of these soldiers felt the same as the officers in James Sedinger's company, the Border Rangers: West Virginia had been sold out -- why should they remain in the army to defend the easterner's interests while their homes were being occupied by hostile Federal troops?

Cox explained one of the reasons for the enormous desterion rate from Wise's army. Most of the valley's population were simply less than enthusiastic about secession from the Union in the first place:

"The population was nearly all loyal below Gauley Bridge, but above they were mostly secessionists, a small minority of the wealthier slaveholders being the nucleus of all aggressive secession movements. These, by their wealth and social leadeship, overawed or controlled a great many who at heart did not sympathize with them, and between parties thus formed a guerrilla warfare became chronic."[38]

There were many others in the region who did not agree with the Confederate cause and these small farmers were relatively quick to rally to the support of the the Union. Cox described the peculiar, isolated situation of these new Unionists:

"In our scouting expeditions we found little farms in

---

37 Jones, Beuhring H., *History of Fayette County, West Virginia*, edited by J.T. Peters and H.B. Carden, Jarett Printing, Charleston: 1926, pg. 229-242

38 Cox, *Military Reminiscences*, pg. 85

secluded nooks among the mountains, where grown men assured us that they had never before seen the American flag, and whole families had never been further from home than church and a country store a few miles away. From these mountain people several regiments of Union troops were recruited in West Virginia, two of them being organized in rear of my own lines, and becoming part of the garrison of the district in the following season."[39]

Wise's rapid retreat from the Kanawha valley obviously left many of the area's Confederate sympathizers and soldier's families in situations dominated by General Cox's troops. One significant family remaining was that of Colonel Christopher Tompkins. Cox explained:

"When Wise had retreated from the valley, Colonel Tompkins had been unable to remove his family, and had left a letter commending them to our courteous treatment."[40]

Tompkins' letter to Cox went straight to the point:

"Gauley Mount near Gauley Bridge
Fayette County, Virginia, July 28, 1861

"Circumstances over which I have no control, have compelled me to abandon my farm, and leave upon it a defenceless family of females and children.

"Should the chances of war direct your columns in their vicinity, it is presumed that these persons would receive treatment befitting their several stations, provided responsible persons were in immediate command. But, should this particular locality be visited by scouting parties or irregular detatchments of your forces, temptations to license or abuse of private rights might be committed without your knowledge or sanction.

"It is to guard against such a contingency, that I have taken the liberty to adress you in this communication, and to call your attention to the propriety of giving such

39 Cox, *Military Reminiscences*, pg. 85
40 *Ibid*, pg. 86

instructions as will doubtless present themselves to an Officer of your rank and reputation. If, however, you should think it out of your power to prevent such abuses of private immunities, I will be obliged if you will apprise Mrs. Tompkins of the fact.

"I have the honor to be very respectfully
Your obedient Servant
C.Q. Tompkins
Colonel 22nd Regiment Virginia Volunteers

To General Cox
Commander Federal Forces KanawhaValley"[41]

General Cox received the letter from Colonel Tompkins and gave orders that the family and property were to be respected by all soldiers under his command. The work of protecting the family was relatively easy at first, but later -- when faced with a Confederate counterattack -- the job of protection became more complex. General Cox wrote:

"Mrs. Tompkins was a lady of refinement, and her position within our outposts was far from being a comfortable one. She, however, put a cheerful face upon her situation, showed great tact in avoiding controversy with the soldiers and in conciliating the good-will of the officers, and remained with her children in her picturesque home on the mountain. So long as there was no fighting in the near vicinity, it was comparatively easy to save her from annoyance; but when a little later in the autumn Floyd occupied Cotton Mountain, and General Rosecrans was with us with larger forces, such a household became an object of suspicion and ill-will, which made it necessary to send her through the lines to her husband. The men fancied they saw signals conveyed from the house to the enemy, and believed secret messages were sent, giving information of our numbers and movements. All this was highly improbable, for the lady knew that her safety depended

41 Tompkins, Christopher Q., A copy of this letter is in the National Archives, Record Group 109.

upon her good faith and prudence; but such camp rumor becomes a power, and Rosecrans found himself compelled to end it by sending her away. He could no longer be answerable for her complete protection. This, however, was not till November, and in August it was only a pleasant variation in going the rounds, to call at the pretty house on Gauley Mount, inquire after the welfare of the family, and have a moment's polite chat with the mistress of the mansion."[42]

Cox had accepted responsibility for the safety of Tompkins' family as if they were his own and he did manage to keep them from being attacked or their property destroyed. There were, however, limits as to what he could accomplish, but generally the Colonel's family fared much better than the families of other Confederates in the area. The war was rapidly taking a nasty turn as hatred began to develop between the two sides and the senior Union command issued orders to confiscate or destroy the property of Rebels under Federal control. Many families were left without food or shelter from the elements when Federal raiding parties burned their farms.

Gauley Bridge was still the key to the military situation in the Kanawha valley. Cox had been ordered to fortify the town and hold it against moves from the east by Wise. Cox felt that an attack was unlikely:

"For ten days after we occupied Gauley Bridge, all our information showed that General Wise was not likely to attempt the reconquest of the Kanawha valley voluntarily. His rapid retrograde march ended at White Sulphur Springs and he went into camp there. His destruction of bridges and abandonment of stores and munitions of war showed that he intended to take final leave of our region."[43]

The construction of fortifications in the town of

---

42 Cox, *Military Reminiscences*, pg. 86-87
43 *Ibid*, pg. 87

Gauley Bridge capable of withstanding a major Confederate attack or seige was ordered by General McClellan from Washington. He warned his replacement in the area, General Rosecrans, that both Lee and Johnston were marching into West Virginia to crush the Union forces and McClellan ordered that both Huttonsville and Gauley Bridge be strongly fortified.[44]

Cox had an engineering officer on his staff and he was soon reinforced by additional engineer officers:

"On the 5th of August Lieutenant Wagner of the Engineers arrived at Gauley Bridge with instructions from General Rosecrans to superintend the construction of such fortifications as might be proper for a post of three regiments. I already had with me Colonel Whittlesey, Governor Denison's chief engineer, an old West Point graduate, who had for some years been devoting himself to scientific pursuits, especially to geology. In a few days these were joined by Captain Benham, who was authorized to determine definitely the plans of our defences. I was thus stronger in engineering skill than in any other department of staff assistants, though in truth there was little fortifying to be done beyond what the contour of the ground indicated to the most ordinary comprehansion.

"Benham stayed but two or three days, modified Wagner's plans enough to feel that he had made them his own, and then went back to Rosecrans' headquarters, where he was met with an appointment as brigadier-general, and was relieved of staff duty. He was a stout red-faced man, with a blustering air, dictatorial and assuming, an army engineer of twenty-five years standing. He was no doubt well skilled in the routine of his profession, but broke down when burdened with the responsibily of conducting the movement of troops in the field."[45]

Once the plans for field fortifications at Gauley Bridge were completed, the Union troops were divided into

44 Cox, *Military Reminiscences*, pg. 89

45 *Ibid*, pg. 88-89

working parties to begin construction. General Cox described the completed works:

"We fortified the post by an epaulment or two for cannon, high up on the hillside covering the ferry and the road up New River. An infantry trench, with a parapet of barrels filled with earth, was run along the margin of Gauley River till it reached a creek coming down from the hills on the left. There was a redoubt for a gun or two was made, commanding a stretch of road above, and the infantry trench followed the line of the creek up to a gorge in the hill. On the side of Gauley Mount facing our post, we slashed timber from the edge of the precipice nearly to the top of the mountain, making an entanglement through which it was impossible that any body of troops should move. Down the Kanawha, below the falls, we strengthened the saw-mill with logs, till it became a blockhouse loopholed for musketry, commanding the road to Charleston, the ferry, and the opening of the road to Fayette C.H. A single cannon was here put in position also."[46]

The entire town was now a federal garrison and Cox's Kanawha Brigade occupied the fortifications in preparation for a general counter-attack by the Confederates under General Wise which would be slow in developing. If Wise were to gather the nerve and troops to attack the Federals, Cox would have been in a difficult position -- there were no troops in the area to reinforce or relieve him as the three remaining brigades of Rosecrans' "Army of Occupation of Western Virginia" were in the northwestern region of the state and could not come to the aid of Cox's single brigade.

The Kanawha Brigade at that time consisted of portions of several Union regiments -- the First and Second Kentucky, the Eleventh, Twelfth, Nineteenth, Twenty-first and parts of the Eighteenth and Twenty-second Ohio infantry and the "Ironton" company of cavalry. While these regiments were committed to Cox's

---

46 Cox, *Military Reminiscences*, pg. 90

command, many of the units were understrength and the Union general had to leave portions of his regiments along the Kanawha River to guard his lines of communications back to the Ohio River. His estimated strength was between 4000 and 5000 troops.[47]

Cox reported that his actual strength at Gauley Bridge and on the turnpike to the east was considerably less:

"... I could keep but two regiments at Gauley Bridge, an advance-guard of eight companies vigorously skirmishing toward Sewell Mountain. a regiment distributed on the Kanawha to cover steamboat communications, and some companies of West Virginia recruits organizing at the mouth of the Kanawha."[48]

General Cox's military problems began to intensify in early August, 1861, when Confederate reinforcements began to arrive in the White Sulphur Springs - Lewisburg area. William Clark Reynolds made a fateful entry in his diary on August 6 of an event that was eventually to determine the outcome of the Kanawha valley campaigns:

"General J.B. Floyd arrived at noon with about a thousand troops."[49]

About the time Floyd arrived with reinforcements, General Robert E. Lee, then commander only of Virginia's state troops, arrived in the area and the Confederate militia units of the counties south of New and Kanawha Rivers were being activated for field duty. Cox was now faced with the possibility of very vigorous manuevering by the Confederates whose goal would be recapturing the entire Kanawha valley. Cox was concerned:

"About the 10th of August we began to get rumors from the country that General Robert E. Lee had arrived at Lewisburg to assume direction of the Confederate

47 Scott, *Philander P. Lane*, pg. 88-90

48 Cox, *Military Reminiscences*, pg. 90

49 Reynolds, *Diary of William Clark Reynolds*, pg. 16

movements into West Virginia. We heard also that Floyd with a strong brigade had joined that of Wise, whose "legion" had been reinforced, and that this division, reported to be 10,000 or 12,000 strong, would immediately operate against me at Gauley Bridge. We learned also of a general stir among the Secessionists in Fayette, Mercer, and Raleigh counties, and of the militia being ordered out under General Chapman to support the Confederate movement upon my line of communications, whilst Floyd and Wise should attack in front.

"The reported aggregate of the enemy's troops was, as usual, exaggerated, but we now know that it amounted to about 8000 men, a force so greatly superior to anything I could assemble to oppose it, that the situation became at once a very grave one for me."[50]

Cox was now in a potentially difficult position. The Rebel army was much larger than his command and General Lee was well-respected by everyone who knew of him for his military ability that he had demonstrated so well in the National army before the war. A large army and a capable general could have made life difficult for the small Union brigade at Gauley Bridge which was hoping to hold the Kanawha valley under Federal control. Cox planned to develop an active defense and kept small units patrolling constantly toward the enemy to give an illusion of strength and confuse the Confederates:

"My reconnoitring parties reached Big Sewell Mountain, thirty-five miles up New River, Summersville, twenty miles up the Gauley, and made excursions into counties on the left bank of the Kanawha, thirty or forty miles away. These were not exceptional marches, but were kept up with an industry that gave the enemy an exaggerated idea of our strength as well as of our activity... By extreme activity these were able to baffle the enemy, and impose on him the belief that our numbers were more than double our actual force."[51]

50 Cox, *Military Reminiscences*, pg. 91
51 *Ibid*, pg. 90-91

Cox's strategy was fairly effective in keeping the larger elements opposite his small force off balance. Neither of his potential opponents -- Floyd nor Wise -- had formal military training. Both were former governors of Virginia and Floyd had been appointed Secretary of War in the Buchannan administration, a political appointee, and they had learned little other than arrogance during the opening rounds of the war. Both were politically-appointed brigadier-generals who were thought to be popular with the inhabitants of western Virginia who could possibly convert some of their previous votes from the region into recruits. They both had capable officers on their respective staffs and could have made matters quite difficult for Cox, but their old political rivalry was renewed with an intensified vigor. The jealosy and intense dislike shared between these two generals prevented any realistic cooperation against the Federals at Gauley Bridge.

Cox was also an inexperienced general officer, but unlike his feuding opponents, he was quite capable. He was described:

"General Cox ... was steadily doing his duty, without complaining and without advertisement of repeating reports, learning by eperience in daily action how to meet and oppose his enemy, and winning the ground by untiring care and persistence."[52]

He knew that if he was to succeed his troops would have to push east on the James River and Kanawha Turnpike. In addition to keeping the Confederates off balance, his scouting operations would be able to locate the forward Rebel outposts and skirmishers. Cox's Eleventh Ohio was under strength and consisted at the time of only eight companies, but they were used in agressive patrolling to the east of Gauley Bridge. Their unit history tells of some of their activity:

"The first scouting expedition sent out in the direction of

---

[52] Scott, *Philander P. Lane*, pg. 39

Lewisburg was a detatchment of the Eleventh, under command of Lieut-Col. Frizell. Going as far as "Locust Lane" on Monday, the 12th of August, the Colonel found his force too small to warrant being so far from support, and on the following day fell back to Mountain Cove. Here the balance of the regiment, with the exception of Company A, which was ordered to remain at "Devil's Elbow" to exchange their old muskets for Enfield rifles, and Company D left at Gauley Bridge, joined the Colonel's party on Wednesday, and another advance to Locust Lane was made.

"The next day a detail of one hundred and twenty (officers and men), under Col. Frizell, continued the expedition to the foot of Big Sewell Mountain. Lieut. John D. Shannon, of Company B, who had command of the advance guard, discovering rebel cavalry a short distance ahead, deployed his men in the thickets on the left side of the road, and advancing, was soon fired upon by a rebel picket guard. Two men of company B, Will. Rae and Augustus Houck, were wounded, one in the right and the other in the left hand. Hearing the firing, the Colonel gave the order to double-quick, and upon turning a bend in the road a squad of rebel cavalrymen were encountered, who gave and received a volley and then retreated. The Colonel formed an "ambush" and sent out scouts from Company H, under Lieut. Weller, who also encountered rebels and received and returned a fire. After waiting for some time and no enemy appearing in the road, it was thought best to fall back to Locust Lane, which was done in the shape if a disorderly retreat while passing the few houses on the route, in order, if possible, to entice the rebels to fall into an ambush which Capt. Drury had been directed to form at a suitable place on the line of "retreat". Not succeeding in luring the enemy on "to their own destruction", our forces were again concentrated at Locust Lane."[53]

The active manuevering on the part of the Union troops

[53] Horton and Teverbaugh, ***Eleventh Regiment***, pg. 37-38

along the turnpike was effectively keeping the forward elements of the Confederate army off balance. The Rebel officers didn't know whether they were forming to advance down the turnpike or were forming to meet a new Federal attack coming up the road. For all of the troop movements, Cox was in a difficult position and he knew it. He was facing a reinforced Confederate army to his east under the command of a general everyone respected for his military knowledge and ability -- Lee! Cox was also receiving pressure from the south as the militia from the counties across the river from his fortifications began to gather under General Chapman.[54]

When General Rosecrans assumed command of the Federal forces in western Virginia after McClellan was ordered to Washington to take command of the Army of the Potomac following the Union defeat at Bull Run, Rosecrans began to plan for more active operations against his opponents. Even as General Lee began to move his regiments from the Cheat Mountain region to the Sewell Mountain area, Rosecrans began to develop plans to shift his army south to join forces with his subordinate, General Cox.

Cox wrote:

"General Rosecrans informed me of his purpose to march a sufficiently strong column to meet that under Lee as soon as the purpose of the latter should be developed, and encouraged me to hold fast to my position. I resolved, therefore, to stand a seige if need be, and pushed my means of transportation to the utmost to accumulate a store of supplies at Gauley Bridge. I succeeded in getting up rations sufficient to last a fortnight, but found it much harder to get ammunition, especially for my ill-assorted little battery of artillery."[55]

In addition to the eight companies of the Eleventh

---

54 Cox, Jacob D., "McClellan in West Virginia", *Battles and Leaders*, Vol. 1, pg. 143

55 Cox, *Military Reminiscences*, pg. 91-92

Ohio under command of Lieutenant-Colonel Frizell operating on Gauley Mountain and beyond, Cox sent troops up Gauley River to scout and make contact with any advance party from Rosecrans' army. Cox wrote:

"Part of the Twelfth under Major Hines did similar work on the road to Summersville, where Rosecrans had an advanced post, consisting of the Seventh Ohio (Colonel E.B. Tyler), the Thirteenth (Colonel Wm. Sooy Smith), and the Twenty-third (Lieutenant-Colonel Stanley Matthews)."[56]

With these multiple regiments positioned over such a wide area, it was only a matter of time before the opposing forces made contact which would develop into a serious battle. There were relatively few roads in the region and the Federal commanders made an attempt to place troops in blocking positions along each approach. Rosecrans was still concerned about the safety of Cox's garrison at Gauley Bridge and started to move his regiments south. Cox described some of the moves ordered by his commander:

"On the night of the 13th of August the Seventh Ohio, by order from Rosecrans, marched to Cross Lanes, the intersection of the road from Summersville to Gauley Bridge, with one from Carnifex Ferry, which is on the Gauley near the mouth of Meadow River. A road called Sunday Road is in the Meadow River valley, and joins the Lewisburg turnpike about fifteen miles in front of Gauley Bridge. To give warning against any movement of the enemy to turn my position by this route or to intervene between me and Rosecrans' posts at Summersville and beyond, was Tyler's task. He was ordered to picket all crossings of the river near his position, and to join my command if he were driven away. I was authorized to call him to me in an emergency.

"On the 15th Tyler was joined at Cross Lanes by the Thirteenth and Twenty-third Ohio, in consequence of

56 Cox, *Military Reminiscences*, pg. 92

rumors that the enemy was advancing upon Summersville in force from Lewisburg. I would have been glad of such an addition to my forces, but knowing that Rosecrans had stationed them as his own outpost covering the Sutton and Weston road, I ordered Tyler to maintain his own position, and urged the others to return at once to Summersville. The road by which they had expected the enemy was the Wilderness road, which crossed the Gauley at Hughes' Ferry, six miles above Carnifex. If attacked from that direction, they should retire northward toward Rosecrans, If possible."[57]

Rosecrans agreed with Cox's suggestion to Smith and Matthews that they move back toward the Federal main force. Tyler was ordered to hold his position near the ferries over the Gauley while scouting for the enemy's presence and if pressed to fall back to Gauley Bridge to the relative safety of Cox's fortifications.

The Confederate regiments under the command of Floyd and Wise had regrouped and refitted in the Lewisburg-White Sulphur Springs area and were now prepared to begin an offensive against the Union regiments positioned between them and the Federal base at Gauley Bridge. The old feud between Floyd and Wise began to increase in intensity and the brigades of each began to move forward separately. Wise and the troops of his legion moved west along the James River and Kanawha Turnpike they had so recently made their "retrograde movement" over as Lieutenant-Colonel Frizell's Ohio soldiers began to pull back. The legion was returning to the valley after their inglorious retreat during the summer.

Wise's "Legion" was a formal military unit of the Confederate army which had ten legions assigned. These legions varied in size and composition, but each normally consisted of infantry, cavalry and artillery elements. Wise's Legion consisted of three regiments of infantry, a cavalry regiment, and artillery.

[57] Cox, *Military Reminiscences*, pg. 92-93

Phillips' Legion was composed of Georgians and were assigned to General Floyd's Brigade toward the end of the Sewell Mountain campaign. This legion consisted of six companies of infantry and four of cavalry.[58] Floyd's Confederate command had two legions assigned to its more conventional military formations.

Floyd moved toward Gauley River from the turnpike by way of Sunday Road. His strategy was relatively sound -- by placing his small army between Cox's garrison at Gauley Bridge and Rosecrans' southbound army, he would be in a position to prevent any reinforcement of the post at Gauley Bridge while Wise manuevered against it from the east. With Floyd's Brigade placed to the north with an open route to attack Charleston, Chapman's and Beckley's militia troops located across New River to the south, and with Wise's Legion closing in from the east, Cox would have a difficult time holding his position. The Confederate manuevering, if successful, would have placed Cox in a situation where his entire command would have been forced to surrender or undergo a prolonged seige while the Confederates moved to re-occupy the strategic Kanawha valley.

Cox was aware of the difficulty that Floyd and Wise were planning for the Union troops under his command:

"Floyd and Wise were now really in motion, though General Lee remained at Valley Mountain near Huntersville, whence he directed their movements. On the 17th they had passed Sewell Mountain, but made slow progress in the face of the opposition of the Eleventh Ohio, which kept up a constant skirmish with them. On the 19th Floyd's advance-guard passed the mouth of Sunday Road on the turnpike, and on the 20th made so determined a push at my advance-guard that I believed it a serious effort of the whole Confederate column. I strengthened my own advance-guard by part of the Twelfth Ohio, which was at hand, and placed them at Pig Creek, a mile beyond

[58] Wallace, Lee A., *A Guide to Virginia's Military Organizations: 1861-1865,* H.E. Howard, Lynchburg: 1986, pg. 150

Tompkins place, where the turnpike crossed a gorge making a strongly defensible position. The advance-guard was able to withstand the enemy alone, and drove back those who assaulted them with considerable loss."[59]

Lieutenant-Colonel Frizell's eight companies on the mountain road had been actively manuevering all along the turnpike to keep the Confederates confused and slow their advance. They were, however, much too small a force to seriously attempt to resist the combined strength of both Floyd and Wise and when the Union officers in charge realized that the main body of the Confederates were marching toward them, they began to slowly withdraw:

"On Sunday morning, August 18th, just after the new guards had 'gone on', at Mountain Cove, word was received that the rebel army, commanded by John B. Floyd, was advancing, being then but three or four miles distant. As the country here was too open for so small a force as ours to succesfully resist such an attack as would probably be made, a retreat to 'Big Creek', some two or three miles distant, was resolved on ... The next day, the 19th, was improved in barricading the road, and running a line of breastworks along the brow of the hill on the Gauley side of the creek. The enemy were seen on a hill a mile or two to the right during the day, but they made no attack. The next morning a detail ... under Corporal Samuel Butler, all from Company B, were sent, by a blundering order from the officer of the day, out the road towards Mountain Cove, and while yet in sight of camp, were fired on by the advance guard of a rebel batallion marching to attack our command. James Roach was killed, and Schultz and Shieler captured, the other three men succeeding in getting back unharmed.

"Roach was the first man of the Eleventh killed by the rebels, and he might have escaped, but he could not resist the temptation to stop and fire at the enemy, who were very near, and in doing so lost his life.

---

59 Cox, *Military Reminiscences*, pg. 93-94

"The rebels turned off the road to the left, and advanced through a thicket of laurel. Firing soon began, but as both parties were pretty well protected no damage was done, although a brisk fire was kept up for an hour, when the rebels retreated.

"During the progress of this 'bushwhacking' fight, Col. Frizell walked out into an open field on our left and challenged the rebels to come out and give us a fair fight! The only response he received was a cursing from the rebel commander, who was hidden behind a tree, and a volley of musketry. The Colonel returned to his command, borrowed an 'Enfield' from one of his men, and watching an opportunity, soon had the satisfaction of repaying, with interest, the cowardly answer to his challenge.

"A road along a ridge to our left that we could not guard, being discovered, by which the enemy could get in our rear, it was resolved to fall back to Hawks Nest. About two o'clock the rebels were discovered to be advancing in force on our new position. Their skirmish line extended across a large corn field, followed closely by cavalry and infantry. Companies A and H, under the command of Major Coleman, were posted along the fence in the edge of the woods, Company C behind a breastwork in the road, the balance of the regiment being some half mile to the rear making barricades across the road. There were two 'Snakehunters' with our advance party who commenced to fire before the enemy had got as close as Major Coleman desired, and the position of our men was thus disclosed. After two volleys the rebels were thrown into confusion, and made a most precipitate retreat. One rebel was badly wounded and left at 'Hamilton's' where he received attention from our assistant surgeon, Dr. Gill.

"About this time, Patrick Callahan, of Company C, was very seriously wounded in the left arm by the accidental discharge of a musket, requiring amputation of the arm near the left shoulder. This difficult operation was performed by Dr. Gill, in the most successful manner. Callahan recovered rapidly, and remained with the regiment until the next spring."[60]

[60] Horton and Teverbaugh, *Eleventh Regiment*, pg. 40-41

The Confederates who made contact with the men of the Eleventh Ohio were commanded by the officer in charge of Floyd's cavalry, Lieutenant - Colonel St. George Croghan, the son of one of the few genuine heroes of the War of 1812. It is unlikely that he would have been the man who let Frizell's challenge pass with only a curse -- he was a skilled and chivilarous officer who would have responded to that sort of challenge. The regiments under his command that advanced against Major Coleman were understrength since large numbers of Confederates were absent from duty -- with measles. The Forty-sixth Virginia had only one-third of the regiment present for duty.[61]

The wounded Confederate left at 'Hamilton's' was Stewart D. Painter. He had been shot through the left lung and was strong enough to be paroled through the lines in order to return to his home to convalesce. He wrote a letter to Dr. Gill to thank him for saving his life:

"I write for the purpose of expressing in written language my gratitude to you for the generous, kindly treatment you bestowed on me, who your enemy, rendered unfortunate by the fate of war, was thrown upon your mercy. Sir, it is impossible for me to express all that my heart dictates. Suffice it to say I can never forget you. No matter what may be my period of life or the circumstances that may surround me, whether in peace or war, prosperity or adversity, the rememberance of Dr. Gill will abide with me ever, and toward him will flow unceasingly my hearts deepest gratitude. May heaven smile upon you Doctor; may your path be strewn with life's choicest flowers; may you pass unscathed through the horrors of this unnatural war, and when you die may these words be your stay and support -- 'inasmuch as ye did it unto the least of these, ye did it unto me'. General Wise and the officers of his staff wish me to convey to you their respectful regards."[62]

61 White, "West Virginia", pg. 35

62 McKinney, Tim, *Fayette County in the Civil War*, Pictorial Histories, Charleston: 1988, pg. 44-45

While Wise moved his legion and attached units to the eastern side of Gauley Mountain in a manuever designed to gain some sort of advantage over Lieutenant-Colonel Frizell's slowly withdrawing companies, Floyd was marching down Sunday Road toward Carnifex Ferry. Cox as not aware of the exact nature of the manuevering of the opposing forces, but mentioned these in his writings done after the war:

"It has since appeared that this movement of the enemy was by Wise's command making a direct attack on my position, whilst Floyd was moving by the diagonal road to Dogwood Gap on Sunday Road where it crosses the old State Road. There he encamped for the night, and next day marched to the mouth of Meadow River near Carnifex Ferry."[63]

Colonel Tyler, commander of the Seventh Ohio Infantry Regiment, had been left in the vicinity of Carnifex Ferry and had small patrols out actively scouting for the enemy's approach. One of these small patrolling elements under the command of Captain John F. Schutte encountered a troop of Floyd's cavalry which was actively screening the movement of the Confederate main force toward the Gauley. Schutte and a private, Charles Rich, were killed as the remainder of the Union patrol were forced to retreat.[64]

The skirmishing on Gauley Mountain on August 19 and 20 was sufficient evidence that the Confederates were returning to the upper Kanawha valley in force and Cox began to shift the units available to him in an attempt to counter the growing threat:

"On the first evidence of the enemy's presence in force, I called Tyler from Cross Lanes to Twenty-mile Creek, about six miles from Gauley Bridge, where it was

63 Cox, *Military Reminiscences*, pg. 94
64 McKinney, *Fayette County*, pg. 42

important to guard a road passing to my rear, and to meet any attempt to turn my flank if the attack should be determinedly be made by the whole force of the enemy. As soon as the attack was repulsed, Tyler was ordered to return to Cross Lanes and resume his watch of the roads and river crossings there."[65]

Unfortunately for the Seventh Ohio, the Confederate army crossed the river while they were at Twenty-mile Creek where Colonel Tyler was delayed an additional day for the issue of shoes and clothing for the men of the regiment. The regiment didn't return to their former positions at Cross Lanes until August 24. This delay was to give Floyd a significant advantage as he manuevered his small army in the general direction of the smaller Union garrison at Gauley Bridge.

Floyd's brigade and attached units had marched down Sunday Road and crossed Gauley River in spite of the advice which had been given to him by his rival, General Wise. Wise had urged Floyd to hold the ferry, but do so by remaining on the south side of the river where Wise felt it could be held by 250 men. Afterwards, Wise wrote to the Confederate War Department to complain that it was "utterly unmilitary to cross unless with a force that could advance; but cross it he would, and cross it he did."[66]

A European officer -- a resident of England, but probably a former resident of Central Europe -- serving in Wise's cavalry, Bela Estvan, wrote about Floyd's crossing at Carnifex Ferry after he had returned to Europe in 1863. Estvan was less than an admirer of Floyd and wrote with some irritation:

"Floyd marched with his brigade rapidly on Carnifex Ferry, which place he reached about noon. He found on his arrival there that the United States troops had made a

65 Cox, *Military Reminiscences*, pg. 94

66 Cook, Roy B., "The Battle of Carnifex Ferry", *The West Virginia Review*, October, 1931, pg. 114

retrograde movement to prevent an attack by our troops on Hawks Nest."[67]

This retrograde movement mentioned by Estvan probably referred to Cox's ordering Colonel Tyler's Seventh Ohio from Cross Lanes to guard the approaches to the Union flank at Gauley Bridge. Estvan continued:

"General Floyd then resolved to raise the boats which the enemy had sunk, and therewith convey his troops to the opposite bank to take possession of the favorable position abandoned by the enemy. As soon as the chief of engineers had informed General Floyd that he had completed that prodigious feat, which took him full twenty-four hours, whilst General Price, in half that time, took an army of 13,000 men across the river Osage, the troops were at once conveyed to the other side. The infantry got safely over, but in conveying the cavalry, one of the large boats was upset, and six men and two horses were drowned. The unfortunate general now found himself in an awkward position: there he was with his infantry on one bank, whilst the whole of his cavalry and artillery remained on the other. The alarm amongst the infantry became every minute greater, for should the enemy get wind of the predicament in which the general was placed, they would not have failed to capture the whole army without firing a shot ... Meanwhile General Floyd set earnestly to work to fortify his position, and set out patrols, to ascertain the movements of the enemy. On the following morning, when all the infantry was safely over, news arrived that the enemy, in great strength, was moving down from Gauley Bridge, and had already occupied Cross Lane. The commander of the Federal troops had already been apprised of General Floyd's mishap with the ferry boats, and hastened to endeavor to cut off his infantry. Colonel Tyler, indeed, felt so certain of Floyd and his infantry that he did not go to work seriously enough. Instead of first ascertaining

67 Estvan, Bela, *War Pictures From the South*, Books for Libraries Press, Freeport, N.Y.: 1971. (1863 edition reprint)

Floyd's real strength and the nature of his position, he was imprudent enough to place his outposts no further than 200 yards from his camp. Floyd, on being informed that the strength of the Federal troops did not exceed 1,200 men, resolved to attack them."[68]

While Estvan correctly described the return of the Seventh Ohio from Twenty-mile Creek, he was incorrect when he wrote this paragraph in 1863. Tyler was not imprudent when he placed his outposts too close to his camp because of over-estimating the difficulty Floyd had when he crossed the river; Tyler was oblivious to the presence of Floyd and was soon to pay a severe price for his ignorance.

The Union newspapers tell the story of the battle of Cross Lanes rather inaccurately, but the general outcome of the fighting is close to reality they depict:

"A battle occurred at Summersville, in Western Virginia, this morning. The Seventh Ohio regiment, Colonel Tyler, was surrounded whilst at breakfast, and attacked on both flanks and in the front simultaneously. The national forces immediately formed for battle and fought bravely, though they saw but little chance of success. The rebels proving too powerful, Col. Tyler sent forward to the baggage train, which was coming up three miles distant, and turned it back toward Gauley Bridge, which place it reached in safety.

"Companies B,C, and I suffered most severly. They particularily were in the hottest of the fight, and finally fought their way, through fearful odds, making great havoc in the enemy's forces. The rebel force consisted of three thousand infantry, four hundred cavalry, and ten guns. The Union forces scattered, after cutting their way through the enemy, but soon formed again and fired, but received no reply or pursuit from the enemy. Not over two hundred were missing, out of nine hundred engaged. The rebel loss was fearful. Lieut.-Col. Creighton captured the rebels'

---

68 Estvan, *War Pictures,* pg. 118-119

colors and two prisoners."[69]

The newspaper reports were not very accurate at the time and each side tended to convert them to little more than propaganda designed to prevent an erosion of popular support. The Confederates were little better at accuracy when it came to reporting war news.

General Floyd had two newspaper editors serving in his headquarters to assure a continual stream of favorable publicity. One of these editors, Major Robert Henry Glass of the *Lynchburg Republican*, arrived in Floyd's camp just in time to report on the battle fought at Cross Lanes. He wrote an article that must have greatly pleased the egotistical general Glass served:

"At 4 o'clock A.M., the Brigade was in motion, and the clear ring of the General's stentorian voice was heard along the lines in the fresh morning air like the blast of a trumpet. We were all instantly to our arms and to our saddles, and advanced rapidly, at double quick. A heavy fog hung over the hills and along the valleys, and we approached almost upon the enemy's pickets before they saw us. They fired and ran, distinctly in our view, and not a hundred yards in our advance. Our men gave a shout at that sort of music, and dashed on with accelerated speed. In a few minutes we discovered the blue coats of the enemy, as they stood drawn up near a church by the road side, while to our right and behind a fence stood another column of the enemy."[70]

Glass described the attack of Confederate regiments toward the hapless Seventh Ohio and the total rout that developed. He expressed surprise at the ratio of killed and wounded to shots fired:

[69] Moore, Frank, *The Rebellion Record*, Vol. III, G.P. Putnam, New York: 1862, pg. 6

[70] Andrews, J. Cutler, *The South Reports the Civil War*, Princeton University Press: 1970, pg. 117

"As we rode through the field this morning, the enemy's bullets could be heard cutting through the corn and whistling by your ears as thick as hail, yet but few of our men were touched. The calculation recently made by some one, that it requires seven hundred balls to kill one man is really true, though the calculation is not of much consolation to the poor fellow who gets the fatal shot."[71]

The news reports of the fighting at Cross Lanes were generally inaccurate, but General Cox wrote a precise review of the battle after the war:

"But Tyler was new to responsibility, and seemed paralyzed into complete inefficiency. He took nearly the whole of the 25th to move slowly to Cross Lanes, though he met no opposition. He did nothing that evening or night, and his disposal of his troops was so improper and outpost duty so completely neglected that on the morning of the 26th, whilst his regiment was at breakfast, it was attacked by Floyd on both flanks at once, and was routed before it could be formed for action. Some companies managed to make a show of fighting, but it was wholly in vain, and they broke in confusion. About 15 were killed and 50 wounded, the latter with some 30 others falling into the enemy's hands. Tyler, with his lieutenant-colonel, Creighton, came into Gauley Bridge with a few stragglers from the regiment. Others followed until about 200 were present. His train had reached the detachment I had sent to Peters Creek, and this covered its retreat to camp, so that all his wagons came in safely. He reported all his command cut to pieces and captured except the few that were with him, and wrote an official report of the engagement, giving that result.

"On the 28th, however, we heard that Major Casement had carried 400 of the regiment safely into Charleston. He had rallied them on the hills immediately after the rout, and finding the direct road to Gauley Bridge intercepted, had led them by mountain paths over the ridges to the valley of

71 Cutler, *South Reports the Civil War*, pg. 116

Elk River, and had then followed that stream down to Charleston without being pursued. This put a new face on the business, and Tyler in much confusion asked the return of his report that he might re-write it. I looked upon his situation as the not unnatural result of inexperience, and contented myself with with informing General Rosecrans of the truth as to the affair. Tyler was allowed to substitute a new report, and his unfortunate affair was treated as a lesson from which it was expected he would profit. It made trouble in the regiment, however, where the line officers did not conceal their opinion that he had failed in his duty as a commander, and he was never afterward quite comfortable among them."[72]

Following the battle, Floyd apparently lost his nerve and moved back to the river area where he proceeded to construct "Camp Gauley". His recent victory left him in an excellent position where he could move along the route taken by Major Casement to Charleston and occupy that place prior to moving to the east to position himself directly in the rear of Cox's position at Gauley Bridge. Cox would have found himself beseiged with Floyd operating on his western flank while Wise manuevered in the area directly across Gauley River. This would have been the probable end for the Federal garrison in the small town -- caught between two large foes far from the prospect of relief. Cox would have had little choice -- capitulate or be destroyed!

Cox was surprised by the lack of a major Confederate attack:

"After the Cross Lanes affair I fully expected that the Confederate forces would follow the route which Casement had taken to Charleston. Floyd's inactivity puzzled me, for he did no more than make an entrenched camp at Carnifex Ferry, with outposts at Peter's Mountain and toward Summersville. The publication of the Confederate Archives had partly solved the mystery. Floyd called on Wise to reinforce him; but the latter dumurred, insisting

72 Cox, *Military Reminiscences*, pg. 96

that the duty assigned him of attacking my position in front needed all the men he had. Both appealed to Lee, and Lee decided that Floyd was the senior and entitled to command the joint forces."[73]

While Lee felt that Floyd was senior and should be in overall command, he did not order Wise to obey the orders of Floyd. Little actually changed in the relationship between the two, but this was of little comfort for Cox as he began to notice the pressure of his situation. He was facing a growing threat with shrinking forces:

"I was not without anxiety ... and was constantly kept on the alert. Rosecrans withdrew the Twelfth Ohio from my command, excepting two companies under Major Hines, on the 19th of August, and the imperative need of detachments to protect the river below me was such that from this time till the middle of September my garrison at Gauley Bridge, including the advance-guards and outposts, was never more than two and a half regiments or 1800 men. My artillerists were also ordered back to Ohio to reorganize, leaving the guns in the hands of such infantry details as I could improvise. I was lucky enough, however, to get a very good troop of horse under Captain Pfau in place of the irregular squad I had before."[74]

Cox resorted to a tactic he had used to his advantage during his initial moves in the area -- he continued with aggressive patrolling in the direction of the enemy and kept them off balance with constant skirmishing by his lead elements. As usual, the men of the Eleventh Ohio under Lieutenant-Colonel Frizell did the best job that could have been expected of them under the circumstances. They had been in nearly constant contact with the Rebels since crossing Gauley River in late July. They had marched and counter-marched as far away as Big Sewell Mountain before returning to the summit area of Gauley Mountain to

73 Cox, *Military Reminiscences*, pg. 97

74 *Ibid*, pg. 98

hold off the impending attack of Wise as Floyd worked his way forward from the north.

The men of the Eleventh Ohio were becoming accustomed to this type of activity. Their unit history:

"But little of general interest transpired until Sunday, the 25th, when being again posted at Big Creek, we were attacked by the rebels, in their usual bushwhacking style, and Charles Allen, of Company A, was killed. Tired of this style of fighting, Col. Frizell ordered a charge, when the rebels retreated *pell mell*, strewing the road with guns, pistols, knives, and everything that would encumber their flight. Following the flying enemy for a mile or more, something near a wagon load of trophies were picked up by our men..."[75]

The men of the Eleventh Ohio had made contact with Wise's cavalry which was under the command of Albert Gallatin Jenkins, a very able cavalry commander at a later time in the war. At this early stage, the Federal skirmishers under Frizell were able to draw them into an ambush, even if the authors of the Eleventh's unit history were unaware of the actual tactic. Cox explained the ambush of the cavalry:

"On the 25th my advance-guard under Lieutenant-Colonel Frizell very cleverly succeeded in drawing into an ambuscade a body of Floyd's cavalry under Colonel A. G. Jenkins. The principle body of our men lined a defile near Hawks Nest, and the skirmishers, retreating before the enemy, led them into a trap. Our men began firing before the enemy was quite surrounded, and putting their horses on the run, they dashed back, running the gantlet of the fire. Wise reported that he met men with their subordinate officers flying at four miles distance from the place of action, and so panic-stricken that they could not be rallied or led back. Jenkins was hurt by the fall of

[75] Horton and Teverbaugh, *Eleventh Regiment*, pg. 41-42

his horse, but he succeeded in getting away; for, as we had no horsemen to pursue with, even the wounded, except one, could not be overtaken. Hats, clothing, arms, and saddles were left scattered along the road in as complete a breakneck race for life as was ever seen. The result, if not great in the list of casualties, which were only reported at 10 or 15 by the enemy, was so demoralizing in its influence upon the hostile cavalry that they never again showed any enterprise in harassing our outposts, whilst our men gained proportionally in confidence."[76]

The Confederate cavalry had recently been reorganized into an official regiment, the Eighth Virginia Cavalry Regiment, and was placed under the command of Colonel Jenkins, a former captain of the "Border Rangers" which became Company E. James Sedinger of the "Border Rangers" didn't elaborate on the ambush on August 25, 1861, but mentioned it:

"...the company was ordered by forced march to join General Wise, near Dogwood Gap on the James River and Kanawha Turnpike, We ran into an ambuscade, but no one was hurt. Colonel Jenkins had his horse killed under him and a number of the boys lost their hats and blankets."[77]

Cox was managing his predicament quite well. His skirmishing units on Gauley Mountain had managed to take the Rebel cavalry out of the action with the loss of only one man as they drew the Eighth Virginia Cavalry into an ambush. Soon afterward, Cox was to make another suprising move deep into enemy territory which was designed to keep the gathering Confederate militia off balance and afraid to assemble into a target for the Federals to attack. This new threat was to his steamboat supply line and he had to prevent any disruption:

---

76 Cox, *Military Reminiscences*, pg. 98-99

77 Sedinger, *Border Rangers*, pg. 7

"Efforts to reach the river and stop our steamboats, kept the posts and detatchments below us on the alert, and an expedition of half the 1st Kentucky, under Lieutenant-Colonel D.A. Enyart, sent to break up a Confederate militia encampment at Boone Court House, 40 miles southward..."[78] "...and he did so on the 2nd of September, completely routing the enemy, who left 25 dead upon the field. Enyart's march and attack had been rapid and vigorous, and the terror of the blow kept that part of the district quiet for some time afterward."[79]

The Confederates were not quite ready to depart from the region and were actively preparing another attempt at the Union force at Gauley Bridge. The Rebels had been successful at Cross Lanes and had been keeping pressure on General Cox at every opportunity. Most of the attempts on Gauley Mountain had been successfully countered, but additional forces were gathering in the area.

The Confederates made a coordinated attack along both sides of New River which utilized units from Wise's Legion and the militia from the area south of the river. Cox wrote:

"We had heard for some days the news of the assembling of a considerable force of Confederate militia at Fayette C.H. under General Chapman and Colonel Beckley. They were reported at 2500, which was a fair estimate of the numbers which answered to the call. On the 3d of September a pretty combined attack was made by Wise and this force; Wise pushing in sharply upon the turnpike, whilst Chapman, assisted by Wise's cavalry, drove back our small outpost on the Fayette road. Wise was met at Pig Creek as in his former attack, the eight companies of the Eleventh Ohio being strengthened by half of the Twenty-sixth Ohio, which was brought from below for this purpose. The effort was somewhat more persistent than before, and Wise indulged in considerable noisy

78 Cox, "McClellan in West Virginia", pg. 144-145

79 Cox, *Military Reminiscences*, pg. 99

cannonading; but the pickets retreated to the creek without loss, and the whole advance-guard, keeping under good cover there, repelled the attack with less than half a dozen casualties on our side, none being fatal. Wise retreated again beyond Hawks Nest."[80]

The Eleventh Ohio had remained on the turnpike with orders to picket the road from "Devil's Elbow" (Chimney Corner) out as far as possible. The approach of the Confederates under Wise in force made this a difficult mission to attempt with only the eight companies available. Lieutenant-Colonel Frizell requested reinforcements which were quickly dispatched from the Federal encampment at Tompkins' farm. The unit's history reported:

"...but the demonstrations by the rebels being vigorous and persistent, Col. Frizell concentrated his forces at the 'Elbow', and requested the General to send him reinforcements. Two companies of the Twenty-sixth Ohio, then stationed at Tompkins' Farm were ordered to act under Col. F,'s orders, and, at Capt. Lane's request, Company K was sent out.

"During the night of September 2d, Wise advanced and stationed his troops just across a ravine in front of our line. One of our picket stations was so situated that the rebels had got between it and the Regiment before the men could escape, and Alex. Gammack and John Helmer, of Company A, laid inside the rebel lines until near morning, when they succeeded in getting away, having *crawled* a long distance through the thickets along side the road.

"Wise opened with his artillery on Tuesday morning, the 3d of September, and continued throwing shell and canister all day without doing the least damage. During the morning a piece of artillery sent out to Col. Frizell arrived, and after firing a few shots, a premature discharge of the gun sent the *swab* whizzing over among the enemy, which, as we afterwards ascertained, frightened them badly, as they thought we were throwing *chain shot*! This

80 Cox, *Military Reminiscences*, pg. 99-100

discharge took off an arm of the "rammer", and a thumb of the "thumber", after which Col. Frizell ordered the gun to the rear, as he found it defective and more dangerous to his men than to the rebels.

"After a day or two, Wise left our front and retreated towards Lewisburg."[81]

The accident with the cannon was probably due to human error rather than defective manufacture. Cox mentioned that his "artillerists" had been withdrawn to Ohio for reorganization and the new gun crews were drawn fron untrained infantry details. This premature detonation of the gun powder propellant was most likely caused by improper swabbing of the bore after a shot was fired. If there were any sparks inside the bore when the rammer pushed a fresh charge into the mouth of the cannon, the smouldering remains of the last shot would have ignited the new charge -- blowing the rammer's swab (as well as his arm) toward the Confederate lines.

Captain Lane and the men of Company K of the Eleventh Ohio had been unable to share the risks of combat with the remainder of Frizell's party. They had been busy with building the ferry over Gauley River and then they were ordered to operate and guard it. Lane wanted to get his troops into combat and requested to be relieved from the ferry duty in order to join Frizell. Lane's biographer recorded an interesting story:

"...but near the end of the month, at Captain Lane's special request, he was relieved there and, with his company, joined the regiment up the road... The Eleventh was getting useful lessons in the arts of war now, -- how to watch the enemy and yet protect themselves, how to meet or make an attack and keep their heads, how to grapple cheerfully with the difficulties and bear philosophically the hardships of the work, thus developing into efficient soldiers. Captain Lane's request to be sent to join the regiment in this active service brought him and his

81 Horton and Teverbaugh, *Eleventh Regiment*, pg. 42-43

company a share in these valuable experiences. Their first real trial by fire he used to describe with humorous appreciation. The Eleventh, being in front, found the enemy in position, sheltered by a thicket, and obstinate. The first two or three companies were thrown into line across the road and ordered to advance, Company K being on the right. On the right of the road was a small spur or ledge of a hill, around which it curved. As soon as this bend was passed the enemy opened fire upon the line. Captain Lane turned to his men, to order them to return the fire, but, to his great amazement, he saw no men. Shocked and bewildered, he yet swiftly scanned the ground to the rear and saw that there were at least some men behind the projecting ridge; and then found the whole company there! They had instinctively taken shelter, just as they would have done individually in civilian life if they had suddenly found shots flying. It was often the case in the war that green soldiers shrank from their 'baptism of fire'. Exceedingly wounded in pride and in great anger (General Cox just then came up), he 'beat' the men back into line, and again led them forward,when they fought well..."[82]

Confederate Captain Joel H. Abbott described events from the rebel side of events. He was serving in the Fayetteville Rifles, a company of the 22nd Virginia. Since Abbott was from the area and was familar with the terrain, he:

"...volunteered to carry a dispatch to General Chapman, commanding the militia of Monroe, Raleigh, and Fayette counties, at Fayetteville, and was detailed to help organize and drill his troops which were stationed at Fayetteville and Cotton Hill.

"About ten days after my arrival at General Chapman's headquarters, we received information that General Cox was marching up the valley and that his advance guard had reached Kanawha Falls. Captain Herndon's company of

[82] Scott, *Philander P. Lane*, pg. 47-48

the 8th Virginia Cavalry, acting as our scouts, was ordered over Cotton Hill. Nine of his men were killed from ambush on Falls Branch and were hauled over Cotton Hill on sleds drawn by oxen and buried on a knoll at the foot of Cotton Hill on the farm of T.S. Robson.

"Two days later three companies of the militia were ordered on a scouting trip over the mountain to Kanawha Falls. I commanded one company, Lieutenant Loughborough, adjutant for General Beckley's brigade, commanded the second, and Captain Richards had charge of the third. We met the advance guard of the Federal troops on Falls Branch, near where Captain Herndon's men were killed. Captain Hunt, who was in charge of the Federals, surrendered to Lieutenant Loughborough when ordered to do so; but he picked his chance, drew a revolver, fired and killed our officer and then made his escape with his men. We brought the lieutenant over the mountain and buried him with the others. The Cox army crossed Cotton Hill and a fight ensued. We retreated to Fayetteville."[83]

Abbott recorded these events after the war and relied on an elderly memory, but the story has considerable truth in it. Captain Loughborough and Captain Hunt were actually involved in a shoot-out in which the Confederate officer was killed. An alternate record of the event was written in the *National Intelligencer* on January 16, 1862:

"Amongst the prisoners lately returned from Richmond, is Capt. Ralph Hunt, of the First Kentucky regiment. In September last, his regiment formed a part of the force under Gen. Cox, encamped near 'Gauley Bridge', in western Virginia. The enemy were desirous of dislodging the General, and about the third of September attempted a reconnoissance in some force. The pickets were driven in, and Capt. Hunt was ordered out with his company to make observations of the force and movements

---

83 Abbott, Joel H., "A Civil War Narrative", *History of Fayette County, West Virginia*, edited by J.T. Peters and H.B. Carden, Jarrett Printing, Charleston: 1926, pg. 215-216

of the enemy, and report thereon. The whole country thereabouts is thickly covered with scrubby pine and cedar, so that a man may escape notice at a few yards distance. Pushing his way through the bushes and scrubby trees until he obtained a position commanding the road by which the rebels must advance, the Captain halted his men where they were well concealed from observation, and ordered them to lie quiet and await orders. A few men had been sent in advance as scouts, but it seems these were bewildered amidst the dwarf pines and bushes, and, in making their way back, unfortunately got into the Captain's rear. The Captain, after posting his men, had gone forward a few yards ... and, hearing an advance upon the road, stepped forward a few paces, in expectation of seeing his returning scouts, but the party advancing along the road turned out to be the leading files of the advanced guard of the rebel forces. With these was a fine-looking officer named Loughborough, who had been sent out to drill the confederate troops in that region. This officer was marching some distance in advance of his men, and catching sight of Capt. Hunt, poured forth a torrent of imprecations, exclaiming, 'Come out, you damned Yankee son of a _____, and be shot!' at the same time raising to his shoulder his Mississippi rifle. The Captain had a musket with him, (the ordinary smooth bore), which he instantly levelled at his adversary. The combatants were about 50 yards apart; each fired at the same instant; the Adjutant's ball whistled close by the Captain's ear, but the Adjutant himself, with a curse upon his lips, fell dead with a bullet through his brain. So instantaneous was the death that not a limb stirred after the body touched the earth. Not less than seven shots were instantly fired at Captain Hunt, none of them, fortunately, taking effect. The enemy, enraged at the loss of a favorite officer, were at first inclined to be revengeful, but the gallantry he had just displayed, and the coolness with which he bore himself when in their power, finally won their respect. The men of Capt. Hunt's company supposed their leader to be killed, and made good their escape to camp. Hunt and the two men with him were so surrounded that escape was impossible. Refusing to give his parole, Capt. Hunt was ironed, and after visiting with his guard several of the towns of Virginia, at length was confined in a 'tobacco-factory' at Richmond."[84]

While there is some difference in the substance of the two stories, the actual truth must lie somewhere between the two. Abbott was over eighty when he told his series of stories and may have had a tendency to exaggerate slightly. The Union newspapers generally told the story to suit the readers of their papers. As in any war, the population remaining at home is in need of "heroes" and stories are embellished as much as is required to satisify the readership. The Hunt-Loughborough duel was a good story and the Union account was probably closer to the facts than Abbott's later tale. Hunt was taken prisoner and later exchanged -- this is generally sufficient evidence that he did not suddenly pull a concealed weapon and basically murder Loughborough. The poorly trained and inexpertly-led country militia would have probably reacted swiftly if Hunt had murdered Loughborough and he would not have made it into captivity, much less be exchanged from Libby prison in Richmond.

The manuevering of the coordinated attack of both Wise and Chapman against Cox's position was nearly over with little concrete results. Cox wrote:

"The irregular troops on the Fayette road were more boldly led, and as there was no defensible position near the river for our outposts, these fell slowly back after a very warm skirmish, inflicting a loss, as reported by prisoners, of 6 killed among the enemy. Chapman reached the bluffs overlooking the river in rear of us, driving in our outposts, but did us little mischief, except to throw a few shells into our lower camp, and on Wise's repulse he also withdrew."[85]

---

84 Moore, *The Rebellion Record*, Vol. VI, pg. 31
85 Cox, *Military Reminiscences*, pg. 100

Cox was far from comfortable, however. He had survived the early stages of what became a half-hearted attack by Wise and the local Confederate militia under General Chapman. He still was threatened by an unfought Rebel army to his north, twenty miles away, at Carnifex Ferry under General Floyd. Cox wrote of his concern:

"I expected Floyd to move at the same time, and was obliged to continue upon the defensive by reason of his threatening position up the Gauley River; I, however, sent Major Hines with his two companies in that direction, and Floyd appeared to be impressed with the idea that my whole force was moving to attack him and attempted nothing agressive."[86]

Cox wrote that he had good reason to feel satisfied with being able to keep all of the Confederate forces facing him at bay. He was actually faced with an overwhelming force and if his opponents had properly coordinated their attacks, the small Federal camp at Gauley Bridge would not have had a chance of survival. Wise reported that his regiments totalled 2200 men and that he estimated the size of the force available to Floyd was 5600. Chapman's militia totalled approximately 2500 men.[87] Cox had managed a minor military miracle with cooperation of the two bumbling incompetent "political generals" set against him. He credits the part-time militia under General Chapman with being "more boldly led" than the full-time troops in the regular Confederate regiments of both Wise and Floyd. General Cox had bluffed and out-manuevered a total of 10,300 Confederates with a force not exceeding 1800 Union soldiers. He did this through an effective system of aggressive patrolling, and risky, but effective feints with smaller elements directed at the enemy's main forces. Cox may have been a political- appointee general like his two opponents, but he was certainly learning to be a

---

86 Cox, *Military Reminiscences*, pg. 100

87 *Ibid*, pg. 98-100

very effective combat leader.

The threat remained essentially unfought in the area and reinforcements from General Rosecrans in the north had not arrived. Cox was forced to keep up the aggressive maneuvering while the men in camp were constantly preparing defensive positions in case the camp came under seige. The Eleventh Ohio's historian wrote of the anxiety developing as the men waited for Rosecrans:

"In the Kanawha Brigade at this time they were looking daily and anxiously for news of the approach of Rosecrans from the north, with more men and guns. Already his march had taken more time than he had set for it. Floyd was strong enough, with good management, to defeat Cox east of Gauley Bridge, or below if he could safely cross the Gauley; but, ... his resolution failed when he had made half the distance, and he turned off to the north, to occupy Summerville, a town twenty-five miles northeast of Gauley Bridge. He may have had an idea that this movement would flank Cox out of Gauley Bridge and compel him to retreat to Charleston; but he seems to have been ignorant of Rosecrans' march, which was directly toward Summerville."[88]

Rosecrans' approach march to the relief of the Federal camp at Gauley Bridge was taking longer than anyone had thought necessary. With the large number of Confederates in the area, Cox had little choice other than to work on his fortifications while the men listened for the arrival of General Rosecrans and the relief force. Cox reported a serious incident during the construction of fortifications:

"In the midst of the alarms from every side, my camp itself was greatly excited by an incident which would have been occasion for regret at any time, but at such a juncture threatened for a moment quite serious consequences. The work of intrenching the position was going on under the direction of Lieutenant Wagner as rapidly as the small

---

88 Scott, *Philander P. Lane*, pg. 49-50

working parties available could perform it. All were overworked, but it was the rule that men should not be detailed for fatigue duty who had been on picket the preceding night. On August 28th, a detail had been called for from the Second Kentucky, which lay above the hedge behind my headquarters, and they reported without arms under a sergeant named Joyce. A supply of intrenching tools was stacked by the gate leading into the yard where my staff tents were pitched, and my aide, Lieutenant Conine, directed the sergeant to have his men take the tools and report to Mr. Wagner, the engineer on the line. The men began to defer in a half-mutinous way, saying they had been on picket the night before. Conine, who was a soldierly man, informed them that should be immediately looked into, and if so, they would soon be relieved, but that they could not argue the matter there, as their company commander was responsible for the detail. He therefore repeated his order. The sergeant then became excited and said his men should not obey. Lieutenant Gibbs, the district commissary, was standing by, and drawing his pistol, said to Joyce, 'that's mutiny; order your men to take the tools or I'll shoot you.' The man retorted with a curse, 'Shoot!' Gibbs fired, and Joyce fell dead. When the sergeant first refused to obey, Conine coolly called out, 'Corporal of the guard, turn out the guard!' intending very properly to put the man in arrest, but the shot followed too quick for the guard to arrive. I was sitting within the house at my camp desk, busy, when the first thing which attracted my attention was the call for the guard and the shot. I ran out, not stopping for arms, and saw some of the men running off shouting, 'Go for your guns, kill him, kill him!' I stopped part of the men, ordered them to take the sergeant quickly to the hospital, thinking that he might not be dead. I then ordered Gibbs in arrest till an investigation should be made, and ran at speed to a gap in the hedge which opened into the regimental camp. It was not a moment too soon. The men with their muskets were already clustering in the path, threatening vengeance on Mr. Gibbs. I ordered them to halt and return to their quarters. Carried away by excitement, they levelled their muskets at me and bade me get out of their way or they would shoot me. I managed to keep cool, said the affair would be investigated, that Gibbs was already under arrest, but they must go back to their quarters. The parley lasted long enough to bring some of their officers near. I ordered them to come to my side, and then to take command of the men and march them away. The real danger was over as soon as the first impulse was checked. The men then began to feel some of their natural respect for their commander, and yielded probably the more rapidly because they noticed that I was unarmed. I thought it wise to be content with quelling the disturbance, and did not seek out for punishment the men who had met me at the gap. Their excitement had been natural under the circumstances, which were reported with exaggeration as a wilful murder. If I had been in command of a larger force, it would have been easy to turn out another regiment to enforce order and arrest any mutineers; but the Second Kentucky was itself the only regiment on the spot. The First Kentucky was a mile below, and the Eleventh Ohio was the advance-guard up New River. Surrounded as we were by so superior a force of the enemy with which we were constantly skirmishing, I could not do otherwise than meet the difficulty instantly without regard to personal risk.

"The sequel of the affair was not reached till some weeks later when...Lieutenant Gibbs was tried and acquitted on the plain evidence that the man killed was in act of mutiny at the time. The court was a notable one, as its judge advocate was Major R.B. Hayes of the Twenty-third Ohio, afterwards President of the United States, and one of its members was Lieutenant-Colonel Stanley Matthews of the same regiment, afterwards one of the Justices of the Supreme Court." [89]

The Confederate column under Floyd hardly had the time to celebrate their victory at Cross Lanes before they realized that they were in some potential peril as well. They had moved into a position near Carnifex Ferry and

89 Cox, *Military Reminiscences*, pg. 101-102

had built some strong field fortifications and some troops were sent to occupy Summersville. The only problem with the position selected to become Floyd's strongpoint in the area was simple to see -- it was on the wrong side of Gauley River and if defeated, the Rebels would have no way to retreat and would have to surrender. This was the reason for the warning from Wise to Floyd not to cross the river, but as Wise later wrote to the Confederate War Department,"But cross it he would, and cross it he did"! The Federals were now assuming the tactical position previously held by the Confederates. With the large Union army under Rosecrans, a general who was not afraid to fight, moving south to relieve Gauley Bridge, the Rebels would be in widely separated locations which would be unable to mutually support one another. Floyd was boxed in on the wrong side of a raging river, Wise was operating, on Gauley Mountain, primarily in one of his "retrograde movements" produced by Cox's advance-guard, and Chapman was learning the lesson that militia troops cannot be kept in the field for long periods successfully. The Union army was about to go on the offensive and Floyd was the first to be encountered as the large army under Rosecrans felt its way southward.

"He had hardly settled himself in Summerville with his pleasing reflections when he was surprised to learn of an enemy near at hand, coming from the north...He immediately abandoned Summerville and fell back to Carnifex Ferry, taking a very good defensive position in a bend of the river, sheltered by a thick wood and covering the ferry crossing."[90]

The battle of Carnifex Ferry became a reality on September 10, 1861, when the lead elements under command of General Benham, recently engineer Captain Benham, of Rosecrans' army came into contact with Confederate skirmishers and pressed forward. Cox explained the outcome:

90 Scott, *Philander P. Lane*, pg. 50

"General Benham's brigade was in front, and soon met the enemy's pickets. Getting the impression that Floyd was in retreat, Benham pressed forward rather rashly, deploying to the left, and coming under a sharp fire from the right of the enemy's works...Charges were made by portions of Benham's and McCook's brigades as they came up, but they lacked unity and Rosecrans was dissatisfied that his head of column should be engaged before he had time to plan an attack...Floyd, however, had learned that his position would be subjected to a destructive cannonade; he was himself slightly wounded, and his officers and men were discouraged. He therefore retreated across the Gauley in the night, having great difficulty in carrying his artillery down the cliffs by a wretched road in the darkness...He reported but twenty casualties, and threw much of the responsibility upon Wise, who had not obeyed orders to reinforce him. His hospital, containing wounded prisoners taken from Tyler, fell into Rosecrans's hands."[91]

Even with the retreat of Floyd, Cox was still isolated at Gauley Bridge and was vulnerable to an attack from Wise and Chapman. As Floyd pulled back from Carnifex Ferry he came closer to joining forces with Wise and they would greatly outnumber General Cox. Rosecrans was obviously concerned about the safety of his subordinate at Gauley Bridge and spent considerable time making up his mind which way to move. He had essentially two options: Cross Gauley River and pursue Floyd or move down the river to relieve Cox. This period of indecision produced grumbling in the ranks of his army:

"As Floyd obviously must be retreating to Lewisburg, and probably in haste, to avoid an attack by Cox on his right, Rosecrans ought to have vigorously pushed a crossing and pursuit. But he was dilatory and ineffective, and it was more than a whole day before he moved over even a detatchment. Yet he was very anxious about Cox,

91 Cox, *Military Reminiscences*, pg. 145-146

fearing that Floyd would strike him with his larger forces above Gauley Bridge; and he sent several messages to Cox during the day.

"But he did not understand Floyd. That general was not at all seeking another fight. Cox was in fact twenty miles above Gauley Bridge, with a considerable part of his brigade, but he had not yet heard of Carnifix, nor even of Rosecrans's arrival. Floyd could have easily given him serious trouble, but he was thinking only of Lewisburg, and hurried by Cox's ground, so near that his movement was easily observed; and Cox was perplexed as to what his great haste could mean. But, feeling sure that it was caused by Rosecrans's advance, he concentrated and followed up the retreat, sending back a courier to get a report to Rosecrans. The next day, the 12th, he had his first news of the battle at Carnifix, in a letter from Rosecrans; but did not yet know that Rosecrans had that morning got one brigade across the Gauley, with orders to reinforce him."[92]

Cox wrote:

"On the 12th communication was opened, and I learned of Floyd's retreat across the Gauley. I immediately moved forward the Eleventh and Twenty-sixth Ohio to attack Wise, who retreated from Hawk's Nest to the mouth of Sunday Road, and upon my approach retired to Sewell Mountain. At the Sunday Road I was stopped by orders from Rosecrans, who thought it unwise to advance further till he made a ferry at the Gauley and succeeded in getting his command over; for Floyd had again sunk the flatboats within reach, and these had to be a second time raised and repaired."[93]

The indecisiveness shown by General Rosecrans after the battle at Carnifex Ferry also produced additional grumbling among the rank and file of Cox's command after

[92] Scott, *Philander P. Lane*, pg. 51

[93] Cox, *Military Reminiscences*, pg. 103

Rosecrans took charge of both Union elements. The men of the Eleventh Ohio were used to quick decisions and risk-taking. They were accustomed to being on the move constantly to deliver an illusion of strength rather than expose their general weaknesses. Moving with caution simply wasn't their style and they resented Rosecrans for imposing it on them:

"On the 13th, Gen. Cox moved out from Gauley to join in the pursuit of Floyd -- Rosecrans taking immediate command of all the troops. The Eleventh was in line at 3 o'clock A.M., and had the Brigade moved at that time many prisoners could have been taken before night. As it was, day light found us only crossing the river, and then we arrived at Mountain Cove just on the heels of the rebel rear guard, and captured a Lieutenant and thirteen men. So *slovenly* was the movement conducted that we did not reach Sewell Mountain until the *tenth* day out from Gauley. Throughout the march the Eleventh had the advance, but were continually held back by orders from the rear."[94]

These were proud, experienced soldiers who had already been on the slopes of Sewell Mountain and at a time when they were only eight companies -- not a full army. They failed to appreciate the caution of the commanding General and dissent must have been buzzing around the Eleventh's campfires. A letter written while on this march explains how the men of the Eleventh felt about themselves. They were hard-fighting veterans who had fought and marched in hostile terrain while being totally outnumbered by their enemy and were proud of their achievements:

"I think we will be permitted to go into winter quarters as soon as the rebels are driven out of Western Virginia, and from present indications that will not be long. Floyd and Wise have been put to flight, and to-day we learn that Lee has been forced to retreat from Cheat Mountain...Our

[94] Horton and Teverbaugh, *Eleventh Regiment*, pg. 45

work last month has made soldiers of us, and we are now always ready to move at very short notice. From our last camp we were ordered to march in twenty minutes, and in ten minutes our Adjutant had the line formed ready to move...We need more men in our little command, but as it is, we have done as much work as any regiment in Virginia, had more skirmishes, killed more rebs, and received less newspaper praise than any other regiment in Virginia. We are now called 'Frizell's Gipsies', as we are here, there, and everywhere, and when the rebs think they have us, we *aint there.* They have tried to surround us three or four times, but as we generally know as much of what they are about as they do themselves, they are rather unfortunate in their efforts. Mrs. Tompkins (wife of a rebel Colonel who has a beautiful place near Gauley) says she never heard of such a set of soldiers as the Gipsey Eleventh, as we know all roads, paths, houses, people, &c., have been over all their big hills, can sleep in logs, behind stumps, in rain or shine, can make the biggest show with the fewest men, and the biggest fight on record!"[95]

The men of the "Gipsey Eleventh" may not have understood caution in this situation, but Rosecrans had a serious problem to consider during the march toward Sewell Mountain. There was one man in Virginia who had to be taken into consideration when tactics were discussed -- Lee! His reputation in the pre-war army was such that most who were aware of him considered Lee the best field officer in the service and second only to General-in-Chief Winfield Scott in ability. All knew that Scott had offered Lee command of all the National Forces, but he was turned down and Lee accepted service with his home state. The phrase, "commanded by Lee in person", was worth several regiments to the Confederates, even at this early stage of the war. Cox wrote of the Sewell Mountain campaign:

"McCook's brigade joined me on the 16th of September, and my own command was increased by

[95] Horton and Teverbaugh, *Eleventh Regiment*, pg. 45-46

bringing up another of my regiments from below. With the two brigades I advanced to Spy Rock, a strong position overlooking a valley several miles broad, beyond which we occupied with an advance-guard on the 20th and in force on the 24th. Before the 1st of October Rosecrans had concentrated his force at the mountain, the four brigades being so reduced by sickness and by detachments that he reported the whole as making only 5200 effective men. Immediately in front, across a deep gorge, lay the united forces of Floyd and Wise, commanded by Lee in person. The autumn rains set in upon the very day of Rosecrans's arrival, and continued without intermission. The roads became so difficult that the animals of the wagon trains were being destroyed in the effort to supply the command. The camp was 35 miles from Gauley Bridge, and our stores were landed from steamboats 25 miles below that post, making 60 miles of wagoning. The enemy was as badly off, and no aggressive operations were possible on either side. This became so evident that on the 5th of October Rosecrans withdrew his forces to camps within 3 or 4 miles of Gauley Bridge."[96]

Rosecrans had little choice in deciding to pull back to positions near Gauley Bridge where the men could be provisioned and supplied adequately. The roads were soaked and the constant rolling of wagon wheels over them had churned their surfaces into a layer of mud which was over one foot deep. Rosecrans gave nothing away when he pulled back. The Rebels now had the problem of supplying their troops over the same impassable roads and were unlikely to advance until spring when better weather would permit offensive operations in the area again. The men in the army didn't understand the reasons behind Rosecrans' decision to retreat and there is some evidence of anger at their commanding general:

"October 5th, an order to strike tents after 'taps' and 'back out' from our position was received. We were ready

---

96 Cox, "McClellan in West Virginia", pg. 146-147

to move at 10 o'clock, but as the Eleventh, as usual, was to take its place in the line nearest the enemy, we did not get off till near morning of the 6th.

"Just after our wagons were packed Gen. Rosecrans came down to our camp, and hearing Col. Frizell using some very *emphatic* language, rode up and inquired the trouble.

"I have the ague, General, and don't feel like lying around in the mud all night,' answered the Colonel.

"Oh, a little quinine and whiskey will set you all right,' replied 'Rosey'.

"I have plenty of quinine, but how do you expect a man to get whiskey in this God-forsaken country,' asked Frizell.

"Well, Colonel, just get a tin cup, put your quinine in it, and I will furnish the whiskey,' answered the General, taking a small 'pocket pistol' from the breast of his coat.

"The Colonel got the cup, shook it over a paper that he took from his vest pocket (the paper was the last 'special order' received), and after pouring out a good strong *dose* from the General's flask, drank it off, thanked the General for his kindness, and assured him that the *medicine* would undoubtedly prove beneficial!"[97]

Lieutenant-Colonel Frizell wasn't any more pleased with the "special orders" he had received that ordered a retreat and he was probably cursing the current situation, his leadership, and life in general when Rosecrans rode up. He had the nerve to tell Rosecrans that he didn't feel like lying around in the mud all night, suggesting that they should be doing something constructive -- like fighting. Frizell definitely wasn't afraid of the Confederates and would prefer to fight as march up and down the roads. Some of Rosecrans' reasoning was later explained:

"His advance finally reached the top of the mountain and found the enemy holding it in a fortified camp; but he did not venture an attack. He seems to have been much mistaken in estimating Floyd's strength and in his belief

[97] Horton and Teverbaugh, *Eleventh Regiment*, pg. 48

that another force, under Lee, was waiting its opportunity to strike from the Huttonville road on the northeast. Lee had come down from the north of the state on hearing of Floyd's defeat, and remained about Lewisburg and Big Sewell until early in November, directing affairs generally, but not taking command of troops in active operations. By his unvarying patience and courtesy he had gained the confidence of both Floyd and Wise, but he could not reconcile them: nobody could."[98]

The two feuding Confederate generals probably contributed to the grey hair that General Lee was rapidly accumulating during the campaign. They simply would not cooperate under any circumstances and would have probably preferred to see one another annihilated than defeat the entire Union army. The Confederates had to separate the two:

"...Lee continued to receive from Wise alarming news of the enemy's advance on Sewell Mountain, and from Floyd reports that Wise would not fall back."[99]

Wise would not forget the insult from Floyd when Wise had concluded his briefing on the general situation following the retreat from the Kanawha valley in late July. Wise had simply asked Floyd what he was going to do -- to which Floyd pointed out the road and said he was going down it. Wise wanted to know what he was going to do on the road -- Floyd said "Fight", implying that Wise had failed to do so. With that insult between them, Wise was not going to retreat to join Floyd at Meadow Bluff. He established "Camp Defiance" and refused to budge and he certainly didn't miss any opportunity to point out that it was Floyd who was now in retreat. Henry Heth wrote:

"Floyd contended that Muddy Creek was the place to receive the attack of Rosecrans. Wise, of course, took

98 Scott, *Philander P. Lane*, pg. 52
99 White, "West Virginia", pg. 42

the opposite view and was for fighting at Sewell Mountain. The council determined on Muddy Creek. Floyd issued orders to this effect. After the council had adjourned, General Wise got on his horse and rode to his command, where he struck the first detachment, halted, raised himself in his stirrups, and in a stentorian voice called out, 'Who is retreating now? Who is retreating now?' "He rode slowly on, and seeing another group of his men, he repeated the same to them. Presently, his entire command had assembled and he said, 'Men, who is retreating now? John B. Floyd, God damn him, the bullet-hit son of a bitch, he is retreating now."[100]

With the Confederate army on Sewell Mountain split into two separate elements, Lee had to do something or face defeat as Rosecrans' larger force simply rolled over each Rebel army one at a time:

"He repaired promptly to the Kanawha valley, reaching Floyd's camp September 21st, and at once wrote to Wise, using these words: 'I beg, therefore, if not too late, that the troops be united, and that we conquer or die together.' To this, the indomitable Wise responded that he would join Floyd there or at Meadow Bluff if Lee would say which, that he laughed the enemy to scorn, and he was ready to do, suffer and die for the cause, but that any imputation upon his motives would make him 'perhaps, no longer a military subordinate of any man who breathes.' Lee then 'went to the mountain,' and on the 23rd, learning that Rosecrans had occupied in force the crest of Big Sewell, brought up Floyd to the mountain position which Wise held with such tenacity. He did this, because it was the most defensible line, and he also caused reinforcements to be sent by Loring, which increased the Confederate strength at Little Sewell to 8,000 or 9,000 men."[101]

Travel in the area was dreadfully slow and Lee was

100 Heth, "Memoirs", pg. 15

101 White, "West Virginia", pg. 42-43

well aware of the time required for any of the reinforcements requested of Loring to march from Cheat Mountain to the area of Sewell Mountain. Lee had previously written Floyd:

"Great efforts have been made to place this column in marching condition. Although the roads are continuous tracks of mud, in which the wagons plunge to their axles, I hope the forces can be united, with a few days' supply of provisions, so as to move forward on Thursday, the 12th instant. I therefore advise you of the probability that on your part you may be prepared to take advantage of it, and if circumstances render it advisable, to act on your side."[102]

The combinations of bad weather, poor roads, and faulty intelligence as to the other's intentions and capabilities prevented any serious action on the part of either commander during the Sewell Mountain campaigns. The inability to supply their respective forces was a constant problem and each side waited for the other to attack.

"General Rosecrans on Big Sewell mountain had about the same number of men as Lee, but each had exaggerated reports of the strength of the other, and it was difficult for either to make an offensive move. Lee naturally anticipated that Rosecrans would attempt to continue his advance, and waited for an opportunity to thwart it. Thus the two forces observed each other across a deep gorge for eleven days, during which period the Confederates, poorly sheltered from the tempests of wind and rain, suffered severely. 'It cost us more men, sick and dead,' General Floyd averred, 'than the battle of Manassas."[103] The Union soldiers had to pull out of the fortifications on Big Sewell during the night to avoid alerting the Confederates that they were vulnerable to attack while the regiments were stretched out along the turnpike. None of them were

102 Hotchkiss, "Virginia", pg. 161
103 White, "West Virginia", pg. 43

very happy about their retreat and felt that General Rosecrans was acting erratically. He was probably afraid that his ruse would be discovered and that his columns would be atacked by Lee while they were strung out in positions where they could not defend themselves. The men, however, were not mind-readers and morale suffered:

"Through mud almost knee deep, the troops wended their way down Sewell's rugged side, halting every few rods till some broken down wagon was turned over out of the way and set on fire. The trains were all in front, and it seemed that the greater effort to hasten them along the slower they went. Riding frantically back and forth among the horses and wagons, ordering mess chests and officer's baggage thrown out, fires built under wagons stalled in the mud, the General (Rosecrans) acted in a strange and unaccountable manner. Among the property uselessly destroyed were the mess chests belonging to several of the company officers, containing all of their provisions, and many valuable official books, papers, &c., and it was only by accident that the box containing the Regimental Books was saved. After arriving at Gauley Bridge an order was received from HEAD-QUARTERS to 'send in all the morning reports' (it having been impossible to make them out while on the march), together with other reports equally impossible to furnish correctly. Here was a fine state of affairs!"[104]

Another reason for the concern of General Rosecrans was the information that he had received regarding the condition of the ferry at Gauley Bridge, a strategic bottleneck in his supply system, where every wagon had to cross the river before slowly creeping over the muddy mountain road to supply the army. The heavy rains had created a serious problem and Rosecrans single option was to get the small army as near to Gauley Bridge as possible where some of the guns from the small town could help hold off a potential Confederate assault against which he

104 Horton and Teverbaugh, *Eleventh Regiment*, pg. 49

would be hard pressed to to repulse. The bad news -- high water had destroyed the ferry on Gauley River.

"...Captain Lane, with his company, was retained at Gauley Bridge, to make sure of the protection and operation of the ferry, since the supply of the army depended upon it. There was a sudden great rise in the Gauley, from a phenomenally heavy rain, and it was with great anxiety that he saw the big torrent rushing down and rapidly rising in height. In spite of the unceasing care and labors of himself and all his men, the swift flood at last carried away the cable, all the boats but one, and the lumber and timbers collected and prepared for reserve. It was said to be the greatest flood the country had known.

"It was now impossible for the army to cross the Gauley, if compelled to retreat, and at the same time impossible to supply it with food and ammunition where it was."[105]

Rosecrans and Cox had every reason to be concerned about their lines of communication back to their supply base at Gauley Bridge. This was the reason for the erratic actions of Rosecrans: he was trapped between a raging river on one side and the Confederate army under Robert E. Lee on the other! The river had swept away the ferry and even though Captain Lane and his company were able to get it back in operation in only a few days, there was a good chance that the river could flood and repeat the performance with the ferry. They were facing a strong enemy in Lee and caution was advisable. Rosecrans felt that they hadn't given up anything that they couldn't take back at any time and felt that the men would be better off at camps along the Gauley where they could get proper clothing and receive their pay.

Few of the men had received any pay since entering the army four or five months earlier and this was also a sore point with them. This lack of pay and the fear that they were going into winter quarters before defeating the Rebels

---

105 Scott, *Philander P. Lane*, pg. 53

were their major complaints:

"The next Sabbath, October 13th, the Regiment arrived at Gauley Bridge, and went into camp just north of 'Scrabble Creek'. A letter written ... gives a very fair account of our condition at that time:

"After several days of toilsome marching we arrived at this place on Sunday last. That morning we broke camp at Mountain Cove, and upon arriving at Tompkins' Farm, were ordered by Gen. Rosecrans to continue our march to Gauley. We were all glad to do so, as we have more room here, plenty of good water, and are some miles nearer *civilization*. ... We have not a Field Officer with us, both Frizell and Coleman being home sick. Our Regiment numbers 717 altogether, but there are only two Captains, 9 Lieutenants, and 281 non-commissioned officers and privates reported for duty to-day...The Seventh Ohio,which has been stationed at this post since the defeat at Cross Lanes, is leaving this morning for Charleston...It seems more like 'old times' just now than at any time since we left Ohio. We have regular Guard mounting, dress parade, &c., daily, and if our officers and men were all together and well, we would be getting along finely...We have been soldiering nearly six months, but have not yet seen the officer called 'Paymaster'. We hear of him occasionally, and hope he is enjoying himself."[106]

While the Eleventh Ohio reacquainted themselves with garrison life, two events were occurring that would have an impact on them. First, General Wise was relieved from command and sent to Richmond where Jeff Davis suggested that the arrogant general may be shot as Wise made a last request -- let him watch them shoot Floyd before being hanged. This event did not affect the Union privates greatly, but it left Floyd in command of a significant portion of the Confederate army facing the camp at Gauley Bridge and would now have a unified command, for the first time. The second would have a day-to-day

106 Horton and Teverbaugh, *Philander P. Lane*, pg. 49-50

effect on them -- their Colonel, DeVilliers, was returning after a stay at Libby Prison in Richmond. He was one of the Union officers who rode into the Confederate lines after the battle of Scary Creek to congradulate them on "whipping the rebs". This was not exactly a confidence inspiring act to witness and since the capture, the Eleventh had been under the command of an excellent officer, Lieutenant-Colonel Frizell, and had accumulated an enviable combat record in the mountains around Gauley Bridge. One of the Eleventh's companies, under Captain Lane, had set records for the number of bridges constructed and had built the ferry over Gauley River on two separate occasions, both in record time. They would have done better in the future if the Confederate jailer had kept DeVilliers.

Cox wrote about the man:

"I had also for a time the services of one of the picturesque adventurers who turn up in such crises. In the Seventh Ohio was a company recruited in Cleveland, of which the nucleus was an organization of Zouaves, existing for some time before the war. It was made up of young men who had been stimulated by the popularity of Ellsworth's Zouaves in Chicago to form a similar body. They had as their drill master a Frenchman named De Villiers. His profession was that of a teacher of fencing; but he had been an officer in Ellsworth's company, and was familar with fancy manuevers for street parade, and with a special drill and bayonet exercise. Small, swarthy, with angular features, and a brusque, military manner, in a showy uniform and a jaunty *kepi* of scarlet cloth covered with gold lace, he created quite a sensation among us. His assumption of knowledge and experience was accepted as true. He claimed to have been a surgeon in the French army in Algiers, though we afterward learned to doubt if his rank had been higher than that of a barber-surgeon of a cavalry troop. From the testimonials he brought with him, I thought I was doing a good thing in making him my brigade-major, as the officer was then called whom we afterward knew as inspector-general. He certainly was a most indefatigable fellow, and went at his work with an enthusiasm that made him very useful for a time. It was worth something to see a man who worked with a kind of dash. -- with a prompt, staccato movement that infused spirit and energy into all around him. He would drill all day, and then spend half the night trying to catch sentinels at fault in their duty. My first impression was that I had got a hold of a most valuable man, and others were so much of the same mind that in the reorganization of regiments he was successively elected major of the Eighth, then colonel of the Eleventh...but it turned out that his sharp discipline was not steady or just; his knowledge was only skin-deep, and he had neither the education nor the character for so responsible a situation as he was placed in. He nearly plagued the life out of the officers of his regiment before they got rid of him, and was a most brillant example of the way we were imposed upon by military charlatans at the beginning."[107]

The good colonel had been captured through his thoughtlessness, a fact which was totally unknown to the men of the Eleventh Ohio. They didn't have the knowledge of the actual capture that the Confederates had and they assumed his capture must have been in the line of duty. His reappearance in October was regarded with some amount of awe which was deepened with the tales of DeVilliers:

"On the 28th of October, Col. de Villiers arrived at Gauley Bridge, and was formally received by the Regiment the next day. Some eight or ten days previously Gen. Cox had issued a general order announcing the Colonel's escape from Richmond. -- and, after many 'hair breadth 'scapes' and wonderful adventures, --safe arrival at Washington. Major Coleman had returned a few days before, and, as eminently proper under the circumstances, paraded the command and gave the Colonel the reception due to his rank.

---

[107] Cox, *Military Reminiscences*, pg. 34-35

"Whether all the stories told by the Colonel concerning his escape are true or not, is of very little moment at this time, but for a while at least he was considered by many as a hero of surprising courage and endurance. Throwing two men at the *same time* into the river, cutting the throat of another whom he met in a corn field, swimming the Potomac four times, and many other incidents of a like nature, were adventures of rare occurrence at that period, and he who successfully performed such feats could not easily escape being lionized, especially when extraordinary pains were taken to give the greatest possble publicity to the most minute particulars of the *grand* affair.

"Assuming command at a time when many of our men were considerably worn down by the hardships of their first campaign; many of the officers sick and absent; winter approaching, and surrounded by other peculiarly depressing influences, many of the men were just in that frame of mind to swallow with avidity the specious promises made by the Colonel of immediate discharge for all who desired it; promotions for those whom *he* chose to elevate, and the removal of the Regiment to Ohio for the winter. Col. de V. may have been entirely honest in presuming that he had the power to effect all of those things, but those men who were examined by Dr. Perkins, and sent home with the assurance that proper discharges would speedily reach them, were soon undeceived when the matter came before higher authority.

"Lieutenant-Colonel Frizell arrived from home about this time, and perceiving that he could be of no benefit to the Regiment under the then existing state of affairs, obtained leave to go to Charleston, where he remained till he learned that the rebels were 'showing fight' at Gauley, when he returned to his post, but did not arrive in time to participate in the 'movement'on 'Cotton Hill".[108]

Colonel De Villiers wasn't necessarily "lionized" by everyone in the Eleventh Ohio:

---

108 Horton and Teverbaugh, *Eleventh Regiment*, pg. 50-51

"One of the grievances of the soldiers at Gauley was removed by the appearance in camp of the paymaster, who arrived near the end of October, and immediately had many of the officers and sergeants busy on the preparation of the 'muster and pay-rolls' required for his use. For the Eleventh Ohio, however, this agreeable experience was abruptly marred by a disaster. Its Colonel returned from his three months captivity, and of course resumed command of the regiment. He had notified the brigade commander he was coming, and the regiment was turned out, on formal parade, to 'welcome' him, tho to nearly all the officers and men the occasion was anything but welcome. At the best there was in his regiment but little respect for him or confidence in him, and what there was had been diminished by the circumstances of his capture. As there was little or no evidence of his adventures after his capture beyond his own story, and, as that story contained many fearful and hairbreadth perils and deeds of daring, he found few believers. He may have been in one of the escapes of officers from Libby Prison, but also may have been merely one of those exchanged: no one seems to have taken the trouble to make an inquiry, and his loquacious boasting was left to free play. He had little or none of the personal dignity that induces respect for an officer, and some of his tales of dangers and daring were openly ridiculed as being only lying inventions."[109]

Cox wrote about DeVilliers escapades:

"Whilst the general and I were talking, Colonel DeVilliers gallops up, having crossed at the ferry and run the gantlet of skirmishers whom he reported as lining the other side of New River opposite the unsheltered part of our road. He had recently reported for duty, having, as he asserted, escaped in a wonderful way from captivity in Libby Prison at Richmond. His regiment was at the bridge and he was the senior officer there; but, in his characteristic light-headed way, instead of taking steps to protect his post

109 Scott, *Philander P. Lane*, pg. 55

and re-establish the telegraph communications, he had dashed off to report in person at headquarters."[110]

The greatly unloved Colonel DeVilliers had returned to a regiment, if not a brigade, that would have preferred to have seen him remain in Confederate hands for the duration of the war. He had returned at the conclusion of a difficult campaign from which the men had been ordered to retreat and morale was not especially high. His erratic commands and approach to discipline did not help the overall situation:

"During his absence the regiment had been finely developed under the Lieutenant-Colonel and Major, and had become at least the equal in discipline and efficiency of any regiment in its army. Now, under the new regime, it fell off rapidly into a bad condition of discouragement among both officers and men. By his erratic performance of his own duties, his rash orders, violent language and many threats of punishments that were never attempted, he broke down discipline instead of strengthing it; and, what with this and his obvious lack of a real knowledge of drill and manuevers, he hampered and irritated the officers; and frequently during the winter got into a quarrel with one or another of them, indulging in the most vulgar and insulting language. During the next four months after his return he made his camp the scene of unhappy turmoil, involving both officers and men. The Lieutenant-Colonel and one of the captains resigned in disgust, seeing no other way to escape their share of the trouble."[111]

A few days after the return of Colonel DeVilliers, the major complaint of the Union troops at Gauley Bridge was about to be resolved. The appropriate forms and rolls had been filled out and the paymaster was about to begin paying them some long overdue wages when the process was rudely interrupted:

---

110 Cox, *Military Reminiscences*, pg. 131

111 Scott, *Philander P. Lane*, pg. 55-56

"With patience and perseverance, however, all was ready in good time, and on Friday morning, November 1st, Major Reese had his strong box opened in the sutler's tent. Just as he began to hand out the first 'greenbacks' that had been seen by us, *zhur-r-r-r, bang*! came a shell from Cotton Hill, striking in the quarters of Company H. Another followed, burying itself in the ground close to Capt. Duncan's tent, where Company B was gathered for the purpose of signing the pay-rolls. At intervals of only a few moments our Regiment shared with the ferry this sort of attention from the rebels during the entire day.

"Col. de Villiers mounted his horse at the first fire, rode off in the direction of the General's quarters, and did not make his appearance again till night."[112]

The Confederates under General Floyd had finally managed to do something significant. They had occupied the small mountain directly across the wide New River from the Federal camp and were rapidly showing Rosecrans the major error he had made by not fortifying it. They were in a position from where they could shell both the camp and the vital ferry across Gauley River and would effectively halt all movement of supplies to the Union camps remaining on Gauley Mountain and along New River.

This Confederate attack was but a single phase of the attempt against the Federal army planned by Lee from his headquarters on Sewell Mountain. Lee had allowed Floyd and his reinforced brigade to cross New River to move along the southern side of the river and bring pressure against the Union camp at Gauley Bridge. He was planning to send General Loring westward along the James River and Kanawha Turnpike in a simultaneous effort against Rosecrans' positions. Unfortunately for the Confederates, there was a serious requirement for reinforcements in the Shenandoah valley and Loring's troops were quickly diverted there. Floyd was permitted to continue his move along the river and was protected to a great degree by the

---

112 Horton and Teverbaugh, *Eleventh Regiment*, pg. 52

swollen river which was impossible to cross.

General Cox went into great detail about this stage of the fighting in the area:

"On the 1st of November the early morning was fair but misty, and a fog lay in the gorge of new River nearly a thousand feet below the little plateau at Tompkins farm, on which the headquarters tents were pitched...I was attending to the usual morning duties of clerical work, when the report and echo of a cannon-shot, down in the gorge in the direction of Gauley Bridge, was heard. It was unusual, enough to set me thinking what it could mean, but the natural explanation suggested itself that it was one of our own guns, perhaps fired at a target. In a few moments an orderly came in great haste, saying the general desired to see me at his tent. As I walked to his quarters, another shot was heard. As I approached, I saw him standing in front of the tent door, evidently much excited, and when I came up to him, he said in the rapid, half-stammering way peculiar to him at such times: 'The enemy has got a battery on Cotton Mountain opposite our post, and is shelling it! What d' ye think of that?' The post at the bridge and his headquarters were connected by telegraph, and the operator below had reported the fact of the opening of the cannonade from the mountainside above him, and added that his office was so directly under fire that he must move out of it. Indeed he was gone and communication broken before orders could be sent to him or to the post. The fact of the cannonade did not affect me so much as the way in which it affected Rosecrans. He had been expecting to be attacked by Lee in front, and knew that McCook was exchanging shots across the river with some force of enemy at Miller's Ferry; but that the attack should come two or more miles in our rear, from a point where artillery had a plunging fire directly into our depot of supplies and commanded our only road for a half-mile where it ran on a narrow bench along New River under Gauley Mountain cliffs, had been so startling as to throw him decidedly off his balance. The error in not occupying Cotton Mountain himself was now not only made plain, but the consequences were not pleasant to contemplate. I saw that the best service I could render him for the moment was to help him back into a frame of mind in which cool reasoning on the situation would be possible...and I now realized how much easier it was for a subordinate to take things coolly...We could not, from where we stood, see the post at Gauley Bridge nor even the place on Cotton Mountain where the enemy's battery was placed, and we walked a little way apart from the staff offices to a position from which we could see the occasional puffs of white smoke from the hostile guns."[113]

A Confederate Captain, D.B. Baldwin, of a Virginia Partisan Ranger unit wrote to his wife and explained the shelling of Gauley Bridge from his side of the river:

"...We have had a verry hard time of it since we came to this place. On the 1st of November all the regiments in the Brigade were ordered out at 3 1/2 O C in the morning. We had taken a Rifle Canon to a point of the mountain commanding Gauley Ferry. This point is just at the junction of Gauley and New Rivers, and is only from 300 to 500 yards from the Yankee Camp. We got the Canon there and mounted without the Yankees knowing it. We marched to the Cols quarters, and reported ourselves ready. Our Company was detailed to go to the Canon. The balance of our Regiment was stationed along the banks of the River. We reached the Canon at daylight, and I was ordered to take our company and coat the top of the battery with black earth, to conceal it as much as possible. I was then ordered to take six of our men and cut the trees in front of the Canon. The moment the trees fell, we commenced firing into the Yankee Camp, and I assure you we created an excitement among them, for up to that time I am certain that they never thought of such a thing as a Rifle Canon that near their camp. I had a good view from where I was, our Company being posted near the Canon on the side next the Yankee Camp. As soon as we commenced

[113] Cox, *Military Reminiscences*, pg. 129-130

firing, they began to run in every direction. I saw some of them upon horses runing down the River, and in about half of an hour, they returned with three ps of brass Canon, and commenced firing at our battery at once. This was about 10 O C in the Morning. They continued to fire upon our battery until about two O C, when they saw our Company posted along the ridge in front of them. They fired into us. The first shot was a round six pounder, and struck the ground near one of our men Jim Grey, and threw the dirt in his face; he dug the ball out, and says that he intends to send it to Bob Smith. The next shot at us was a 12 pound shell filled with musket balls, and exploded among us without hurting any of us. They then fired a Rifle canon ball into us, then fired at us no more that evening. We layed all night at the Canon, it rained the whole night and all next day. The next morning Gen Floyd sent orders to have a right and left wing built to the battery. Our Company being there, we were ordered to cut large trees and put up the brest work, which was intended to protect the Artilery-men. When they commenced work it was verry early in the Morning, and before the fog was off the River. Abour 9 O C it cleared up and when our men were at work thick around the Canon, the Yankees fired into us. We had to leave the work, and get as good position as we could. They fired into us three times that day only two however come near us. A shell bursted among us and come verry near killing some of us; I was sitting near James Gillispee and a ps of it struck his hat and passed between two more of our men. The Yankees come down to the New River banks and hid themselves, and shot Minie balls at us all evening. We had canon posted at other points up and down River, and had Men posted on the banks for about 8 miles.

"...The Yankees then run their Canon at different points along the River, and just in front of our forces, and pitched shell into them for two days. The most remarkable thing connected with this brush is that we did not have a single man killed. We killed a good number of Yankees. I saw some of them fall myself. I had my glass and could see them verry distinctly. We laid out there two days and nearly two nights.

"...I have just received the socks and shirts. They come in good time. I am very much obliged..."[114]

Cox continued to explain events from his side of the river and the long-range conflict that was developing:

"From our camp the road descended sharply along the shoulders of steep hills covered with wood for a mile and a half, till it reached the bottom of the New River gorge, and then it followed the open bench I have mentioned till it reached the crossing of the Gauley. On the opposite side of New River there was no road, the mass of Cotton Mountain crowding close upon the stream with its picturesque face of steep inclines and perpendicular walls of rock. The bridge of boats Rosecrans had planned had not been built, because it had been found impossible to collect or to construct boats enough to make it. We were therefore still dependent on the ferry. Whilst the General and I were talking, Colonel De Villiers galloped up...he was willing to take the risks of the race back again, he was allowed to go, after being fully instructed to set up a new telegraph office in a ravine out of range of fire, to put the ferry-boat out of danger as soon as he should be over, and prepare the ordance stores to be moved into the valley of Scrabble Creek at night. I begged the general to be allowed to go back with De Villiers, as the thing I feared most was some panic at the post which might result in the destruction of our stores in depot there. He, however, insisted on my staying at headquarters for a time at least.

"...Benham, who was nearest, was ordered to send down part of his brigade to meet the efforts of the enemy to stop our communication with Gauley Bridge. The battery of mountain howitzers under Captain Mack of the regular army was also ordered to report to headquarters, with the intention of placing it high on Gauley cliffs, where it could

114 Kelley, Donald B., "Rifle Cannon and Yankees: Captain D.B. Baldwin in the Skirmish at Gauley Bridge", *West Virginia History*, Vol. XXIV, No. 4, pg. 353-354

drop shells among the enemy's skirmishers on the opposite bank of the river."[115]

If the letter of Captain Baldwin is any indication, Captain Mack was quite successful in dropping shells among the Confederate skirmishers along the south bank of New River. The Union counter-measures were beginning to have an effect on the Rebel strategy. Scrabble Creek was nearby, actually within the town and the ordinance would not have to be hauled very far to get it into a safe location. The ferry was another matter. It was at the mouth of Gauley River and would be hard to protect from direct hits from the Confederate cannon firing downward from the tops of the cliffs only five hundred yards away.

The work of rescuing the ferry fell to the man who constructed it, Captain Lane:

"Captain Lane had been relieved of duty at the ferry (as there was no movement of troops now, the operation of it was only routine work for a small party) and was in camp with his regiment at some distance. When the shells began to strike near the ferry, some one there sent a messenger in a rush to tell him. He could answer only that he had no authority and that the message should have gone to Colonel DeVilliers. He had taken no action in the emergency, and did nothing now but send the man to Captain Lane with authority to do what he thought best. Angered by this cowardly shuffling off of responsibility, but seeing the importance of instant action, the Captain at once ran down to the ferry. He found thirty or forty men there, sheltered, but in a helpless state of mind, while the ferry-boat was at the other side of the river, clearly in sight from the rebel battery. A shell had just struck dangerously near it. He called four men to go over with him and move the boat out of range. Three did volunteer, and with these he crossed on the 'walk' attached to the cable, which, like the boat, was fully seen from the battery, and, with strenuously rapid labor, they released the boat and hauled it up stream and

115 Cox, *Military Reminiscences*, pg. 131-132

behind a projecting point of rocks. The movement took time enough, however, to enable the rebels to get in three more shells, which he describes as two very close and one wild."[116]

General Rosecrans was still showing that he had been taken by surprise by Floyd's occupation of Cotton Hill and revealed a personal characteristic that was later to seriously affect his career. He did not respond well to the unexpected and when placed under severe pressure, his frustration could cause him to argue with his superiors and hesitation and excessive caution replaced his aggresssiveness. After a near-disaster at Chickamauga, he was relieved by General Grant and had no active role for the remainder of the war. Cox was beginning to discover this side of Rosecrans' personality as the shocked general tried to recover his balance:

"An hour or two passed and the detachment from Benham's brigade approached. It was the Thirteenth Ohio, led by one of its field officers, who halted the column and rode up to General Rosecrans for orders. The General's manner was still an excited one, and in the rapidity with which his directions were given the officer did not seem to get a clear idea of what was required of him. He made some effort to get the orders explained, but his failure to comprehend seemed to irritate Rosecrans, and he therefore bowed and rode back to his men with a blank look which did not promise well for intelligent action. Noticing this, I quietly walked aside among the bushes, and when out of sight hurried a little in advance and waited at the roadside for the column. I beckoned the officer to me, and said to him, 'Colonel, I thought you looked as if you did not fully understand the general's wishes.' He replied that he did not, but was unwilling to question him as it seemed to irritate him. I said that was a wrong principle to act on, as a commanding officer has the greatest interest in being clearly understood. I then explained at large what I knew

116 Scott, *Philander P. Lane*, pg. 57-58

to be Rosecrans's purposes. The officer thanked me cordially and rode away. I have ventured to give this incident with such fulness, because subsequent events in Rosecrans's career strengthened the impression I formed at the time, that the excitability of his temperament was such that an unexpected occurrence might upset his judgement so that it would be uncertain how he would act, -- whether it would rouse him to a heroism of which he was quite capable, or make him for the time unfit for real leadership by suspending his self-command."[117]

Cox was always the loyal subordinate to General Rosecrans. When he provided the supplemental briefing of the colonel from the Thirteenth Ohio, he used the approach that the colonel was at fault for being unwilling to question Rosecrans "as it seemed to irritate him" rather than point out that being clearly understood was really the responsibility of the general, himself -- not the colonel's. Cox related one of the most fascinating stories of the war, at least in the western Virginia campaigns:

"Soon after noon I obtained permission to go to Gauley Bridge and assume command there; but as the road along New River was now impracticable by reason of the increased fire of the enemy upon it, I took the route over the top of Gauley Mountain, intending to reach the Gauley River as near the post as practicable. I took with me only my aide, Captain Christie, and an orderly. We rode a little beyond the top of the mountain, and sending the orderly back with the horses, proceeded on foot down the northern slope. We soon came to the slashing which I had made in August to prevent the enemy's easy approach to the river near the post. The mist of the morning had changed to a drizzling rain. We had on our heavy horseman's overcoats with large capes, cavalry boots and spurs, swords and pistols. This made it toilsome work for us. The trees had been felled so that they crossed each other in utmost confusion on the steep declivity. Many of them were very

117 Cox, *Military Reminiscences*, pg. 132-133

large, and we slid over the great wet trunks, climbed through and under branches, let ourselves down walls of natural rock, tripped and hampered by our accoutrements, till we came to the end of the entanglement at what we supposed was the edge of the river. To our dismay we found that we had not kept up stream far enough, and that at this point was a sheer precipice some thirty feet high. We could find no crevices to help us climb down it. We tried to work along the edge till we should reach a lower place, but this utterly failed. We were obliged to retrace our steps to the open wood above the slashing. But if the downward climbing had been hard, this attempt to pull ourselves up again,

'*...superasque evadere ad auras,...*'*

was labor indeed. We stopped several times from sheer exhaustion, so blown that it seemed almost impossible to get breath again. Our clothes were heavy from the rain on the outside and wet with perspiration on the inside. At last, however, we accomplished it, and resting for a while at the foot of a great tree till we gained a little strength, we followed the upper line of the slashing till we passed beyond it, and turned toward the river, choosing to reach its banks high above the camp rather than attempt again to climb through the fallen timber. Once at the water's edge we followed the stream down till we were opposite the guard post above the camp,when we hailed a skiff and were ferried over."[118]

The northern slope of Gauley mountain is indeed a formidable obstacle during the best of times. Descending this very steep slope in the rain while being forced to cross interlocking fallen trees which had been set in place as an intentional barrier to a military force would certainly have required serious exertions of the general and his aide. Most of the mountain is steeper than forty-five degrees and in several areas the slope varies between sixty degrees and vertical. If Cox had been delayed in his descent until after dark, there is an excellent chance that he would not have

* "Conquer and Ascend to the Heavens"

made it across without receiving an injury -- or worse! He continued his narrative about the condition of the Union camp which had been under Confederate cannon attack for most of the day:

"It was now almost dark, but the arrangements were soon made to have the wagons ready at the building on the Kanawha front used as a magazine, and to move all our ammunition during the night to the place I had indicated in the ravine of Scrabble Creek, which runs into the Gauley. The telegraph station was moved there and connection of wires made. We also prepared to run the ferry industriously during the night and to put over the necessary trainloads of supplies for the troops above. A place was selected high up on the hill behind us, where I hoped to get up a couple of Parrott guns which might silence the cannon of the enemy on Cotton Mountain. I was naturally gratified at the expressions of relief and satisfaction of the officers of the post to have me in person among them. They had already found that the plunging fire from the heights across the river was not a formidable thing, and that little mischief would happen if the men were kept from assembling in bodies or large groups within range of the enemy's cannon.

"The fatigues of the day made sleep welcome as soon as the most pressing duties had been done, and I went early to rest, giving orders to the guard to call me at peep of day. The weather cleared during the night, and when I went out in the morning to see what progress had been made in transferring the ammunition to a safe place, I was surprised to find the train of wagons stopped in the road in front of the camp. General Rosecrans's ordinance officer was of the regular army, but unfortunately was intemperate. He had neglected his duty during the night, leaving his sergeant to get on without guidance or direction. The result was that the ordinance stores had not been loaded upon the waiting wagons till nearly daylight, and soon after turning out of the Kanawha road into that of the Gauley, the mules of a team near the head of the train balked, and the whole had been brought to a standstill. There was a little rise in the road on the hither side of Scrabble Creek, where the track, cutting through the crest of a hillock, was only wide enough for a single team, and this rise was of course the place where the balky animals had stopped. The line of the road was enfiladed by the enemy's cannon, the morning fog in the valley was beginning to lift under the influence of the rising sun, and as soon as the situation was discovered we might reckon upon receiving the fire of the Cotton Mountain battery. The wagon- drivers realized the danger of handling an ammunition train under such circumstances and began to be nervous, whilst the onlookers not connected with the duty made haste to get out of harm's way. My presence strengthened the authority of the quartermaster in charge, Captain E. P. Fitch, helped in steadying the men, and enabled him to enforce promptly his orders. He stopped the noisy efforts to make the refractory mules move, and sent in haste for a fresh team. As soon as it came, this was put place of the balky animals, and at the word of command the train started quickly forward. The fog had thinned enough, however, to give the enemy an inkling of what was going on, and the rattling of the wagons on the road completed the exposure. Without warning, a ball struck in the road near us and bounded over the rear of the train, the report of the cannon following instantly. The drivers involuntarily crouched over their mules and cracked their whips. Another shot followed, but it was also short, and the last wagon turned the shoulder of the hill into the gorge of the creek as the ball bounded along up Gauley valley. It was perhaps fortunate for us that solid shot instead of shrapnel were used, but it is not improbable that the need of haste in firing made the battery officer feel that he had no time to cut and adjust fuses to the estimated distance to our train; or it is possible that shells were used but did not explode"[119]

The Civil War artillery was to do much to make the war the deadliest up to that point in history. There was a wide varity of ammunition available which ranged from solid shot to canister which resulted in gigantic shotgun

119 Cox, *Military Reminiscences*, pg. 134-136

blasts fired directly into the ranks of attacking infantry. Other shells included explosive charges which produced large blasts of fragments into the target area when the shell impacted. Some varieties of ammunition had "time fuse" which could be shortened to time the explosion as the shell passed directly over the enemy. These explosions could result in shell casing fragments or a shower iron balls called case shot which produced large numbers of casualties if employed properly against troops in the open. The range of the artillery used in the war was greater than most would have believed. A Parrott gun was capable of firing a 9 3/4 pound shell for 5000 yards with considerable accuracy against enemy targets. Many of the Civil War gunners became excellent at estimating the range to their target and by using the firing tables included in each ammunition chest to determine the average flight time of a shell, they could cut the fuse to a proper length to ensure airbursts directly over their targets. All of their aiming was, however, directly at the enemy. A soldier in the Confederate army, Milton W. Humphries of Bryan's Battery, later developed the art of indirect artillery fire during the second major campaign against targets in the Kanawha valley.

Cox continued to explain the tactical situation as Gauley Bridge came under an artillery seige from the Confederates under General Floyd:

"During the evening of the 1st of November General Benham's brigade came to the post at Gauley Bridge to strengthen the garrison, and was encamped on the Kanawha side near the falls, where the widening of the valley put them out of range of the enemy's fire. The ferry below the falls was called Montgomery's and was at the mouth of Big Falls Creek, up which ran the road to Fayette C.H. A detatchment of the enemy had pushed back our outposts on this road, and had fired upon our lower camp with cannon, but the position was not a favorable one for them and they did not stay long. After a day or two we were able to keep pickets on that side with a flatboat and hawser to bring them back, covered by artillery on our side of the

Kanawha."[120]

The Twenty-second Virginia Infantry which was commanded by Colonel Tompkins, the owner of the farm where Rosecrans was camped at this time, and since the Colonel was on a short leave to meet his wife who had been held on the farm until a few days previously, Major Isaac Smith was in command. The Twenty-second Virginia was no favorite of General Floyd and he had sent one of his favorites, Colonel John McCausland, to press Major Smith's men as close to the enemy as possible. This very advanced movement of the Twenty-second resulted in Cox's outposts on the Fayette Courthouse road being pushed back toward and probably over the river. These Confederates were far in advance of any reinforcements which would be needed in case of a serious Federal attack that they had to be pulled back closer to the top of the mountain or be lost. As they were moved back, Cox was able to put his pickets back on the south side of the river, but they were covered by Federal artillery.

Rosecrans began to collect all of the information available to him on the numbers and intent of the Confederates facing him and potential reinforcements for the Rebel forces across the river:

"During November 2nd Rosecrans matured a plan of operations against Floyd, who was now definitely found to be in command of the hostile force on Cotton Mountain. It was also learned through scouting parties and the country people that Lee had left the region,with most of the force that had been at Sewell Mountain. It seemed possible therefore to entrap Floyd, and this was what Rosecrans determined to attempt. Benham was ordered to take his brigade down the Kanawha and cross to the other side at the mouth of Loup Creek, five miles below. Schenck was ordered to prepare wagon bodies as temporary boats, to make such flatboats as he could, and get ready to cross the New River at Townsend's Ferry, about fifteen miles above

120 Cox, *Military Reminiscences*, pg. 136-137

Gauley Bridge. McCook was ordered to watch Miller's Ferry near his camp, and be prepared to make a dash on the short road to Fayette C.H. I was ordered to hold the post at Gauley Bridge, forward supplies by night, keep down the enemy's fire as far as possible, and watch for an opportunity to co-operate with Benham by way of Montgomery's Ferry. Benham's brigade was temporarily increased by 1500 picked men from the posts between Kanawha Falls and Charleston. He was expected to march up Loup Creek and cut off Floyd's retreat by way of Raleigh C.H., whilst Schenck should co-operate from Townsend's Ferry. On the 5th the preparations had been made, and Benham was ordered to cross the Kanawha. He did so on the night of the 6th, but except sending scouting parties up Loup Creek, he did nothing, as a sudden rise in New River made Rosecrans suspend the concerted movement, and matters remained as they were, awaiting the fall of the river, till the 10th.

"For a week after the 1st, Floyd's battery on Cotton Mountain fired on very slight provocation, and caution was necessary in riding or moving about the camp. The houses of the hamlet were not purposely injured, for Floyd would naturally be unwilling to destroy the property of West Virginians, and it was a safe presumption that we had removed the government property from the buildings within range, as we had in fact done. Our method of forwarding supplies was to assemble the wagon trains near my lower camp during the day, and push them forward to Gauley Mount and Tompkins farm during the night. The ferry-boat at Gauley Bridge was kept out of harm's way in the Gauley, behind the projection of Gauley Mount, but the hawser on which it ran was not removed. At nightfall the boat would be manned, dropped down to its place, made fast to the hawser by a snatch-block, and commence its regular trips, passing over the wagons. The ferries, both at the bridge and at Montgomery's, were under the management of Captain Lane of the Eleventh Ohio and his company of mechanics. We had found at points along the Kanawha the gunwales of flatboats, gotten out by lumbermen in the woods and brought to the river bank ready to be put into boats for the coal trade, which had already much importance in the valley. These gunwales were single sticks of timber, sixty or eighty feet long, two or three feet wide, and say six inches thick. Each formed the side of a boat, which was built by tying two gunwales together with cross timbers, the whole being then planked. Such boats were three of four times as large as those used for the country ferries upon the Gauley and New Rivers, and enabled us to make these larger ferries very commodious. Of course the enemy knew that we used them at night, and would fire an occasional random shot at them, but did us no harm.

"The enemy's guns on the mountain were so masked by the forest that we did not waste ammunition in firing at them, except as they opened, when our guns so quickly returned their fire that they never ventured upon continuous action,and after the first week we had only occasional shots from them. We had planted our sharpshooters also in protected spots along the narrower part of New River near the post, and made the enemy abandon the other margin of the stream, except with scattered sentinels. In a short time matters thus assumed a shape in which our work went on regularly, and the only advantage Floyd had attained was to make us move our supply trains at night. His presence on the mountain overlooking our post was an irritation under which we chafed, and from Rosecrans down, everybody was disgusted with the enforced delay of Benham at Loup Creek. Floyd kept his principal camp behind Cotton Mountain...in an inaction which seemed to invite enterprise on our part. His courage had oozed out when he had carried his little army into an exposed position, and here as at Carnifex Ferry he seemed to be waiting for his adversary to take the initiative."[121]

This was a common reaction of Floyd when placed into a difficult situation. He was full of courage going into an assault position, but actually engaging the enemy was

[121] Cox, *Military Reminiscences*, pg. 138-139

difficult for him to order. He was so concerned about being placed in that "iron cage" the Federals had reserved for him that he could normally be expected to lose his nerve in a tight spot. He lost it at Carnifex Ferry, during the retreat to Sewell Mountain, on Cotton Hill, and he was to repeat this practiced performance for a last time at Fort Donelson in 1862 and be relieved of duty by Jefferson Davis.

Cox went on to explain his preparations for an amphibious operation across the wide river to land troops to support an attack on Floyd:

"To prepare for my own part in the contemplated movement, I had ordered Captain Lane to build a couple of flatboats of a smaller size than our large ferry-boats, and to rig these with sweeps or large oars, so that they could be used to throw detachments across New River to the base of Cotton Mountain, at a point selected a little way up the river, where the stream was not so swift and broken as in most places. Many of our men had become expert in managing such boats, and a careful computation showed that we could put over 500 men an hour with these small scows."[122]

The men of Captain Lane's company had provided excellent service to Cox and the Federal army and were again ordered to make an attack across the river possible by building assault boats for materials at hand. They had the small boats ready for use shortly and Cox ordered Lane's men to make a reconnaissance of the enemy-occupied shore:

"The shelling and sharpshooting having ceased late on the 7th and the two guns having apparently disappeared from the brow of the hill, a reconnoissance was ordered. Why it was not made from Benham's brigade, already on that side of the river, is not learned. Captain Lane was chosen for this service, probably by General Cox, because of his skill in the use of boats (both rivers being then high

122 Cox, *Military Reminiscences*, pg. 139-140

from the recent rains) and his proven courage. At night of the 9th he received an order to move at three a.m., with his company, cross the river by boat, and find what the enemy had done on the hill. He was ready on time, but found only 37 men of his company fit for duty (the regiment was much reduced at the time, from hard service, detachment &c, and mustered for duty much below 300), but with the 37 he set out in the two boats he had built. He was to run down the Gauley and pull with oars across the mouth of the New, but a heavy rain that day had raised the Gauley to a very swift current, the boats were caught in it and swept down the Kanawha toward the falls. This was great danger, and it was only with desperate efforts that the boats, after a mile or more, could be worked out of the flood of the channel and into slower current at the side. They finally escaped the peril and reached the shore on the side they started from. But the Captain was not daunted; he was intent only on obeying his order. With great labor they hauled the boats up along the shore to the Gauley, up that river to a possible crossing place, pulled over to the left side, and again ran down, this time taking great care to keep in the shore current and to work up into the New River along its right shore with every energy. This brought them into comparatively easy water, and, with the strongest men at the oars, they got over the New without mishap, and landed at the upper side of the foot of Cotton Hill."[123]

"From the 5th to the 10th Rosecrans had been waiting for the waters to subside, and pressing Benham to examine the roads up Loup Creek so thoroughly that he could plant himself in Floyd's rear as soon as orders should be given. Schenck would make the simultaneous movement when Benham was known to be in march, and McCook's and my brigade would at least make demonstrations from our several positions. From my picket post at Montgomery's Ferry I had sent scouts up the Fayette road, and by the 9th had discovered such symptoms of weakness in the enemy that I thought the time had come to make an effort to

123 Scott, *Philander P. Lane*, pg. 61-62

dislodge the battery and get command of the crest of Cotton Mountain overlooking my camp. On the 10th I made a combined movement from both my upper and lower camps. Colonel De Villiers was ordered to take all of the Eleventh Ohio fit for duty (being only 200 men), and crossing by the small boats, make a vigorous reconnoissance over the New River face of Cotton Mountain, reaching the crest if possible. Lieutenant-Colonel Enyart of the First Kentucky was directed to cross below the falls with a similar force, and push a reconnoissance out on the Fayette road, whilst he also should try to co-operate with De Villiers in clearing the enemy from the heights opposite Gauley Bridge. The place at which De Villiers crossed was out of sight and range from the enemy's battery. His first boat-load of forty men reached the opposite shore safely, and dividing into two parties, one pushed up the New River to a ravine of the rocks where they landed."[124]

The men of Captain Lane's scouting party had landed after a serious delay in crossing the river during which they were nearly swept over the dangerous falls. The delay was serious as daylight was near:

"But several hours had been lost and dawn was now appearing. Captain Lane was very anxious to get to the top of the hill without being met or seen by the enemy. Leaving a small guard with the boats, with the remainder he climbed the hill as fast as possible, tho its steepness and roughness, -- small, difficult ravines, rocks and tangled thickets -- made the work slow at the best. The gun of one of the men was fired by accident. This halted him for an anxious minute or two, but no sound from the enemy following, he was reassured and hurried on to the top. Here, in the misty light of early day he found the field abandoned, the guns gone, and no enemy in sight.

"Taking a position with prudent care for retreat, if compelled, he sent out small parties to scout in several directions; and, finding no sign of the enemy near, he

[124] Cox, *Military Reminiscences*, pg. 140-141

advanced himself, and found him about a mile from the Gauley front, at the interior or southeastern end of the hill (where it is highest) and sheltered by a wood."[125]

The climb of Captain Lane's patrol up the face of Cotton Hill was a very difficult and dangerous ascent. The mountain face is extremely steep and remains entangled with heavy brush to this day. The trees are large and crowd the steep slopes to the top of the mountain. It is fortunate that the Confederates had pulled their skirmishers back from the crest of the mountain or when the musket was accidentally fired, the Confederates would have learned of the presence of the small patrol and would have captured or destroyed it.

Once Cox realized that Lane had met with no resistance, he began to push over a larger Union force to take and hold the top of the mountain:

"The remainder of the men of the Eleventh were put over as fast as possible, and joined their colonel in the ravine mentioned, up which they marched to a little clearing high up the hill, known as Blake's Farm, where the advanced party had found the enemy."[126]

Cox was confused when he thought the men had joined their colonel in the ravine. It was De Villiers, the less than heroic figure from the battle at Scary Creek, who had crossed the river in a rowboat and showed his lack of leadership qualities immediately on landing:

"The Colonel came over in a rowboat with three , two at the oars and one steering. On landing he ordered these men to remain in their seats, then called off the sergeant commanding and one man from the guard Captain Lane had left in charge of his two large boats, directed the man to hold the bow of his rowboat to the bank, ready for instant use, and the sergeant to remain there in command of

125 Scott, *Philander P. Lane*, pg. 62-63

126 Cox, *Military Reminiscences*, pg. 141

the four and shoot at once any of them who attempted to leave, while he provided for the sergeant himself by declaring his intention to cut his head off if he failed in any of these duties. This rediculous stuff seems almost incredible...The men directly concerned in the Colonel's careful provision at the boat account of it upon the simple tho harsh theory that he was thinking only of his personal safety."[127]

Once Lane had determined the positions of the enemy's pickets and reasoned from this the location of their main position, he spread his men out in locations where they could observe the Confederates, but could quickly rally at a point where they could defend themselves, if discovered, or retreat down the mountain. He took the first opportunity to send a messenger to the rear to report his findings from the scouting operation. The messenger encountered Colonel De Villiers on the river bank (probably near his boat) and the colonel sent the man *back* to the top of the hill with an astonishing order for Captain Lane to report in person. This was stupidity -- recalling a field commander who would have to leave his troops in the face of the enemy while they were greatly outnumbered! It would take Lane an hour to descend from the top of Cotton Hill to reach the bottom for his short discussion with the seemingly demented colonel.

"As it was, the Captain hurried down to the river, and the Colonel, without asking for further report or information, at once began to berate him for not getting across the river earlier, and filled the air with violent and vulgar abuse and epithets, applied to the Captain and his men and all the regiment...In the coarse and profane language he was given to, he declared the Captain was unfit to command, and that he had failed to cross the river and get up the mountain from cowardice; and all the time he was flourishing in the air a cavalry sabre (he carried it constantly, instead of the proper infantry officer's sword)

127 Scott, *Philander P.Lane*, pg. 64

as 'wildly as a madman'. Captain Lane at first tried to speak, but seeing the uselessness of it and unwilling to lower his dignity in a quarrel, he was silent, only keeping his hand on his pistol 'if the fellow came near me.' "When the truculent little Colonel's wind was spent, he was so far from ordering any one to execution that he directed the Captain to take that portion of the regiment now landed to the position of his company on top of the hill and command the whole till further orders. It was barely in time, for the enemy was showing signs of activity. Closer skirmishing followed, soon afterward Major Coleman appeared -- an experienced soldier and very capable officer -- and took command; and finally Colonel DeVilliers came, as he ought to have done long before. There was a good deal of desultory fighting, with no definite gain that day."[128]

Cox now had a considerable force on the mountain. Portions of both the Eleventh Ohio and the First Kentucky had ascended the mountain slope and were holding their own against the Confederates skirmishers. Cox had ordered the First Kentucky to move up the road toward Fayette Courthouse and these troops reported no resistance. Both the cannon and Floyd's infantry had pulled back from the mountain and were no longer able to shell the Federal camp. General Cox advised Rosecrans:

"I reported our success to Rosecrans, and doubtful whether he wished to press the enemy in front till Benham and Schenck should be in his rear, I asked for further instructions. General Rosecrans authorized me to take over the rest of my available force and press the enemy next day, as he was very confident that Benham would by that time be in position to attack him in rear. Accordingly I passed the Second Kentucky regiment over the river during the night and joined them in person on the crest at daybreak. The remainder of the First Kentucky, under Major Leiper, was ordered to cross at Montgomery's Ferry later in the

---

128 Scott, *Philander P. Lane,* pg. 65-66

day, and advance upon the Fayette road as far as possible. My climb to the crest of Cotton Mountain was a repetition of the exhausting sort of work I had tried on Gauley Mount on the 1st. I took the short route straight up the face of the hill, clambering over rocks, pulling myself up by clinging to the laurel bushes, and often lifting myself from one great rocky step to another. This work was harder upon the officers who were usually mounted than upon the men in the line, as we were not used to it, and the labor of the whole day was thus increased, for of course we could take no horses. Resuming the advance along the mountain crest, the enemy made no serious resistance, but fell back skirmishing briskly, till we came to more open ground where the mountain breaks down toward some open farms where detachments of Floyd's forces had been encamped. Their baggage train was seen in the distance, moving off upon the Fayette turnpike. As we were now in the close neighborhood of the whole force of the enemy, and those in our presence were quite as numerous as we, I halted the command on the wooded heights commanding the open ground below, till we should hear some sound from Benham's column. Toward evening Major Leiper came up on our right to the place where the Fayette road passes over a long spur of the mountain which is known in the neighborhood as Cotton Hill. Here he was halted, and nothing being heard from co-operating columns, the troops bivouacked for the night.

"Rosecrans had informed Benham of my advance and ordered him to push forward; but he spent the day in discussing the topography which he was supposed to have learned before, and did not move. Schenck had not been put across New River at Townsend's Ferry, because Rosecrans thought it hazardous to do this whilst Floyd was near that point in force, and he intended that when Floyd should be forced to attack Benham (whose command was now equal to two brigades), it would withdraw the enemy so far that Schenck would have room to operate after crossing. But as Benham had not advanced, toward evening of the 11th Rosecrans sent him orders to march immediately up the Kanawha to my position and follow Major Leiper on the road that officer had opened to the top of Cotton Hill, and as much further toward Fayette C.H. as possible, taking Leiper's detatchment with him; meanwhile I was ordered to keep the remainder of my troops on the mountain in position already occupied. Benham was expected to reach Leiper's position by ten o'clock that evening, but he did not reach there in fact till three o'clock in the following afternoon (12th). After some skirmishing with an outpost of the enemy at Laurel Creek behind which Major Leiper had been posted, nothing more was done till the evening of the 13th. Floyd's report shows that he retired beyond Fayette C.H. on the 12th, having conceived the mistaken idea that Benham's column was a new reinforcement of 5000 men from Ohio. Abandoning the hope of using Schenck's brigade in a movement from Townsend's Ferry, Rosecrans now ordered him to march to Gauley Bridge on the 13th, and joining Benham by a night march, assume command of the moving column. Schenck did so, but Floyd was now retreating upon Raleigh C.H. and a slight affair with his rear-guard was the only result. Fayette C.H. was occupied and the campaign ended."[129]

The "slight affair" with Floyd's rearguard was fought at McCoy's Mill and there was only a single fatality recorded, but there was a great deal of emotion associated with this death. Confederate Colonel St. George Croghan was the son of one of the few actual heroes of the War of 1812 and the father had served in the regular, pre-war army as a career soldier. He had died while still on duty and was serving as the army's Inspector-General.

Young George Croghan was a brave officer who had served under William Henry Harrison in the Battle of Tippecanoe and was recommended for a commission by Harrison for his courage under fire. Harrison later planned to have him shot for disobeying an order to abandon Fort Stephenson which was located near Sandusky Bay.

[129] Cox, *Military Reminiscences*, pg. 141-143

Croghan was from a military family: his father had fought in the Revolutionary War; his uncle, William Clark crossed the continent with Meriwether Lewis and a second uncle was General George Rogers Clark -- the officer who secured the northwest territories for the young republic. These fighting Irishmen were unlikely to retreat when threatened by the enemy and George Croghan wasn't about to surrender the fort under his command to the British and indians beseiging it, even if the commanding general ordered it.

This was a dangerous position in which to be -- surrounded by hostile indians barely under the control of the British during the best of times. During a discussion under a flag of truce, a British officer attempted to convince the American garrison to surrender by claiming that they would be unable to prevent a massacre after the inevitable capture of the fort. The American officer answered quickly, "When the fort shall be taken, there will be none to massacre."

The opening fire convinced Croghan that he knew where the actual assault would occur and he moved his cannon into a position where it could rake the approach from behind a concealed port hole. By dawn, the British had moved three cannon into range and began to fire approximately five hundred balls at the fort during the day. Croghan stuffed the cannon to its muzzle with grape-shot, double slugs, and even pieces of pottery and settled down to await the inevitable attack.

The British regulars climbed into a ditch which was directly in front of the Fort's palisade and rushed to hack at the individual posts as their commander ordered "no Quarter"! and fell into the ditch with dozens of others as the cannon's blast ripped them with projectiles. He wrapped a handerchief around his sword to surrender, but the American troops heard his no quarter order and a second volley from the cannon killed him. More than fifty men were dead in the ditch while the Americans had lost only a single man. Croghan's victory was the start of a national celebration for the American public which was caught in a depressing conflict that was short of heroes. Croghan was to receive the thanks of Congress, a gold medal, and a sword from the ladies of Chillicothe, Ohio, for his heroism.[130]

His son was St. George Croghan, the cavalry commander attached to General Floyd's small army, and the son was made of the same stern miltary material as the father. During the retreat of the Confederate army over roads which were really streams of liquid mud, the men were rapidly becoming disillusioned with their commander and were beginning to desert. Floyd had to abandon his military stores and wagons in the mud as the retreat continued past a schoolhouse which retained its' name even through the Confederate occupation, Union schoolhouse, and the soldiers straggled through Fayette Courthouse toward saftey in southwestern Virginia.

A West Virginia historian, Forrest Hull, tells the story best:

"The morning of the thirteenth found Floyd nearing McCoy's Mill, ten miles from Fayette...All night the tired troops had laid on the wet ground, unprotected from the elements. At the first streak of dawn, they were in motion.

"At nine o'clock a report came from the rear that the enemy was close and about to attack...Henningsen (the famous Nicarguan filibuster) of Floyd's staff, ordered the small cavalry force to the rear. This force was commanded by a dashing young officer, Colonel St. George Croghan, son of a distinguished soldier of the war with Great Britain. The debonair colonel saluted, wheeled his horse and, followed by his small band of gray-clad horsemen, galloped to the rear.

"Two miles north of McCoy's Mill, there was a bend in the road and the view beyond was hidden by a heavy growth of timber. Around this bend the cavalry dashed and collided with a heavy skirmish force, the 13th Ohio, under

130 Burton, Pierre, *Flames Across the Border: The Canadian-American Tragedy -- 1813-1814*, Atlantic Monthly Press, Boston: 1981, pg. 141-146

Colonel Gardner. The Federals instantly poured a heavy fire into the surprised cavalry men. Several of the horsemen were wounded and the rest became panic-stricken. Seeing this, Colonel Croghan spurred his horse to the center of the road, and in plain view of the enemy, ordered his men to dismount and return the fire. Responding to his stentorian voice, his men drew carbines, dismounted, found cover, and opened on the enemy massed down the road a few rods. Colonel Croghan remained in the saddle, a martial figure and a fine target...

"On the other side of the road was a field, and some two hundred yards away, a house. Across these fields the Federal lines began to spread out in a v-shape to flank the cavalrymen. Colonel Croghan was calling on his men to fall back when, suddenly, he reeled in the saddle, clutched at his horse's mane, and slid slowly to the ground with his foot caught in the stirrup. The frightened animal leaped and dragged the officer into the weeds beside the roadside, where his foot became dislodged and he lay covered with blood from a terrible wound in his abdomen and another in his wrist. Instantly four of his men ran to him and, lifting him up, bore him to the house in the field. Unmindful of the enemy fire and the frightened cries of the occupants of the home, they entered and laid the wounded man on a bed. It was seen that his injury was mortal. He was beyond human aid.

"The gunfire was growing heavy and a cavalryman, glancing out a window, cried out, 'they are flanking us. We will be captured!' The wounded leader lifted himself on his elbow and pointed to the door.

"Go, men!' he gasped. 'Save yourself, for I am dying!'

"No time was to be lost. With a groan of pity for the officer, the soldiers sprang out of the house and ran to join their comrades. But they were too late. The Confederates had been forced to fall back down the road and they could not reach their horses. All over the fields the muskets were cracking and a hurricane of bullets swept around the four men. Whirling, they ran for the rear of the house, crossed a field, and reached the shelter of the woods and safety. The skirmish of McCoy's Mill was over."[131]

The death of Colonel Croghan revealed the horror of this war to many observers and served to bring some reality to the conflict while dampening any residual romanticism remaining in the minds of most of the people on both sides. It was reported in the newspapers on both sides and this article was in the Cincinnati *Gazette*:

"As I telegraphed you, Floyd retreated the night of the skirmish at Cotton Hill, leaving a strong rear guard behind him. Next morning discovering from our scouts that he had vacated his position, we followed up to Union School House, still apprehensive that he might attack us, knowing that in point of numbers his force was superior to our own.

"A scouting party under Sergeant Lambert...got on his track, killed one of his scouts, and brought information that induced the General to order a forward movement. We left Union School House late in the afternoon, marched some four miles to Col. Dickerson's place, well known through this part of the country, the Colonel being probably the most influential secessionist in this part of the country. Here we obtained some items, and captured a few secesh guns. After halting for a couple of hours we took up the line of march, and, tired as we were, toiled on until four o'clock in the morning, when we again halted to allow the men and horses to refresh themselves. Soon after daylight the order to march was given, and we pushed on over roads rendered almost impassable by the heavy rains, and cut to pieces by the recent passage of Floyd's artillery and wagon trains. Our skirmishers, under the command of the gallant Capt. Gardner, of the Thirteenth Ohio, were in advance of the column on both sides of the road, and proceded cautiously. Just as they reached a bend in the road, one of the company (private Seig, of Company F) crawled over and espied two squadrons of cavalry under Col. Croghan, of Kentucky, and here commenced the battle of McCoy's

131 Hull, Forrest, "The Death of Colonel Croghan", *The West Virginia Review*, Vol. XXIV, No. 1, pg. 20-21

Mills.

"A volley was instantly opened on the enemy, who were, as their wounded afterward acknowledged, taken completely by surprise. At the first fire several saddles were emptied, and Col. Croghan fell mortally wounded in the abdomen. The rebels, though surprised, showed fight and retired slowly, firing as they went; but our men having possession of the elevated ground on both sides, exposed them to a galling cross-fire, and forced them back. The main body then advanced, having, as before, strong parties of skirmishers. Col. Croghan was carried to the nearest house, and was cared for as well as the state of the case would admit by Surgeon Chase, of the Thirteenth Ohio. He was a gallant man and an accomplished officer, and, though an enemy, the sight of his dying agonies 'drew tears from the eyes of men unused to weep'. The colonel's father and Gen. Benham were old acquaintences...and the interview between them was, of course, quite painful. We did all we could for the unfortunate man, but human aid was vain, and he expired in the same afternoon. We brought down the body on our return, and Gen. Benham intends forwarding it to his friends at once."[132]

General Benham had been a Captain in the pre-war regular army and would have known of or had some previous association with the elder Croghan, who had spent much of his life in the army. He took the time on November 15, 1861, to write a letter to Floyd to let him know of Croghan's fate:

"Sir: In the skirmish which occurred yesterday between the United States forces under my command and your brigade, I regret to be obliged to inform you that Colonel St. George Croghan, commanding your cavalry regiment, as he stated to me, was mortally wounded. He was shot through the right wrist and side of the upper portion of the abdomen, the ball passing entirely through the body, and lived from half-past nine A.M., when he was wounded, till

132 Moore, *Rebellion Record*, Vol. III, pg. 383

half-past two P.M.

"I saw him in passing, a few minutes after he was wounded, and he recognized me, conversing freely, but with pain, and, shaking my hand on leaving him, he requested me to state that he 'died the death of a brave soldier,' -- as he did, in every way worthy of his gallant and noble father. "I left him in charge of my brigade and one other surgeon, with hospital attendents and a guard, and on my return this morning from my camp ground, the hospital steward handed me a small blank memorandum book, in which was a history made by his request, of which I enclose you a copy. He left his adress, with the chaplain of the Tenth (Col. Lyttle's) Ohio regiment, Rev. H.E.O. Higgins, and told me that his family were residing in Newburgh, New York. I will endeavor to communicate with them as early as possible, and send each a little memorial from him as I shall be able to collect them, for I yet cannot ascertain where most of his property has gone, as the people of the house where he died would not attend to it. I have sent his remains toward Fayetteville, where they will be interred, if we are not able to take them to Gauley; though I will, if possible, place the body there in a box with salt, to preserve it for his friends. It will be subject to the order of Gen. H.S. Rosecrans.

"And now, having for the third time the opportunity of extending courtesies somewhat of this character to your officers -- as first, in returning the baggage, uniform, &c., of Colonel Porterfield, at Philippi, and afterward, of preserving the sword, effects, and body of General Garnett at Carrick's Ford -- I trust your officers will appreciate the desire thus exhibited of mitigating in every way the horrors of this fratricidal strife, as I think you yourself will do me the justice to believe that I most earnestly wish it.

"I send this by a private citizen, as I thought you would prefer it to a flag of truce, and on account of uncertainty of the means do not send forward any of the little memorials preserved."[133]

133 Moore, *Rebellion Record*, Vol. III, pg. 385-386

Historian Forrest Hull told of Croghan's last hours:

"...Of his watch, money and other valuables, nothing is known, although General Benham tried to find them. The only blot on the record of a noble enemy -- someone stole the meagre belongings of the dying man.

"As the day wore on the dying officer grew quiet. Outside the rain fell in torrents. Above the storm could be heard the sounds of the wagon trains moving up. Within the room a candle had been lighted to dispel the gloom, The light fell on the pale features on the bed; on the sympathetic faces of the watchers; on the glistening accouterments of the guard who had come in out of the rain. Members of the family stood in the shadows or moved about softly. The dying man stirred. His mind was wandering and he talked in a low voice of home and wife, of days past and gone. Again he imagined he was in battle and his voice would grow strong with authority as he gave orders to his command. Once the Chaplain bent to smooth his hair and give him a drink, and he opened his eyes and smiled faintly. The Chaplain bent to catch his words:

"It's cold and I am far from home --' he murmured.

"At half past two, while the rain beat on the clapboard roof and log walls of the house and the moving columns churned the highway to liquid mud; while whips cracked and drivers cursed and bugles sang off in the storm, the gallant Colonel Croghan died. Far from loved ones and in the hands of his enemies."[134]

The 1861 campaign of the Confederates to regain the Kanawha valley was at an end. Organized resistance to the Federals in the area came to a halt as the Rebel forces under Floyd moved swiftly to safer areas in southwestern Virginia. They had narrowly escaped capture or destruction by the Federal army assembled against them. General Cox completed the story:

"It would appear from official documents that Floyd did

[134] Hull, "The Death of Colonel Croghan", pg. 21

not learn of Benham's presence at the mouth of Loup Creek till the 12th, when he began his retreat, and that at any time during the preceding week a single rapid march would have placed Benham's brigade without resistance upon the line of the enemy's communications. Rosecrans was indignant at the balking of his elaborate plans, and ordered Benham before a court-martial for misconduct; but I believe that McClellan caused the procedings to be quashed to avoid scandal, and Benham was transferred to another department. It is very improbable that Schenck's contemplated movement across New River at Townsend's Ferry could have been made successfully; for his boats were few and small, and the ferrying would have been slow and tedious. Floyd would pretty surely learn of it soon after it began, and would hasten his retreat instead of waiting to be surrounded. It would have been better to join Schenck to Benham by a forced march as soon as the latter was at the mouth of Loup Creek, and then to push the whole to the Fayette and Raleigh road, Rosecrans leading the column in person. As Floyd seems to have been ignorant of what was going on in Loup Creek valley, decisive results might have followed from anticipating him on his line of retreat. Capturing such a force, or, as the phrase then went, 'bagging it,' is easier talked of than done; but it is quite probable that it might have been so scattered and demoralized as to be of little further value as an army, and considerable parts of it might have been taken prisoners."[135]

The Federal forces were able to move into their winter quarters in the Kanawha valley for some well deserved rest. The soldiers of the Eleventh Ohio had borne the brunt of the marching and fighting during the campaign which had ranged from Scary Creek in the west to Sewell Mountain in the east. These men, under the command of Lieutenant-Colonel Frizell, had marched and counter-marched to keep the Rebel regiments off balance. They were the men called on to cross New River at Gauley

[135] Cox, *Military Reminiscences*, pg. 143-144

Bridge and climb the steep slopes of Cotton Hill to assault the cannon positions which had been shelling the Union camp at the town.

They lost several men from their depleted ranks in the fighting on the mountain. Three were killed or died from their wounds and four were captured by the Confederates. They told many stories of their first year in the war -- and most of them were from the area around Gauley Bridge.

One of the stories repeated while the men were in winter quarters concerned the adventure of Sergeant George Cart of Company D of the "Gipsy Eleventh":

Cart was assigned to a picket post of Cotton Hill which was attacked by a Confederate squad, reported to be from the Second Virginia, but probably from the Twenty-Second since the Second Virginia was in the "Stonewall Brigade" at the time. The story of Cart's adventure was widely published in Union newspapers at the time:

"Sergeant Cart, of Tippecanoe, Ohio, was upon the post first attacked by the enemy. The advance-guard of the Second Virginia (rebel), consisting of twelve men, came suddenly upon him and his three companions. The bright moonlight revealed the flashing bayonets of the advancing regiment. He was surrounded and separated from his reserve. With great presence of mind he stepped out and challenged, 'Halt! Who goes there?' The advanced guard, supposing they had come upon a scouting party of their own men, answered, 'Friends, with the countersign.' At his order, 'Advance and give the countersign!' they hesitated. He repeated the order peremptorily, 'Advance and give the countersign, or I'll blow you through!' They answered, without advancing, 'Mississippi!' 'Where do you belong?' he demanded. 'To the Second Virginia Regiment.' "Where are you going?' 'Along the ridge.' They in turn, questioned him, 'Who are you?' 'That's my own business,' he answered, and taking deliberate aim, shot down the questioner.

"Calling his boys to follow him, he sprung down a ledge of rocks, while a full volley went over his head. He heard his companions summoned to surrender, and the order given to the major to advance with the regiment. Several started in pursuit of him. He had to descend the hill on the side toward the enemy's camp. While thus eluding his pursuers, he found himself in a new danger. He had got within the enemy's pickets! He had, while running, torn the U.S. from his cartridge box, and covered his belt plate with his cap box, and torn the stripes from his pantaloons. He was challenged by their sentinels, while making his way out, and answered, giving the countersign,"Mississippi, Second Virginia Regiment.' They asked him what he was doing there. He answered that the boys had gone off on a scout after the Yankees, while he had been detained in camp, and in trying to find them had lost his way.

"As he passed through, to prevent further questioning, he said, 'Our boys are up on the ridge -- which is the best way up?' They answered, 'Bear to the left and you'll find it easier to climb.' Soon, however, his pursuers were again after him, 'breaking brush behind him', this time with a hound on his trail. He made his way to a brook, and running down the shallow stream threw the dog off the scent, and, as the day was dawning, came suddenly upon four pickets, who brought their arms to a ready, and challenged him. He gave the countersign, 'Mississippi', and claimed to belong to the Second Virginia Regiment. They asked him where he got that belt (his cap box had slipped from before his belt-plate), to which he replied that he had captured it that night from a Yankee. They told him to advance, and as he approached, he recognized their accoutrements, and knew he was among his own men, a picket guard from the First Kentucky.

"He was taken before Colonel Enyart, and dismissed to his regiment. He said his plan was to give intimation to the reserves of their advance, that they might open upon them on their left flank, and so, perhaps, arrest their advance."[136]

---

136 Hazelton, Joseph F., *Spies Scouts, and Heroes of the Great Civil War*, Star Publishing, Jersey City: 1892, pg. 407-408

The men of the Kanawha Brigade were to return for a short campaign against the invading forces of General Loring the following autumn, but this task didn't require either much time or effort. They were soon assigned to duties in the western armies and fought in some of the bloodier campaigns of the war.

Sergeant George Cart of Company D, of the "Gipsy Eleventh",was to die in the battle of Chickamauga, Georgia, on September 20, 1863. He was only one of many from this regiment which had gained its first experience in the Kanawha valley who was to die in the war.

It had been a long and difficult campaign for everyone involved. General Cox had learned much about managing troops in combat and proved that he had the ability to lead his regiments successfully. He was soon to be reassigned out of the Kanawha valley -- to the Army of the Potomac -- with his "Kanawha Brigade" and they would see combat in the large battles in the eastern theater, One of the senior officers of the Eleventh Ohio, Major Coleman, would die in the battle at Antietam with many other Union veterans of the fighting in the Kanawha valley.

The Federal soldiers of the Kanawha Brigade were chosen to attack the bridge on the battlefield which became known as "Burnside's bridge" because of their strong opening attack the previous Sunday at South Mountain. Cox was elevated to command of the IX Corps in the battle, a command accidentally shared with General Burnside -- the Corps had two commanders through a mistake -- after the death of General Reno at South Mountain.

The Union soldiers who served on Gauley Mountain were now caught up in the bloodiest battle of the Civil War and were to see a great deal of combat before the end of the war -- as would their gentleman general.

---

[137] Lyle, W.W., *Lights and Shadows of Army Life*, Cincinnati: 1865, pg. 401

Fig. 1. Union regiment on parade near Montgomery's Ferry, just downstream from the falls on the Kanawha River. (Print done by J. Nep Roessler, 47th Ohio Volunteer Infantry.) West Virginia Archives

Fig. 2. Union soldiers doing laundry adjacent to one of the area's streams, probably Laurel Creek. (Print done by J. Nep Roessler, 47th Ohio Volunteer Infantry.) West Virginia Archives

Fig. 3. Federal guard post located near Gauley Bridge. These soldiers have recently been in an engagement. (Print done by J. Nep Roessler, 47th Ohio Volunteer Infantry.) West Virginia Archives

Fig. 4. Union Soldiers crossing Little Birch River on their march to Carnifex Ferry where they engaged the Rebels. (Print done by J. Nep Roessler, 47th Ohio Volunteer Infantry.) West Virginia Archives

Fig. 5. Teamsters move wagons along the James River and Kanawha Turnpike after crossing the ferry at Gauley Bridge. (Print done by J. Nep Roessler, 47th Ohio Volunteer Infantry.) West Virginia Archives

Fig. 6. Federal troops crossing Miller's Ferry as they march to Fayette Court House, the local county seat. (Print done by J. Nep Roessler, 47th Ohio Volunteer Infantry.) West Virginia Archives

Fig. 7. The Federal camp at Gauley Bridge contained more soldiers than the town had inhabitants. (Print done by J. Nep Roessler, 47th Ohio Volunteer Infantry.) West Virginia Archives

Fig. 8. Union pickets were posted along the road from Gauley Bridge to Tompkins' farm at Gauley Mount. (Print done by J. Nep Roessler, 47th Ohio Volunteer Infantry.) West Virginia Archives

Fig.9. Union pickets were also posted farther east on the turnpike at Lover's Leap which is located near Hawk's Nest. (Print done by J. Nep Roessler, 47th Ohio Volunteer Infantry.) West Virginia Archives

Fig. 10. Union soldiers occupied the log house at Miller's Ferry, the crossing from the turnpike to Fayetteville. (Print done by J. Nep Roessler, 47th Ohio Volunteer Infantry.) West Virginia Archives

Fig. 11. Camp Tompkins was located on a gentle slope on Gauley Mountain. Gauley Bridge is in the right rear. (Print done by J. Nep Roessler, 47th Ohio Volunteer Infantry.) West Virginia Archives

Fig. 12. Union soldiers guard Hawk's Nest. The scene faces downstream toward Gauley Bridge. (Print done by J. Nep Roessler, 47th Ohio Volunteer Infantry.) West Virginia Archives

Fig. 13. Union artillery on Hawk's Nest. This scene is facing upstream in the general direction of Sewell Mountain. (Print done by J. Nep Roessler, 47th Ohio Volunteer Infantry.) West Virginia Archives

Fig. 14. Union regiments under General Rosecrans assault Rebel positions at Carnifex Ferry. (Print done by J. Nep Roessler, 47th Ohio Volunteer Infantry.) West Virginia Archives

Fig. 15. Union troops skirmish with Confederate militia across New River at Miller's Ferry. (Print done by J. Nep Roessler, 47th Ohio Volunteer Infantry.) West Virginia Archives

Fig. 16. Union officers observe Rebel positions on Sewell Mountain during the typical weather of that campaign. (Print done by J. Nep Roessler, 47th Ohio Volunteer Infantry.) West Virginia Archives

Fig. 17. Union regiments advancing in the woods near Gauley Bridge. (Print done by J. Nep Roessler, 47th Ohio Volunteer Infantry.) West Virginia Archives

Fig. 18. Federal pickets along New River just to the east of Gauley Bridge. (Print done by J. Nep Roessler, 47th Ohio Volunteer Infantry.) West Virginia Archives

Fig. 19. A waterfall located between Gauley Bridge and Tompkins Farm. (Print done by J. Nep Roessler, 47th Ohio Volunteer Infantry.) West Virginia Archives

Fig. 20. Hawk's Nest as seen from its base near New River. (Print done by J. Nep Roessler, 47th Ohio Volunteer Infantry.)

West Virginia Archives

## CONFLICTING DUTIES

*The battles of the Kanawha Valley had been fought and the Confederates under the command of General Wise had managed their "retrograde movement" east along the James River and Kanawha Turnpike where they had joined with the forces of General John Floyd. Under Floyd's less than enlightened leadership, the volunteers from the state's western counties had participated in the battles fought at Cross Lanes and at Carnifex Ferry after which they again withdrew into the mountains to begin to prepare for the anticipated attack by the combined forces of both Generals Rosecrans and Cox.*

*The second-in-command of the Twenty-Second Virginia Volunteer Infantry, Christopher Tompkins assistant, Major Isaac N. Smith had been writing to his young wife, Callie, who was in Union-occupied territory at Charleston. Since he seldom had opportunities to slip letters through the Union lines to his family, he began to prepare a diary that he would send to his wife whenever he discovered a method to deliver it. He began the diary while in the Confederate camp on Sewell Mountain and he described the events that occurred before, during, and following the battle fought between the Union troops under Rosecrans and the Confederates under Floyd at Carnifex Ferry on September 10, 1861.*

## Conflicting Duties

*Fight on Brave Boys with out a doubt*
*On til you gain the field*
*The god of Battle he is stout*
*He will caus our foas to yield*[1]

"Camp Sewell - Sept 15, 1861

"A letter written to my dear wife written last Monday gave some particulars about my own movements and those of the army. I propose to write from day to day upon these pages and when an opportunity comes, send them home.

"We had just been ordered back to Floyd's camp when I last wrote, after having just reached Wise's camp,and the whole regiment, officers and men, was filled with indignation at the manner in which the poor volunteers were treated by the two legions, being ordered to and fro continually."[2]

Major Smith's regiment, the Twenty-second Virginia Volunteer Infantry Regiment, was the only Confederate regiment recruited exclusively from the counties west of the Alleghenies. Currently, the men were caught up in a long-running political squabble between two of their generals, Floyd and Wise. These two rivals, both ex-governors of Virginia, were manuevering in the same operational area with the same rank, but since Floyd's commission was presented prior to that later given to Wise, Floyd was in command and his rival resented his position passionately.

Wise's forces, after winning the South's first land victory in the war at Scary Creek had recently retreated under pressure from Federal units from Ohio that began to move into the Kanawha Valley. Wise had been legitimately concerned that additional Union troops operating under the

---

1 Howe, *Times of the Rebellion in the West*, pg. 48

2 Childers, William, "A Virginian's Dilemma", *West Virginia History*, Vol. XXVII, No. 3, April, 1966, pg. 176-177

command of General Rosecrans in the northwestern sections of the state would move into the Confederate rear by marching south through Sutton and Summersville to Gauley Bridge. This manuever would trap the small Confederate army between the Ohio regiments of both Cox and Rosecrans. Faced with the prospect of this military disaster, Wise decided to withdraw into the mountainous region to the east of the small town of Gauley Bridge.

While Wise was retreating. the troops of his political enemy, Floyd were advancing toward the west. Ex-Governor Floyd had been commissioned specifically by Jefferson Davis to recruit an infantry brigade from southwestern Virginia where he was popular.[3] Floyd accomplished his assignment by recruiting a large force and was then ordered to move his troops into western Virginia - into Wise's territory - and then the real problems began.

Wise's legion included attached regiments of volunteers recruited from the Kanawha Valley and adjacent areas in western Virginia. These units included 22nd Virginia, originally designated the "First Kanawha Regiment", and a sister regiment,the "Second Kanawha", and a third regiment was in the process of being organized when the Federal invasion of the Kanawha Valley began. All of the Kanawha Valley forces were under the command of Gauley Bridge resident, Christopher Tompkins. He had been placed in command after General Lee and Governor Letcher had commissioned VMI instructor, John McCausland and Cadet John Thompson, to move into the valley to recruit and train troops for the Confederacy.

All had gone relatively well until the arrival of the bickering generals, Wise and Floyd. Wise was a good politician and knew how to manage people. He placed leaders in command positions and listened to the advice of the military professionals on his staff. Once they had made a recommendation, it appears that Wise would adhere to their advice. His units were composed of volunteers from Virginia's western counties, and the various units were

3 White, "West Virginia", pg. 33

assigned to his "Legion". (A legion in the Confederate army was a "combined arms team" and was capable of independent action. Wise's Legion consisted of both infantry and calvary elements and also had artillery support assigned to the independent command.) State volunteers from the Kanawha Valley, such as the First and Second Kanawha Regiments, were initially attached to Wise's command, but when Floyd demanded reinforcements from his "subordinate", Wise, he was normally sent the Kanawha volunteers.

The First Kanawha later was redesignated the Twenty-second Virginia and the Second Kanawha became the Thirty-sixth Virginia Infantry Regiment. Colonel Tompkins was commander of the Twenty-second and John McCausland commanded the remaining Kanawha regiment.

As Floyd's personality began to have its' detrimental effect on the morale of the volunteers and the personal conflict between Floyd and Wise began to be superimposed on the difficult military situation, the state volunteers began to bear the brunt of the problems. Major Smith, Tompkins' good friend, and actual second-in-command of the Twenty-second Infantry, as well as the remaining officers and men of the regiment were not very happy with the treatment that they were receiving at the hands of the two Confederate generals.

"...being ordered to and fro so continuously..." was a common complaint as the volunteers were sent first to reinforce Floyd and then, after the danger was past, were returned just as quickly to Wise's command. Both the officers and men were quick to recognize the incompetence of both commanders, but most would have preferred Wise - if they were to make such a choice. At least he was able to make them feel like they were actually men and soldiers, unlike his rival. For most of the men from the Kanawha Valley, Floyd was simply an incompetent fool who sent them on long and useless marches. These men were veterans of Scary Creek, Barboursville, Charleston, Cross Lanes and were probably confident that they could stand against any Federal force marched against them. They did not, however, enlist simply for the opportunity of marching back and forth between Floyd's and Wise's different headquarters.

Major Smith continued with his diary which began to explain the recently fought battle at Carnifex Ferry:

"We were told that some 6000 men were approaching to attack Floyd but did not believe it -- thought the whole affair was a false alarm. About one o'clock PM the regiment was put in motion. We marched about 8 miles to a camp, about 2 1/2 miles from Carnifex's Ferry in Gauley, near Floyd's camp -- next morning moved on, the men ferried over, and hurried up the hill. As we crossed going one way - wagons filled with sick haggard men were being ferried the other. I remained after the Regiment had started up, to see that our wagon train was started across -- had them all drawn up at the landing, so as to exclude others, got the first waggon over and then followed the Regiment. As I went up the steep narrow road, it was almost impassable with sick men, fugitive citizens, and waggons and calvarlry. I was astonished at the numbers and learned that the pickets had all been driven in. The enemy were within a mile of the works. Reached the top of the hill with great difficulty and found the men all drawn up along breast-works, the cannon in position, and the gunners at their posts. The position of our Regiment had been defined some time before, and I rode up to it hastily -- found them in position, hitched up my horse and took my place in the line."[4]

Rosecrans' Union brigades were moving in on Floyd's position at "Camp Gauley". The brush and trees were quite thick and the Union troops leading Rosecrans' column were unable to spot the Confederate field fortifications until they were relatively close to them. General Benham's Brigade was in the lead. Actual combat had not yet begun when Isaac Smith arrrived with his regiment:

4 Childers, "Virginian's Dilemma", pg. 177-178

"It was the opinion of nearly all with whom I conversed that the enemy would not dare attack us in our position, but would simply amuse us with a feint, whilst their waggon train passed down the road from Summersville to Gauley Bridge, and then would follow the waggons. We had a strong position. I will try to give you some idea of it - Gauley river like New river runs between most precipitious and lofty mountains, with high ranges of cliffs on both sides."[5]

Like most soldiers just before a battle, the men assigned to Smith's regiment attempted to convince themselves that the enemy would simply attack their strongly fortified position in an attempt to protect their supply train rather than bring on a general engagement in which there would be many casualties. The supposed destination of both the Union wagons and troops was an obvious one. Union General Cox had a substantial Federal garrison at Gauley Bridge and combining both of the Union elements would give Rosecrans a numerical superiority along the route of the James River and Kanawha Turnpike, the single major road that passed through the rugged mountains into Virginia. There was only one problem with this simple analysis of the current military situation: Rosecrans didn't know exactly where Floyd had positioned his regiments, and of lesser importance,Rosecrans would have enjoyed attacking Floyd in return for the successful Rebel attack on Colonel Tyler's Seventh Ohio Regiment at Cross Lanes recently. Defeating Floyd would also prove that he was a worthy successor to McClellan after "Little Mack" was called to Washington to take command of the Army of the Potomac. Additionally, these Union troops were actively looking for a fight!

Smith's diary continues:

"The enemy were cautious in their approach. After waiting some two or three hours, the men hungry and thirsty, Col Tompkins sent me back to hurry up our

5 Childers, "Virginian's Dilemma", pg. 178

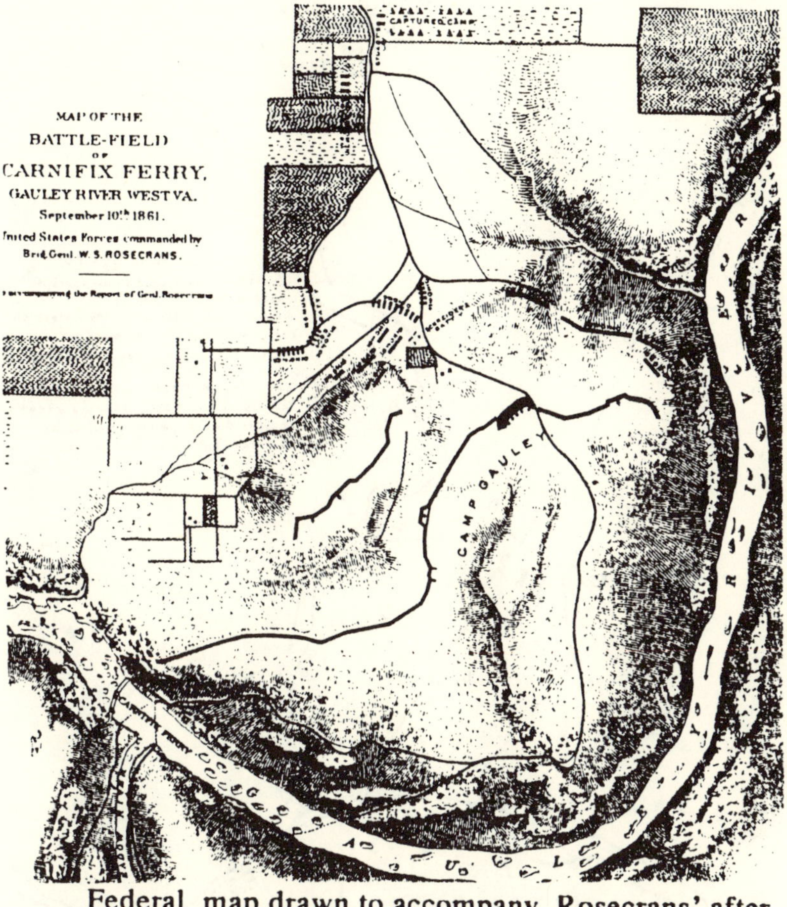


Federal map drawn to accompany Rosecrans' after action report on the battle fought at Carnifex Ferry. The site of the Confederate fortifications was on the top of a bluff which ended in both steep slopes and cliffs which ended at the edge of Gauley River. The stream was impossible to ford or swim at the ferry as an extensive set of rapids were just downstream from the ferry site. Rebel General Floyd couldn't have selected a better trap for himself if he were a West Point graduate like his opponent.

The map is in the Atlas of The Official Records of the War of the Rebellion.

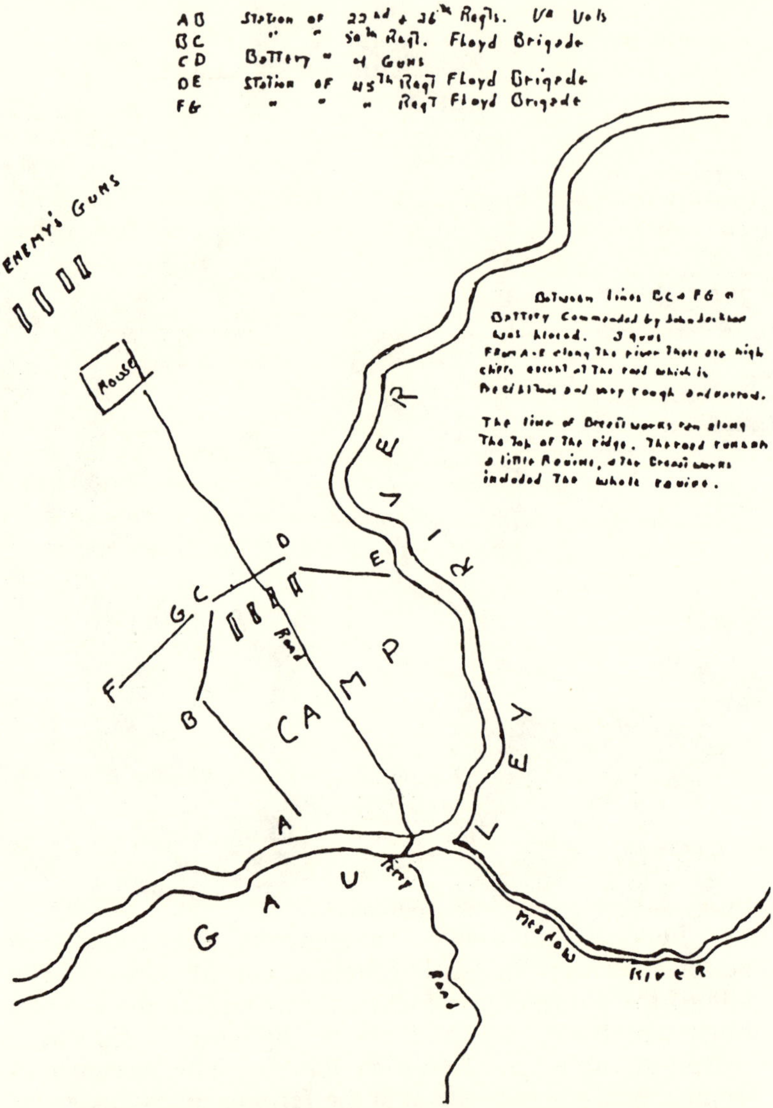


Map drawn by Isaac Smith of the Confederate fortifications at Camp Gauley at Carnifex Ferry. The letters are the key to understanding many of his descriptions of his and the 22nd Virginia's movements prior to, during, and after the battle that was fought there in 1861.

waggon, which was first to cross the ferry.

"In order to reach the road from our station (near to A), it was necessary to ride along the lines, and close to them until the road was reached, and then go down the road. I had just got to the first gun at C, when I saw one of the men start up saying 'there they are'; and looking over the breastworks (for on horseback I was high above them) I saw - one - two - three men coming, just at the edge of the forest. The General ordered the men not to fire without orders"[6]

The three men were skirmishers moving in advance of General H.W.Benham's First Brigade which had been marching most of the day to attack the Confederate camp. Benham's troops began their march at four o'clock that morning starting from a camp located approximately eight miles north of Summersville. After nearly a two hour halt one mile from Cross Lanes, the scene of the Seventh Ohio's recent rout by Floyd's army, Benham moved his brigade toward the Rebel positions. After making a personal reconnaissance, Rosecrans authorized Benham to move forward. Benham later reported that he had been authorized to be "using my best discretion in the case." Benham was a West Point-trained engineer and as he had no engineering officer, he remained at the front of his lead regiment as it moved into position. Benham later wrote:

"I kept with the head of the regiment to avoid ambuscades, and to judge myself of their position and arrangements. After advancing about one-fourth of a mile to the end of the woods, I halted the command, and could perceive that a heavy crossfire had been prepared for us at the open space at the debouch from the roads."[7]

Isaac Smith was on the opposite side of the field

---

6 Childers, "Virginian's Dilemma", pg. 178

7 Benham, H.W., "General Benham's Report", *The Rebellion Record*, edited by Frank Moore, G.P. Putnam, New York: 1862, pg. 38

fortifications, primarily earthworks and trenches, that were being evaluated by Benham. Smith was on his horse and was enroute to the rear to check on the status of the unit's wagon when the two armies made their initial contact:

"I of course started back to my regiment in haste, the firing began at once. The line AB is not visible from the forest. We had to cut it out of the thichest brush I ever saw, but observe its position, and you will see that the enemy's guns were so placed as to rake the line from one end to the other. The position was higher than line CD, the enemy directed their fire at the guns mostly, and as they always shot too high, the cannon balls, shell, etc. all came up along our line, and rather low too. There was scarcely a gun fired by them which did not send its rifle cannon balls, grape cannister or fragment of shells among us. We could not see the enemy nor could they see us, but we expected after each fire a ball among us. We could not tell the explosion of our guns from theirs and could see neither."[8]

There was similar confusion on the Union side of the field. Benham reported to Rosecrans after the battle:

"Within five minutes of this time, (nearly half-past three o'clock,) while carefully examining the earth-works on the road in front, and their intrenchments on our left, a tremendous fire of musketry was opened on us, which in a few minutes was followed by a discharge of grape and spelter canister from a battery of some six pieces of artillery. This caused a break in the line for a few minutes, though for a few minutes only, for the men immediately returned to their ranks, under the lead of their officers, to their former position, where I retained them, as I was certain that the fire at us through the close woods was without direct aim, and because they were needed for the protection of our artillery, which I immediately ordered up... throwing their shells well into their intrenchments on

[8] Childers, "Virginian's Dilemma", pg. 178

our left".[9]

Benham's lead regiment had been quickly engaged as they first ventured into the view of the Confederates concealed behind their fortifications. This Union regiment, the Tenth Ohio Volunteer Infantry, was commanded by Colonel W.H.Lytle and he, although seriously wounded, sent his report of the battle to General Rosecrans the following day, September, 11. His report included the following:

"After passing through the woods for half a mile, our skirmishers were suddenly engaged in front, and I pushed on to their relief until I reached a cleared space on the summit of a hill, where, for the first time, the enemy came into view, posted in force behind an extensive earthwork with twelve guns in position to sweep the road for over a mile. A ravine separated the hill, by which we approached from the right of the breastworks of the enemy, which was composed of logs and fence rails, and extended for over a mile to the right and left of their entrenchments, affording secure protection to their infantry and riflemen.

"When the head of my column reached a point opposite the right centre of their earthwork, their entire battery opened on us with grape and canister, with almost paralyzing effect, my men falling around me in great numbers."[10]

Union regiments assaulted different portions of the Confederate line in a rather uncoordinated way, but Lytle's regiment, the Tenth Ohio, was probably the most heavily engaged. The four advance companies from the Tenth Ohio were observed by a reporter from Cincinnati:

"...these skirmishers ... peering through the bushes ...

---

9 Benham, "Benham's Report", pg. 39

10 Lytle, W.H., "Colonel Lytle's Report", *The Rebellion Record*, Vol. III, edited by Frank Moore, G.P. Putnam, New York: 1862, pg. 40

found themselves about two hundred and fifty or three hundred yards in some sort of fortification; exactly what, it was impossible to see. The enemy seemed to discover them about the same time. For a few moments there was a resumption of the sharp but scattered firing, then suddenly there came a terrific crash of musketry, and a perfect storm of lead. The enemy had opened along his whole front ... Gen. Benham ... sent back orders for the Thirteenth, Colonel Smith, and the Twelfth, Colonel Lowe, to come rapidly forward... The angry peals of musketry, sharp as the peals of heavy thunder, grew fiercer, till the sound became one tremendous, incessant roar; while speedily, at least one full battery of heavy field-pieces sent in their swelling, deep-toned notes to mingle with the crashing rattle of the small arms. Fortunately, neither the artillery nor the infantry of the enemy fired with much accuracy at this period of the engagement, and though the poor boys suffered severly, yet, under the partial cover of the trees, their loss was far less than would have been expected from the tremendous fire that was directed upon them."[11]

Colonel Lytle was much closer to the enemy's position than the reporter travelling with Rosecrans' headquarters. His official report quite vividly describes the action occurring in Isaac Smith's right rear:

"I ordered the colors to the front for the purpose of making an assault on their battery, perceiving which, the entire fire of the battery was directed upon us.

"The men rallied gallently on the hill-side, under withering volleys of grape and small arms, amid a part of three companies, A, E, and D, actually moved up to within pistol-shot of the intrenchments, and for some time maintained an unequal contest.

"Both my color bearers were struck down; the bearer of the State color - Sergt. Fitzgibbons - had the staff shot away

11 Reid, Whitelaw, "Cincinnati *Gazette* Narrative", *The Rebellion Record*, Vol. III, edited by Frank Moore, G.P. Putnam, New York: 1862, pg. 46-47

and his hand shattered, and in a few moments afterwards was shattered in both thighs while waving his color on the broken staff. The bearer of the National color - Sergt. O'Connor - was, at the same time, struck down by some missile, but recovered himself in a short time, and kept waving his colors in front of the enemy's fire; about this time I received a wound in the leg, the ball passing through and killing my horse."[12]

Initial reports of the fighting reaching Rosecrans' headquarters were terrible. Stragglers brought

"...enormous stories of the fearful slaughter, from the midst of which they had so gallantly escaped; the terriffic firing, which some experienced military men pronounced the heaviest they ever heard; the mystery of the position which nobody could understand; the news of Lowes' death, and the uncertainty about Lytle's fate, had all combined to create a general feeling of depression, and a conviction that the battle was going against us."[13]

The heavy volume of both musket and cannon fire aimed against troops massed in the open would naturally be thought to produce a "fearful slaughter", but terrain and thick vegetation apparently prevented accurate aiming by the Confederates manning the fortifications being assaulted by the Ohio soldiers. As in any battle, there was considerable confusion during the fighting --on both sides. Isaac Smith explained some of it in the next entries in his diary:

"The enemy attacked each line separately and late in the evening, we supposed, got around to our line. We have reason to believe that what we supposed was the enemy was our own scouts -- The scouts were certainly there, and received a heavy fire from us. When our fire opened, the enemy, who had almost ceased firing, opened upon us, and

12 Lytle, "Lytle's Report", pg. 40-41
13 Reid, Cincinnati *Gazette* Narrative, *Rebellion Record*, pg. 48

some of our own guns were directed to that part of the ground so as to help us, but our men had the benefit of both fires as we were not in sight of either battery. This affair ended the engagement which had continued about three hours, sometimes very active, at others desultory and almost without the report of a single gun."[14]

The Kanawha Valley volunteers, the 22nd and 36th Infantry Regiments, were placed on the west side of the Confederate perimeter and this was the last section of the line to be probed by the Union Regiments. These western trenches were on the Federal Army's right flank and what Isaac Smith "supposed" to be Confederate scouts was probably a "provisional brigade" assembled from companies from several of General Rosecrans' Union regiments and placed under the command of Colonel W.S. Smith. Colonel Smith explained the attack against the Confederate right flank in his report written the day after the battle:

"A brigade ... was extemporized by General Rosecrans, and I was placed in command, and ordered to carry the works on the right by assault.

"I formed the command as above constituted in the ravine, and was the ordered by General Rosecrans to halt and await further orders. We remained in this position for about one hour, when General Rosecrans ordered us to move forward to the atttack. I reached the head of my column and started just at dusk. Before we could march down the ravine, through we had passed before, and countermarch up the right hand slope, so as to draw out my line on the flank, and in front of a portion of the enemy's line, it became so dark, and the men so weary, having marched from three o'clock in the morning, that it was found impossible to ascend to their line; the ground was covered with rocks and a dense underbrush of laurel, and Col. Moore reported that it would take until two o'clock in the morning to get two companies of his regiment up. I

[14] Childers, "Virginian's Dilemma", pg. 178

then ordered the whole column to "Face About!" and march out just as it had marched in, and crossed the ravine to the rear of the column to lead it out, when a shot or two from the enemy's skirmishers, or an accidental shot from one of our own pieces, caused the whole column, doubled as it was into a "U" shape, to open fire, killing two, and wounding about thirty of our own men."[15]

Colonel Smith's action against the Confederate positions filled with the men from the 22nd and 36th Infantry Regiments was witnessed by a reporter from the New York *Times*. He wrote:

"... Col. Smith worked off to the extreme right of the rebels under a furious fusilade of rifles and musketry, and was laboriously engaged in scaling a precipice which protected the rebel position in that direction. It was twilight before he got into a position for an assault, but his men lay on their bellies in the thicket playing away at the enemy not a hundred yards from them. The order for assault did not come, and the brave thirteenth had wasted its energies and showed their pluck for nothing".[16]

Both sides had the misfortune to fire into their own troops in the closing minutes of the battle. Isaac Smith thought that they had opened fire on their own scouts and was sure that the Confederate artillery had fired into their section of the line in an attempt to assist with repulsing the Union attackers.

The Union troops had similar misfortunes. While manuevering away from the Confederate fortifications, two segments of the attacking Federal "provisional" brigade -- a mixed unit from several regiments who were not familar with one another -- fired accidentally into their own ranks.

15 Smith, William S., "Colonel Smith's Report", *The Rebellion Record*, Vol. III, edited by Frank Moore, G.P. Putnam, New York: 1862, pg. 43

16 Western., "New York *Times* Narrative", *The Rebellion Record*, Vol. III, G.P. Putnam, New York: 1862, pg. 52

Accidental deaths and wounds were quite common during these early days of the war as the soldiers of both sides began to learn the basic skills of the soldier. It is very common to locate references to accidental gunshots that caused a serious wound or a fatality in the books and diaries of that period. The rates that the accidents occurred probably diminished as the troops on both sides gained experience and survivors became veterans.

The reduced visibility and exhaustion among the Union assault columns brought the fighting to a halt as darkness fell. The Federal troops remained close to the Confederate positions in order to renew the attack early on the morning of September 11. While the Union assault columns rested, the Rebels began to re-evaluate their general position and strategy. Isaac Smith entered the results of the afternoon's combat into his diary:

"The breast-work, except in front of the artillery, was very incomplete, made of log rails and brush, and on our line afforded no protection as the enemy's fire came in behind us or along the line. John Thompson, son of Dr. Thompson of Putnam and acting adjutant of our Regt, was wounded almost in the beginning of the fight by a ball shot at our gunners from a point near the house. It is about 3/4 of a mle from the house to the place at which Thompson stood."[17]

John Thompson had been a cadet at the Virginia Military Institute in Lexington and accompanied John McCausland into the Kanawha Valley to assist in the training of volunteers expected to rally to the support of the new Confederacy. He survived the effects of this wound and returned to active service with the 22nd Regiment. Later, he was seriously wounded at both Lewisburg and Droop mountain and was cared for by his Brother-in-Law, Andrew Barbee , a company commander in the 22nd Virginia during the battle at Carnifex Ferry.

Smith continued to describe the fighting in his diary:

17 Childers, "Virginian's Dilemma", pg. 178-179

"No one else was hurt in our regiment, no one was killed, and I believe but four wounded on our side, none mortally. Two of those terrible rifle-cannon balls passed nearly the whole length of our line, just high enough to have knocked the heads off the whole line of men -- one ball went about 10 feet in rear. The last passed just over Plus' back as he threw himself on the ground and about three feet from Col. T. Plus acted as aid to the Col. during the engagement and was constantly with him as he was walking up and down the line. A ball passed just over the head of all three of us while at my end of the line (the rightwing a half of the regiment) discussing the progress of the fight. A piece of bomb shell fell between Wm Reynold's knees as he was sitting on the ground, he sat still and dug it out of the ground where it had buried itself."[18]

This type of incident must have been fairly common during the battle as William Reynolds didn't bother to mention it in the diary he was keeping on his service in the war. His only mention of the battle of Carnifex Ferry was his exaggerated estimate of federal casualties.

Isaac Smith was not as hesitant to describe the events that occurred during the fighting:

"A canister shot or piece of shell fell just before me a few feet and buried itself in the ground so deep I could not dig it out with my sword."[19]

The Confederates were fortunate that they did not have numerous casualties from Federal artillery. The Union battery attached to the infantry regiments fired an enormous quantity of shells and solid shot into the Confederate works. Colonel Smith's report mentioned the activity of the two cannon assigned to his command:

"... my section of two rifled cannon, under command of Capt. Schneider, and supported by his company (E,

18 Childers, "Virginian's Dilemma", pg. 179

19 *Ibid*, pg. 179

Thirteenth regiment)was ordered by General Benham to take a position in the road ... about four hundred yards from the enemy's works; several shots were fired from this position with good effect ... Schneider found a better position for his guns, about one hundred paces to the right, and cut a road with his sword and hatchet, and from this new position, in full view of the enemy's battery, he fired seventy-five rounds of solid shot, and fifteen of shells; his shot ploughed through the parapet of the enemy's battery, spreading consternation among those who served the pieces."[20]

Carnifex Ferry's fighting would have been far more bloody if the participants had been more experienced at the time of the battle. With one Union participant describing the Confederate fire as the heaviest he had ever heard and a two gun Federal battery firing ninety rounds in a little over three hours, casualties on both sides would have been much greater if the troops participating had been more experienced. It is very unlikely that Captain Schneider's guns could have moved into an open position four hundred yards from a fortified Confederate battery and survive to fire ninety rounds, if this had occurred later in the war. If the battle had been fought in 1863 or 1864, it would have been far bloodier and the outcome would have probably been less than favorable for the Rebels.

The Confederates were in a difficult position following the end of the day's fighting. Their fortified position, while relatively strong, was situated with a deep gorge to their rear which effectively prevented any attempt at an orderly withdrawal while under fire, if the Federal regiments renewed their attacks in a co-ordinated manner the following morning -- which appeared to be the case. At a minimum, Floyd would be placed in a tactical situation where he would be forced to sacrifice a substantial portion of his small army as a rearguard while the remainder tried to escape -- down the steep slopes and across the ferry or newly completed footbridge to safety. The potential loss of

20 Smith, "Colonel Smith's Report", *Rebellion Record*, pg. 43

several regiments, his wagon trains, and artillery was not a possible outcome Floyd wished to discuss. Reinforcements from his rival, General Wise, may not have arrived in time to affect the outcome of the second day's fighting or they might not come at all. The choices were obvious -- remain behind the strong defensive fortifications and attempt to destroy the attacking Federal army the following day or begin a quiet retreat in the night.

The best description of the Confederate positions was written by a New York *Times* reporter travelling with General Rosecrans' headquarters:

"The defenses consist of a parapet battery, three hundred and fifty feet in front and centre, flanked by breastworks of logs laid in direct line with the front, and curving back until they terminated in the cliffs of Gauley. The exterior slopes are screened by slanting rails. The defenses are on the westward crest of a horseshoe mountain, which mounts up precipitously on the west side of the Gauley River, in front of Carnifex Ferry. They embrace almost a square mile of territory. The rear is protected by gigantic cliffs, shooting up in perpendicular line three hundred and fifty feet above the river, and where there are no cliffs the surface of the mountain, except on two narrow lines which lead to the ferry, are so steep and rugged that an armed man could not scale them if opposed with a broomstick. The mountain curves off on either flank to similar cliffs, and the defenses are carried to them. On the left, the position is comparatively accessible, and double lines of breastworks were constructed -- Col. Wharton occupying the extreme left, with a regiment of infantry and a battry. The lines on the right flank were carried down until they pitch off the rocks several hundred feet down. A trench, of course, protected the battery epaulement. Gauley River, a wild, roaring, beautiful torrent, also covers the rear perfectly. The rapids are dangerous above and below, but at the ferry the stream is wide and very deep. The interior of the works where the rebels are encamped is concave, excepting on the wings -- The depression in the centre of the mountain forming a perfect cover against missiles, excepting shells.

In front the mountain pitched off into a deep jungled ravine. On the right and left, however, there were ridges outside of the lines which were cleared and protected by abatis. The dense thickets and heavy forests in front so completely masked the position that it could not be seen at all until we ran directly into its embrace."[21]

A retreat under fire from a place such as this would be nearly impossible. It was an excellently fortified position with equally excellent natural fortifications, but as General Floyd and his staff were learning -- it was on the wrong side of Gauley River to adequately defend against the Federal attacks. If a man "armed with a broomstick" could hold off an armed soldier coming up the mountain, a well-positioned Union regiment would be able to decimate any retreating Confederate units caught packed on the ferry road leading off of the mountain. If a decision to withdraw was made, the timing of the troop movement would be critical.

Isaac Smith continued to explain events in his diary:

"I have no idea what effect our fire had upon the enemy -- some think it was very fatal. I do not. I believe we made no great impression upon them. At any rate night only stopped the engagement and the enemy evidently held their ground for the purpose of renewing the attack next morning. The men were kept to their places behind the breastwork -- had nothing to eat, but little water since early that morning with the certainty of a severe battle the next day. Our wagons had been ordered back to re-cross the ferry. We sent men down to bring up something to eat and all the axes that we might strengthen our breastwork which was extremly weak and afforded little or no protection. About 10 o'clock a message came for Col T and myself to come to headquarters. On our way we met Mike coming up with food for us--sent him on to wait our return. At headquarters found Genl Floyd's tent filled with officers.

---

[21] Western, "New York *Times* Narrative", ***Rebellion Record***, pg. 54-55

He was wounded slightly in the arm and had it bandaged in a sling. Everything was stiller and more solemn than a funeral. Genl Floyd then told Col T that from good sources he had learned that Genl Rosecrans with nine regiments had formed the attacking party and that without additions to our small force of about 1800 men we could not whip them and that a retreat had been determined on by the officers and asked his opinion."[22]

Floyd had an additional factor influencing his decision to retreat rather than risk defeat and possible capture by Union troops. Floyd had recently been Secretary of War in the Cabinet of President Buchannan and was involved in some "questionable transactions". He had managed to allow the states -- primarily southern -- to purchase converted flintlock muskets "in excess of the proper quota" from the Federal government. His order permitted the states to trade green musket stocks for seasoned and in one of his final actions while in Federal office, he ordered the transfer of 124 cannon from Pittsburg to posts in the South.[23]

Two other questionable incidents resulted in indictments against Floyd and investigations by the House of Representatives. He had secretly sold the Fort Snelling reservation to a New York syndicate and he was accused of misusing $870,000 in Indian Trust Bonds. He was saved from possible arrest and prosecution by the disagreement within Buchannan's Cabinet over a course of action regarding the need for reinforcing Fort Sumpter that provided a convenient excuse for resignation and his return to Virginia.[24] He was never tried, but was sure that the Federal courts would want to review the outstanding indictments if he was ever to come under their control.

---

22 Childers, "Virginian's Dilemma", pg. 179

23 _______, "Generals Wise and Floyd", *West Virginia Legislative Handbook and Official Register*, 1929, pg. 881

24 Klement, Frank, "General John B. Floyd and the West Virginia Campaigns of 1861", *West Virginia History*, Vol. VIII, No. 3, April, 1947, pg. 323

Floyd's tendency to retreat rather than to fight and risk capture lead to his undoing. He was in command at Fort Donelson the following year when it was surrounded by Federal soldiers. Floyd turned over command and escaped with his Virginia troops, but the new Rebel commander, General Buckner, was captured when the fort surrendered.[25] Floyd was relieved shortly afterwards by an angry President Davis. Floyd *definitely did not want to be captured* by the Union troops.

Major Smith described the preparations and the retreat:

"The retreat was then ordered and as usual it was decided that our regiment should bring up the rear. In a retreat this is the most dangerous service, as the rear guard must keep everything before them, waggons, cannon and everything, and are held responsible for the safety of the whole train. Floyd sent his own regiments first -- McCausland (who is a sort of favorite) next and ours last. We had no waggons of our own to guard -- They are all over the river and had been ordered away by Col T. but we had to wait until everybody else got off before we could move. It was also necessary that everything should get over the river before daylight, and without the knowledge of the enemy for after we left the top of the hill, a few hundred men could station themselves on the cliffs and shoot us down like dogs -- either with cannons or small arms. Our Regt did not move until about 12 1/2 o'clock. Col T and I expected most certainly to be taken prisoners with the whole regt, knowing it would be almost impossible to cross before day. I forgot to mention that during the day a foot-bridge had been finished across the river, by which the soldiers could cross but waggons and horses had to take two little flatboats which could ferry one waggon at a time."[26]

Fortunatly for the small Confederate command, soldiers recruited primarily from a mining company in southwestern

---

25 _____, "Floyd and Wise", *Legislative Handbook*, pg. 881

26 Childers, "Virginian's Dilemma", pg. 179

Virginia were able to complete a footbridge made of split logs as the fighting went on above. Without the bridge, the 1800 men would have been forced to cross on the two small flatboats at the ferry.[27] There would not have been enough time to get everyone across the Gauley River before daylight would allow the Union soldiers to enter the abandoned breastworks and discover the Rebel regiments trapped below at the crossing. The river was simply too dangerous to attempt wading or swimming and the flatboats were too small and slow to permit the rapid evacuation of the small Confederate army.

Smith continued:

"Of course the greatest silence was necessary lest the enemy hearing the commotion in camp, should suspect our design and attack us in the confusion. Col T and I had no time to eat, but sent Mike down with our horses and the food so as to save the horses if possible. There were seven guns (4 and 6 horses each) beside the waggons of each regiment."[28]

With the regiments of Floyd's brigade, the artillery, the wagons, and McCausland's 36th Virginia Infantry Regiment moving out of the fortified camp before the rearguard, composed of Smith's unit, the 22nd Virginia, could begin moving, there is little wonder that both Smith and his commander, Colonel Tompkins, felt that they would probably be captured along with the entire regiment before reaching the safety of the opposite bank of the Gauley River. The darkness, steep road to the ferry, and the need for slow, quiet movement, all combined to work against their escape. Smith wrote about their close call from the relative safety of the new camp on the top of Sewell Mountain on September 18, 1861:

"I have never felt anxiety such as was experienced that

---

[27] Davis, James A., *51st Virginia Infantry*, H.E. Howard, Lynchburg: 1984, pg. 4

[28] Childers, "Virginian's Dilemma", pg. 179

night. The safety of the whole regiment was involved, and the honor of its officers and of the service depended on the issue of that movement. If we were even successful in getting everything over, we would be so long delayed as to make a fight or surrender inevitable -- to fight down in that ravine would have been almost madness -- to surrender would have laid us open to reproach, no matter what might have been the circumstances. Floyd does not like Col T because he knows that Col T despises his character as a man and has no respect for his qualifications as a soldier, and it would suit Floyd's view to leave Tompkins to bear all the blame which might attach to any mishap in the retreat".[29]

Colonel Christopher Quarles Tompkins, unlike General Floyd, was a professionally-trained military officer. He had graduated from West Point if 1836 -- the year prior to the graduation of General Benham, the commander of the Union column that had been attacking the forward positions at Carnifex Ferry.[30] Tompkins believed in taking care of the men in his regiment and while he thought that the Virginia militia who had volunteered to serve in the Confederate army were "rabble", they were his rabble and did not deserve the treatment they were receiving at the hands of the "political generals". Floyd was an unscrupulous character with a less-than-unimpeachable past who possessed few characteristics that Tompkins would acknowledge in a commander. The frequent misuse of the 22nd Virginia, the shuttling of the regiment between both Floyd's and Wise's independent commands, and the common use of the 22nd as an expendable rearguard or lead regiment during an advance -- hazardous duties that other regiments didn't share -- created a situation between the Colonel and the General that had to be eventually resolved. Floyd's leadership qualities did little to endear him to any of the Kanawha Valley volunteers. Smith pointed out one special quality of the General in his next

29 Childers, "Virginian's Dilemma", pg. 179-180

30 *Registry of Graduates*, West Point Library, pg. 230

diary entry:

"*The general went over the river first* -- we had nothing for it but to await preparations, and march of the other regiments -- tho we could have started in ten minutes after the order, and have crossed the river within an hour after it was given. After a long delay of about 2 1/2 hours, during which our anxiety was greatly increased, we started our regiment on the march from the left at A: At B found the 36th which was to march before us, halted about 15 minutes for them, moved off again, they being in front. Everybody was perfectly still, no talking above a whisper allowed, the night rather dark and somewhat threatening. Instead of marching around the breastwork we crossed the hollow from B in direction a little to the left of E. This was done to keep the enemy from hearing us if possible. Down in the hollow, we were again halted to wait, as we understood, for some waggons -- and we waited and waited, every moment increasing our anxiety and lessening our chances for escape. I felt then that every moment's delay was probably at the cost of one man's life or liberty.

"If we had been drawn up in fair battle array, to meet the men, it would not have occassioned fear in the opprobrious sense of that term, but I know we should get down into the pen before morning, and when there, that escape was utterly hopeless if the enemy chose to attack. In the most intense impatience of men and officers, we waited in that hollow for at least 3/4 of an hour. We could hear some commotion among men and horses up along the artillery line, but none moved. I made up my mind finally that death or prison was my fate -- went forward to where Col T was sitting, found that he had abandoned pretty much all hope of saving the regt -- but at the same time found it was the artillery we were waiting for and not the waggons of the 36th Regt as supposed."[31]

For the combat soldier, waiting is the most difficult time. Waiting to move out of a potentially hopeless

31 Childers, "Virginian's Dilemma", pg. 180

situation before discovery by the enemy is infinitely worse on the nerves than actual combat. Each minute of delay makes it more likely that death or capture would be the fate of everyone in the rearguard. The feeling of hopelessness could have been overwhelming, except for the steadying presence of senior officers such as Tompkins and Smith. Their calming influence went a long way to preserve both the nerve and the fighting spirit of their men while they were caught in this situation. The Confederate privates obviously had confidence in their regimental officers and that something would be done to get them out of their predicament. Major Smith requested permission from Colonel Tompkins to check on the cause of the delay:

"I proposed to go up and see what was the matter to which the Col gave a hearty assent. Went up -- found some of the men lying on the ground, the horses not harnessed to the guns, and many of them without harness on -- The baggage lying about in every direction -- the Capt not on the ground -- called for an officer. After some time found a lieutenant sitting on a stump drumming his heels against it. Remonstrated with him -- told him I believed his guns were lost unless the movement was made immediately and that his caissons would almost certainly be lost -- explained the danger he was in of losing everything and our connection with it. The men seemed perfectly astounded, seemed to know nothing of what was going on, and as I have learned says they had no orders to move. Went back and reported these facts after taken the authority to order the guns off immediately. Col T sent me back to repeat my order in his name also -- found the Capt this time. The men were in great confusion -- I went to each gun, hurried up the men (none of the guns were limbered) and staid there until I saw them all start off. All of this of course occupied more precious time before daylight. Again set out down the road to the ferry, stopping every moment or two on account of the crowded condition of the road before us. The waggons, guns, caissons, etc. made it almost impassable even to those who had a right to go forward."[32]

An artilleryman assigned to the battery at Carnifex Ferry later wrote about the events during the evacuation:

"Many of us were asleep behind our breastworks when the evacuation was ordered, broken down from fatigue and excitement, and nothing disturbed our slumber save some groans of the wounded, not far from our fortifications, until an officer of the guard awoke us, saying that we had orders to evacuate our position as soon as possible. Orders were obeyed accordingly as with as little difficulty as could be expected under the circumstances ... in coming down this dangerous road to the ferry that dark night, we only lost one caison, besides a good deal of baggage, which went over a precipice."[33]

Major Smith described the evacuation route for his wife in the diary:

"The road down to the ferry is steep and worse than any road you have ever travelled on Poca, and just wide enough to admit a single waggon. It is precipitous above and below, and down in between the two high mountains in the dense shade, the darkness was most intense, it was impossible to see anything. From our start after the artillery, until we reached the river, is about one mile perhaps not more than 3/4 mile -- we were at least two hours on the march. You can imagine the suspense during its slow progress. In order to find a place to sit, we passed the waggons and guns, and reached the banks of the river. The 36th Regt passed on over the bridge. Gauley River is just like New River in its character at this place; Meadow River empties into it, and there is smooth but swift water for about two hundred yards. Above and below there are rapids and falls -- the falls below are about 1/2 mile long,

[32] Childers, "Virginian's Dilemma", pg. 180-181

[33] Riddle, Thomas J., "Floyd's Operations in West Virginia", *Southern Historical Society Papers*, Jan-Dec, 1883, pg. 94

full of tremendous rocks. There is no escape for the unfortunate man who should be drawn into them. The frail and narrow bridge was about 50 or 75 yards above, the water running swiftly under it. A few dim lights were burning along the bridge -- There was no railing. Some four or five poor fellows fell over -- I heard some were drowned but believe they were rescued."[34]

With the arrival of the 22nd Virginia, all of the Confederate troops had left the narrow mountain trail and were waiting to cross the river. McCausland's 36th Virginia had crossed the footbridge and only the artillery and wagons remained for the 22nd to guard. Tompkins quickly saw that the ferry used for the wagon crossing could be guarded best from the opposite shore and suggested this to Floyd. Major Smith continued his account:

"We, of course, remained -- Col T more and more impressed with the danger of losing the whole force by capture and seeing plainly that the ferry could be defended so much better from the other side and with only the ordinary dangers of the battlefield, crossed and mentioned his views to Genl Floyd, who co-incided with him and ordered us across. It was beginning to clear up for daylight, and you can imagine the gratification of the men when they discovered that they were not to be sacrificed but to fight on fair terms. I started them over the bridge single file about 5 feet apart. In about half an hour the whole force had crossed, and after calling out again and again along the shore to see that none were left. Plus (who had stood at the end of the bridge with a light to see that the men went single file and at proper distance) and I walked over arm in arm. The last of the 22nd Regt and of the forces (except for some artillerists) to cross. I have never experienced relief so great as when I set my foot onshore on this side, knowing that my whole regiment was safely across, not one lost or injured. From a seeming certainty that all would be

[34] Childers, "Virginian's Dilemma", pg. 181

lost, suddenly all were found safe. The crossing soon progressed so far as that Genl Floyd ordered us to leave a ferry guard of one company to remain and destroy bridge and boats when all were over and to march on. On top of the hill we stopped for about an hour when the men took a little something to eat. Here I found Mike who had arrived with the horses just a short time before us, having been since 8 o'clock the night before in going about two miles. The delay was at the ferry of course. I was determined if the Yanks took me, they should not get my new calvalry saddle I had purchased two days before."[35]

The small Confederate army was safe. The 22nd Virginia, Tompkins and Smith, had composed the army's rear guard and were able to successfully extract the entire force from a very difficult situation. Southern newspapers reported the retreat in glowing terms:

"I think that the public and all military men will agree that our fight and our fall back to the other side of the river are among the most remarkable incidents in the history of war. Seventeen hundred men, with six inferior pieces of artillery, fought back four times their number, with much superior artillery, for more than four long hours, repulsed them three times and remained masters of the ground. They then retired their numbers, baggage, stores, and more than two hundred sick and wounded across the river, from ten P.M. to four A.M., along one of the steepest and worst single track roads that a horse's hoof ever trod or man ever saw. Four o'clock found these men three miles from the enemy, with our newly-constructed bridge destroyed and our boats sunk behind us."[36]

While these accounts may not be entirely accurate -- Floyd had newspaper editors travelling with his headquarters to ensure adequate coverage for his efforts.

---

35 Childers, "Virginian's Dilemma", pg. 181

36 _____, "Lynchburg (Va) *Republican* Account", *The Rebellion Record,* Vol. III, edited by Frank Moore, pg. 56-57

The article on the battle seems to have a pro-Floyd bias. It ended with:

"I think these facts show a generalship seldom exhibited anywhere."[37]

Floyd was *not* a good general. His "Camp Gauley" where he planned to meet and defeat Rosecrans was not a position where he could have "...defied the world, the flesh, and the devil".[38] Far from it -- the breastworks occupied by the 22nd and 36th Virginia Regiments were unfinished and Floyd built his fortress without an escape route. If the log footbridge had not been completed on the day of the battle, retreat would have been impossible and without substantial reinforcements, the Union forces would have probably overrun at least one wing of the trenches the following morning. Floyd also bungled the retreat. He failed to get proper orders to his artillery batteries and if Isaac Smith had not had the presence of mind to check on the delay in the retreat, the small army would have lost both its rearguard and its artillery at dawn when the retreat was discovered. The newspapermen travelling with Floyd were wrong. Floyd definitely was ***not*** a good general.

Major Isaac N. Smith and Colonel Christopher Q. Tompkins were the Confederate officers actually responsible for making the rebel withdrawal a success. Isaac Smith was the "Officer of the Guard" who awakened the privates of the "Goochland artillery" and on his own authority ordered them to prepare to move. Tompkins had the leadership ability to recognize the value of Smith's suggestion that he should "go up and see what was causing the delay" -- as well as sending Smith back to order the artillery departure in his own name (probably to protect Smith from any retribution from Floyd) as well. He was also able to cross the river and convince Floyd that his regiment -- the rearguard -- would be in a better position to

---

37 ____, "Lynchburg (Va) *Republican* Account", pg. 57

38 Reid, Whitelaw, "Cincinnati *Gazette* Narrative", *Rebellion Record*, Vol. III, pg. 45

defend the ferry from the east bank (in relative safety) rather than being trapped on the western shore and being forced to fire nearly straight up if the Union regiments discovered the retreat. Floyd was a useless general, but Isaac Smith and Christopher Tompkins were excellent officers and in spite of the inept handling of their regiment by Floyd, both continued to do their duty and were able to salvage the retreat -- in spite of the fact that General Floyd was the ***first*** to cross to safety.

The battle of Carnifex Ferry was over. Both sides claimed victory, but it was actually a stalemate in which both sides won something. The Confederates survived intact as a military force and were able to withdraw eastward along the James River and Kanawha Turnpike past the road junction where the Wilderness road from Summersville entered the turnpike. This position was chosen in order to prevent any Union troops from marching easily into their rear and trap the rebel forces between them and the soldiers of General Cox at Gauley Bridge and on Gauley Mountain.

Major Smith continued to write about the retreat:

"We marched to a place on the turnpike about two miles above Vaughan's, but as we were in the rear of everything, the march was provokingly slow. We were all day making the 8 miles. Camped here and remained until Thursday night -- were ordered then to march from there at about 10 1/2 PM. Marched all night -- The men were terribly fatigued with loss of sleep. Stopped about 1 1/2 miles below Frank Tyree's at about 10 in the morning of Friday. Remained here all day and night. Next morning (Saturday) moved on to the top of Big Sewell. Remained here Sunday and Monday -- The men were engaged in fortifying. Monday night 10 o'clock again ordered off. Just as we got the men formed a terrible rain came upon us, the poor fellows had to stand and take it without shelter or motion for about two hours waiting for the slow regts who were to move before us to get off, and when we did start, the men were marching in mud over shoe tops, and the rain drenching them beside.

"Whilst we were drawn up waiting, the quick report of three guns in the direction of our pickets was heard, and presently the calvalry picket of 3 or 4 near the camp, came dashing in saying the advanced guard of the enemy was approaching within a mile, and they had fired into it. This was startling news indeed and I believe I became nearer being scared than at any time since the war began. Everything was in such utter confusion, part of the force gone, and the other part just leaving, and the 22nd Regt occupying a position which would force them to engage the enemy first, and so situated that the enemy would be entirely protected by woods whilst we should be in open ground. I thought we stood a poor chance, but I got all right pretty soon and after a great deal of alarm and apprehension all around it was discovered that the calvalry dragoon had fired upon our own infantry picket which had been stationed beyond, and were returning to camp to join in the march."[39]

Another mishap between friendly units had occurred. A cavalry patrol fired by mistake into infantry pickets returning to their regiments to continue the march. Killed or wounded soldiers from this incident were not mentioned in Smith's diary, but accidents such as these frequently produced casualties.

Smith continued:

"This march was decidedly terrible. Mud, rain, cold. hunger, and loss of sleep combining to make it an uncomfortable as possible. You will observe that in one week we march three nights. If the march could begin and then the men go on until they came to a stopping place it would not be so hard, but each regiment and its wagons have their place in line, and must not pass it, so that the toiling up hill of heavily loaded wagons keeps the men constantly on the move, but never stopping for any length of time. One stalled waggon stops everything behind it.

---

39 Childers, "Virginian's Dilemma", pg. 181-182

Each regiment follows its own waggons. We marched to Meadow Bluff, where the Blue Sulphur Road turns off. The object of coming here is to prevent our rear being reached by the road from Nicholas Courthouse which also comes here. The men had scarcely prepared for bed last night, hungry and tired, when another order came for another forced march to begin at 3 o'clock next morning and for four days rations to be cooked -- The poor fellows of course would have to cook all night before the march and thus get no sleep at all. Fortunately however an order came first to postpone time of march to 5 o'clock and afterward countermanding it altogether, for good reasons.

"I might say much about these matters but it would be neither prudent or proper."[40]

The bungling Floyd and his staff's incompetence were beginning to have an impact on Major Smith. He, like most of the soldiers, were there because they chose to be -- volunteers -- and they were willing to give their lives for a cause they believed in, if that should prove necessary. No one was willing to die because of a stupid decision made by an incompetent general and they were beginning to view Floyd this way and Smith was beginning to have doubts.

He was also about to lose his slave who was accompanying him:

"Mike after many expressions of faithlessness, etc. left our wagon on the march from Dogwood Gap last Thursday night and has not returned. He sent me word that he was sick and had to stop but took good pains to keep out of my way, although he knew I was behind at the head of the column. He had a wagon to ride in and many a poor sick fellow I saw dragging himself along that day who had no other way to come. Col Tompkins' brother-in-law saw him marching back down the road toward and near the enemy and turned him back. Genl Wise did the same and put him in charge of a soldier to bring back but the fellow escaped him. Dr. Wilkins told him to go back to the hospital which

---

40 Childers, "Virginian's Dilemma", pg. 182

was near and he would give him medicine and a good wagon to carry him on -- The sickness was all false, but he was making it for the Yankees. Look out for lies from him. He will use every means to run his wife and children off, and will doubtless be aided by the Yankees. You know he is liable to confiscation by their law, as he has been actually used in the service. Watch out for the rascal and believe none of his lying excuses for leaving."[41]

Isaac Smith had been accustomed to slavery all of his life and was fighting to preserve a way of life that involved slaves. His view was much like any other Southerner who was missing an expensive piece of property and wanted "it" back. Smith's father, Benjamin H. Smith, was a staunch Unionist and the elder Smith went to Gauley Bridge, the Federal headquarters during the Sewell Mountain campaign, to request that General Cox return Mike, the slave, to his rightful owners. Cox wrote of the event after the war:

"A negro man was brought to my camp by my advance guard as we were following Floyd to Sewell Mountain in September. He was the body-servant of Major Smith, and had deserted the Major with the intention of getting back to his family in Charleston. In our camp he soon learned that he was free, under the Act of Congress, and he remained with us, the servants about headquarters giving him food. When I returned to Gauley Bridge, Mr. Smith appeared and demanded the return of the man to him, claiming him as his slave. He, however, admitted that he had been servant to Major Smith in the rebel army with his consent. The man refused to go with him, and I refused to use compulsion, informing Mr. Smith that the Act of Congress made him free. The claimant then went to General Rosecrans, and I was surprised by the receipt, shortly after of a note, from headquarters directing the giving up of the man. On my stating the facts the matter was dropped, and I heard no more of it for a month, the man meanwhile disappearing.

41 Childers, "Virginian's Dilemma", pg. 182-183

"Soon after my headquarters were moved to Charleston, in December, I received another note from headquarters, again directing the delivery of the fugitive. Again I gave a temperate and clear statement of the facts, adding that I had reason to believe the man had now taken advantage of his liberty to go to Ohio. Mr. Smith's case was thus ended, butit left him with a good deal of irritation at what he thought a wrong done to him as well as insubordination on my part."[42]

Mike, the slave, was freed by an Act of Congress that allowed for the confiscation of any slave serving with the Confederate army. Mike apparently left for Ohio to enjoy his freedom, but his wife and children probably remained with the Smith household until after the end of the war.

Isaac Smith went on with his entry for September 18, 1861:

"Since Thompson was wounded it has been the duty of Sergeant-Major (Plus) to act as Adjutant and he has done well. He has called forth praise from Col Tompkins for his promptness, which is in itself a volume of commendation, for he seldom praises anything in these rabble hosts as he regards all militia.

"I have written this for the family generally, thinking the narrative would be gratifying. Read it to them. I have expressed opinions somewhat too freely for a junior officer, but am speaking to those whom I know will not permit me to be made instrumental in injuring the service. Such things of course should not be generally discussed lest they might get to Yankee ears."[43]

Such things did, however, get to Yankee ears. The entire diary fell into General Cox's hands with some captured rebel mail. Cox had encountered Isaac Smith's father, Benjamin Smith, during the episode over the slave, Mike. The captured diary was probably carefully read and

42 Cox, *Military Reminiscences*, pg. 158-159

43 Childers, "Virginian's Dilemma", pg. 183

later passed to the elder Smith and Cox later wrote that"...we became good friends."[44] Smith was a leader in the movement to form a new state from the western counties of Virginia which remained loyal to the Union. The Unionist sentiment was far from unamious in the area and many families were split over the issue. Cox described the situation of Benjamin Smith and other leaders of the "new state movement":

"Even the leaders of the Unionists found their "house divided against itself", for scarce one of them but had a son in Wise's legion, and the Twenty-second Virginia Reginent was largely composed of the young men of Charleston and the vicinity."[45]

Western Virginia's families were caught up in a brutal Civil War. Families were split, father and son in different armies; brothers, cousins, uncles, and extended family members split into two bitter camps. Loyal Union regiments were raised in western Virginia and the troops from the region on both sides fought one another frequently. For example, the Confederate raid on Guyandotte against recruits for a Union Virginia regiment was conducted by Rebel cavalry troops also recruited from the same region of the state. The Civil War in western Virginia was literally fought within families --brother against brother and father against son. There was a great strain placed on the Rebel soldiers who were recruited from the Kanawha Valley and their lack of confidence in their commanders as well as their lack of respect for their two generals -- compounded by bad weather, disease, families caught in Union-controlled territory, and lack of food lead many to re-evaluate their political position. It was probably not a single, isolated event that caused a man to resign, if he were an officer, or desert from the army, if enlisted, but normally several inter-related pressures caused a man to overlook his special pride in belonging to his regiment and

44 Cox, *Military Reminiscences*, pg. 158

45 *Ibid*, pg. 158

the influences of friends who would remain behind after he left. The feeling of deserting friends to their fate was frequently sufficient to hold many of the men to the regiment to the end, but pressures were beginning to build in the Confederate army on Sewell Mountain.

Major Isaac Noyes Smith wrote faithfully in his diary. Perhaps the time spent writing notes for his wife's eventual reading allowed him to feel close to her. Regardless of his motivation, Major Smith was an excellent reporter of the events developing around him. He continued his account on September 19, 1861:

"A quiet pleasant day yesterday, no exciting news or rash orders. This morning came news that the enemy were marching rapidly upon Wise, that Wise was determined not to retreat, but to await their attack. Our whole force was therefore ordered out to prepare for the attack upon our lines, and have been actively engaged in throwing up breastworks all day. We are fortifying the east bank of Meadow River on both sides of the turnpike just this side of Little Sewell Mountain. The lines are about three miles long. Our left has about 400 yards on the right flank, where a road comes in from the Wilderness road. The boys worked well to-day although they have only about 10 axes. Every other regiment was supplied with quite a number of shovels, picks and axes. Our point is one of great importance, and especially so under the news received this evening that the enemy were advancing in force along the road from Nicholas CH, an outlet of which we are to defend. If they have no artillery we can whip them -- with artillery they will hurt us considerably as the hills on the other side of Otter Creek completely command our position. The place we occupy is condemned by every Col in the forces I believe -- It is a selection of General Floyd's.

"I must go to bed for there is every probability there will be commotion tonight perhaps some movement. It is very certain we will hear Wise's guns tomorrow -- and we may probably fight ourselves. May God preserve us all. In him is my trust."[46]

This diary entry was the first that begins to reflect a subtle change in the outlook of Major Smith. Previously, he wrote about hardship and danger, but he continued to do his duty without complaint. Now, following the mismanaged retreat from Carnifex Ferry, the poorly planned marches to Sewell Mountain, and his total lack of faith in the ability of General Floyd, Smith invokes the Almighty for the first time. Even as he related his fear of death or capture during battle, he didn't mention his faith and his trust in God. The stress of the campaign coupled with the misuse of Smith's regiment --leading advances, rearguard in retreats -- now defending the most likely avenue of attack without sufficient tools to prepare adequate defenses in a location selected by the bungling Floyd, even though the majority of the army's colonels disagreed with the position, all began to erode Smith's morale. When this was combined with very bad weather, poor food, and some homesickness for the family in Union-held territory, it was beginning to cause Smith (as well as several others in the small army) to gradually lose confidence in the path they had chosen. We have Smith's diary to evaluate, but the pressures felt by him had to be common throughout the entire 22nd Virginia.

His next entry was dated three days later on September 22:

"Contrary to expectations no fight yet -- Wise has not even engaged the enemy although 12 miles in our front. We have had a more quiet time than usual. No orders at night -- everything regular and quiet as though we were 100 miles from the enemy. Everyone is more or less surprised at their inaction -- can't understand why they don't attack or try to outflank us and get in our rear.

"Genl Lee of the Northwest army and Commander of the forces in Virginia arrived at our camp last night. This morning the field and staff officers and Captains of our

46 Childers, "Virginian's Dilemma", pg. 183

regiment called upon him in a body to pay our respects. He was known to be the most talented man in the U.S. Army after Genl Scott -- is about 6 feet high, a most perfect figure, straight without stiffness, full chest, trim built in every respect, decidedly the handsomest figure I ever saw -- his features equally handsome, and his face and eyes are full of intelligence -- courteous and perfectly easy in his manners, and with the most remarkable faculty of keeping his own counsel I have ever known -- perfectly circumspect in all he says, answers all questions civilly, but with good care that no one shall find out more than he intends them to know. One thing is certain that not the least symptom of the politician appears in his manners or conversation but on the contrary everything that characterizes a gentleman. We shall all feel every confidence in his opinions and directions, and the whole army will act willingly upon his suggestions. We are not advised what his course will be, whether he will remain here or return immediately to his command. It is probable he will straighten up matters here, set these two political generals on the right course in the right way and then leave us."[47]

Smith must have felt that his prayers had been answered. In Lee, he saw a soldier's general -- a man who could be trusted to make the right plans, select proper positions, and make correct decisions. Here, finally, was a general who had no evidence of politics about him who would soon straighten out both Floyd and Wise -- political-appointee generals who were rapidly losing the Kanawha Valley and western Virginia to the invading Yankees. He and most of the men in the small Confederate army had very high hopes in Robert E. Lee.

Unfortunately, Major Smith received news from a friend in the army that would eventually change his relationship with the Confederate army. He wrote:

"I am much depressed today from various causes. This unhappy war is growing more and more fierce every day,

[47] Childers, "Virginian's Dilemma", pg. 183-184

and there is less prospect of peace than ever. Vile passions are aroused and terrible scenes yet to be enacted. West Virginia is to be red with blood before the end is yet my source of constant trouble is that my father will be in danger. Wicked and unscrupulous men with whom he has lived in friendship for years absolutely thirst for his blood, as I truly believe. He and Summers, as one of their friends remarked to me today, are especial objects of hatred and aversion to men here. I am actually leading a set of men one of whose avowed objects is the arrest and judicial of lynch murder of my father. The situation is a terrible one and I cannot continue in it. Much as I regret the differences of views which we may hold, yet it is not proper for me to be so situated. My father has been neutral and committed no act which would subject him to imputation but in this war, prejudice and passion decide everything on both sides; reason and facts none."[48]

Here was an additional problem for Major Smith. His father was a strong, outspoken Unionist who was becoming active in a movement to form a new state from the western counties of Virginia, but his father, Benjamin Smith (who had previously visited General Cox in an attempt to reclaim the escaped slave,Mike) was not a member of any military unit and as a "neutral" was not to be attacked. Major Smith's wars were fought with other soldiers -- not civilians -- and he was one of the last of the age where chivalry entered into warfare.

Emotions -- Smith's "vile passions"-- were definitely aroused and the war was becoming something that no one had envisioned at the outset. It was becoming a bitter,serious, and bloody family feud fought out among many different families simultaneously. Isaac Smith's family was no exception. Smith had a cousin Joab, a member of Captain W.H. Lipscomb's company, who also participated in the Kanawha Valley and Sewell Mountain campaigns. Like his cousin, Joab also kept a journal in which he wrote about seeing his "Uncle Ben" as his

48 Childers, "Virginian's Dilemma", pg. 184

company marched through Charleston during Wise's retrograde movement:

"I saw that notorious traitor and cold-blooded villain who seemed delighted at our misfortune. In fact, the hoary-headed scoundrel could not conceal his delight. Great God! to think that I should be related to this infernal demon in human form!"[49]

If a close relative could have feelings as strong as this, one would be afraid to examine the emotions of strangers who were really angry at the elder Smith. Isaac Smith was probably correct -- men under his command would probably attempt to harm his father -- neutral or belligerent -- because of his pro-Union activities and opinions.

Union General Cox wrote of Mr. Smith:

"Colonel Benjamin F. Smith was a noteworthy character also. He was a leading lawyer, a man of vigorous and aggressive character, and of tough fiber both physically and mentally. He shared the wish of Summers to keep West Virginia out of the conflict if possible, but when we had driven Wise out of the valley, he took a pronounced position in favor of the new state movement."[50]

Isaac Smith completed his diary entry for September 22:

"This is Sunday -- no preaching, no service, no godly conversations, no Christian considerations are a part of the day's duties. Our Chaplain has never been near us since we left White Sulphur and only there for a few days. Everybody is intent upon the shedding of blood, upon war and its evils, upon the follies of earth and not upon the love, the mercy and goodness of God.

"I am in no humor to write -- the future is terrible. I have no control over my own fate -- if free from the army

49 Clark, W.C., "Impressions of a Soldier of 1861", *The West Virginia Review*, November, 1930, Vol. VIII, pg. 52

50 Cox, *Military Reminiscences*, pg. 156

could not visit my friends or even hear from them; have no conception from day to day where the morrow will find me or even the next few hours -- and the future of my life (if God's mercy gives me length of days here on earth) how utterly darkened inscrutable -- I can have no plan."[51]

Major Smith had reached a low point in his military career. Even with the presence of a soldier's general such as General Lee, the overall situation combined with the dilemma regarding his father's political activities and enemies were nearly enough to overwhelm him.

General Cox described the situation facing the Smith family very well:

"The family distress and grief revealed by accident in this case is only an example of what was common in all the families of prominent Union men."[52]

This particular type of grief was widespread through western Virginia as politics, oaths sworn, and loyalty to regimental comrades held young men with conflicting duties to the Confederate army. Faced with these serious problems, it is amazing that many of them were able to remain on active service and fight on to the end. It was an especially cruel war!

Major Smith's duties and depleted morale kept him from recording any additional entries in his diary until the following Sunday, September 29. He wrote from General Wise's fortifications on the eastern summit of Big Sewell Mountain, Camp Defiance:

"How remarkable that we are here. What is written above shows my ignorance of what was to happen. On Monday night (23rd) received orders to have tents, baggage, and everything packed in waggons, one day's rations in haversacks, and every man and company ready to start at 5 o'clock next morning -- got the men ready by the

51 Childers, "Virginian's Dilemma, pg. 184

52 Cox, *Military Reminiscences*, pg. 157

time fixed but had no orders to move. Waited longer, had the men formed and waiting -- in about two hours or more received orders to march -- our regiment in advance, and then ascertained for the first time that Genl Wise was about to be attacked at Big Sewell, and we were to go to his relief. You will notice that our regiment usually is put in front on an advance and in the rear in a retreat.

"Moved the regiment and went about 100 yards, and found the waggons were not to go. Col Tompkins had two biscuit in his haversack -- was sent back by him for a canteen, and took occasion also to get three biscuit with a small piece of meat in each, in my hurry. This was the only stock for Col T. Plus and myself. Marched rapidly -- met men and waggons from Wise's camp at almost every turn. Many of the men had great stories to tell of how the pickets were shot etc., etc. The waggons hurrying to the rear -- and we met some going rearward very rapidly whom we thought ought to be going forward."[53]

While Smith may have had doubts, he was not afraid of moving forward with his troops to face combat. He had doubts about those moving to the rear -- a coward does not bother to pass judgement on others who begin to shirk their duty.

He went on:

"At the top of Sewell or near it (Mrs. Buckingham's old place) halted for a moment to rest the men, had scarcely sat down when the booming of a cannon was heard, the Col jumped to his feet called out "forward" and we were off again.

"It was about 2 or 3 o'clock when we reached the first troops. We were marched off into the woods, and shown our place along the top of the ridge, no breastworks or defenses had been made. The men were deployed behind logs, trees, or in open ground along the the line, aand stood awaiting the attack. Continual firing among the pickets was heard -- one poor lieutenant carried along dying in a litter,

53 Childers, "Virginian's Dilemma", pg. 184-185

shot at the outpost -- every gun created the impression that the enemy was upon us. The men moved to their posts and with hand upon the locks of their guns, watched for the enemy to show himself before them -- we were in the woods where the enemy had even chances with us.

"On the way down Col T and I had together eaten one biscuit -- late in the evening I ate another. Neither water or food except that, from 3 o'clock in the morning -- the evening wore away and no attack. The men had set to work, one half watching, the other working, with about four axes had managed to do something towards a breastwork. Many of the poor fellows had nothing to eat all day. They had relied upon the waggons, and had started out on the march when the waggons were ordered back. Guard out all night. Slept on a few leaves with Col T, in the middle of the ridge road, just behind our lines -- troops and horsemen were passing at all times during the night within 2 or 3 feet of us.

"Up at 4 o'clock -- almost certain of attack -- had the men along the lines. Same expectation and anxiety and watchfullness of day before, jumping to the guns and breastworks at every gunshot. The men worked hard and by night had made an excellent line of breastworks fully protecting the whole line of some 3 or 4 hundred yards. Still nothing to eat. Some time in the forenoon Gen Wise sent some flour and beef -- men were sent to cook -- They used the barrel heads to cook upon, and about night some warm dough and some beef burned upon the coals were distributed -- no salt either in the bread or on the meat. A piece of bread about the size of one's hand, and a small piece of meat were given to each man. Some received none until after night -- this was the meal of the second day -- 3rd day (Thursday) about the same scenes -- food of the same character but a little more of it. I cut my dough into thin slices, browned it thoroughly and ate it with water -- could eat no more beef. In the afternoon it was evident rain was coming on. We got some men to build us a brush camp -- the rain sprang up before it was finished, and in a short time it was saturated and came pouring through as badly as though there was no shelter. In a short time we were saturated. Tried to sleep but could not -- water almost running under us, and a leak dropping in my face, and many others running upon my body. At about midnight all gave up. Plus tried to sleep and probably did; after 12 the balance of us sat up -- the dough was thoroughly saturated by morning -- took it wet and upon a chip cooked it once again.

"This was the remains of the night before, when we had some bread with salt in it, and some potatoes (quite a feast). The rain poured on pitilessly; the poor fellows were shivering in the wet and cold -- the blankets of many were in the waggons at Meadow Bluff. All day it poured on. A more merciless, cheerless rain, and more miserable day could scarcely have been experienced by anyone -- The poor, half-frozen, half-starved men had to stand it. We were all thoroughly drenched, and with difficulty kept the rain from extinguishing our fire. Some of the men seeing our destitute condition came and offered to build us a slab camp. Just after this, to the joy of all, some of the waggons came in, bringing tents and provisions for the boys. Our waggon came along, our tent was pitched, and in a short while we had a nice supper of excellent hot coffee, good bread and butter, and cold turkey and ham. We enjoyed it, of course. This is Sunday and this morning it was reported that the enemy had made a movement, and an attack was expected, and everyboby put on the alert. I have been writing here, expecting at any moment to hear the guns. This morning we felt almost confident of attack, and every falling tree (the men were strengthing the breastworks) made us start."[54]

A week had passed since Smith's previous entry in the diary and he seems to have recovered from his depression which was recorded so vividly the previous Sunday. During the week, there had been a great deal of marching and preparing to receive an attack from the formidable combined armies of both Rosecrans and Cox. Both of

[54] Childers, "Virginian's Dilemma", pg. 185-186

these Union generals had proven that they were willing to fight aggressively and they had moved their troops eastward along the James River and Kanawha Turnpike to confront General Wise at his "Camp Defiance".

Wise and his legion had refused to fall back to Meadow Bluff with the remainder of Floyd's small army after the retreat from Carnifex Ferry. Wise sent reports of his potential peril to General Lee who was managing Confederate operations in the northwestern portion of the state and at the same time Lee was also receiving letters from General Floyd complaining that Wise wouldn't obey commands to fall back and re-unite the small forces. The frustrated Lee soon moved his headquarters to Sewell Mountain in order to attempt to more closely manage the two feuding, political generals. Lee arrived on the mountain on September 21, 1861 and shortly wrote to Wise:

"...I beg, therefore, if not too late, that the troops be united, and that we conquer or die together."[55]

Wise agreed to join forces *under Lee* at either location, but when General Lee learned that Rosecrans had moved a large force into the Sewell Mountain area, he ordered Floyd to march his command to Wise's assistance. This was the troop movement recorded by Isaac Smith in his diary. Now, with Lee in command things might be diffferent. This could have been the reason Smith's morale was so much higher than it had been the previous Sunday. Lee was the hero of the Southern soldiers even at this early time and his reputation as a soldier was unequalled on either side. Facing the strength of the combined Federal forces in the area, Lee sent for General Loring and his regiments from the Cheat Mountain area of the northwest and their arrival brought the Confederate strength to 8,000 or 9,000 men.

It is obvious from Smith's diary that there was a good relationship between the officers and men of the 22nd

---

55 White, "West Virginia", pg. 42

Virginia Regiment. Colonel Tompkins might have considered them "rabble", but obviously took care of his command. Smith was also worried about the welfare of the "boys" and that affection was returned. Several of the men volunteered to erect a "slab camp" for the officers during the worst of the bad weather on the mountain. It is doubtful that they would have done as much for Floyd -- even if ordered. Smith was relatively inexperienced (he had started his military career as a private in the Valley's militia), but had learned to become a good officer very quickly.

He went on to describe the area and the nearness of the Federal camp:

"There are two tops to Sewell Mt, one about a mile from the other, the enemy are camped on the western, we on the eastern -- the enemy are camped where I wrote the first part of these pages. From many places in our line, we can see their whole camp -- large number of tents, all over the hilltop, and men walking about among them. Last night we heard the band playing with great distinctness -- the bugle playing 'tatoo' and 'extinguish light' signals. It seems so singular that we should be here so near and for so deadly a purpose. I feel so much more like shaking them by the hand, urging them to let us alone, to go home, end this fratricidal war and whilst they live under their government, to let us live under ours unmolested.

"The trip, as you may see, has been one of great hardship. Genl Wise's folly has occasioned it -- he refused to obey Floyd's orders, and go back with him to Meadow Bluff, and the consequence is the enemy found him here -- he was not able to withstand them, and had to send for re-inforcements. This Friday the poor old man had orders from Jeff Davis, to report at Richmond immediately, and turn over his command to Floyd. Nothing could be more humuliating -- he despises Floyd, and now while all of his ambitious hopes have been ruined, he goes back to Richmond in disgrace, and his old enemy takes his command."[56]

The bitter feud between the two political generals was at an end. Wise was recalled to Richmond and there was no ambiguity in the message written in Richmond on September, 20, 1861:

"Sir: You are instructed to turn over all the troops heretofore immediately under your command to General Floyd, and report yourself in person to the Adjutant General in this city, with the least delay. In making the transfer to General Floyd you will include everything under your command.

By Order of the President,
J.P.Benjamin
Acting Secretary of War

General H.A.Wise"[57]

Wise wrote a note to General Lee asking for advice. Lee's response was simple:

"Obey the President."[58]

Wise departed shortly afterward and while in Richmond, he explained everything in detail that had transpired between Floyd and himself. Henry Heth, a Confederate Colonel under the command of General Floyd later related a story about Wise's interview with Jefferson Davis:

"When Wise called to see Mr. Davis in Richmond, Mr. Davis said, I presume, in a playful way, 'General Wise, I think I will have to shoot you.' General Wise started from his seat and said, "Mr. President, Shoot me. That is all right, but for God's sake let me see you hang that damned rascal Floyd first!'"[59]

---

56 Childers, "Virginian's Dilemma", pg. 186
57 Humphries, *Military Operations in Fayette County*, pg. 6
58 *Ibid*, pg. 6
59 Heth, "Memoirs of Henry Heth", pg. 18-19

The request that Wise had previously submitted for his legion to be transferred to another theater of operations was shortly approved and the firey Wise was soon facing new Federal troops on the Outer Banks of North Carolina with his general's commission intact along with his legion. He retained his rank and was with Lee at Appomatox.[61]

The diary went on:

"Gen'l Lee is in command here, and the troops have every confidence in him. Our position is remarkable -- I believe if we could go back with honor, we should so, but the Genl cannot turn while thus face to face with the enemy, and we believe the enemy are in precisely the same situation. We can get no provisions here -- the bridges along the meadows have been washed away, and the road overflown -- waggons cannot get along. Our last barrel of flour goes to-day (not ours but the troops of the 22nd Regt). The poor horses are starving. In two days mine has had six ears of corn, and a small armful of hay. Chestnut leaves is all they get. The woods of course will be wretched after this rain, even when the water recedes. We could get the food if it could be hauled.

"I have but little hope (indeed none) that the troops will reach the Kanawha this fall --(I must go for some horse feed somewhere). May God preserve you all.

"I am writing in the slab camp, Plus is smoking -- Dr. McDonald reading my bible. We have just had a good dinner -- ham and potatoes -- remains of turkey, bread and butter, and good molasses.

"Slept better in this camp last night than at any time since leaving home. At night it is impossible to realize that I am in 3/4 mile of an enemy who may kill me in a few moments -- feel and seem to miss Uncle Brad.

"This is a strange and unnatural war."[62]

All wars are strange and unnatural, but a civil war is generally more fierce and bloody than ordinary conflicts

61 Humphries, *Military Operations in Fayette County*, pg. 7

62 Childers, "Virginian's Dilemma", pg. 186-187

between nations. This civil war was to be no exception to the general rule as passions began to take a more specific role in governing the limits of the conflict.

The week of heavy, cold rains brought a halt to active operations on both sides. With bridges out and roads flooded, even the horses didn't get enough food. Troops on both sides began to get sick -- measles, typhoid fever, pneumonia -- but it was the poorly equipped Confederate army that suffered most. General Floyd later reported:

"It cost us more men, sick and dead, than the battle of Manassas."[63]

The Confederate positions were well-entrenched and Lee's strategy was to wait for Rosecrans to attack him. A Richmond *Examiner* reporter wrote:

"If they would attack us, we could whip them without, perhaps, the loss of a man; but, if we have to attack them, the thing would be different."[64]

Sewell Mountain was one of the most unlikely locations for a major battle. Both armies had stretched their supply systems past its effective limits and the bad weather compounded the transportation problem. It was a strange autumn. Ice had formed on Valley Mountain during the night of August 14-15 and because of the heavy rains, both New and Kanawha Rivers were at their highest stages in history as Lee and Rosecrans awaited the others attack on Sewell Mountain.

The transportation problems facing the Union side was probably more complex than that facing Lee at the time. The Confederates had to contend with flooded meadows and washed out bridges on creeks along their route to the depots on the eastern slopes of the Alleghenies, but the Federal supply officers had serious problems with which to contend. The Union supply route entered a bottleneck at

[63] White, "West Virginia", pg. 43
[64] Klement, "Floyd and the West Virginia Campaigns, pg. 330

the flooded Gauley River where a slowly functioning ferry used to replace the bridge burned as Wise retreated. What supplies were getting across the swollen river and over the mountainous, muddy turnpike would rapidly vanish if the ferry at Gauley Bridge became inoperable because of the high water. This would leave the Federal forces in an untenable position from which they would be forced to retreat -- back to a potentially uncrossable river. Rosecrans was too able a general to overlook this possibility.

Major Smith continued to record events as he observed them beginning the following day, September 30, 1861:

"A few moments after I ceased writing on yesterday learned that Col Spaulding had just been killed by the enemy's pickets. He commanded one of Wise's regiments. Has been intoxicated for several days and on yesterday, ordered out one of his companies and started towards the enemy -- went some distance beyond our lines, met the pickets turned his Co back and rode up to within a short distance of the pickets three of whom fired at him killing him almost instantly -- his horse wheeled and ran back to the Co and he fell into the arms of his men. The whole thing was unauthorized and of no use but very sad.

"I am officer of the day to-day and as such it is my duty to visit all of the guards -- I have looked forward to it with some apprehension as at one of the pickets a number of men have been shot by the enemy and at another several of our own men and officers have been shot by our own guards, when they were going to relieve or visit the sentinels. This morning went to the advanced picket -- (that which is nearest to the enemy's line) and was shown where one of our men had been shot by the enemy -- expected every movement to draw their fire as we (the officer and I) were in full view and good range. The officer informed me that I was the first officer of the day who had visited that advanced guard, much less the advance sentinel. From this point there is a fine view of the enemy's camp because so near -- can see men and horses plainly and the "Star spangled banner" (in spite of my position I love it yet) waving in the breeze -- will have to visit the guard again tonight after 12 o'clock. This is one of the regulations of war. Don't fear anything from the enemy on this visit but have much to fear from the guard itself.

"One regiment have shot two lieutenants and one man in a week of their own body, at the same post."[66]

Smith was performing a very dangerous duty. Moving up to the forward positions to inspect the readiness of the Confederate guards was doubly dangerous. Either an alert Federal soldier or a jittery Rebel guard could shoot at any moment. His sense of duty caused him to inspect even the most remote forward outpost even though none of the other regimental officers assigned this duty had taken similar risks.

Isaac Smith was a very complex individual. He had been a private in a volunteer militia company, the Kanawha Riflemen, and the entire company had volunteered to support the state of Virginia when the seccession vote was ratified. He had been a member of that company -- not as an officer -- since 1858 and had developed his military skills to the point that he was now a Major in Confederate service. He, his original commander, Captain George S. Patton, and the remainder of the Kanawha Riflemen had issued a strong statement of their intentions as they all volunteered for state duty at the opening of the Civil War:

"We, the Kanawha Riflemen, hereby declare it to be our fixed purpose never to use arms against the State of Virginia, or any other southern state, in any attempt of the administration at Washington to coerce or subjugate them. That we hereby tender our services to the authorities of the state, to be used in the emergency contemplated."[67]

66 Childers, "Virginian's Dilemma", pg. 187

67 Cohen, Stan, "Colonel George S. Patton and the 22nd Virginia Infantry Regiment", *West Virginia History*, Vol. XXVI, No. 3, April, 1965, pg. 178-179

Virginia had not quickly joined the new southern Confederacy and the convention which met in Richmond to discuss the possible need for seccession initially rejected the concept. The catalyst which forced many of the on-seceding southern states to withdraw from the Union was President Lincoln's proclamation requesting that 75,000 state volunteers be provided to the Federal Government to force the seceding states back into the Union. After this appeal for troops was made, many volunteer companies in the south -- like the Kanawha Riflemen -- were issuing similar statements and the Seccession Convention in Richmond reversed itself and voted to join the Confederacy. The Civil war became a reality and everyone involved in the voting process understood that Virginia would become the major battleground in the war.

Isaac Smith, however, was still torn between the oath he had taken as a Confederate officer ("...in spite of my position...") and his loyalty for the nation and the flag which represented so much to Americans ("...I love it yet..."). He, like many others in the Confederate army, was beginning to feel torn between the two loyalties and had to make difficult choices.

He finished the daily entry:

"Last night Frank Noyes, Dave Ruffner, Donaldson, J. Doddridge, Alline Brown and others came to our camp and we sang a number of excellent hymns, had one prayer book and nothing else for words; it was decidedly a pleasing way of winding up the Sabbath, illy as it had been spent.

"It is thought probable by some we shall fight within a day or two -- we will probably attack them if they do not attack us. I was told so today but not upon decided authority. If we attack it will be with great loss of life -- for the enemy are strongly entrenched -- Something will surely be done for we have a large force here now and re-inforcements coming every day."[68]

---

68 Childers, "Virginian's Dilemma", pg. 187

A large battle was the most likely outcome to all of the military manuevering in reinforcing of both sides in this strange war for the possession of the mountaintop. The reinforcements were arriving from the remainder of Lee's split command that had stayed in the area of Cheat Mountain. These soldiers were under the command of Confederate General Loring and they were entering the Rebel fortifications daily. With the constant arrival of Loring's troops and the expected reinforcements from across the mountains, the Rebel army under Lee was becoming a credible force. Loring and a total of 9,000 additional men had arrived by September 29.

Lee was in a strong natural position which had been extensively fortified and he was willing to wait for Rosecrans to attack as the Union general had attacked Floyd at Carnifex Ferry. Rosecrans, however, had learned a severe lesson regarding assaults on fortifications since the previous battle and the presence of Lee as the commander -- combined with the tenuous Federal supply situation -- made the Federal commander cautious.

Lee's reputation with the regular U.S. Army officers serving with Rosecrans was as strong as it was with the Confederates and alone was sufficient to make the Union commander cautious. The two opponents settled into a waiting game -- neither willing to risk the huge losses which would result from a direct assault on the other's fortifications.

Waiting for the order to attack or prepare to be attacked left little for Major Smith to do. He found time to write again in his diary on the following day, October 1, 1861:

"Visited the outposts of our line of sentinels last night. Plus had said he would go with me to be on hand if anything occurred and at one o'clock we set out. There were such a number of outposts that it would take three days to visit all so I suggested to Genl Lee that I should only visit those next to the enemy which he approved, the others being of less importance we were out about 2 1/2 hours much less time than I expected, nothing unusual occurred and today I was relieved at 8 o'clock AM. Will not have to go on duty again for a long time as there are so many officers here now.

"There are many indications of early actions here. Genl Floyd has moved with his troops making a movement to the rear and I am very much afraid we shall be ordered to join him. When we fight again I wish it to be under Genl Lee not a politician."[69]

This section is interesting because of several factors -- First, General Lee was apparently involved in the management of the army down to the smallest detail in its' daily activities. He was contacted by Smith for permission to shift the number of posts visited by the Officer of the Day, a decision which could have been made at a significantly lower level in the Confederate army. There were probably so many untrained, unqualified officers present that the commanding general even had to plan the duty roster for the Officers of the Day. While he was obviously qualified to make such rosters, it should have been the resonsibility of his staff to plan such activities.

Second, the entry shows the dislike that the average field officer had for the political appointees such as General Floyd. Fighting was inevitable in the upcoming campaign, but the Virginia volunteer officers would have preferred to serve in combat under the command of a professional soldier such as Lee, even at this early stage of the war.

Smith went on to record some information about personal friends of both him and his wife:

"Wm H. Ruffner came into camp today from Rockingham, bringing bedding, lint bandages for sick or wounded -- hear from him that Miss Julia has reached Ashland.

"Jim Lewis stayed here all day yesterday and last night trying to get a discharge from the service -- a violent "secesh" -- and so it is with many others of that ilk who

69 Childers, "Virginian's Dilemma", pg. 188

hang about the army and run to the rear when there is a fight. By the way when Plus and I got back last night -- found Lewis on my bed tick with his shoes on and all my covering and Plus' over him -- he paid no attention to either of us, but slept on. Plus and I were cold and sleepy, and I got no more rest. At 4 1/2 had to get up and warm and have not lain down since. Col Tompkins from this and some other little matters took a violent dislike to him."[70]

Lewis, who had apparently advocated a hardline approach to the North-South problem, was not willing to back up his position with deeds. Lewis had been a member of the Kanawha Riflemen in 1858, but was now attempting to convince the military authorities that he should be dismissed from the army. Men like Tompkins and Smith would have little respect for this type of individual who would take a position advocating war, but would then let others with less strong political convictions do the actual fighting. It is not surprising that Tompkins took a violent dislike for the man. Smith did not refer to James F. Lewis in the remainder of his diary which was continued on October 2, 1861:

"Rain again today -- waked up by it at 4 o'clock this morning -- continued all day -- dull and dispiriting. It is probable the meadows will be again overflown, and we shall be troubled about provisions. I cannot see how we shall fight here to any purpose if half starved. Under the circumstances we certainly could not pursue the enemy if we ever defeated him. Deserters (I hear) have come into camp saying they were famishing in their camp.

"I am afraid continually that I shall never see the loved ones at home again. If we attack the enemy there will be terrible slaughter -- why should I again survive when so many are certain to be lost. It is my great trouble when about to go into action that my separation from all was so unexpected. How little we thought when I left the house on Monday morning that it was our last meeting for so long a

70 Childers, "Virginian's Dilemma", pg. 188

time, and very possibly forever. I dread an action on this account than any other. Floyd's troops have joined us here. Our large force cannot long remain inactive."[71]

Smith's fears are no different from any other soldier about to go into combat. All have mentioned regrets that they may leave sadness behind with their survivors poorly prepared emotionally for their loss. He has little actual fear of death while performing his duties, but he has severe regrets because of the unhappiness that his potential death would produce among those who love him. He worries that he did not prepare his new wife for his long absence during their confident, but short farewell that Monday morning. These thoughts are more difficult for a combat soldier to manage than the thought of dying in the fighting. Generally, a soldier who writes such passages in a diary or in a letter home is trying to say goodby -- possibly from the grave when a diary is delivered to relatives.

Smith did not have an opportunity to write in the diary again for three days. He began once again on October 5:

"Yesterday and the evening before was a busy and exciting period. We had received intimations that the enemy would attack the following morning (yesterday). I was greatly depressed for I am afraid of never meeting you all again, but was active and ready to do my duty as I believe hitherto on such occaisons I have faithfully performed. The battle when it comes, will be severe, and hotly contested. I feel pretty confident of the issue being favorable to us. We can hardly be whipped here. At quarter past three o'clock we were all up, and ready very shortly after to receive the enemy. Every moment we awaited the opening of the enemy's guns, and so continued until late in the day. At 12 o'clock I thought it more than probable no attack would be made during the day. You have no idea of the excitement such a state of things produces, but I have been so long accustomed to such things that the effect is nothing like it would be to the

71 Childers, "Virginian's Dilemma", pg. 188

inexperienced person. We looked for the enemy to-day but not so much as yesterday. A prisoner taken today says the enemy have 24000 men and more on the march, and will attack when all their forces arrive."[72]

Waiting for a battle to begin is the most difficult time for any soldier. That alone produces the excitement that Smith refers to in the diary. He also attempts to reassure his family that he will be doing his duty faithfully and is sufficiently experienced to be able to defend himself. He appears to try to let his inner feelings about the pending battle come through, but Smith must also reassure his family who will later receive this diary that even though he is concerned about his possible fate, he still will remain true to his duty as an officer.

Isaac Smith continued with more personal notes:

"We have been told here that Mr. Quarrier has been arrested and sent to Colombus. I have never believed it; have heard of Major Parks' and Goshorn's arrest, and today that Goshorn had been returned. Did not believe this, until informed they were sent to Wheeling not Colombus. The Major had Cox's safe-conduct and guarantee but the most outrageous baseness would permit to be violated."[73]

Mr. Quarrier was probably Isaac Smith's father-in-law. His wife was the former Caroline S. Quarrier, the daughter of Alexander and Caroline W. (Shrewsbury) Quarrier, one of Charleston's most prominent families.[74]

Isaac Smith didn't have the complete story regarding Major Parks' arrest and confinement at Wheeling. The "baseness" began when General Wise ordered the arrest of a prominent Unionist, Colonel Thomas A. Roberts. Wise had informed Richmond that "from the moment he entered

72 Childers, "Virginian's Dilemma", pg. 188-189

73 *Ibid*, pg. 189

74 Laidley, W.S., ***History of Charleston and Kanawha County, West Virginia and Representative Citizens***, Richmond-Arnold Publishing, Chicago, pg. 937

upon his mission that no snakes should lurk in the grass of the soil which he came to defend to sting him when his back is turned or when his head is up and at the enemy. Accordingly, many have been arrested and subjected to examination."[75]

Colonel Roberts had been commissioned a colonel of the Ohio militia and was a delegate to the Second Wheeling Convention when the loyal government of Virginia was organized. He returned from the convention to begin recruiting soldiers for the Union army and was arrested by the order of General Wise:

"Arrest, forthwith, all or every person who took part or supported that Wheeling convention; take them dead or alive and send them to Richmond, where we will bury the dead and hang the living."[76]

When the Union forces arrived in Charleston, one of their first acts was to arrest Major Andrew Parks, a former State senator, as a hostage for the safety of Colonel Roberts. Parks was sent to Wheeling and on October 19, 1861, loyal Virginia's governor, Francis H. Pierpont, wrote to Virginia's Confederate governor, John Letcher:

"Major Andrew Parks was arrested in Kanawha and brought a prisoner to Wheeling, Virginia, and is here now a prisoner. Parks was arrested for his complicity in the rebellion of the Southern States, and especially in Virginia. T.A. Roberts, Esq'r., of Roane County, who was a member of the Wheeling Convention, was arrested by Henry A. Wise on his expedition into the Kanawha Valley and sent to Richmond a prisoner. On the return of Roberts to his home in Roane County, Virginia, by the Confederate authorities at Richmond, Parks will be released. Otherwise, the same course will be pursued toward Major Parks by the authorities in Virginia that is taken toward Roberts by the

---

75 Stutler, Boyd B., "Annals of the Mountain State", *The West Virginia Review*, Vol. VII, No. 4, January, 1934, pg. 124

76 *Ibid*, pg. 108

authorities in Richmond."[77]

Smith certainly did not have the whole story of the summary arrest of Major Parks and may have more understanding if he had been able to put the two arrests into proper perspective.

Smith went on to discuss another family friend, Creed Parks, who had fallen ill during the campaign. Parks had also been a member of the Kanawha Riflemen since it was organized in 1858.

Smith wrote of Parks:

"Creed Parks has stood the whole campaign like a brave fellow as he is, until a few days since, when he has been obliged to go to Meadow Bluff on account of sickness. I think the hardship and exposure just after we came here has occasioned his illness. Tell Cousin Margaret that as soon as I learned of his illness, I did what I could for his comfort. Yesterday he was sent back, out of harm's way in case of an engagement, and where he could receive better attention and food, and is of course beyond my aid. If he gets worse, he will be sent to Lewisburg to the hospitals established there. Creed will probably get into some house, and be well attended at Meadow Bluff. Looking every moment for the enemy yesterday I could not go to see him before he left, but was told he had a place to which he could go. Creed was threatened with fever, and was not seriously sick when he left, but may so hereafter. He was growing better when sent away and may recover at once."[78]

The Sewell Mountain campaign produced many sick soldiers from the Confederate army and the hospitals were filled with them. The weather was the primary culprit and when combined with the unprepared state of the Rebel army and a set of recruits who came from rural areas where they had never been exposed to several diseases, epidemics developed. Measles and complications from this disease

77 Stutler, "Annals of the Mountain State", pg. 124

78 Childers, "Virginian's Dilemma", pg. 189

resulted in many casualties and other diseases took a similar toll among the young Rebel troops who had no natural immunities to the illnesses which were killing them.

Smith's cousin, Joab Smith, (the soldier who regretted being related to Uncle Ben while his company retreated through Charleston) had been sick with dysentery and on September 23 was sent White Sulphur Springs for a period of convalescence and was put in charge of a hospital ward. He made his last entry in his personal diary on October 10, 1861. He died shortly afterwards of the illness.[79] Isaac Smith may have not known that his cousin was in the Rebel army with him. There is no mention of Joab in Smith's diary.

Isaac Smith continued:

"These two armies will suffer terribly here when Sewell begins to show itself in its true light. At present the weather is delightful.

"Tomorrow is the Sabbath again, I lose all account of the week days about the middle of the week, but hunt up the day (by comparison with others) towards the end so as to know the Sabbath. We shall have no service unless Mr. Ruffner will come up and preach for us. He is on Little Sewell awaiting a battle, and will be here to aid in taking care of the wounded. O how I long to spend one more Sabbath at home -- to hear the old familar church bell, to meet my old friends in God's house in preparation for the duties of the day -- to sing the songs of praise with old familar voices and faces, to hear my my own kind pastor from our own sacred desk -- to enjoy the calm tranquility of a home Sabbath. Indeed to meet once more the loved ones at home and once more with them endeavor to devote to God the holy day he has set apart for his worship.

"I have just finished making a haversack -- cut it out, sewed it entirely myself and it is a good effort. Made it of a piece of torn linen. Am delighted with my success in this new business.

"Have just learned of an opportunity to send this and

---

79 Clark, "Journal of a Soldier of 1861", pg. 66

will now write a short letter to Callie with it. The opportunity comes at exactly the right time as the paper has given out."[80]

Here again, Smith opens up to his wife about his wishes to be home for the Sabbath -- especially the "calm tranquility" of being safe at home rather than face another day of potential violence on Sewell Mountain. At the same time, however, he attempts to reassure his family that he can take care of himself -- after all, he made a haversack entirely by himself and appears to be self-sufficient.

Major Smith didn't have an opportunity to write again until October 16. His military duties, manuevering, and lack of paper delayed additional entries into the diary until his regiment moved into camp near Richmond's Ferry on the south side of New River:

"When I last wrote my paper was used up. I believe the same evening I wrote the last sheet I was perfectly astounded to receive an order detailing me as Officer of the Day to fill up Col Read's tour who had gotten into some trouble and had to be taken off duty. This was the second time in one week, when I had supposed I should not be called upon for nearly a month. At one o'clock that night I set out alone to visit the pickets, mad and lonely, and found that one of the pickets, Capt John Quarrier's Co now commanded by Lieut Ray (Quarrier sick and gone to Richmond) had heard great rumblings of waggons etc. and had reported it. The other pickets had heard waggons but thought there was nothing unusual as they had heard them nearly every night. Went to all the pickets near the enemy and consulted the officers, none of them thought anything of the matter but Ray and Ray thought no great deal of it. I thought of going at once to report at headquarters, but concluded to consult Col Tompkins who thought it best to say or do nothing about it. I left orders with the picket to send me a messenger immediately if anything happened. I sat up a long time waiting for a messenger.

80 Childers, "Virginian's Dilemma", pg. 189

"The camp was really surprised next morning when daylight showed the opposite hill perfectly bare which had been filled with tents and moving men the day before. Col T regretted not having permitted me to report and said he would tell Genl Lee about it. The Genl afterwards said I should have advanced the pickets and felt the enemy -- just think if I had known that was the way to manage the matter I should have been the first man to occupy the enemy's camp, but live and learn -- if I had known better how to manage these things we should have had an exciting time that night."[81]

The Confederates missed a great opportunity during the night of October 6 as the Union troops under the command of General Rosecrans withdrew from their fortified positions on Sewell Mountain under the cover of darkness. Rosecrans used the exact tactic that Floyd employed during his retreat from Carnifex Ferry earlier that fall. The quiet movement of the Federal army in the night enabled Rosecrans to extract his troops from a difficult situation. Smith probably recalled his own anxiety during the prolonged rearguard manuever from Carnifex Ferry and was aware of how vulnerable the Union army was as it stretched out along the mountain road leading to Gauley Bridge. It was a lost opportunity -- an attack on the Federal army while it was in disarray would have resulted in a major Confederate victory. Better timing for a victory would have been difficult to arrange. The Union had just been seriously defeated at Bull Run and a Confederate victory on Sewell Mountain could have been disasterous for the National government's efforts to win the war. Rosecrans' problem with supply delivery -- an over-extended line of communications -- and sickness among his troops facing a numerically superior Confederate army were major factors which induced him to withdraw his entire force to the Gauley Bridge and Hawks Nest region. This move shortened considerably his supply lines and if Lee chose to advance his forces, Confederate

81 Childers, "Virginian's Dilemma", pg. 189-190

supply problems would increase with every mile.

Lee was now presented with an opportunity to move his troops forward into the upper Kanawha Valley in an attempt to force the Federal army to withdraw into Ohio. His large force was soon divided into two manuevering elements and his plan of attack was carefully planned.

General Floyd's brigade and attached regiments -- a force which included portions of Russell's Mississippi Regiment, Phillips' Legion, the Fourteenth Georgia, and the Fifty-first, Forty-fifth, Thirty-sixth, and Twenty-second Virginia Regiments as well as 55 cavalry. Floyd's force totalled about 4000 men and they crossed the New River on October 16.[82]

Lee had planned to send General Loring's regiments down the James River and Kanawha Turnpike in a move to support General Floyd as both elements manuevered against the Union forces on Gauley Mountain and at Gauley Bridge. The total plan was disrupted when Lee was forced to divert Loring's troops from the valley campaign to protect the vital railroads at Staunton, Virginia.[83]

Floyd was permitted to continue along the southern side of New River without support on the northern side. The river was in flood and the high water afforded some protection against a Federal attack. Floyd moved his force past the small town of Fayetteville and on to positions on the slopes of Cotton Hill where Isaac Smith finally found time, paper, and composure to continue his diary after a break in writing of eleven days. He began recording events at the new Confederate camp on Cotton Hill on October 27:

"Don't recollect what stopped my writing before but will continue now. Supposedly hunger had driven the enemy away. Our whole force remained here a number of days longer. Floyd was busy in getting up a scheme to enter Kanawha Valley. At last we received orders to march on Friday I think (October 11th) by Richmond's Ferry. No information was given whether we were to cross New River

82 White, "West Virginia", pg. 45

83 Ambler, "Lee's Northwest Virginia Campaign", pg. 112

or not or what our destination was. I ought to say that in the meantime I had been again detailed as Officer of the Day but this time went to headquarters and demanded a change which was readily made. We set out on Friday, marched slowly along through a rich and finely rolling hill country along the Sewell ridge. The land is positively excellent and nearly level -- Travelled about eight miles, stopped away down in the valley of a New River creek. It rained considerably and we had an unpleasant night. Next day marched about ten miles and stopped on Lick Creek (see it on the map). Camped here Saturday night -- next day (Sunday) each regiment was ordered to send fifty men and two field officers to work on the road. Our regiment has but one and of course I had to go and was off at six o'clock, and actually worked hard until about 2 1/2 PM this evening. How often I thought of the dear ones at home, and the surprise all would feel if they knew how I was engaged, but it was my duty and unpleasant as it was I obeyed orders. The next day we marched to the Ferry our Regt in advance, the road was barely wide enough for one waggon and where the road led down to New River,steep precipices were on the lower side -- a misstep might have been fatal -- the romance of the place is charming -- to my surprise found New River here a broad stream as wide as our loved Kanawha flowing smoothly along its channel. Have an idea this is the place Uncle Bill and Aunt Ellen crossed at, though possibly it may have been at Pade's Ferry higher up. We were occuppied the larger part of the day crossing our troops and train but reached a point about 3 miles from the ferry on the South Side at which Camp I commenced this sheet. We were here some time waiting the crossing of the other troops. Thursday morning Oct 10th marched under orders for the turnpike some ten or twelve miles distant. Moved very slowly, the road being dreadfully cut up by the trains which preceded us and very indifferent originally. About three o'clock went down a big hill into a gloomy laurel hollow and found about 3 or 4 pieces of artillery with as many caissons and some 15 ordinance and baggage waggons closely packed in the same hollow and utterly unable to get up the terrible hill which led out of it. We had neither room nor authority to pass and in the midst of rain which now set in awaited the movements of those before us. Col Tompkins had gone on ahead to select our camp ground on the turnpike 5 miles further on. After about two hours I ordered the men to pitch their tents upon the slippery hillside and we remained there all night. Awoke for an early start next morning but the waggons and guns were still there. Sent forward men to work the road around them and to help them up and finally about 3 o'clock in the evening set out ourselves. We had to help the other waggons before us and actually only marched about a mile and a half to the top of the hill. Col T met us on the way up and left us for Lewisburg to meet Mrs. Tompkins whom he had just learned was at that place. I was therefore in command of the regiment and dreaded the responsibility. Plus rode forward in great haste to tell Col Tompkins the news about his wife and the Col frequently alludes to it, says he will never forget Plus for his kindness."[84]

Tompkins' wife, Ellen, and his family had remained on the family farm on the mountain overlooking Gauley Bridge when it was occupied by Union troops as the Confederates in Wise's Legion withdrew from the area. She and the family had been cared for by General Cox who had assumed responsibility for their safety after receiving a letter requesting assistance was sent to the Union commander by Colonel Tompkins. After several months of separation. Ellen and Christopher Tompkins were to meet in Lewisburg. She had been allowed to travel to Richmond on her "parole of honor" from General Rosecrans in order to purchase winter clothing.

Isaac Smith was now the commander of the 22nd Virginia Infantry Regiment while Tompkins was on leave in Richmond with his wife. Smith would now have to deal directly with the "political general" he disliked so much. He began to record some of the mismanagement he

84 Childers, "Virginian's Dilemma", pg. 190-191

observed in his diary:

"Next morning, Saturday, marched from the turnpike expecting to go about four or five miles, camp in a pleasant place with the troops ahead and await the arrival of those yet behind. Up to this time we knew nothing definite as to our destination. When about one mile from the turnpike Capt Jackson came up, said Genl Floyd had ordered all the troops forward and our regiment must join him as early as possible. Under this order I pushed the men and jaded teams along wretched roads to a point one mile east of Raleigh Court House in all about seventeen miles and the teams very poorly fed before starting. Reported for orders and was told to keep my camp -- found the other troops had orders to march at six o'clock next morning (Sunday) with two days rations cooked -- was much surprised at our being left to rest. At about 9 1/2 next morning Floyd rode up, sent Plus to him for orders and he said we must move forward at once. In a half hour we were in motion, and that day we marched sixteen miles having nearly caught up with the troops who started 3 or 4 hours before us. All of this haste was because Floyd had heard the enemy were at Fayette Court House. The men were thoroughly worn out, never saw them so used up. They could scarcely stand up long enough to receive orders for the night. Floyd camped about 150 yards from us across the creek and yet the order to cook provisions and march did not reach me until 11 o'clock that night. I determined not to awaken the poor fellows and did not, but had them up early the next morning. Could not possibly get off at the hour and could not get the cooked rations ordered the night before. Next morning learned the enemy were not on this side of the river and Floyd told me when I asked for a delay of an hour in my march that I must start at once and come on leisurly as the present state of things did not require the haste he had intended. The men declared it was impossible for them to march any distance and some thought they would not be able to move at all. We expected that all the troops would camp two miles east of Fayette Court House.

"I went along leisurly with the men and about a mile this side of Fayette Court House found all the waggons of all the troops stopped and learned that the troops had marched forward. This of course indicated an expected engagement. I inquired of everyone for any orders left for me, could get none and could not even get information except that the troops were ahead. They had provisions cooked. We had none, but I soon determined my course, left the waggons behind with the cooks and ordered provisions to be cooked and sent forward to the men. Told the men that the enemy were probably ahead and we must rush forward to be in the battle. Moved off and directly after met John Carr with orders from Col McCausland to bring up the men quickly and Carr said the Col had put his men to the double quick. Rode up and down the line to encourage the men. Cheered them up and got them off again at a quick trot and with a cheer. I was astonished that the poor wearied men could move so readily and rapidly. We went on farther and farther and about two miles this side of the Court House I halted and made them load. Finally about 4 or 5 miles from Fayette C H whilst I was encouraging the men forward expecting every moment to lead them into action I was mortified and astonished to have Col McCausland ride up and without a word to me, commenced giving commands to the regiment, actually assuming the command. In a short time I mentioned the subject to him and said I presumed he took command as the senior officer of the Brigade. The 22nd and 36th regiments have been brigaded and placed under the command of Col Tompkins and of course when Col Tompkins was absent Col McCausland would command the brigade. Col Mc said he did not act in that capacity, but Genl Floyd had sent him to aid me (of course I understood that). This depressed me greatly for I saw that it was an insult I should be obliged to notice. McCausland of course was bound to obey, but the order was so utterly contrary to all decency or usage or propriety and Floyd cared for none of these things. The men and officers under my sole command had acted well: had given me no trouble had obeyed my commands with readiness and deference in spite of the fact that I had pushed them most severely and had been obliged several times to speak more harshly to all of them than ever before. I had brought them forward with alacrity and enthusiasm and I am satisfied they would have followed me into battle with full confidence and reliance and just as we were nearing the point of danger another man is ordered to assume command over my troops and I am marched through the two or three regiments ahead of us with a stranger, my superior, in command."[85]

It is probable that Smith and the 22nd Virginia were caught up in the dislike between Floyd and Colonel Tompkins. Tompkins was a well-trained and experienced officer, obviously respected by his superiors in the War Department in Richmond. Tompkins would have a great deal of protection from the type of harassment that Smith was undergoing in his absence. The vindictive Floyd had no opportunity to attack Tompkins, but took advantage of the Colonel's absence to vent his bitterness on Tompkins' friend and subordinate, Isaac Smith. This was the reason Smith dreaded taking command while Tompkins was on leave with his wife. Smith was aware of the bad feelings between his Colonel and Floyd. He had written in a previous diary entry:

"Floyd does not like Col T because he knows that Col T despises his character as a man and has no respect for his qualifications as a soldier, and it would suit Floyd's view to leave Tompkins to bear all the blame which might attach to any mishap..." [86]

If Floyd was unable to get even with Tompkins while the West Point graduate was present, he certainly was wasting no time in the attempt to discredit Tompkins by creating confusion regarding the combat effectiveness of the 22nd Virginia and the ability of its acting commander,

85 Childers, "Virginian's Dilemma", pg. 191-192
86 *Ibid*, pg. 180

Isaac Smith. After being relieved and riding past the other Confederate officers with McCausland (of whom Smith had previously written was "a sort of favorite of Floyd's" ) in command of his regiment which was obviously an insult which had to be "noticed" by Smith, but the continuing harassment of both the Major and the 22nd Virginia Infantry Regiment didn't stop after McCausland took charge. He obviously had been ordered to teach them a lesson in discipline. Smith wrote about the remainder of the march:

"We hurried on, and strange to tell my poor wearied men without food or a moment's halt are pushed forward past men who had been well rested and had food with them and were marched on, without stopping to within about 1 1/4 miles of Kanawha River at a house on Fall's Creek, and about seven miles in advance of the other forces. We halted here, the enemy picket was at the turnpike on this side and their tents whitening every level spot on the other side of New River.

"One hundred of this little band was sent on still farther as a picket with orders to push up as close to the enemy as possible. Our ranks of course were greatly thinned by many causes. We were out of the way of the relief seven miles behind. A cold rain had set in, the pickets were not allowed fires and they were to follow a road every turn of which might disclose an armed foe and if possible get sight of the river that night. I was opposed to the position, but McCausland had command. The top of the mountain was a strong place and there I would have stopped if in command. When we did stop we were in a trap. The main body had marched 21 miles that day, the picket had advanced about a mile further on the most dangerous duty in the service.

"You can imagine the anxiety with which the night was passed, every moment we were expecting to hear the guns which would indicate our pickets had met. Early next morning (daylight) Col Mc and I went to visit the picket. Col Mc thought it had not advanced far enough and we undertook to push it farther. We moved down beyond our outside man, not knowing but that every turn of the road would bring a volley upon us and then planted the picket much nearer than it was before. This morning provisions came at last the first the men had eaten in more than 24 hours. Every day seemed to convince me that our position was most wretchedly chosen for our main body -- and it was a subject of earnest consultation between some of the Captains and myself and my views were pretty well known to Col Mc. The enemy seemed to know nothing about us and we actually pushed the picket almost to the last turn where the road turns down to the turnpike. On one morning I went to our outpost man, climbed a tree and thought I could plainly discern a sentinel about 150 yards off at the turnpike with his gun in his hand.

"During our stay here in examining our position Col Mc, Capt Sam Miller, and myself and two others went along the ridge leading to Cotton Hill and looked down upon the enemy at Stockton's and Gauley and above all else could see the old Kanawha river and see it dashing along away down below. How my heart leaped to think how near the loved ones were and yet how far away. I looked on the noble stream and sent my h_ _ _."[87]

Major Smith and the 22nd Virginia had into their positions in what was to become the battle of Cotton Hill. They had moved directly above the turnpike crossing at Montgomery's Ferry located approximately one-half mile downstream from the falls on the Kanawha River. The other regiments assigned to Floyd's small command were to the rear of the 22nd Virginia and remained on top of the ridge across the river from Gauley Bridge.

The Federal garrison in the area under the command of General Rosecrans were in camps on the opposite side of the rain- swollen New and Kanawha Rivers and "their tents whiting every level spot". Union camps were located at the falls, at Stockton's Inn near the falls, at Gauley Bridge, and at Colonel Tompkins' farm on Gauley Mountain. Additional Federal regiments were positioned upstream on

---

87 Childers, "Virginian's Dilemma", pg. 192-193

New River and small detachments guarded the Miller's Ferry crossing to Fayette Court House and guards were posted farther upstream on New River at Townsend's Ferry.

Confederate cannon were placed on the crest of Cotton Hill and the Rebels began firing on the numerous Federal camps near Gauley Bridge and at the falls. A Confederate soldier briefly described the action:

"About October 27 Rosecrans learned that Floyd was advancing from Raleigh towards Cotton Hill. On the 29th Floyd drove some Federal outposts down near to the mouth of Great Falls Creek, and on November 1 he occupied Cotton Hill. By means of artillery he made it impossible in the day time for ferry boats to run at the mouth of Gauley or wagons to pass along the road. Floyd claims to have destroyed the ferry boat. This state of affairs with constant skirmishing continued for some time. Floyd says three weeks, but his own account makes it not more than ten days. The cause of Rosecrans' failure to dislodge Floyd earlier has been explained, but as soon as he learned that there was no danger of a Confederate advance from the direction of Lewisburg, he took steps to end the situation. Already on November 4 he had posted Brigadier-General H.W. Benham (first honor West Point graduate of 1837) with 3000 men opposite the mouth of lower Loup Creek to prevent Floyd from getting in his rear if he were attacked by Loring. Now that this danger no longer existed, he formed a plan by which he hoped and reasonably expected to capture or disperse Floyd's entire force. Brigadier R.C.Schenck was posted with an adequate force far enough up New River for him to get in Floyd's rear, and complete preparations were made for rapidly crossing, while Benham, also well prepared for crossing the Kanawha, was to press the Confederates in front. Fortunately for Floyd, just as this plan was to be put in operation, New River rose to such a height that it was impossible for Schenck to cross ... The plan was then changed, and Benham was to cross the smoother Kanawha and pass around to his right around to the rear of Floyd and Schenck was to come down, cross at the same place, and press him in front ... On November 10, under the supervision of General Cox, Colonel C.A. DeVilliers and Lieutenant-Colonel D.A. Enyart crossed the river, each with 200 men, and somehow caused the Confederate artillery to withdraw... He [Floyd] fell back before this small force, was re-inforced by 6 companies after dark, and skirmishing continued until midnight, the Federals having gained possession of the mountain as far as Blake's farm. On the 11th at day-break the advance was resumed, the Confederates skirmishing as they retired, but making no determined stand. When the Federals reached the edge of Cotton Hill proper, Floyd's wagon-train was seen moving on the road towards Fayetteville."[88]

Active skirmishing continued between the two contending forces, but the clever General Cox halted his advance before the Confederates were able to determine exactly the size of the units doing the attacking. Floyd's greatest concern, however, was the possibility that Benham's large Union force would be able to get into his rear and cut off his line of retreat. The Confederate attempt to attack the Union camps and supply line along the James River and Kanawha Turnpike had been relatively unsuccessful and a disenchanted Major Smith recorded much of the campaign in his diary. He began writing again on November 9, 1861, after a two week pause in writing:

"Many misfortunes have befallen me since I last wrote here. Something stopped me suddenly, I know not what at this time.

"I have felt unwilling to continue this little history, as it involves so much if my unhappiness and trials, and nothing but utter want of employment now permits me to write. Without employment my thoughts are painful. But I will hurry over these events."[89]

Smith's problems with General Floyd were increasing

---

88 Humphries, *Military Operations in Fayette County*, pg. 8-9

89 Childers, "Virginian's Dilemma", pg. 193

in intensity. This conflict, combined with the difficulty of leading the 22nd Virginia while being closely observed and monitored by Colonel McCausland combined with the strong likelihood that serious combat was imminent had begun to weigh down the young Major. He went on:

"On Thursday (I think) just after dinner, we were all sitting quietly in Huddleston's house, the men lounging about outside and in without their guns. So long a time had elapsed during our stay at this dangerous place, without anything of moment occurring, that we all felt much more secure; true the picket had fired twice on Yankees who had sauntered up the road, but the Yanks seemed to pay no attention to our presence here. That morning two men had been fired on, in a most shameful manner, and suffered to escape after they had surrendered themselves, but it had occurred early in the morning and no notice was taken of it.

"Suddenly the rattling crash of musketry was heard all around us, and the greatest uproar and confusion prevailed. Men were crowding in the house, others rushing out all confused and (I may well say as to many of them) terrified. I was upstairs, and seizing my sword and pistol, rushed out, to make my way down; the narrow staircase was a perfect jam, men rushing up with and after their guns, and others seeking to get out. I found it impossible to get out. An effort to do so would have impaled me upon the bayonets, which were bristling above the heads of the men. I stood at the head of the stairs urging the men to get their guns and clear the house. Finally forced my way through the mass and rushed out into the road. To my surprise and mortification, the men were flying in every direction. I had no idea where the enemy was, supposed they occupied the hills on both sides of the hollow, and had surrounded us - Couldn't see the enemy though. They were firing continually, and some of our men were firing back. A few brave fellows had taken their station (Mr. Quarrier prominent among them) under the bank in front of the house. Found out pretty soon that the enemy were only at the hill in front of the house, and immediately ordered these brave fellows to fall back that we might occupy the hill on the other side. They fell back and we found a stone fence would fill our purpose better and halted there. Just then for the first time, I saw the enemy though I had been exposed to their fire for some time, and immediately jumped on the stone wall and called upon the men to follow me, and charge up the hill upon them. I stood urging the men for some seconds before any of them came. Young Reynolds says whilst standing there he saw a minnie ball strike right at my feet which dashed the dirt into his eyes as he came up to me - The boys came up following me, and the enemy who had begun to run were soon out of sight. I sent two large parties out to intercept them, but they escaped. Their trace where they crossed the hill on their return was bloody, showing they had wounded men along. They left one fellow dead in the field shot in the center of the forehead, and one mortally wounded through the body. We had one man shot slightly through the foot and another scratched in the hand. The house had a number of bullets through it. I felt great pity for the poor wounded man, he was in great agony - about 20 and fine-looking, fair skin, dark hair, and intelligent face. I talked to him kindly - he said he would soon die.

"The enemy had crossed the hill behind our pickets, and thus surprised us. I had expected them to surprise us in some such way for it was impossible for us to guard against it."[90]

The 22nd Virginia had let its guard down that day. Their pickets had previously been probed by the Federal troops and the two Union escapees had obviously informed their commander of the location of the Confederate regiment's main body. Given the circumstances of the enemy situation and their probable knowledge of the Rebel situation, Smith or McCausland should have been more alert for an attack. Major Smith was fortunate that only a small Union force crossed the hill to fire into Huddleston's house. If the Federal commander had moved in a full

---

90 Childers, "Virginian's Dilemma", pg. 193-194

regiment, it is probable that the diary would never have been finished. The shock of coming under fire so suddenly apparently terrified most of the volunteers and a major Union assault at that time would have taken the 22nd Virginia off of the Confederate army's rolls for the remainder of the war.

Smith went on to explain the closing events of the small fight:

"McCausland who had not been with us since the night before soon came up, and to my gratification gave it as his opinion that we ought to leave immediately and go to the top of the hill. I told him my opinion had always been that the top was the only proper place for us, and we drew in our pickets, and moved off at once. I went up the hollow and made provision for having the wounded man taken care of, and the dead man buried -- fixed both in the best way we could -- The poor fellow died about midnight as I since know.

"On the hill we were without tents, and but little fire and bitter cold."[91]

Colonel John McCausland -- acting under the orders of General Floyd to assist Smith during Tompkins' absence -- had probably pushed the 22nd too far down the mountain toward the river. They were also too far forward -- about 7 miles -- from any potential reinforcements if they should come under any serious attack. McCausland was commander of the 36th Virginia, also a Kanawha Valley regiment, and he probably had little love for the 22nd which was commanded by his superior officer, Colonel Tompkins. McCausland was apparently a "favorite" of Floyd's and he had probably decided to give the rival regiment a rough time. He had little fear of combat, but knew that the small Confederate force couldn't afford to lose a full regiment and when his error of placing the 22nd too far forward became apparent he agreed that a strategic withdrawal to the top of the mountain was in the best

91 Childers, "Virginian's Dilemma", pg. 194

interests of everyone. The possibly demoralized 22nd had another difficult bivouac "without tents, and but little fire and bitter cold." Smith's commander and friend, Colonel Tompkins, returned from leave the following day:

"On Friday Col Tompkins came at last, and brought me Pa's letter with Maj Park's papers, and Ma's excellent letter. I read with much concern. Col Tompkins had heard how I was treated, and was very much vexed -- he knew that I intended to resign in consequence, and I told him so again, he thought no other course possible or admissible. I had only waited for his return in order to resign. That night we heard of Clarkson's return from a trip down the Kanawha, and Plus whispered me that the captured poll books had Pa's name as a candidate. I need not say how this intelligence grieved me -- his friends all said they were satisfied he had not authorized it and said so I fondly hoped. I saw too that this fact was to have an unfortunate influence upon my resignation. That night I was very sad. Next day my resignation was handed in. Sunday passed and I heard nothing, but that Gen. Floyd had forwarded it to the Department for acceptance without comment, which insures prompt acceptance. Next day Monday I applied for the usual leave of absence granted on such occasions and on Tuesday received an order giving me leave. This I supposed happily ended the matter. I was forced however to remain several days to settle up my affairs. I had just paid 200 dollars for a horse, now useless to me, had just received a saddle and bridle for which I paid 60 dollars about two months before, had a uniform on the way for which I had paid 85 dollars at the same time and another military saddle for which I paid 35 dollars. I remained here to sell these articles. On Thursday Ben Turner and John Noyes arrived, and I heard the startling intelligence that Pa was actually and fully identified with the Pierpont government. Those with whom I was connected call and curse him as a traitor, and he knew it would surely be so. Why my dear father had chosen to place me in this terrible situation is beyond my comprehension. I have been shocked beyond description in contemplating the awful consequences to the peace safety and happiness of both of us. I cannot write all that crowds upon my mind in this connection. It is all terrible."[92]

Clarkson, Ben Turner, and John Noyes had all been members of the Kanawha Riflemen since 1858 and had served since that time with Isaac Smith. They had returned to duty at Cotton Hill after apparently slipping quietly down the Kanawha Valley -- probably to Union-held Charleston -- and they brought back the news that Smith's father, a prominent Unionist, was involved with the pro-Union Pierpont administration and was "fully identified with the new state movement."[93]

This became a very difficult time for Isaac Smith. At the very time he was attempting to resign his commission for Confederate service, the news that his father was not only an active Unionist, but was working with the Pierpont government to split western Virginia from the original state to form a new, Unionist state. This was enough to cloud his original motivation for resigning with many of his peers and perhaps his loyalty was questioned along with his father's. Unfortunately for Smith, worse was still to come. He continued:

"On that morning Wm Quarrier who had also just reached here told me that General Davis at Headquarters would buy my horse. I immediately rode up there. Whilst there the Adjutant handed me an order revoking my furlough, and ordering me to rejoin my regiment. I was astonished. Went to Floyd for explanation. At first he endeavored to put me off with an unjust insinuation about my resigning in the presence of the enemy and when an engagement was expected, knowing as he well did that it was the gross insult he had put upon me, and my regiment, that forced me to resign, and that I had awaited Col Tompkins return, under great exposure to danger, and

92 Childers, "Virginian's Dilemma", pg. 194-195

93 Cox, *Military Reminiscences*, pg. 156

experiencing the only fighting we have had here where there was a danger, before I had offered to resign."[94]

Apparently Smith had decided to resign the proper way -- by waiting for the return of Colonel Tompkins in order to hand over the responsibility for the regiment to him. His loyalty to Colonel Tompkins and to the men he commanded required that he delay his departure until the regiment could be properly handed over. After the resignation was submitted and the furlough was approved, the unheard of happened -- his leave was revoked by Floyd. This was simply harassment, but Smith was helpless when the General applied his power. Smith's difficulty with Floyd over the issue of the resignation was just beginning. He wrote further:

"I insisted on more explicitness, then began a conversation in which was evinced the coarsest brutality, the most outrageous tyranny, injustice and meaness. He grew excited and angry, used his position and rank to treat me with the coarsest severity, knowing that I could not resist. He declared that my father was engaged in an effort to defeat the great cause in which his army (and I was a member of it) was struggling and had made himself a traitor, and that he intended I should remain in the Confederate army as long as he could possibly keep me there, that I should stand in the front of battle, and meet my father face to face -- that he would immediately write to the department not to accept my resignation, and keep me here. This and much more was said in a most brutal and unfeeling manner, and here I am held as sort of hostage or prisoner, yet pretending to command a regiment. I could write pages on this affair, for I have suffered most intensly under it -- but I have just learned that an opportunity of sending my letters can be had today, and I must hasten. Here I have remained since that day, perfectly miserable. I am hoping for deliverance in a day or two, but fear it will not come. Col Tompkins insisted I should have a Court of

94 Childers, "Virginian's Dilemma", pg. 195

Inquiry, but that involves a six or twelve months task in attending to it. I have been expecting ever since to be ordered on dangerous service, for the malignity of the man who could take pleasure in keeping father and son in open hostility is ready for anything."[95]

John B. Floyd wasn't the sort of man anyone would want to get angry. He didn't forgive and once he had made up his mind, it was too late to save the victim. Smith already had two serious shortcomings in the eyes of the bitter general: he was a close and loyal friend of Christopher Tompkins and he was an officer in Tompkins' regiment, the 22nd Virginia. When the final evidence of the pro-Union activities of Smith's father began to be whispered in the camp, poor Isaac came to the attention of the general.

Floyd was the type of commander every officer dreads to serve under: a harsh, demanding, and incompetent general who took great pleasure in pointing out the shortcomings of others. In this case, Smith was to be punished for the political affiliation of his father and for the simultaneous poor timing of his resignation from the Confederate army, but the real target of Floyd's wrath was Tompkins -- the military professional who was untouchable.

Tompkins encouraged Smith to demand a review of the affair by a military court which would decide the correctness of Floyd's reasoning in this case. Perhaps this was an attempt by Tompkins to get back at his regiment's tormentor, someone he had "no respect for as a man", but this was more likely the professional soldier advising an amateur how to rely on the military system to ensure that justice was done. By this time, of course, Smith didn't want to remain under Floyd for 6-12 months for the court to convene and arrive at a decision. He simply wanted to get out of a very difficult personal and professional situation by resigning from the army.

Smith continued to explain the sequence of events on

95 Childers, "Virginian's Dilemma", pg. 195

Cotton Hill:

"Our regiment remained on the mountain until ordered out after a party of Yankees, who appeared within our lines and we marched 11 or 12 miles in rain and cold over the roughest hills, brush, rocks and cliffs -- were lost -- staid all night on top of a high hill, could get no farther, were hungry and cold and without shelter -- and reached our comfortless camp about 11 o'clock next day, more than 24 hours without food. We are now camped in the hollow, but the men have their arduous duty to perform on the hills.

"On Wednesday last Col Tompkins asked for leave of absence to make arrangements for his family in Richmond -- his means had been lost to him by the war, and he needed to make some provisions to provide their necessities. This leave was refused him, and he resigned and has gone, leaving my condition much more hopeless and miserable than before. I, a prisoner commanding men who were commanded by so excellent a Colonel, and the men placed in circumstances making the command infinitely more difficult."[96]

Tompkins' family were located on a mountain across the valley from the Confederate position on Cotton Hill. The family farm was now a Union camp and the family, while protected by General Rosecrans and General Cox, was in a hazardous position.Once released by the Federals, primarily General Rosecrans, Ellen Tompkins and her children made their way to Richmond where they were joined by Colonel Tompkins after he resigned. His long-standing problems with General Floyd and two additional key events lead to his decision to resign. First, the difficulty that Isaac Smith was stoically enduring from his tormentor and the constant ungentlemanly harassment and second, the constant misuse of Tompkins' regiment, the 22nd Virginia, was certainly enough to cause anyone to resign. The final problem came when Floyd ordered cannons fired at the Union camp at

96 Childers, "Virginian's Dilemma", pg. 195-196

Tompkins' farm -- while the family was still in the house.[97]

Tompkins resigned immediately and left the Confederate camp at Cotton Hill without waiting for the formality of having the resignation being approved by the Confederate War Department. He was an officer with a known reputation who knew his version of events would be heard, if there was ever to be a court of inquiry regarding his sudden departure. Smith, a former militia officer, did not have the reputation which would have insulated him from charges of desertion that would have been lodged against him by Floyd if he had tried to do the same. Smith had no choice except to remain in service and endure the worst abuse that Floyd could aim at him.

Isaac Smith continued the diary entry with a final paragraph designed to ensure that his family would keep the information he provided confidential. Even though he had decided that his personal circumstances required that he leave the Confederate army, he did not want to harm the cause for which he had fought with the men of his regiment. This did little actual good since the diary was later captured by Cox's troops and carefully read by the Federals.

The paragraph was similar to a legal document that Smith was so familar with:

"I shall close for the present. I demand that nothing written here shall be read outside the family and that any statements here about the army shall be kept strictly secret, though I have endeavored throughout to avoid mentioning any facts which would be at all prejudicial to the interests of the Confederate States. I am aiming to give a sort of personal narrative of what has befallen me in this campaign more than a history of the war."[98]

Smith, the civilian attorney, was beginning to take few

97 Tompkins, Ellen W., "The Colonel's Lady", *The Virginia Magazine of History and Biography*, Vol. 69, No. 4, October, 1961, pg. 419

98 Childers, "Virginian's Dilemma", pg. 196

chances. He was faced with an enemy more dangerous than the Union army across New River -- the general -- and he realized that he could be charged with spying because of the diary. If General Floyd was to gain possession of his notes, a case could be made that the resignation was simply an excuse to leave the service to deliver the notes on the army to his Unionist father. This entry would give Smith some protection and the well-known fact that many of the soldiers were also keeping journals on the war would make it difficult for Floyd to bring up the charges. Isaac Smith was in a very dangerous position with a personal enemy who could probably convene a field court martial for espionage and execute him without appeal, if he chose to make the attempt. Smith was wise to take no chances with this extremely dangerous and possibly deranged man.

Misfortune had accompanied Smith through most of his military service, but he did not lose his loyalty to the cause which he served. He was sufficiently intelligent to be able to understand that all of his problems could be traced to a single personality, General John B. Floyd, not an idea -- a second American Revolution. He knew that there was a great deal of useful information in the notes he kept that could be valuable to the Union government which his father served willingly. His final paragraph would also ensure that the father, also an attorney, would respect his wishes and keep the diary confidential.

Smith was now the commander of a regiment in Floyd's small army and they were facing a large Union army which was soon to take the offensive. The regiment was so recently lead by "so excellent a Colonel", Tompkins, and the responsibility was great for anyone. Smith was burdened with the constant threat of Floyd's retribution hanging over his head as he tried to lead the regiment, but he was soon to receive good news. He wrote about it on Saturday, November 16:

"We moved on about two miles where all of the troops were camped. Sunday (a happy day for me) late in the afternoon Col Jackson came from Headquarters, and handed me a paper. I opened it supposing it was some order relative to the troops generally and read (and with what delight) the order from the Secy of War accepting my resignation. I immediately began to fix up, and Monday morning at about 9 o'clock bid farewell to the 22nd and as I hope to military life forever. I was determined to let no delay give an opportunity to Floyd for further persecution. Came to Pack's Ferry in Monroe County that night (that I am sure is the place where Uncle Bill and Aunt Ellen travelled) -- from thence I came last night to this place where I happened to see old Mr. Henderson of Pt Pleasant. He told me I could get lodging at this house, and I am now comfortably fixed by a great fire writing to the loved ones at home. This morning the rain was falling fast and I had some of the most utterly filthy (no other word will suit) clothes to have washed, I determined to remain here a day more especially as I have no particular purpose or destination in view. At Mr. Pack's house I ate under a roof and slept in a bed for the first time since the middle of August, when we left the White Sulphur. The luxury of these two things is perfectly tremendous and overpowering. And now how can I be sufficiently grateful to the Merciful God, who has brought me thus far in perfect safety and health through so many dangerous hardships and trials. May God give me grace to praise him for his mercies, and trust him for deliverance from all troubles."[99]

The newly discharged Major remained at Mr. Pack's home for two days before travelling on to Centreville, also in Monroe County, before continuing with his "personal narrative of what has befallen me in this campaign." The diary entries began once again on November 20, 1861:

"Free at last I hope -- restored to civilization once more. Out of the army and comfortably housed and fed. You can scarcely conceive the intense relief and enjoyment of my freedom. Not a soldier within 20 miles of me and the army forty miles away. Unless I am persecuted by Floyd's

[99] Childers, "Virginian's Dilemma", pg. 198-199

malignity upon false pretenses and without a shadow of right of law -- I am again a white man."[100]

Smith was out of the army and could now escape from Floyd. He went on to explain how he had carefully arranged for his resignation to be accepted by the authorities in Richmond and he continued the story of the fighting on Cotton Hill:

"The day that Floyd revoked my furlough I made arrangements to send William Quarrier to Richmond to secure the acceptance of my resignation. He and Miller and myself fully agreed that was the better course -- The next morning Nov 1st he left. I remained in command of the regiment nothing of moment occurring until Sunday Nov 10th when Col Wm. A. Jackson of Charleston of the Jenny Lind mansion back street was assigned to the command of the regiment. This relieved me very much of all the responsibility and annoyance was shifted to his shoulders. Poor man he had nothing in the world -- not a blanket, no towel, soap, or any of the indispensibles of camp life. I shared my scanty stock with him. That night at about one o'clock he received orders to have everything ready for a movement at daylight next morning. Were ready accordingly and after some time were ordered to march to the rear -- went about one mile back and were drawn up in order of battle to await an attack of the enemy (if any was made) whilst the guns on Cotton Hill which had been playing Hot Ball across the river for about a week could be extricated. These guns had been placed in position with great difficulty and had to be watched continually by 300 to 500 men exposed to every hardship and had been firing away thousands of dollars worth of ammunition and so far as I knew or heard never struck anything or did any one any harm. The guns were finally extricated (and the enemy deserves to be sneered at for permitting it) and we moved on about 3 or 4 miles and encamped at what was said to be a very strong position. We had just fairly gotten our tents

100 Childers, "Virginian's Dilemma", pg. 196

pitched when the enemy began to throw shells into our camp from the opposite cliff of New River. It rather struck some of the army that under such circumstances the position was not so terribly strong after all. However we put up breastworks working after night and next day some men were sent down to feel the enemy and we were kept at the breastworks. At about eleven o'clock AM the enemy began to shell us again and they shot very handsomely too -- Their range was exact upon the camp of the 22nd and 36th -- we could not get our waggons and horses in any position to keep out of harm's way. One shell fell under a wagon but did not burst -- a large piece of an exploded shell fell about 20 steps from our tent where we were at dinner and about 5 or 6 steps from our wagon and horses. The firing was not kept up by the enemy or they could have damaged us greatly."[101]

Once again, General Floyd was retreating rapidly to avoid losing his troops to the advancing Federal army. He knew that he was still anxiously awaited in Federal court to answer for several of his decisions while he was Secretary of War. As at the battle fought at Carnifex Ferry, Floyd withdrew from new, strong positions which could have been held against the Union force moving against him. Floyd definitely did not want to risk capture and repeated his habit of retreating the following year at Fort Donelson when his garrison was surrounded by General Grant's army.

The withdrawal from Cotton Hill became a general retreat over bad roads in miserable weather and the marching of the Confederate army did not stop until Floyd's small army had completely left western Virginia. Isaac Smith wrote about the early stages of the retreat:

"About dusk a council of war was called and about 8 o'clock we were ordered to pack up wagons and prepared for marching. News had reached camp that the enemy had gotten in behind us and we were to retreat at once. A number of regiments had no transportation and were

101 Childers, "Virginian's Dilemma", pg. 196

obliged to burn nearly everything they had. We were in the rear with the 36th and saw piles of tents, with broken cooking utensils and articles of every description blazing away as all had to be consumed and destroyed. As we marched along that night we could see where flour had been thrown away, tents and along the line of march blankets, overcoats and etc even were destroyed and many of our poor ragged fellows got hold of some good things thus thrown away. We trudged through the mud and cold, and stopped next day at about 11 o'clock AM after a march of about 15 miles. It is impossible to tell what became of all the sick and stragglers. I fear many of them have fallen into the hands of the enemy.

"On Thursday Nov 14th continued our march, a heavy rain began to fall shortly after our start and the road (before most wretched) became a mass of liquid mud (such as the streets of Charleston in mid winter) through which the poor soldiers were obliged to wade. We had not marched far before a courier pushed through the ranks at full speed hunting General Floyd and shortly after he appeared returning to the camping ground and gave us orders to halt at a place designated further on and about 5 1/2 miles from where we had camped the night before. We then heard of the skirmish in which Col Crogan was killed and that the enemy were about to attack our rear. This was a very dismal camp ground. I felt very anxious about our baggage. Every regiment had lost a large part of their equipments. We had lost none but rather gained, for our fellows picked up everything valuable and carried it. I was very anxious to have the wagons move on so that the old 22nd could come out of the campaign right side up.

"Col Jackson had it arranged finally that the wagons should move on that night. After some time we found that all the trains were to move forward, and all the troops but the 22nd and 36th. We were to remain and in the morning fight the enemy from a position some distance back and after checking them fall back to another point where we would find another regiment and some artillery and there we were to make a decided stand."[102]

The Kanawha Valley volunteers were once again being used as a rearguard while Floyd continued his retreating pattern with his other troops. The western regiments were expendable and Floyd would not have regretted their loss. The troops were beginning to understand this and their morale was probably not much higher than that of Major Smith. It is surprising that they remained together as a fighting force when their continuous mistreatment by Floyd is considered.

Colonel St. George Croghan was the commander of Floyd's calvary and he was killed in a short, but sharp, skirmish in a rearguard action at McCoy's Mill with some of Benham's advance troops. Croghan's father had been one of the few heroes of the War of 1812 and had served as Inspector General of the pre-war army. General Benham had known the father while young Benham had been a student at West Point and arranged for the transfer of the body so that it could be returned to the family for burial.

Smith continued to describe the retreat:

"The night was cold and dark, the black clouds filled the heavens. Our tents were taken down and the wagons sent off to make their way through the mass of mud in front, if possible, and if not to be destroyed. The Quartermaster General was utterly and hopelessly drunk, Miller had great difficulty to keep away from him so as to manage his train in his own way. Very soon the heavy rain began to fall. I laid down upon some straw, covered up head and feet with my old shaggy blanket and the rain poured down upon us in torrents. The most vivid lightening and tremendous peals of thunder were seen and heard every few moments. Added to all this the Officer who was to command us the next morning was foolishly drunk, perfectly childish and silly. I regard my position that night as the most unfortunate of my life. It seemed that God was against me, and I felt the contest of the morning would be fatal to me.

102 Childers, "Virginian's Dilemma", pg. 197

The great probability of the destruction of our train, the personal discomforts of my position, the gross injustice and tyranny which placed me there, God's terrible presence in the heavens, the anticipated desperate fight of the morning and a drunken commander seemed to leave no hope, no prospect of escape. I was not afraid as cowards are, for this war I believe has assured me that I am not afraid of the battle field, but I was superstitious and felt God had declared against me. With all of this (thanks to my good old blanket) I slept soundly and sweetly during a part of the night. I surrendered my fate to my heavenly father and slept in peace. Plus slept by my side and poor fellow seemed to feel very much as I did. Our situation was truly desolate."[103]

Smith and the other volunteers were in a desperate situation. They were ordered to form Floyd's rearguard and to prepare to fight a larger Union army which was rapidly approaching from across Cotton Hill and from along Loup Creek. With the high probability of combat the following morning, the spirits of the regiments were hardly raised when the unnamed rearguard commander got drunk. This was a situation that would inspire confidence in few soldiers and most of the troops of the rearguard probably sensed the hopelessness of their situation and were as demoralized as Major Smith and his friend, Plus.

Smith continued to describe the events of the following morning:

"Next morning before daylight all were astir. Plus and I were the only persons with dry clothes in the officer's mess. We marched off through the mud just at dawn to meet the enemy. Took our positions to await the attack. We could see far down the road from our elevated position and watched for the enemy with some eagerness (for strange to say there is a sort of excitement in battle, which makes a man rather court the contest, when the first anxiety has passed away) but we watched in vain. At 9 o'clock no

103 Childers, "Virginian's Dilemma", pg. 197-198

enemy in sight and calvalary scouts reported none within 1 1/2 miles. We were marched back to the second position reported how matters stood and were ordered on."[104]

The commander of the Union pursuit, General Benham, was incredibly slow in developing a strategy to follow and engage theretreating Confederates. General Cox moved troops over Cotton Hill and Rosecrans sent impatient orders to Benham to move rapidly. Cox later wrote of Benham's slowness:

"Rosecrans had informed Benham of my advance and ordered him to push forward; but he spent the day in discussing topography which he was supposed to have learned before, and did not move ... It would appear from the official documents that Floyd did not learn of Benham's presence at the mouth of Loup Creek until the 12th, when he began his retreat, and that at any time during the preceding week a single rapid march would have placed Benham's brigade without resistance upon the line of the enemy's communications. Rosecrans was indignant at the balking of his elaborate plans, and ordered Benham before a court-martial for misconduct..."[105]

Benham was never tried for his lack of effectiveness during the Confederate retreat from Cotton Hill. General McClellan was responsible for having the charges dropped, but General Benham's slow response in going after the retreating Rebel force caused the Union army to lose an opportunity to capture or destroy an entire Confederate army. Isaac Smith and his regiment were spared the battle all had dreaded as the Union pursuit failed to materialize. Smith went on:

"On this march we saw the true character of our retreat. The road and road side was strewn with articles of every description -- tents, boxes, guns, clothes,

104 Childers, "Virginian's Dilemma", pg. 198
105 Cox, *Military Reminiscences*, pg. 142-143

provisions,knapsacks, broken harness, cooking utensils, dishes. Waggons were left fast in the mud with their loads untouched -- at one place twelve wagons were left, most of them turned upside down, and at the same time a number of horses had drowned in the mud, that is had sunk beyond hope of extrication and had been shot. At some places mudholes were filled with tents to make a passage for the wagons. All this was a perfect harvest for the 22nd. Being in front of the regiment we noticed this was only a fragment following up, and halted for the stragglers to catch up, waited a long time and they did not appear -- went back and found the fellows resting behind. The rascals claimed to be tired down as a reason for their halt, and no wonder, for when I started them out again I found about every other man loaded down with flour, frying pans, buckets, mess kettles, and such things. I found myself, eleven good percussion guns, and gave them to the men, but made them carry their flint locks also. This regiment has by captures from the enemy and otherwise, gained about 100 good percussion guns, a number of them Enfield rifles. Had I commenced earlier, I could have secured many more guns, but it never occurred to me the men would leave their guns. Those that were left so far as I know were those of sick men turned over to the Master of Ordinance or which could not be transported with the men.

"We camped that night (Friday) about two miles this side of Raleigh Court House --- heavy snow that night. Many of the poor fellows are entirely barefoot, or nearly so as to make what they wear an encumberance rather than a benefit. I begged from a Georgia Col four pairs of shoes for some poor fellows who had been marching barefoot, with their feet bleeding almost as they walked. These political brigadiers give every comfort and priviledge first to their own troops, who take good care to leave nothing for the poor Va Vols who have been a sort of shuttlecock between them."[106]

Smith remained a good officer even though he had requested a furlough following the submission of his letter

---

106 Childers, "Virginian's Dilemma", pg. 198

of resignation from the army and had been so rudely treated by General Floyd. He had worked to prepare his regiment for the rearguard battle under a "drunken commander" and his attitude toward the "political brigadiers" -- politically appointed generals -- was beginning to resemble that of his friend and former commander, Christopher Tompkins. It was obvious that the politician's troops had better equipment , were given preferred positions during long marches, and were generally able to avoid dangerous duty such as the the rearguard action that had recently faced the 22nd and 36th Virginia Regiments. These western volunteers were constantly misused while the other regiments in Floyd's force were obviously given preferential treatment throughout the campaign.

His concern for his men was obvious. He obtained shoes which had to be "begged from a Georgia Col" for some of his soldiers who had remained in the retreat rather than drop out or desert and were continuing to march barefoot -- in November. When most of the 22nd fell behind during the retreat, he found them "resting" and referred to them affectionately as "rascals" -- as if they were tardy schoolboys instead of soldiers who fell out during a march because they were overloaded with the loot they had collected from the abandoned materials of the lead regiments. Smith also continued to be a good soldier as well. He found "eleven good percussion guns" and had his soldiers carry them along with their outdated flintlocks to increase the number of these excellent weapons in his regiment and to avoid abandoning them to the enemy. He mildly criticized himself for not collecting more "had I commenced earlier". All of this was from an officer who had been mistreated to the point that he had requested to be permitted to resign from the Confederate army. He had not left the army yet and duty required that he be the best commander he could be until the resignation was approved. Duty was obviously more than only a word to Isaac Smith.

He soon left for Lewisburg where he was able to go to church for the first time since leaving Charleston. He wrote from Lewisburg on November 24, 1861:

"Came to this place on Friday, and am at the hotel with a good room, but the country is so eaten out by soldiers that one nearly starves at the hotel. This is the Sabbath day, and I thank God from my heart that I have been permitted once more to visit his holy sanctuary, and hear Jesus Christ and him crucified preached. The religious destruction of the army is awful, and I have felt my heart swell with thankfulness this day (wickedly as I have spent it) for the grace which permits me to be where God's holy name and day are honored. Am waiting here for the evening church bell to ring, but it is now almost too late -- the snow storm has doubtless prevented service tonight. Will probably go up to Mr. Matthews, and sit with Misses Jennie M and C our acquaintences of Richmond. Called on them yesterday, and they made many kind inquiries for Callie and Emma. This day finished the bible fourth time of regular reading. Began either on my wedding day or the day after."[107]

Smith was able to locate a room for rent on a farm owned by Matthew Arbuckle which was located five miles south of Lewisburg. He completed his diary from there on November 29:

"This is my wedding anniversary. How strange that the day which gave me my dear wife should upon its recurrance find us separated so far and with so little hope of meeting. How little any of that gay throng which assembled to witness the completion of our happiness anticipated the misery which has followed so soon. Oh how this day especially makes us long for home, for my long-lost wife and the other dear ones. Poor Callie, you cannot feel the pangs of to-days separation more than I and you cannot realize the bitterness so deeply for you do not know the difficulties yet to be surmounted ere we can meet again.

"I am boarding at this place -- after some disappointment in my efforts to get cheap boarding in the country. I have settled here and am very comfortable. Mr.

[107] Childers, "Virginian's Dilemma", pg. 199

Arbuckle has no children but has an adopted nephew whom they raised from an infant eight days old. Both he and his wife are kind and pleasant and sensible and well-informed. They have a number of excellent books which I cannot more than finish in a year's stay. They keep an excellent table -- plenty of milk, honey, butter and all the excellences of a good farm and have them cooked particularly well. The house is one of those time-honored log house structures with good sized fireplaces and large hearths where a big blazing fire is always ready to greet you. The floor undulating to a most remarkable degree tells of old age and seems to be the more comfortable for its very irregularity. I am located in a newer part of the house -- in fact I have the parlor which is snugly and neatly furnished. My bed room opens into it and there I have everything as neat and comfortable as one could wish (linen sheets) a luxury unheard of by me since my departure from home until now. Mr. Arbuckle has a splendid farm 2000 of the best land in Greenbrier. Many of the fields are now covered with the most magnificent grass long enough to mow if not so trampled or fallen down. You can see I am comfortable and my poor horse too is literally "in clover". All of those comforts only serve to remind me the more of Callie and home.

"Nov 30th

"Went to town today and heard something about Mr. N B Cabell's family starting for Kanawha. I shall again make an effort to send home this diary. I am applying for leave to come home not that it is necessary to obtain leave, but that no one can say I have slyly deserted a cause, in which I have borne arms, or sneaked away from it. My hope is to find some quiet spot, where with Callie, parents, and sisters we may all live through this terrible war, without participating in it. My intentions and desires will all be disclosed to this government.

"My great trouble will probably be with the Yankees. Will they permit me to live under the jurisdiction of the U S, simply upon parole not to bear arms against them, during the war, and can there be any certainty that the government will not repudiate the acts of their generals when it suits their convenience. I believe Genl Rosecrans would appreciate my position, but he is not President. I cannot take any oaths, but I do not expect to take up arms again. Apart from my own wishes on the subject, I could not do so with any propriety, maddened as the people are against my father.

"It is impossible for me to say whether my unfortunate situation here will be so far appreciated to secure me the permission I seek. I hope it may, but even then a long time must elapse, and many difficulties be overcome, before I can find out what the Yankees would do with me."[108]

Isaac Noyes Smith had now returned to the civilian world, but his problems were far from over. He was separated from his family by hostile armies and with the memory of the imprisonment of Major Parks in spite of a safe conduct pass after he had appempted to return to the Kanawha Valley so fresh in his mind, Isaac Smith was uncertain of his immediate, as well as his long-range, future. He had been forced out of the service by the malice of General Floyd toward Christopher Tompkins and because of this intense hatred for a single officer, all of the volunteers from the western counties of Virginia had been cruely used. As all of this was beginning to put a great deal of pressure on him, Major Smith remained a good soldier and an effective officer determined to do his duty properly. Even after Floyd had denounced both him and his father, Smith continued to lead the 22nd Virginia to the best of his ability. He demonstrated his loyalty to both his duty and to his regiment when he felt the sting of the original incident when McCausland was sent to take command of the 22nd during the march to Cotton Hill and remained with the regiment until the return of Colonel Tompkins before submitting his resignation.

Smith was out of the army, but was unable to go home. He was aware of what could happen when he came under the authority of the Federal officials... Major Parks had a

108 Childers, "Virginian's Dilemma", pg. 199-200

safe conduct pass issued by General Cox and was still imprisoned at Wheeling. Smith expected the same type of treatment from the Union authorities if he came into their hands and was afraid to go home to Callie and his family.

He did, however, manage to send the diary home -- probably with the N.B. Cabell family mentioned in the November 30 diary entry. His careful instructions to keep the diary's contents away from the "Yankees" did little good as it was captured by Union troops and given to General Cox. As previously mentioned, Cox knew Smith's father and after reviewing its' contents, probably gave the diary to the elder Smith. Smith remained in contact with Colonel Tompkins during the remainder of the war and there is some circumstantial evidence that on the suggestion of General McCausland that Isaac Smith was engaged in some activities -- possibly espionage -- which kept him from being drafted into the Confederate army later in the war as a private. There is a paper written by Colonel Tompkins on the fall of Richmond that mentions the name Isaac N. Smith and hints that he may have used the alias "Jason N. Snead" as he attempted to avoid capture by Union troops in hot pursuit. This, unfortunatly, is very difficult to document due to the destruction of most of the records of the Confederate espionage service. It is very unfortunate that Smith's diary ended at the time it did. He had a great deal more to tell as the war continued.

And General Floyd -- the cause of all of the misfortune that happened to Isaac Smith: he continued to retreat out of western Virginia and effectly lost the area to the Union for the remainder of the war. The total loss of control by the South was to result in the development of the new state of West Virginia in 1863.

Floyd was soon ordered to move his brigade to Fort Donelson in Tennessee and managed to avoid capture there by his usual retreat. He escaped with his Virginia troops (including Colonel McCausland and the 36th Virginia) while General Buckner was left to surrender his command of nearly 14,000 soldiers unconditionally to General Grant.

As a result of this pattern of retreats that was becoming apparent, Floyd was relieved of his command

and he returned to his home. He continued to be a problem for the Confederate authorities, however. In July, 1862, Brigidier Henry Heth said Floyd was working against the Confederate army because of disappointment and was trying to break the army down in southwestern Virginia by his opposition to the new conscript law. Later, when John McCausland was attached to Heth's command, he accused Floyd of trying to prevent men from reenlisting under Heth's command.[109]

Floyd was later given a minor command over state troops, the "State Liners" but accomplished little. He died from an illness in April, 1863.[110]

Both Tompkins and Smith saw the uselessness of the man and others began to notice his problems as well.

William Clark Reynolds also witnessed the 1861 campaign, but as a private. He had joined the Kanawha Rifles in Charleston as the war was breaking out and later his company was assigned to the 22nd Virginia where he was under the command of both Tompkins and Smith.

Reynolds also kept a diary and at the completion of the winter retreat from Cotton Hill, the resignation of both Tompkins and Smith left the 22nd Virginia without a senior commander that the men knew and trusted. All of their problems -- other than the disease and bad weather -- could be traced back directly to the poor management abilities of General John B. Floyd -- a former governor of Virginia.

Reynolds wrote an interesting entry into his diary on November 28, 1861:

"The old Governor killed his hogs and scalded them in hot water and hung them up to dry, he did."[111]

William Reynolds was not in the mood for writing at the

---

109 Brown, James E. "Life of Brigadier John McCausland", *West Virginia History*, Vol. IV, No.4, July, 1944, pg. 252

110 Klement, "Floyd and the West Virginia Campaigns of 1861", pg. 332

111 Reynolds, *Diary of William Clark Reynolds*, pg. 20

time. He went back to reading his bible -- he had completed seven chapters the previous day.

Floyd had made several men religious during the Kanawha Valley campaigns.

## MISTRESS OF THE MANSION

*Ellen Wilkins Tompkins lived near the small village of Gauley Bridge, Virginia, at the onset of the Civil War and was a witness to the opening campaigns of that conflict. She lived on a eight hundred-twenty acre farm with her family which was located on Gauley Mountain to the east of the small town. The farm had been purchased by her husband, Christopher Quarles Tompkins, in 1855. He was a West Point graduate and had resigned from the regular army in 1847 and began to work in the iron and steel manufacturing business in Richmond. He relocated into western Virginia in 1855 when he was appointed superintendent of collieries on Paint Creek in Kanawha County.*

*Christopher Tompkins had served with his regiment in the Seminole Wars in Florida and was later sent for recruiting purposes to Fort McHenry, Maryland, and it was probably during this recruiting duty that the young Lieutenant met the twenty-two year old Ellen Wilkins of Baltimore. It is relatively easy to visualize the romance that developed between the twenty-seven year old professional officer and the intelligent and lovely Ellen. Tompkins was reassigned to his regiment in Florida and the long absences from Ellen during the campaigns of his regiment must have been a major factor in re-evaluating his career in the army. Their son, Joseph, was born in 1844 and a daughter, Ellen, followed in 1846. Tompkins was then reassigned to Monterey, California, on a deployment which was especially long. The trip aboard the Sloop of War, Lexington, required travelling around the Cape of Good Hope and the voyage alone lasted six months. He submitted his resignation from the army and this was accepted in 1847.*

*Christopher Tompkins was a man who possessed unusual values along with a highly developed personal and military sense of honor. In addition to the desire to have a normal family life with Ellen, he was probably disillusioned with the bureaucracy of the army and the politics that entered into most officer's careers. He left the* military *career he had chosen at the end of the Mexican War while serving in a safe location -- California -- while his friends and West Point classmates were being killed and wounded in Mexico. These three factors: army politics and bureaucracy, long absences from Ellen, and being unable to share the dangers of his classmates in combat reinforced his decision to leave the army.*

*He returned to Richmond where two additional children were born before the family relocated into western Virginia. They moved to the farm near Gauley Bridge in 1855 and by the time war was beginning to threaten, Tompkin's farming efforts had progressed considerably. A large house had been built along with an overseer's house, a large barn with outbuildings, and the farm had an extensive vinyard.*[1]

*As with the majority of Virginians in 1861, Christopher Tompkins had little desire to join the more militant southern states that were seceding from the Union. Unfortunately, President Lincoln's call for 75,000 volunteers to enforce the laws of the United States was the catalyst that forced Virginians into action. The Virginia Convention then considering seccession was meeting in Richmond at the time and had voted against separating from the young nation, but after the call for volunteers by by Lincoln, the convention rapidly approved the Ordinance of Secession and the Civil War moved closer to reality.*

*The Tompkins family was soon to experience a very close relationship with the competing sides and would be observing many of the early events of the war from a unique perspective. Christopher Tompkins had offered his services to the state of Virginia following his resignation from the regular army and as a West Point graduate and experienced officer, he was soon appointed a Lieutenant-Colonel in Virginia's militia and as a militia officer, he was probably automatically activated to full duty*

---

1 Tompkins, Ellen W., "The Colonel's Lady", *The Virginia Magazine of History and Biography*, Vol. 69. No.4, October, 1961, pg. 387

*when Virginia's Governor Letcher called for volunteers. Virginia's western counties had two strategic lines of communication from the western states remaining in the Union which were of military value to either side. The northern military axis was along the east-west route of the Baltimore and Ohio railroad and the first land battle of the war was fought as opposing forces maneuvered to control or interdict this vital military artery. The second strategic target was the Kanawha Valley. Unfortunately for the Tompkins family, the upper Kanawha Valley began at their farm, Gauley Mount.*

*Robert E. Lee's Adjutant General, Robert S. Garnett, sent a letter to Tompkins in early May, 1861, commissioning him a Colonel and placed him in charge of Virginia's military forces being organized in the Kanawha Valley.*

*Tompkins had to be at that point in his life when many men begin to re-evaluate their lives as compared to others they have known. He probably had doubts about giving up the prestige and status normally associated with the army career he had chosen even after fourteen years. A key indicator is located in a letter to West Point biographer, G.W. Cullum:*

> *"...I regret that my autobiography is so meagre..."*[2]

*The conflicting emotions of the newly commissioned Confederate Colonel must have been enormous. He had left home and family once before because of military duty and he had friends who would obviously choose to remain in the Federal army, but his loyalty to the state of Virginia was probably the compelling factor which lead him to his decision. The attraction of war also gave Tompkins an*

[2] Tompkins, Christopher Q., Personal letter to G.W. Cullum which is dated 25 October 1855. A copy is located in the West Point Library.

*opportunity to fill out that "meagre autobiography", but unfortunately a war does not only impact on its direct participants -- in this war the families were also affected.*

*The Confederacy sent out a former governor, Henry A. Wise, to the Kanawha Valley and he proceeded to mismanage Rebel forces there into a major retreat. Advancing Federal forces threatened to cut off the small Confederate army and they withdrew, Wise's "retrograde movement", from the valley and they burned the large, covered bridge at the town of Gauley Bridge[3] and left the Tompkins family under Union army contol.*

*Ellen Tompkins left a vivid and unique record of a short and forgotten period of history that began when Union General Cox received a letter from Colonel Tompkins which requested that Cox assume responsibility for the family trapped on the farm or:*

*"...if, however, you should think it out of your power to prevent such abuses of private immunities, I will be obliged if you will apprise Mrs. Tompkins of the fact."[4]*

*Ellen Tompkins' letters sent from Gauley Mount provide a unique insight into the early fighting in the upper Kanawha Valley. Most of her letters which have been preserved were sent to her sister, Sarah, who lived at "Cooch's Gap" in Delaware. Her letters to her sister were delivered unopened, but letters sent through the lines to her husband under a flag of truce were subject to Federal inspection and were far less detailed than the ones which went to Delaware. Ellen normally asked that her letters be destroyed, but fortunately these unique records of a little known period of history were preserved.*

---

3 Hotchkiss, Jed, "Virginia", *Confederate Military History*, pg. 59

4 Tompkins, "Colonel's Lady", pg. 390

*Our Wives and sweet hearts*
*tell us go and fight like a man*
*And keep the nothern negro crue*
*off of Virginue land*[5]

"They looked mad, asked if he was here. I said, 'No.' 'When did he leave?' I said, 'I am not here to answer such questions. I should not be worthy of the name of wife if I betrayed my husband.' The officer seeing I was not in a trifiling mood said,'Ask the lady no such questions; she won't answer you. Give us some whiskey."[6]

The Union soldiers were probably from the 2nd Kentucky Volunteer Infantry Regiment. They were recruited from the river front in the Cincinnati area and at this early stage of the war, they were more an undisciplined rabble than soldiers.

Ellen continued to describe her initial encounter with the newly arrived Federal army:

"I told them I had none as I sent it away when I heard they were coming, if they wished milk or bread or meat, that they should have it. A party rushed into the kitchen. I asked the officer very politely to request his men to leave the kitchen, food should be brought to them in the porch. Some had gone to the vinyard house (no one was in it however). A party rushed into the stable yard with shovels, etc. Three went to Dickert's house, the white man who has lived here for two years, broke open his trunk, took his watch, breastpin, 437 dollars in notes due in Cincinnati, 95 dollars in bank notes. I told the officer that Mr.T. had written to General Cox and that as a gentleman my greatest protection was in my entire defencelessness, and showed him the note left the day before by the officers. One was his captain, fortunately. He called his men off and left. Mr. Dickert went after them, but they were going to run him

5 Howe, *Rebellion in the West*, pg. 48
6 Tompkins, "Colonel's Lady", pg. 391

through. I sent a letter for him, to stop the payment of the 437 dollars, the 95 he lost, of course. I told him if faithful I'd give him a watch."[7]

August was a very active month for people in the area of Gauley Bridge, Virginia. The Confederate commander was able to come away from the battle of Scary Creek which was fought below Charleston with what was essentially a stalemate. He and his forces were now faced with a situation in which they were threatened with being surrounded by troops sent from the Sutton area. If these Federal troops were able to march south to Gauley Bridge, the small Confederate force would be cut off and would probably have been forced to surrender. General Wise, his Legion, and the newly recruited Confederate regiments from the Kanawha Valley began their retreat.

As in any retreat, the Confederates destroyed bridges in their rear to prevent the development of rapid pursuit and the bridge across Gauley River was not to be an exception. It was burned early on the night of July 27, 1861[8] and the blaze from the burning structure was spectacular. The glow was seen as far away as Woodville (Ansted) and the flames would have been quite visible from the Tompkin's home.

A.B. Roler, a member of Wise's Legion, recorded the destruction of the bridge in his diary:

"...When all of the companies were over the bridge with their baggage and commissary stores, the bridge was set on fire at about 11 p.m. It burned very fast, and the first arch that was fired fell in about one half hour. The whole length of the bridge was at least 150 yards, and ten minutes after the torch was first touched, the whole bridge was one sheet of flame, and for five or ten minutes afterwards presented one of the most beautiful sights I have ever saw. The night was somewhat cloudy and very damp from the recent rain, though it had stopped raining by this time. The smoke arose

7 Tompkins, "Colonel's Lady", pg. 391

8 Cook, Roy B., "The Destruction of Gauley Bridge", *The West Virginia Review*, October, 1925, pg. 5

from above in heavy spiral columns which lingered a moment over the burning wreck, affording time to be lit up in the most gorgeous colors, and then passed off into the air. The curve of the wind was S.E. and was right against the side of the bridge which caused the smoke from the flooring of the structure to circle beneath the arches in beautiful curves, and to mingle with that of the roofing after it had passed across. Our position was on the windward side. With the smoke thus circling around and before the bridge had burned sufficiently to obscure all the heavy timbers in the side walls, it had the appearance of a bridge of gold with frescoed work of the finest skill -- The exclamations of all present was what a beautiful sight! I could not but feel for the loss of the property -- though I admit of its being a military necessity..."[9]

Christopher Tompkins and the remainder of Wise's small army continued the retreat to Bunger's Mill (in the vicinity of Lewisburg) and Wise submitted a written report to Richmond:

"In thirty minutes after we fell back from Tyler Mountain, the enemy took possession and nearly succeeded in cutting off Colonel Tompkins' command at Coal River. We left Charleston last Wednesday week (July 24), and Gauley last Saturday, destroying the bridges behind us. This I was obliged to do ... owing to gross inefficiency of the quartermaster's department of my brigade, I have come on slowly."[10]

Federal troops under the command of General Cox moved quickly into the military vacuum produced as the Confederates pulled out. Portions of the 11th Ohio and the 2nd Kentucky Volunteer Infantry Regiments were pushed across Gauley River to continue to press the Rebels -- keeping them off balance.

[9] Roler, A.B., *The Diary of A.B. Roler*. The diary is in the collection of the Virginia Historical Society.

[10] Cook, "The Destruction of Gauley Bridge", pg. 5

Elements of the Kentucky regiment were the visitors to the Tompkins farm who demanded liquor from Ellen. This group of soldiers was little more than a mob and at least one member of the 2nd Kentucky's sister regiment, the 1st Kentucky -- Private Gatewood -- was later executed by firing squad in Charleston for serious violations of military discipline.[11] Another was later killed at Gauley Bridge by an officer for refusing to obey orders.[12]

General Cox claimed in his memoirs that these soldiers were later extensively drilled and with experience, they became skilled soldiers, but at the time of the farm visit they were highly undisciplined and the fact that General Cox had sent orders that the Tompkins family was not to be harmed meant very little to these men.

The visiting Kentucky troops broke into the overseer's house and robbed his savings while others went to the stable yard with shovels. This is probably the source of the story that there was a quantity of silver buried on the Tompkins' farm that has persisted to the present. (The location of the treasure was alleged to be marked with a buried musket.)

Ellen described her rather strange situation to her sister:

"Major Leiper came up at dinner time to say that General Cox had received Mr. T.'s letter, recognized his right to send it, and would see me protected, that his horse would not cross the ford or he would have called himself. He called the next day with several of his staff officers and took dinner, and is an elegant, accomplished gentleman, withal very handsome. Strange to say General Wise always sat at table on my left hand (the seat of honor I believe) and General Cox, his enemy, took the same seat two days after. I smiled to think how the table was filled with men in so

---

11 Cox, *Military Reminiscences*, pg. 149-152. Cox gave a full description of the military execution of Private Gatewood in his book; Moore, Frank, *The Rebellion Record*, Vol. 3, G.P. Putnam: 1862, pg. 117

12 Cox, *Military Reminiscences*, pg. 101-102

short a time anxious to cut each other's throats."[13]

Cox had received a letter from Tompkins and had accepted responsibility for the safety of the Tompkins family. The letter was written at Gauley Mount on July 28, 1861 and was sent to Cox. He was probably given the letter as he entered the town of Gauley Bridge:

"Sir:

"Circumstances over which I have no control, have compelled me to abandon my farm, and leave upon it a defenceless family of females and children.

"Should the chances of war direct your columns in this vicinity, it is presumed that these persons would receive treatment befitting their several stations, provided responsible persons were in immediate command. But, should this particular locality be visited by scouting parties or irregular detatchments of your Forces, temptations to license and abuse of private rights might be committed without your knowledge or sanction.

"It is to guard against such a contingency, that I have taken the liberty to address you in this communication, and to call your attention to the propriety of giving such instructions as will doubtless present themselves to an Officer of your rank and reputation. If, however, you should think it out of your power to prevent such abuses of private immunities, I will be obliged if you will apprise Mrs. Tompkins of the fact."[14]

Tompkins' letter was written the day after the bridge was burned and Cox had dinner there two days after Wise had eaten at the same table. Cox must have been on the farm on either July 30 or August 1. The pursuit was not very far behind and the burned bridge was only a temporary obstacle to the continued Union advance. The

[13] Tompkins, "Colonel's Lady", pg. 391-392

[14] Tompkins, Christopher; the letter to Cox is in the Military Records Section of the National Archives.

Federal officers who visited the farm were described by Ellen as "...very respectful and really kind, thank me for all that I do for them..."[15] but Ellen's position within their lines was precarious. Her family and property had to be guarded by troops from each side. When the area was occupied by the Confederates, General Wise's son, O. Jennings Wise, the commander of the "Richmond Light Infantry Blues" provided guards to prevent property damage "fearing Union men would burn the house as they threatened it."[16] Now, the Union officers must attempt to guard the private property from their own troops. Ellen described them best:

"...but the soldiers are cut-throats, villainous looking indeed. They are very angry, say it is a pretty kind of war, here is a seccession Colonel and they are not allowed to pillage anything..."[17] A guard force of twenty soldiers was posted to keep the farm safe from looters.

Ellen Tompkins continued to explain the unsual aspects of her situation to her sister, Sarah:

"A man dined here who told me he ordered one hundred guns to be fired at Mr. T., described his horse exactly, knew he was an officer by his orders to the men, and said, 'Is it not strange that here I am dining at his table?' He said the twigs of the trees flew, but the range was too high. They are very respectful and really kind, thank me for all that I do for them, But the soldiers are cut throats, villainous looking indeed. They are very angry, say it is a pretty kind of war, here is a secession Colonel and they are not allowed to pillage anything, not even a chicken. The apple orchard is the only sufferer. Four are there to guard it, but, somehow, few apples are left. The stock, horses are all preserved. The guard is sent at nine o'clock every morning to relieve twenty men in three places. Two lieutenants or captains, besides the officer of the day, come up twice besides and

---

15 Tompkins, "Colonel's Lady", pg. 392
16 *Ibid*, pg. 392
17 *Ibid*, pg. 392

once in the night to see all is right. The officers eat at the table and sleep on matresses on benches in the porch, the men on the lawn or in the road. Ellen is *never* seen. They do not know I have a daughter. When our troops were at Gauley Bridge, where these are now, Captain O. Jennings Wise sent me a guard every night, fearing union men would burn the house as they threatened it. So we have been highly honored by both parties. Captain Wise is General Wise's son."[18]

It was beginning to be a strange war for all participants. Here was the wife of a Confederate Colonel, eating at the same table with a man who described how he had ordered his unit to fire at her husband in an effort to kill him. Ellen felt they were"very respectful and really kind..." in spite of the fact that they were enemies. Her daughter, Ellen, was constantly concealed from the Union soldiers as her mother feared for the safety of the fifteen year old girl if she were seen by the ordinary soldiers who were "cut throats ... villainous looking".

She continued the letter to her sister in Delaware:

"The greatest trial is I am cut off from all communication with Mr. T. The mails are stopped from here to Lewisburg. Except a message, I have heard nothing from him. I do not know where he will be ordered. Sometimes my heart almost gives out. Then I feel I must rally as all depends on me now. Whether these troops will go to attack Mr. T. or remain here, I have no idea. The children tell me 'I am a prisoner of war but don't know it.' It is true -- I ought not to leave here , all is lost if I go, but I am so anxious about Mr. T. Yet we cannot afford to lose this place if by remaining two months all may yet be well. I suppose you know that the dear old state is to be divided. Governor Pierpont is for the union and this fact is certain, the forces will go as far as the sword will cut. What about Washington? Is it to be taken? I dread the bloodshed

18 Tompkins, "Colonel's Lady", pg. 392

following it. Do pray write to me. Tell me who is living, who is dead, and where Henry is? Caroline, I heard , was doing well. I get papers from Cincinnati, sent by the officers to me. Indeed, I call them socially friends and am puzzled to draw the line of their political enmity. I look at them and think here General Cox makes it a personal matter to protect the wife and children of a man he may kill next week. I know and believe many of the officers would spare him now for my sake. It is a matter for thought.

"Now for business. How does the blessed estate get on? Do write me a real *long* letter. Remember how I am situated and how thirsty I am for news of every kind. Your letter must be directed to Mrs. Colonel C. Q. Tompkins, Care of Brigadier-General Cox, Gauley Bridge, Fayette County, Virginia, It will come safely through Cincinnati. General Cox sent a letter to Mr.T. from me to relieve his anxiety, and lets me send to mill or store, but worded the pass so as to throw me on my honor. He sends this letter and says I may seal all I write. I admire him truly, for such men have a happy effect for peace. Please send this letter to Ann Tilyard and tell her not to show it, burn it but to go to see Louisa and Achsah and tell them the news, also Jane. Goodby with love to Mr. Cooch, Wilkens, Helen, and all the family. I wonder if we will ever meet again."[19]

Ellen Tompkins had nearly completed the letter to her sister, but as became her habit she included interesting post-scripts:

"Write the day you get this for General Cox may leave and my letter might not arrive so safely. Ellen received a letter from Florence last week. She was so delighted. "The people intercept my letters from Mr. T., I fear to gain some news. He could write nothing to instruct them, of course. They burn my fences, to let the stock out, make fires near the barn in hopes to burn it. I get angry sometimes. The officers put things to rights for me. Oh,

[19] Tompkins, "Colonel's lady", pg. 392-393

what an awful curse war is. How I envy you with your husband and children at home..."[20]

Ellen Tompkins had a real fear of the Union soldiers on her farm and she took serious risks whenever she caused the Union officers to confront the enlisted men on her behalf. She was aware of the risks she was taking by remaining on the farm and took extra precautions by keeping young Ellen hidden and out of sight. Like any normal person, Ellen Tompkins wanted to leave for a safer location, but in the absence of Colonel Tompkins, she felt that the family's fortunes were her responsibility. She was sure that they would lose their farm and possessions to looters or arsonists if she abandoned the property and she apparently planned to remain there to "see if all may be well". Most people felt that the war wouldn't last very long and would be settled in favor of the South. If she could hold out for a few months, the farm in which they had invested most of their money could be safe. If they abandoned it, they would probably lose everything they had there. Ellen Tompkins had excellent reasons to remain on the farm when the Federal troops took possession of Gauley Mountain.

A second reason for remaining rather than move to Richmond (as the Confederates withdrew) or travel through Union-controlled territory to Baltimore (as offered by Federal offficers) was the nearby presence of Colonel Tompkins. They apparently had a very close marriage and with all of her pressing problems, she confided in her letter to her sister that her "greatest trial" was being cut off from all communications with her husband. At the time the letter was written, Tompkins was probably at Bunger's Mill near Lewisburg where Wise's regiments had halted after their long retreat, but there was no way to send mail through the hostile lines.

It is quite likely that Ellen and Christopher Tompkins were more than simply husband and wife. It appears that they were romantically in love with one another since

---

20 Tompkins, "Colonel's Lady, pg. 392-393

before their marriage. Christopher gave up his army career to return to Richmond to be with Ellen and she had accompanied him into the rough, sparsely populated area of Fayette County, Virginia, to make their home near Gauley Bridge. Occasional hints are present in her letters that indicate their romance was still strong. After her trip to Richmond to collect winter clothing, she wrote her sister that she "spent some blissful days with Mr. T."[21] and she worried constantly about his welfare.

Following the dinner where the Federal officer described how he had "...ordered one hundred muskets to be fired at Mr. T. ,described his horse exactly..."[22] Ellen warned her husband in a note: "Remember you must not ride that horse. It is too well known." Later in another short letter to her husband, she wrote "I hope you have sold that horse."[23]

These short warnings were the best that she could do to help protect her husband from harm as her letters had to be sent through the Union lines unsealed. She remained unsure of the actual location of Colonel Tompkins, but sent a letter through the lines to him at Lewisburg from Gauley Bridge on September 1, 1861:

"My Dear Husband,

"I have not had the pleasure of hearing from you since the third of August. Various reports have reached us of your presence in this region, but none reliable. My impression is that you are with General Lee, therefore I shall direct this to Lewisburg.

"We are treated with much kind consideration by the officers and a guard is kept here to prevent intrusion. I shall remain here until I know your wishes on the subject. We are all well. The children long to see you. I need not tell you how I wish to see you, for that you know full well.

"How does John[24] get on? Give our love to him, and

21 Tompkins, "Colonel's Lady, pg. 413

22 *Ibid*, pg. 392

23 *Ibid*, pg. 394

24 John Wilkins, Ellen's Brother, was a physician with Wise's Legion.

Mr.Grimme[25] sends his respects. I am tired of this war, and yet see no hope of peace, all looks dark to me, however, I hear no news from the east except a few papers from Cincinnati, newspaper reports I do not credit. I wish I could suggest a way to send me a letter, but I am entirely at a loss."[26]

She completed the letter with "With much love your devoted wife" and continued with one of the usual postscripts:

"My judgement still approves of my remaining here, but the difficulty of hearing from you is a severe trial. My health is rather better, for I have no spells of nausea, therefore feel no uneasiness about me. Remember you must *not* ride that horse. It is too well known."[27]

Ellen's letters to her husband were subject to Federal censors/reviewers and were kept short and straight forward. Her brother, John, was a physician assigned to General Wise's command and his presence in the Confederate force operating in the area gave her additional cause for concern, but her major complaint centered on her inability to communicate with her husband.

Elements from both armies were maneuvering into positions in the area from Hawk's Nest to Sewell Mountain. Two major transportation routes intersected in that region-- the James River and Kanawha Turnpike and Sunday Road (which connected northern areas) where the Federal forces under the command of General McClellan were operating. Wise had to ensure that his small Confederate army did not get caught on the turnpike between General Cox (at Gauley Bridge) and the Federal army under McClellan which could move from the north on Sunday Road and trap the Rebel force in a very

25 Mr. Grimme was the Tompkins' children's tutor.
26 Tompkins, "Colonel's Lady", pg. 393-394
27 *Ibid*, pg. 395

inaccessible area where retreat or maneuver would be nearly impossible.

Cox, with a smaller military force at his disposal, kept several of his regiments out in front of his main element, constantly skirmishing with the Confederate pickets to keep Wise off balance. Cox was concerned that the combined Confederate army would be able to attack his force in Gauley Bridge and push the Federal forces out of the upper Kanawha Valley. While Cox was a volunteer general, his military instincts were quite good and he was able to keep the less qualified General Wise guessing about his actual strength and intentions.

During this period of maneuver and counter-maneuver, Tompkins and Ellen's brother, John, arranged for a note to be sent to General Cox requesting that the Tompkins family be allowed to pass through the Union lines to rejoin her husband in safety. The letter was sent by Colonel C. F. Henningsen, an Englishman who had joined the Confederate army following several years as a "Soldier of Fortune".

Henningsen's most recent experiences included the invasion of Nicargua along with a group of Southerners lead by Willian Walker of Tennessee. The note was hand-carried to General Cox's headquarters in person by Ellen's brother, Dr. Wilkins. The message from Henningsen has not been located, but Cox's reply explained a great deal about Ellen's situation, Cox's protection, and advised that she would not be allowed to cross into Confederate-controlled territory. It was written at Cox's headquarters in Gauley Bridge on September 6, 1861:

"To Colonel C. F. Henningsen:

"Your note dated 4th was brought in today with a flag of truce by Dr. Wilkins. I have endeavored to save Mrs. Tompkins from any of the inconveniences or dangers which might result from hostilities in her neighborhood, and have spared no pains to keep her family and property from molestation. She has been allowed every latitude I could reasonably grant and subjected to only such restrictions as seemed necessary.

"The very fact that she has been allowed to remain so long with her family within our lines, makes it improper for me now to grant the request that she should pass over to your forces. I will however see to it that she is not left in any personal danger in any event, or will even allow her a safe conduct to go to her friends in Baltimore, by way of Ohio. More than this I must be excused from granting at present, however I may regret the duty of refusing any request her husband or friends might make. Of course I include her family in the assurances above given."[28]

There were several reasons that Cox was uncomfortable in releasing Ellen to travel into the Confederate lines at this particular point in the mountain war. Ellen was probably aware of the general weakness of the Federal forces in the Gauley Bridge area at the time. If she were able to tell Confederate General Wise of the Union positions in the area of her farm, the Rebels would shortly realize that they had a definite advantage and would probably be able to force the relatively weak Federal garrison out of the upper valley.

Cox, however, was a gentleman who promised to protect Ellen or permit her to slowly travel through Ohio to Baltimore -- a prolonged trip which would protect the military positions his soldiers were holding. He told Henningsen that he regretted his duty of refusing to allow Ellen and her family to join Tompkins,but this might be slightly incorrect. Actually, Cox was able to derive some benefit by holding the Tompkins farm and family within the Federal camp. While Ellen and the children were there, it was very unlikely that General Wise's forces, with Christopher Tompkins as a senior officer, would place the family in danger by attacking. Cox, the gentleman, may have realized the tactical advantage he was gaining by holding Ellen and the family within the Union camp.

During this period, large military forces from Virginia began to maneuver into the area. Confederate General John

28 Tompkins, "Colonel's lady", pg. 394

B.Floyd, like Wise -- a former governor of Virginia -- moved his troops into the region after arriving at Sewell Mountain. There had been some animosity between Wise and Floyd in the past and since Floyd's commission as a general predated that of Wise, Floyd was now in command. An intense rivalry to the point of hatred developed between these two Confederate commanders.[29]

Following Federal victories in the northwestern section of the state, General McClellan was able to "self promote" himself into command of the Army of the Potomac. General Rosecrans took command in western Virginia and began to move troops south toward the Kanawha Valley.[30]

Christopher Tompkins remained in the area with his regiment, recently reorganized and redesignated the 22nd Virginia Volunteer Infantry Regiment -- formerly the First Kanawha Regiment. This regiment was unique in Confederate service as it was formed exclusively from volunteer companies recruited from western Virginia counties.

Tompkins was able to get a letter passed through the lines to Ellen which was handcarried to Gauley Mount by the commander of the 26th Ohio Volunteer Infantry Regiment, Colonel Fyffe. Ellen replied to her husband from the farm on September 10, 1861:

"My dear husband,

"I had the pleasure of receiving your letter from the hands of Colonel Fyffe, and was much gratified to hear that you and John were well.

"The children send much love and have enjoyed good health and, not withstanding the exciting times, continue their studies quite industriously. They seem much interested in their music and play *Dixie* and various airs.

29 White, "West Virginia", pg. 33

30 Husley, Val, "Men of Virginia -- Men of Kanawha-- To Arms", *West Virginia History*, Vol. XXV, No. 3, April, 1974, pg. 220

General Cox and his officers treat us very kindly and made us as comfortable under the circumstances as possible. The General thinks however that it will be most judicious for us to remain here for the present, and I agree with him, feeling quite safe under his protection. As for my going to Baltimore it is entirely out of the question. If nothing occurs to drive me away, I would like to remain here as late as possible, although it forces me to forgo the pleasure of seeing you and John, especially as Mr. Grimme and Mr. Dickert think they could not remain here with advantage without the family. The stock is all in good condition, and the crops were quite abundant, but not equal to the demands made upon them. Of course I will write when ever there is an opportunity. In the meantime I hope you will feel no unnecessary anxiety about us as I feel sure in case of sickness General Cox would allow me to let you know. My own health is rather better. The servants give me no trouble. All desire their respects to you and John.

Yours devotedly,

Ellen Tompkins

P.S. I hope you have sold that horse. Sarah wrote me all were well and our property in Baltimore right."[31]

Tompkins apparently missed being able to communicate with Ellen to the degree that she missed his letters. He asked her to write and she assured him she would do so whenever there was an opportunity. She also took the opportunity to warn him again about his well-known horse which had caused him to become a special target for Union soldiers.

Ellen's letters to Colonel Tompkins were delivered through the Union lines and were delivered in an unsealed condition. Since these were coming from inside Union territory and could contain military information, they were probably read before being delivered to the Confederates. Ellen was obviously aware of this practice and didn't write the open, frank letters such as were sent to her sister. Since

31 Tompkins, "Colonel's Lady", pg. 395

the letters to her husband would be read by Union officers and perhaps General Cox, himself, Ellen took the opportunity to let them know that she had been well treated and expected the same sort of care in the future.

There was a great deal of activity occurring in the vicinity of the Tompkins' farm at the time, but Ellen never referred to it in the letters sent to her husband. She wrote a more extensive letter to Sarah that same day -- September 10 -- in which she advised that Sarah's letter had been received and that the war was heating up in the area:

"My dear Sarah,

"I was delighted to hear from you once more. We have had a terrible time here, skirmishes within a few miles of us. You heard that Colonel Tyler was routed by General Floyd's brigade 18miles from us. Ben Ficklin is his Lieutenant Colonel. The federals had their arms stacked, eating their breakfasts, and the *rebels* in their midst before they knew it. But for timely aid from Camp Gauley their wagon trains would have been cut off."[32]

This was the battle of Cross Lanes, where the 7th Ohio Volunteer Infantry Regiment was attacked by a very superior force under General Floyd. Ellen was correct in reporting that the Federal troops were caught by surprise while eating breakfast and suffered a bloody defeat. The entire regiment was scattered, killed, or captured. Initially, the Union officers feared their losses were far greater than it turned out, but Major John Casement was able to rally nearly 400 Union survivors from the surrounding countryside and march them over the mountains to Charleston where they rejoined the Union army.[33]

Until they were able to return to Union control, Cox's headquarters was nearly in a panic -- only the 7th Ohio's commander, Colonel Tyler, his Lieutenant-Colonel, and 200 Union survivors of the Confederate attack had arrived

32 Tompkins, "Colonel's Lady", pg. 395-396

33 Bailes, "Cox in West Virginia", pg. 28

at Gauley Bridge.[34]

It had taken on the appearance of a terrible defeat until Casement's group appeared in Charleston.

General Floyd, obviously pleased with the results of his initial battle of the war, sent a report on the action to General Robert E. Lee:

"I determined to attack them, which I did yesterday about sunrise. They were posted about three miles from my camp in a commanding position, but our men made the attack with spirit and soon carried it. The enemy were completely routed... The enemy's killed and wounded number upward of 30 men. Amongst the killed is a captain. The prisoners number over 60 ... we captured some of their wagons and hospital supplies. The result of this fight will enable me to hold this quarter of the country, I think certainly, and cut off effectively all communication between General Cox and the forces toward the north."[35]

Ellen was unaware at the time that she was writing this letter that her husband's regiment was attached to Floyd's Brigade and had participated in the rout of the Seventh Ohio. Later she was to learn of his humanitarian actions at the time of the battle which saved many Union soldier's lives and this display of gallantry was to be of benefit to Ellen and the children.

The September 10 letter to Sarah continued with a description of the skirmishing that went on along the eastern boundary of the farm -- in the area of Chimney Corner:

"September 3rd we heard the cannon roaring two miles above us, actually on the farm which extends three miles on the turnpike. The 11th Ohio and two other regiments were concealed in the bushes each side of the road expecting our troops to come down and attack Gauley

34 Cox, *Military Reminiscences*, pg. 96
35 Bailes, "Cox in West Virginia", pg. 28-29

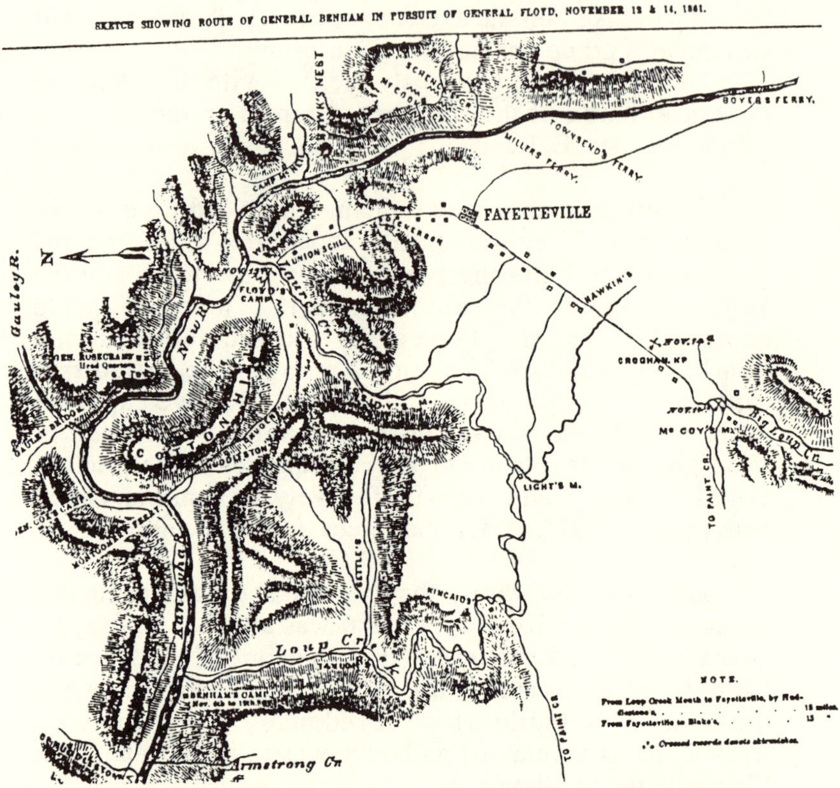


Map of the battlefield of Cotton Hill. Floyd and his small army occupied the crest of the mountain above the Federal camp at Gauley Bridge and fired on the Union soldiers with cannon for approximately two weeks. Union Generals Cox, Benham, and Schenck were ordered to cross the New and Kanawha Rivers at three points and surround the Rebel army on the mountain -- "bagging it" as the soldiers used to say.

Benham blundered his movement and Floyd was able to escape the "iron cage" he was sure the Union authorities had for him in the North.

Col. Croghan was killed near McCoy's Mill.

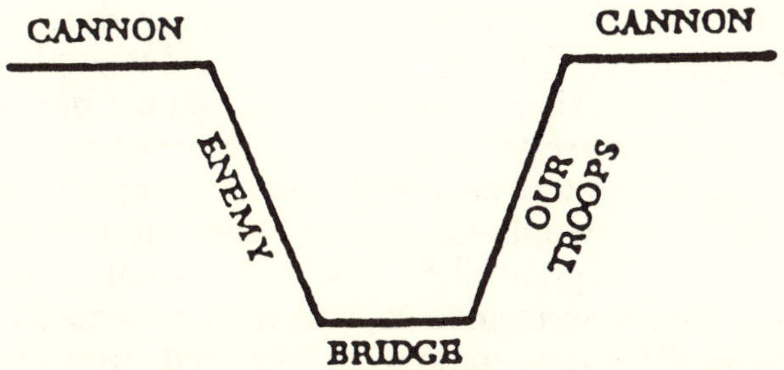


Sketch map done by Ellen Tompkins to illustrate the positions of both sides during the skirmishing on her farm. This a sketch of the "Devil's Elbow", a sharp turn on the James River and Kanawha Turnpike, which is now called "Chimney Corner".

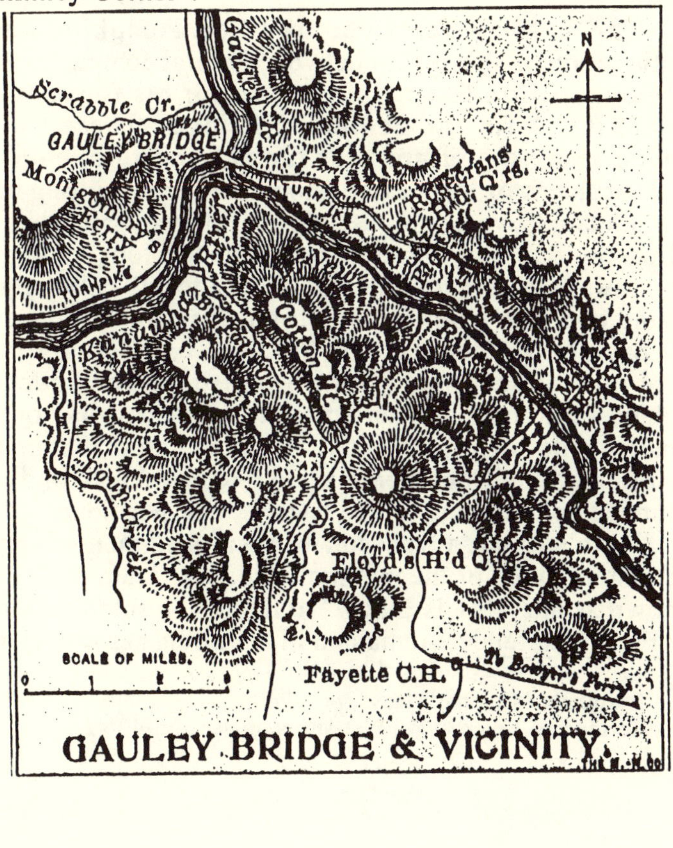

Camp. Our troops, it seems, followed the same plan. When either showed themselves, were honored with a volley. The road ran in this way. Both were surprised at the reception they met. The idea of six thousand men playing bow peep at each other. The federals blame a boy who went to mill a *hundred* times a day, said they heard cow bells all night which was the *rebels*' signal, complain of the ingratitude of the people to an army sent here to *protect them*!. I am truely grateful for one! The country people run in, close doors and windows, will answer no questions. Neither party did much, some were wounded, none killed. But the best thing was a cannon taken from General Wise was true to the southern cause. It hung fire and blew off the arm of the cannoneer and another man's thumb. Better them than our forces should suffer."[36]

The fighting described by Ellen Tompkins was a continuation of skirmishes between several companies sent by General Cox to act as a screen for his force at the Tompkins' farm and at Gauley Bridge. These troops moved along the turnpike as far as Locust Lane on the western slopes of Big Sewell Mountain before pulling back to Mountain Cove on August 13. A 120 man patrol left the following day and marched as far as the foot of Sewell mountain before encountering Confederate calvary and having two men wounded in a brief skirmish. They again fell back to Mountain Cove, but the Confederate forces were now advancing. The Union troops continued to withdraw and halted to set up a line of breastworks on the "Gauley side" of Big Creek. A six man patrol sent up the road toward the Confederates had one man killed and two wounded before being forced back to their positions.[37]

Wise's forces advanced and positioned themselves on the eastern slope of the mountain sides at Chimney Corner (known as the "Devils Elbow" to the Union soldiers) while the Federal defenders remained in their trenches across the

36 Tompkins, "Colonel's lady", pg. 396

37 Horton and Teverbaugh, *Eleventh Regiment*, pg. 40-42

valley to the west. Wise's artillery fired all day at the Federal troops with "shell and canister", but did no damage to either the field fortifications or the men in them.[38]

The Union artillery batteries began a defensive counter-battery fire against the Confederate guns which were deployed against them and during their firing, there was a premature discharge which Ellen Tompkins referred to in her letter. Union eye-witnesses tell the story best, however:

"During the morning a piece of artillery sent out to Col.Frizell arrived, and after firing a few shots, a premature discharge of the gun sent the *swab* whizzing over among the enemy,which, as we afterwards ascertained, frightened them badly, as they thought we were throwing *chain shot*! This discharge took off the arm of the "rammer" and the thumb of the "thumber", after which Col. Frizell ordered the gun to the rear, as he found it to be more dangerous to his men than the rebels."[39]

Wise's regiments remained in the immediate area for a few additional days and again withdrew to the east. The 11th Ohio was replaced opposite the enemy by the 26th Ohio (commanded by Colonel Fyffe, the officer who had delivered Tompkins' letter to Ellen). The 11th Ohio returned to their camp at Gauley Bridge on September 8 following an active month of skirmishing with the Confederates under General Wise that occurred from Gauley Mountain to Sewell Mountain and back, again.[40]

Ellen reviewed her opinion of the current tactical situation facing the Federal army under General Cox in her letter to her sister:

"They have to keep a tremendous force here, 1000 men in Charleston. The people are very sulky to them there. They are being attacked on all sides up Gauley, from New

38 Horton and Teverbaugh, *Eleventh Regiment*, pg. 42
39 Ibid, pg. 42-43
40 Ibid, pg. 43

River etc. Their supplies fired into daily and they fear they will be cut off entirely".[41]

Being cut off was a major concern for General Cox. With the bulk of his small army at Gauley Bridge, he was afraid that General Wise would continue to move against his fortifications on Gauley Mountain to hold his attention while General Floyd moved his regiments along the route to Charleston taken by Major Casement following the Union defeat at Cross Lanes.[42]

If this were to occur, the Union forces in the Kanawha Valley would be trapped between Wise and Floyd in a very narrow valley with few avenues for escape. It was a valid fear for the Union commander at Gauley Bridge to consider. Cox was sufficiently concerned about the Confederate maneuvering near his lines to send the following dispatch to his commander, General Rosecrans, on August 29:

"There are reports that Wise's force has gone south of the river and is strong enough to take Loop, Paint, and other creek roads, with designs on our trains so often rumored. There are reports of an intent to bring artillery over Cotton Hill.".[43]

Cox's small Union army was facing a crisis and the officers guarding Ellen were sufficiently talkative to keep her accurately informed as to the current military situation. Her letter continued:

"Their pickets are fired into and their forces scattered, as the foe appears where least expected. General Rosencranz sent them word he would reach them yesterday with reinforcements by the Somerville road. They are in a bad way today. The *rebels* have got between them and Rosencranz and cut off communication with Gauley. Their

---

41 Tompkins, "Colonel's lady", pg. 396
42 Bailes, "Cox in West Virginia", pg. 29
43 *Ibid*, pg. 29

wagons are fired on (I saw the wounded horses) a mile above this house on the farm but across the river at the narrow falls. Our troops have pickets within two miles above us, the camp two miles and a half off"[44].

General Cox was rapidly finding himself in a difficult situation. His relatively small force of Ohio and Kentucky volunteer regiments was nearly surrounded at Gauley Bridge (and vicinity) and promised reinforcements from General Rosecrans' northern-based troops were unable to get through quickly to provide help. General Floyd's regiments had slipped between the two Federal groups and demonstrated both a willingness to fight and tenacity when they attacked the unfortunate Ohio regiment located at Cross Lanes. Cox was pleasantly surprised by the lack of serious attention he was receiving from the numerically superior Confederates, but did not find out until after the war why his small command was spared. After reviewing some captured Confederate correspondence which was written during this dangerous period, he concluded:

"Wise had a capacity for keeping a command in hot water. If he had been half as troublesome to me as he was to Floyd, I should indeed have had a hot time of it."[45]

The letter to Sarah went on to explain the situation at the farm:

"Now I must tell you how we are situated. Four days ago they put a camp of nearly two thousand men on the field next to my kitchen, with nearly one hundred tents. When I saw them measure the field, I sent Joe[46] to tell the superior officer to come to me. I asked him by whose authority he was acting. He showed me General Cox's order. I told him I did not acknowkledge the right to

44 Tompkins, "Colonel's Lady", pg. 396
45 Cox, *Military Reminiscences*, pg. 97
46 Ellen's son Joseph, was seventeen years old.

intrude on me according to General Rosencranz Order no. 3, which I had cut out of the American".[47]

Rosecrans announced on August 20, 1861 from his headquarters at Clarksburg that among other things:

"... you must remember that the laws are suspended in Eastern Virginia, which has transferred itself to the Southern Confederacy. The old constitution and laws of Virginia are only in force in Western Virginia. These laws you must maintain...Unarmed and peaceful citizens shall be protected, the rights of private property respected ..."[48]

This must have been the approximate content of the General Order Ellen had so cleverly cut from a newspaper for use in protecting her home from the Union troops. Unfortunately for Ellen, military necessity at a time when the Confederates were a severe threat overwhelmed the intent of Rosecrans' order. Cox was in a tight spot and the Tompkins' farm was the best open area where a military post could be constructed for miles in any direction. Cox had no choice other than use the open fields adjacent to Ellen's house, but Ellen felt otherwise:

"He said it was military necessity. I told him to say *convenience.* I fought long to save us the annoyance, but their motto is "*might is right.*" I told him they had taken my corn crop, hay, wheat, etc. and if I could protect nothing I had no resort but to cut the throats of my horses, etc. I then sent a message by an officer I knew was my friend to General Cox to say that I would give up the use of one stable, the vinyard house for a hospital, the overseer's house for the commissary, but there must be a division. I must have my part undisturbed. The Colonel called on me to say General Cox agreed and that he would station sentinels anywhere I said. So they walk night and day in front of the kitchen and really considering, I am not much

47 Tompkins, "Colonel's Lady", pg. 397
48 Moore, *Rebellion Record*, Vol. 2, pg. 540-541

intruded on. But Colonel Fyffe is a gentleman and so is his Lieutenant Colonel. They killed five sheep the first day. So I keep the flock in the front yard, my carriage horses in the turkey house. Sometimes I have to laugh at my contrivances to secure our things. Mr. Dickert, the overseer, could not stay here if I left. They curse him, and threaten him, every day he is true to our interest. He cut off the grapes by the bushel (just turning) as the soldiers were tearing down vines and all. It looked like such a shame"[49]

A great deal of both time and expense had gone into the Tompkins' farm to get it to its' current point. With the constant foraging of the undisciplined Union troops looking for food to supplement their army rations, Ellen could see the farm's rapid erosion in spite of her best efforts to keep it intact. She continued this very long letter to Sarah and attempted to explain her predicament:

"The Generals of our army have sent in three flags of truce to General Cox for him to allow me and the family to pass out of his lines, four miles, and join our forces, but he positively refused, says I may go to Baltimore but not to Lewisburg. I told him I refused entirely to go to Baltimore (he sent Colonel Fyffe to me) that I could not hear from Mr. Tompkins nor could I take the servants. Yesterday General Cox called with three of his officers to apologise for not coming to report to me, as he was much engaged. He certainly is an elegant man, but I think he made a mistake to refuse to let us go. I told him I felt badly as I feared I was in the way of our forces making a military movement. For it stands to reason our troops can't attack Gauley with me exposed between two fires. Of course under these circumstances my presence protects the camp more than Rosencranz' reinforcements. General Cox told me to prevent such a condition of things, in his answer to our Generals, he had told them he would be certain to move me in time out of all danger. They have four cannon and entrenchments on the hill by the kitchen. Mr. T. told

49 Tompkins, "Colonel's Lady", pg. 397

General Wise I was to be depended on in any danger, was thoroughly game. I think I am severely tested."[50]

Cox could hardly permit Ellen to move into the Confederate camp after having seen all of his military preparations to meet the impending Confederate attack. He would have agreed to her travelling to Baltimore, however, as he had explained in a previous letter to Confederate Colonel Henningsen. She had both family and property there. Maryland, while essentially a southern state, had not seceded from the Union and while many of her citizens were Confederate sympathizers, the Federal government was in control. By the time Ellen would have arrived after a journey through part of Ohio, into Pennsylvania, and into Maryland any military information she could have possibly relayed to the Confederate army facing Cox would have been greatly outdated.

She was probably correct when she wrote that "my presence protects the camp..."from any Rebel attack. Cox was too much a gentleman to keep her and her family at risk in order to gain a military advantage, but as long as Ellen Tompkins was living on the farm the Federal troops were not likely to be attacked by the confederate army.

The letter went on to explain her brother's visit under a flag of truce:

"John came with a flag of truce, and as he heard the house was burnt to the ground ventured to see. They fired at him and the ball just grazed him. Again he came with five cavalry and they did not see the flag and they were covered with Enfield rifles. His uniform being like the federals saved him and the flag was seen. He begged so hard to see one of the boys Colonel Fyffe told Captain Simmons to put one on his horse and take him up, but one of the General's aids would not allow it, even at my portico forbid it. I told General Cox he must allow me to go up in the carriage with one of his officers to see John, or let him be brought here blindfolded. The officers were amused to

50 Tompkins, "Colonel's Lady", pg. 397-398

hear me talk to him as they treat him with such deference, not even sitting down without he invites them. He laughed a good deal himself. He said he could not break his rule, but I told him I was an exception to every general rule and to consult policy less, his heart more. He said he would consider it favorably but yesterday sent his Adjutant to say he must ask to delay it for a few days. I sent him word I could not take a refusal and if delayed John might be moved. The Adjutant said the General would be up himself to see me in a day or two. But our troops have made a move, fallen back to Hawk's Nest, and these have sent some companies up to hide in the bushes".[51]

Ellen's brother, Doctor John Wilkins, had been captured while trying to determine the condition of the family after rumors were heard in the Confederate camp that the house had been burned. She did not hesitate to use her charm and power of persuasion on General Cox in order to be permitted to see him. John Wilkins rode in under a flag of truce and was later released to return to his regiment. This is seen by comparing dates of entries in Isaac Smith's diary with the dates of Ellen's letters. She reported the capture in a letter written on September 10 and Smith's diary entry on September 18 referred to Dr. Wilkins offering to treat Smith's malingering slave, Mike, during the march on the previous Thursday.[52]

This probably occurred on September 12 or 13 as the Confederates pulled out of the area. General John B. Floyd arrived in the Gauley Mountain region with his infantry brigade on August 6 and the political infighting between Wise and Floyd began to disrupt the Confederate effort against the Federals holding the Kanawha Valley. At the time Ellen wrote this letter, the two commands had split. Wise and his legion remained in the Hawk's Nest area to keep pressure on Cox's troops in and near Gauley Bridge while Floyd's Brigade marched up Sunday road, crossed the Gauley River at Carnifex Ferry, and routed the

51 Tompkins, "Colonel's Lady", pg. 398
52 Childers, "Virginian's Dilemma", pg 182

7th Ohio at Cross Lanes. Rather than advance on Charleston as Cox feared, Floyd's troops withdrew to Carnifex Ferry and erected field fortifications.

Wise's regiments and the local Confederate militia units under General Chapman and Colonel Beckley operated at will in the area and fired on Union wagon trains moving from Gauley Bridge to the camp at Tompkins' farm. Ellen witnessed the increasing tension as the Federal regiments prepared to be attacked by the numerically superior Confederates:

"September 11: The news is General Rosencranz is cut off from Gauley camp, at least no dispatches can reach him, our troops between. The wagons are shot into, the federals do their hauling at night. Orders have just come to this camp here, to be ready to move at a moment's warning. The batteries above us on the hill are manned, 4 cannon, and three thousand troops on this farm. How would you like to be in our place? I keep the trunks packed as a shell may set fire to the house at any moment. It requires much thought to act rightly. I dare not speak without thought. I know John won't be allowed to come now. The officers express much sympathy for our situation, say they would not have their wives or families in our place. General Cox won't let us go, so I make the best of it. All agree the house would go, if I left, in twenty hours. General Cox says with us here, it is comparatively easy to protect us. There is even amongst the soldiers a feeling for us. I am a great coward naturally, I know, but never have I known a sensation of fear since Mr. T. left. To part with Mr. T. and to have him exposed to their bullets has given me a feeling of desperation. It is true at times all hope forsakes me of seeing him, but I lock myself up until I have cried my heart out fairly, and never give way before the children. Indeed, I dare not, for it would but make matters worse and they are bad enough. I shall have to send this letter today or may not get it off. I regret I cannot relieve your anxiety about us, but I will write again if they let me. Don't allude to a word I have written in your answer. Love to all. "Ellen"[53]

She was much like the Union soldiers in the area. She was expecting an attack at any time and had her more important possessions packed in preparation for an immediate family evacuation she knew would be ordered when the first shells hit the farm. Even with the fear and uncertainty, Ellen still worried about the safety of her husband who was "exposed to their bullets."

Ellen continued the letter with one of her most unusual postscripts:

"Please send this to Wilkins Glenn but do not direct to him, under cover to someone else, as times are such in Baltimore. What is Anne Tilyard's direction? Excuse all mistakes. I have no time to read or correct. Send the slips of paper *To be burnt* by W.G. Mr. Grimme has such a knowledge of the world he is a great advantage, but he and Mr. Dickert refuse to stay if I leave. Mr. Grimme is never willing to see the officers even. Colonel Fyffe brought me a letter from Mr. T., not sealed, telling me he wished me to abandon the property, and could not let me be exposed to such terrible trials. General Cox says"No". Colonel Fyffe sent an answer for me to him, open of course."[54]

The postscripts on Ellen Tompkins' letters generally included instructions to pass her letters to someone with instructions that each be burned. Wilkins Glenn is frequently mentioned as a second recipient and in this case, Sarah is directed to send the letters to someone other than Glenn who should be instructed to deliver the letters to him in a less than obvious way "as times are such in Baltimore". The special instructions that were also provided (and complied with as there is no record of what was written) "Send the slips of paper *To be burnt* [her emphasis] by W. G." is a particularily intriguing phrase.

53 Tompkins, "Colonel's Lady", pg. 398-399
54 *Ibid*, pg. 399

Ellen was later accused of espionage by some Ohio newspapers and while active spying on her "Federal hosts" could probably have been possible, it was discounted by Cox after the war.[55]

Ellen probably would not have hesitated to send notes regarding Union military dispositions to the Confederate military by way of her sister in Baltimore. It is more than simply interesting that Ellen would have used an identical system of message delivery that was utilized by the Confederate espionage service -- except that her letters went the opposite direction.

The operations of the Confederate Secret Service Bureau remain shrouded in mystery. Most of the records of their agent's activities have not been revealed because the acts of espionage which were committed were punishable by hanging at the time and few knew what would happen to them after the war, if their actions became known. With the exception of a few celebrated cases, the files of the Confederate espionage service remain a mystery. There are a few documented cases which shed light on their methods of operation. One that has become known involves a leg of a very efficient courier system which operated along the eastern shore directly across from Confederate territory. The farm of Thomas A. Jones was located directly across the Potomac River from a Confederate debarkation point that was used to start both people and correspondence into the infiltration network that branched out into the North. Jones had been arrested by the Federal authorities early in the war for ferrying travellers across into Virginia who were evading Union warrants or possible incarceration as Southern sympathizers. While he was in prison, his wife had died and he became a willing recruit for the Confederate Secret Service Bureau. His farm was only one mile away from the Virginia shore and he quickly determined the watch schedules of the Union pickets sent to guard the river. A black cloth hung in a neighbor's attic window warned any boat departing from the Virginia side that there were Federal guards in the vicinity and with this

55 Cox, *Military Reminiscences*, pg. 87

simple, but effective warning system in effect, travellers and information crossed the river safely. Packets of northbound letters would be deposited in the fork of a dead tree and when the area was clear of any Federal pickets, Jones would simply walk to the tree, pick up the information, and place it in the Federal mail system to be delivered to Confederate agents and sympathizers throughout the northern states.[56]

It does not stretch the imagination to picture Ellen Tompkins using the exact same mechanism only in reverse in order to get her letters to Confederate authorities in Richmond who could make use of the information contained in the "...slips of paper *To be burnt...*"which went to Wilkins Glenn. This could simply be a coincidence, but the discovery of the identity of Wilkins Glenn tightens the available circumstantial evidence to something which can be believed.

William Wilkins Glenn was a resident of Baltimore and was a co-owner of the newspaper, the *Daily Exchange.* He was obviously a Confederate sympathizer -- a vocal supporter as he was imprisoned by the Union authorities for his political activities. He and Ellen shared the same middle name -- Wilkins -- and it is safe to assume that they were cousins. He was probably very familar with the Confederate courier system operating out of Maryland which was so efficient that New York newspapers could be delivered to Richmond within 24 hours of their publication.[57]

He had the capability of simply placing Ellen's letters into the Federal mail system to have them delivered to Farmer Jones, but too much mail in a rural area can create suspicion, so Glenn probably sent the information provided by Ellen through the courier system. It was probably placed in the fork of the dead tree -- a dead letter drop -- with a bundle of mail for the Confederate capital and the "loading signal"-- the black cloth in the attic window --

---

56 Time-Life, *Spies, Scouts, and Raiders - Irregular Operations*, pg. 51-52

57 *Ibid*, pg. 51

was set up to indicate that the dead drop needed to be serviced. Rebel boatmen rowed across the narrow stretch of river, retrieved the bundle, and Ellen's information was soon in the hands of the Confederate army.

Whether Ellen was briefed carefully on the actual mechanism to be used to send out information will never be known, but there can be little doubt that she actively delivered information that she discovered to the Confederate authorities in Richmond. This could account for much of the anxiety on the part of Colonel Tompkins to get her out of the farm safely when she was being accused of being involved with spying. He was probably aware of the plan to transmit casual information to the South. He had told General Wise that Ellen "was to be depended on in any danger, was thoroughly game."[58]

If the circumstantial evidence is correct, Ellen's motivation was probably explained with her comment regarding the Union cannoneer who lost his arm in the premature discharge : "...Better them than our forces should suffer."[59]

The next obvious questions must go without answers:

A. Was Ellen a deliberate "stay-behind" agent?

B. Had she been carefully briefed as to the method to use to get her letters into the Confederate courier system or was all of this simply a coincidence?

C. Was William Wilkins Glenn a major player in the Confederate Secret Service Bureau and how did Ellen know to send her letters to him?

D. Since all of this occurred quite early in the war, how would the Confederates have known to prepare Ellen for any future role?

It is unlikely that any preliminary thought had been given to the development of Ellen Tompkins as a potential stay-behind agent who would remain within the Union camp and report as she was able on their activities. It is far more plausible to believe that a hasty plan was conceived at the Tompkin's dinner table when General Wise had a final

58 Tompkins, "Colonel's Lady", pg. 398
59 *Ibid*, pg. 396

meal at the house the day before the Union soldiers visited the farm for the first time. A hastily conceived plan was explained to her on a system which could possibly be used to communicate safely if she were able to observe and record any significant military activity. She learned to work like a professional in a very short time.

All of the aspects of a professional espionage network were present in the system used by Ellen. It is far too complete to have been simply a coincidence or the hasty assembly of ideas on the part of a housewife. She used her special status well and quickly "recruited" many of her Union officer contacts. She gave letters directly to General Cox for mailing through the Federal postal system to her sister in another Union state knowing that the letters would not be opened. These crossed no hostile lines and at the time no "gentleman" would ever consider reading the private thoughts of a lady. She had her sister forward the letters with the special slips of paper which had to be destroyed to another person who would then deliver the letters to Wilkins Glenn. She now had a mechanism which would reduce the chances of her discovery, if the letters should be intercepted by Federal authorities. Wilkins Glenn had every opportunity to slip the notes into the Confederate courier system -- perhaps not identical to the "line" worked by Mr. Jones, but something similar. Letters would move down Maryland's eastern shore and be ferried across the river to Virginia for a quick trip to Richmond. It is very unlikely that Ellen Tompkins developed this special delivery system alone.

She continued to ask that her letters be sent to third parties, ordered that each be burned, and occasionally asked if her letters had been received and identified them by the name of the person scheduled to be the receiving party. This was an interesting system for accounting for forwarded letters and a simultaneous reminder that she had wanted them forwarded.

There is some evidence that the courier system worked back to Ellen with some information. She was later to tell her sister to forward a letter to "Cousin Henrietta Glenn as I know they are attached to Mr. T." Again there are questions: How did she know that Henrietta Glenn was travelling with Colonel Tompkins'regiment and if her sister, Sarah, was instructed to send the letter to Colonel Tompkins' camp, how did Ellen know that her sister was able to get the letter sent through or around the Union lines?

The Confederate courier system was probably involved and may have been more extensive than anyone could have imagined. There is no other obvious method for accounting for the two-way flow of information that appears to have been occurring. If all of this conjecture is true, Tompkins' statement he made to General Wise at the time of their final dinner was correct. Ellen "was to be depended on in any danger, was thoroughly game."

The next letter to be sent to Sarah contained news of the battle fought at Carnifex Ferry between General Rosecrans' troops and the Confederates under General Floyd. Union forces were held off until after darkness halted the fighting and the Confederates withdrew. Rosecrans had a superior force and was able to get a cavalry force through to Gauley Bridge to order General Cox to send his regiments east on the turnpike in an attempt to cut off and trap Wise and Floyd between the two advancing Union forces.

Ellen explained the fighting to her sister quite accurately in a letter dated September 13:

"I find it impossible to find a trusty person to send this by, therefore send you the news. General Rosencranz with four thousand men attacked our forces Sunday afternoon and fought until seven, then fell back a quarter of a mile, intending when his troops came up to fight his way through to Gauley (this was at Cross Lane's) but our troops did not allow him to find them but yet managed to cut off his communication until yesterday when a company of his cavalry came in and ordered General Cox to advance up this road with the 11th Ohio, 26th Regiment (the one camped here) 2nd Kentucky and one more and meet

General Rosencranz who hopes to hem our troops in as he advances on the Somerville road which enters this turnpike. They were passing here all night with their wagons with provisions, ammunition, cannon, then seven ambulances with surgeons followed, looking like hearses with their black covers. I cannot find out where our troops are. Mr. T. sent me a letter by a flag truce, but as my letters and his are examined by the Generals our correspondence *is very formal, not dated.* I am filled with anxiety of course. The batteries on our hill are manned. They say one good victory here, then on to Richmond. They will never get there. General Cox sent his Adjutant General up to me, with his compliments, to say he hoped in a few days to give me a pass to Richmond, and also sent a letter from Florence Fuller. Do you know, the soldiers believe General Cox is my brother-in-law; he is so attentive to protect me. I must confess my situation has elicited much kindness from the officers, but I trust few and ask favors from none but General Cox and three others. Go to the highest in command is the safest for me. The mistake was in ordering General Wise to abandon this valley. They could not have advanced to save their lives, but now Governor Letcher is deposed, acording to them, Governor Pierpont wants *all* Virginia. Can he get it? I won't pay my taxes to him. They hope to get to Dogwood Gap, 14 miles from here, and surprise our troops. Could I but have warned them, but no doubt they are up to them. I can't tell if I will accept the pass as General Cox kept me here to oblige his views, I may stay to favor my own. He has not got the victory yet. To add to my troubles Willie[60] has been very sick, caught cold. All the rest are well and get the name of being such bright, gentlemanly children. Joe passes current as he never names politicks.

"The soldiers are much excited about not being paid for four months, fed on pork and beans and stale crackers, sleeping on the ground and targets at all times. They earn eleven dollars a month. They say the politicians get it. The troops have exhausted three wells and now use the ice dam

60 "Willie" was the eleven year old son of the Tompkins.

and spring. A sentinel has to protect my well to secure us water. Write again as I may remain, for I can't tell what Mr. Tompkins wishes me to do now, and will remain if he desires it. But I really cannot in a letter tell you our trials. Two of our servants just escaped a few moments ago being shot. They were getting fire wood and not recognized as their backs were that way. The order is to shoot all not in uniform. A sentinel stopped the soldiers just in time. I keep the children in sight all the time, as they would be shot by accident. The servants are tempted to sell everything they can get to the soldiers. How I envy any one who can rest without a feeling of apprehension. These officers tell me if they could but get Mr. Tompkins, he wields so much influence here, musters the militia, etc. and that Judge Summers and all union men speak of him so highly. If taken prisoner, he would be sent to Colombus as they won't exchange prisoners. But they have not got him yet, and I feel sure they won't. The country people are all devoted to him, tell these officers, 'Pray never shoot Col. T.' All tell me of his popularity.
"Send this to Wilkins Glenn. He must burn it. Your second letter has arrived, mine must be burned."[61]

Ellen was unable to locate someone she could totally trust, so she told Sarah "...therefore send you the news." What would she have mailed her sister if she had found a trustworthy person? Probably a great deal more information than just the news. It is interesting that there were no slips of paper in addition to the letter to be passed on the Wilkins Glenn.

The Union commander in the valley, General Cox, genuinely appreciated the predicament of Ellen and the children and did many things to assist them. As a man of honor, he had accepted the responsibility of protecting the family when asked by Colonel Tompkins. He went as far as receiving Ellen's mail at his headquarters in Gauley Bridge, delivered the letters *unopened* to her at Gauley Mount, and ensured that there were sufficient armed guards

61 Tompkins, "Colonel's Lady", pg. 399-400

on hand to provide adequate protection at all times. It is little wonder that the common soldiers of the Federal regiments on the farm thought that the general was Ellen's brother-in-law. Strangers normally would never receive such protection.

Cox later explained the relationship:

"When Wise had retreated from the valley, Colonel Tompkins had been unable to remove his family, and had left a letter commending them to our courteous treatment. Mrs. Tompkins was a lady of refinement and her position was far from being a comfortable one. She, however, put a cheerful face upon her situation, showed great tact in avoiding controversy with the soldiers and in conciliating the good will of the officers, and remained with her children and servants in her picturesque home on the mountain. So long as there was no fighting in the near vicinity, it was comparatively easy to save her from annoyance; but when later in the autumn Floyd occupied Cotton Mountain and General Rosecrans was with us with larger forces, such a household became an object of suspicion and ill will..."[62]

Ellen's situation became increasingly precarious as the month of September continued. The military situation was far from stable as the Confederate forces withdrew after the stalemate at Carnifex Ferry. Union troops were maneuvering to attempt to trap Floyd and Wise's commands between Cox and General Rosecrans' larger Union army which was continuing to pursue southward along Sunday road toward the James River and Kanawha Turnpike. Cox's smaller Federal force moved east from Gauley Bridge and Gauley Mount along the turnpike in an attempt to hold the Confederates until Rosecrans could attack their rear. The political situation was also becoming undesirable for Ellen Tompkins and people in the region with convictions similar to hers. Attitudes toward southern sympathizers were beginning to harden as the war

62 Cox, *Military Reminiscences*, pg. 86-87

began to lengthen along with the casualty lists. A new Federal administrative unit, the Mountain Department, was created by the government primarily to provide a command for the blundering John C. Fremont.

Fremont had come a long way from the heroic "trailblazer" who found new routes through the continental interior to the west coast and he had been the new Republican party's first Presidential candidate in 1856. He had failed in a western command in the early stages of the war and was being given a final opportunity to redeem himself as a military leader. He began to take and advocate a hardline against secessionists and ordered arrests as well as property confiscations.

Ellen's Union protectors were able to shield her from the effects of Fremont's proclamation, but the threat of property seizure hung over her head constantly.

She explained her latest problems to Sarah in a letter written on September 16, 1861:

"I have not met a man I could send this by without the risk of being opened. I think they have a great respect for our talent to outwit them. They have guards all round the house at night. I go into the front and back porches the last thing at night. As I walked out last night, each side of the front door was a sentinel. I did not speak nor did they. I walked around as usual, for if I let them see me afraid I should be imposed on directly. I was obliged just now to send for the officer in command and told him I would allow no one to impose on me beyond a certain point. I should report it to General Cox as a nuisance. He made me apologies at once. I told him once before an officer went beyond his orders, but I reported it to General Cox and he was not allowed to come here again, as he was told that he was objectionable to me. One of their guards climbed into the bedroom of Mr. Dickert. He seized an axe and he got out of the window. Yesterday four officers came to see me on business. I am tired of such a responsible situation, for Mr.Grimme never sees them I have to depend upon myself. I have to act with policy yet be independent, they are so imposing. All acknowledge the soldiers are friendly to me as I never omit doing them a kindness, especially for their sick and a number are sick. This camp is being moved away to my great relief. General Cox and three thousand men went up four days ago and found the camp of *rebels* nine miles from here deserted, as they had started a few hours before on a retreat to Lewisburg. They had three thousand men of General Rosencranz employed in putting up barracades to fight behind, then by a side road called the Sunday road had advanced a regiment to cut off the retreat, but our troops got round another side road and escaped the trap they set for them. The federals now are camping about thirty miles from here and the reports vary about their plans. Some say they are to go to Richmond, others to East Tennessee, if successful, but I believe the main body of General Rosencranz is in a fix and they are trying to relieve him.

"The camp at Gauley is still manned, but I could promise one thousand men could take it. The federals are not boastful at present. At Cross roads they lost one hundred men besides Colonel Lowe. They report that General Lee was defeated at Cheat Mountain with great loss on both sides. What do you think of the proclamation of General Fremont? Is it not outrageous? Orders have arrived here to take all secessionists and to confiscate all property. The soldiers are not pleased with General Fremont's act, as they say they have friends on both sides and would not like their friends shot. Write again, but always put my name on the outside, care of General Cox, Gauley Bridge, Fayette County. The letters are sent me. A new officer has just come in and I will send this by him as I believe he can be trusted as well as any for all my best friends are above. Please put me a few of the new stamps in your next letter. My letters must be burnt. As I hear there is such times in Baltimore, I shall certainly remain here as cannot pass through two armies on the road to Lewisburg. Write at once. I can't read this over as I have no time."[63]

---

63 Tompkins, "Colonel's Lady", pg. 401-402

The Union officers were certainly developing an awareness of Ellen's ability to stay one step ahead of them. They also began to suspect that she was able to get messages to the Confederates about Federal strength and preparations in the area. Most of this could have been based on camp rumor, but Ellen was located in an excellent position and was a keen observer. Her remark to Sarah in a previous letter must always be remembered when trying to decide if the flimsy evidence shows she was spying benignly on her hosts: "Better them than our forces..." This will help in making the decision regarding whether she arranged for information to be passed directly to Wise's forces. There was an additional comment made in a letter which was suggestive:"...Could I but have warned them..." was sent to Sarah as Cox's troops marched past the farm in an attempt to trap the retreating Rebels.

The Union soldiers certainly believed that messages and signals were used to aid the rebels. Cox later wrote:

"The men fancied they saw signals conveyed from the house to the enemy, and believed that secret messages were sent, giving information of our numbers and movements."[64]

Cox's small Federal garrison had been in a difficult situation. They had been out-numbered, cut off from immediate re-inforcement, and the Union soldiers *knew* that they were in a poor tactical situation. Confederate strength in the immediate area was reported to be in the vicinity of 10,000 or 12,000 men and additional reports reaching Cox warned

"...of a general stir among the secessionists in Fayette, Mercer, and Raleigh counties, and of the militia being ordered out under General Chapman to support the Confederate movement by operating on my line of communications, whilst Floyd and Wise should attack in front."[65]

64 Cox, *Military Reminiscences*, pg. 87
65 *Ibid*, pg. 91

Given the general perception of peril among the Union garrison, Ellen Tompkins was fortunate to have been allowed to remain on the farm. Cox informed Ellen in a letter on a later date that while she had won the respect of his officers, the troops were in a constant state of irritation and Cox was afraid that her property if not her person might be endangered. Cox took many special precautions for the safety of the family that Ellen didn't know about.

As previously mentioned, the privates in the Union army were an unruly group. Rosecrans had appointed a future President, Rutherford B. Hayes, as his Judge Advocate (a military prosecuting attorney) and he was kept busy with courts martial of the undisciplined soldiers. Hayes recorded in his diary some unpleasant details about some of his cases from only a single regiment in Cox's small army, the Ninth Ohio Infantry Regiment, a totally German unit:

"... one man shot resisting a corporal, two men in irons for a rape ..."[66]

Many of the enlisted men in the Union army were not necessarily nice people to be around. They were relatively uneducated, generally hard-drinking, and had to be managed with rigid discipline from their officers. Ellen Tompkins was taking a great risk by remaining on the farm in what was rapidly becoming an important Union military post. She and her family were quite fortunate to have had as friends General Cox and a few of his senior officers. If their protection had not been there, the outlook for the family may have been grim.

Ellen sent another letter to Sarah a few days later which was written on September 22:

"Dear Sarah,

"I wrote to you ten days ago, but I expect it was not

66 Hayes, Rutherford B., *Diary and Letters of Rutherford Birchard Hayes*, edited by Charles R. Williams, Ohio State Archaeological and Historical Society: 1922, pg. 83

sent as a great scamp took it. I asked you to send it to Cousin Henrietta Glenn as I know they are attached to Mr. T. I have tonight over a hundred wagons camped here, but they go tomorrow. The guard has to be very active, I tell you, to keep the teamsters right. The two officers here I know I can fully depend on. Would I not suffer if they had their way. A secession Colonel is fair game. Mr. Tompkins' character and position secure me much consideration. Even the roughest teamsters will call to tell me Mr. T. is well. Say they have wives and feel for my situation. The country people send me messages if they hear of Mr. T. or John who is very popular."[67]

Union supply trains apparently stopped overnight at the farm as the wagons ferried supplies from the nearest point of steamboat navigation at the mouth of Loup Creek eastward to the area where active combat operations were being prepared. The teamsters were generally a rough, hard-drinking, disorderly group who would have carried away any loose object they could get their hands on. "A secession Colonel is fair game" simply meant that Ellen understood that any of her property could be carried off without any threat of punishment if someone was apprehended during the theft.

As Colonel Tompkins had resided in the area since 1855, was a prominent citizen, and a Lieutenent-Colonel in the area's militia,[68] he was liked and well respected by all of the county's residents. It is not surprising that the country people would try to get word to Ellen when they heard anything about Tompkins. This, incidentally, could have been an opportunity for Ellen to send verbal messages through the lines. The local people would know all of the safe routes through Union pickets and would have willingly carried word about Ellen and the family to Tompkins -- possibly with other information, as well.

Ellen's long letter continued;

---

67 Tompkins, "Colonel's Lady", pg. 402

68 Personal correspondence between Tompkins and George Cullum on 25 October 1855.

"The whole camp is ordered to be moved and now these regiments are to advance, take Lewisburg and the railroad and go to East Tennessee. But providence interfered for us. General Rosencranz sent a dispatch to General Cox to advance on our troops up this road and he would send three thousand men by a road to get them between, attack front and rear at once. Well! Twelve cavalry started with this dispatch and a German picket (*of their own*) fired into them not being able to understand English. They shot ten, the other two remained in the woods twenty-four hours and that gave our troops time to retreat beyond the place where their plans were laid. Were not they mad? I outwit them in finding out the news, guard us as they may. I make friends in curious ways. No one was allowed to speak to us except before a commissioned officer, but I still heard the news. When I found out that our troops had escaped the trap, you can imagine my joy. Still my anxiety is terrible as there is to be a battle at Lewisburg or the end of the railroad. They are so confident of success that I have trouble to be silent. The 26th Regiment camped here nearly three weeks and took off with them the most valuable man I have. General Cox says he shall be returned, but the soldiers have him hid in the woods now. He will be so demoralized that he will be of no value."[69]

Even though Ellen and the children cannot speak with the Union troops unless there is a Union officer present, she took pleasure in being able to continue to gather militarily-significant information which was mailed to her sister. She carefully worded the information so that it will appear as "news"or idle gossip between two women, but there is significant information in the letters which are sent to Sarah.

Ellen apparently had a great ability to draw people into conversations where they would eventually let a few facts slip. It is probable that most of her information came from the commissioned officers detailed to prevent any

[69] Tompkins, "Colonel's Lady", pg. 403

conversation with the enlisted guards. They were naturally talkative about their "exploits" and probably talked freely around Ellen when they visited her home or were invited to dinner. Most men are eager to impress a pretty, cultured woman and will generally "slip" during a conversation.

She was concerned about the loss of a valuable piece of property, a male slave who was being hidden in the woods by the soldiers. She was not any different from any other person of her class at the time. She had grown up with slaves held as property and obviously saw nothing wrong with the institution. The Federal soldiers felt differently.

The letter continued with some details of the bloody rout of the Union regiment surprised earlier at Cross Lanes:

"Mr. T. was at the battle of Cross Lanes with General Floyd's brigade. Lieutenant-Colonel Ben Ficklen led the charge. The Seventh Ohio was surrounded and had to run. They say the charge was so handsome they forgot the danger in sight. But two companies ran to get to a mountain pass and the soldiers (the remainder of the 7th guard us now) told the boys, Joe and Chris, that there was, to their surprise, Colonel Tompkins' regiment drawn up and had he fired, the slaughter would have been murderous, but he ordered the men not to fire and called out, 'Throw down your arms, boys, and you shall not be touched.' Was it not noble and like him? The officers told me he won the respect of the men by that order. You may imagine the trial to have these men at every meal and then to know they are trying to take Mr. T."[70]

Several of the men from the Seventh Ohio who were captured by Colonel Tompkins' regiment at the battle of Cross Lanes escaped or were recovered by Union troops after the battle fought at Carnifex Ferry. The word of Tompkins' chivilarous act would have quickly spread in the Federal camp and this single act of compassion did much to win friends for Ellen in the Union army. Many may have

[70] Tompkins, "Colonel's Lady", pg. 403

felt that they owed a debt of honor and were repaying it by protecting Ellen and his children.

The episode related by Ellen in the letter regarding the German picket (a group of soldiers on guard in an advanced position) and the shooting of their own cavalry couriers resulted in a delay of an order from Rosecrans to his field units that, if delivered, could have resulted in a battle in which the Confederates would have been outnumbered and probably defeated. Ellen was elated over this stroke of luck as the Union error resulted in her husband being safe for a longer period.

Accidental woundings and deaths were common occurrences in these early stages of the war. The men were not familar with "challenge and password" systems and the most dangerous duty in either army facing junior officers was making the rounds of his advanced pickets. These officers were frequently shot by accident by their own soldiers and since the picket posts were normally close to the enemy's forward positions, the young officers were also in danger of being killed by the opposing forces.

Ellen continued:

"How I envy you a quiet home and your family at home with you. My trials are terrible. Willie is much better, but looks delicate. The rest are well and I am no worse. Write anything you like in your letters. Both of yours arrived safely, also one from Helen to Ellen. She will write soon.

"Major Leiper dined here yesterday and told me his wife in New York had sent him a column of the Exchange with an extract of a letter from me. I expressed surprise, but took it very cooly. He said there was a Southern spirit through it. What else could he expect? Do pray send me a copy, for I wrote in haste, as I always do, and feel ashamed not to copy often. They all know General Cox will protect me and amongst his staff and high officers I really can depend on being treated kindly. That is the only redeeming feature in the situation we are placed in. I wrote you three flags of truce had been sent in about letting us pass through their lines. General Cox refused, but said I could go to

Baltimore. I refused as I should be cut off from Mr. T. As it was General Cox I submitted. He is a refined, elegant gentleman and very handsome. Colonel Tyler commands at Gauley, but still direct as before, without General Cox's name as he is away. Please send me a few of the new stamps. There are none here and my letters have to be franked. Let me know if you received the third letter, that one I wished sent to cousin Henrietta Glenn, not this. Burn this.[71]

Ellen Tompkins' situation worsened toward the end of September and in early October. General Rosecrans, General Cox'superior, had moved his headquarters into the Gauley Bridge area. With him came some more hardened, less gentlemanly officers who were not in sympathy with Ellen's plight. Among these was Rutherford B. Hayes, a former lawyer who appeared to see things in terms of "right and wrong". He didn't feel that it was proper for U.S. troops to be standing guard over a rebel Colonel's property. He wrote in his diary:

"Why devastate the homes and farms of poor deluded privates in the rebel army and protect this property? Treat the lady well, as all women ought always to be treated, but put through the man for his great crime".[72]

The burning of rebel property was a common occurrence during the war. A typical patrol in the western Virginia area was described in a soldier's diary:

"Scouting party of eighteen men. Went out about ten miles where we burned a schoolhouse and a stillhouse and captured fifty chickens and a number of turkies."[73]

71 Tompkins, "Colonel's Lady", pg. 403

72 Williams, Harry T., *Hayes of the Twenty-third: The Civil War Officer*, Alfred A. Knopf, New York: 1965, pg. 92

73 *Ibid*, pg. 64

The destruction of rebel property was to provoke anger and hatred that lasted through the war and beyond. The southern sympathizers in the area were outraged at these raids, but were too weak militarily to defend themselves and their property. In response to these depredations carried out by their Unionist neighbors or the Federal troops, they sought revenge for the arbitrary arrests and arson by resorting to "bushwhacking" or the ambushing or murdering sentries, neighbors, or officials blamed for the destruction. These acts of revenge generally provoked Union reprisals and an extremly vicious cycle of violence became common. Bushwhacking became a common tactic of the guerrilla warfare that began to be used against the "arsonist" Union troops. The reprisals generally consisted of more killings and arson and the cycle of hatred continued throughout the war in western Virginia and remained after the war to spawn some long-running feuds.

Burning or pillaging the property of the rich rebel Colonel or worse must have been a common thought among the Union privates. They were moving through a largely Southern sympathizing region like a swarm of locusts when they encountered rebel property. Remember that Ellen had described them as "...very angry, say it is a pretty kind of a war, here is a secession Colonel and they are not allowed to pillage anything, not even a chicken..."[74]

Ellen was indeed fortunate that General Cox and his senior staff officers had taken extra precautions to protect the family from the ravages that constantly hovered nearby.

The first two pages of a letter written by Ellen in late September or early October, 1861, are missing, but the pages that are left reflect some of the change of attitude toward Ellen and the farm with the arrival of Rosecrans' veteran troops following the battle at Carnifex Ferry. She related a meeting she had with one of Rosecrans' brigade quartermasters who was attempting to procure supplies from the farm:

"I had a stormy interview with a quartermaster, He

[74] Tompkins, "Colonel's Lady", pg. 392

said he wished to buy hay and corn. I told him I regretted I could not oblige him, but my new corn crop (about four or five hundred bushels) was eaten green by the soldiers; I had given all the hay away I could spare. He said, 'Well, I will replace it.' I said I could not run that risk as a long winter was ahead and as horses could not eat money, I should have no resort but to cut their throats. He said, 'Well, Madam, I shall take it.' 'Why,Sir,' said I, 'did you call to ask me about it if such was your determination? By whose authority do you act?' 'My own,' said he, 'as brigade quartermaster, for I did not ask General Cox as I feared he would refuse.' I said, 'I don't acknowledge your authority, Sir, you shall not have my corn or hay.' He said,'You should remember you are treated differently from every one in your peculiar situation.' I said, 'General Cox attends to that.' He said, 'Every officer agrees that you are a real lady and that is another reason.' 'By them I am treated as one,' I said. He lost his temper, repeated his threats in a most disagreeable manner. Then my indignation got beyond my control. I told him he should not touch my corn or hay and I knew my rights and he should see I'd maintain them. He left at once. The officer with him did not open his lips. I called the officer of the guard in, told him I'd look to him to carry out General Cox's orders to protect me and my property. He said he would certainly do it. The officer in charge of the camp here said he would turn out every man to protect me, I had been kind to them. I told Major Leiper the next day not to send him here again, I would have no business transactions with him, we were strangers forever. He regretted it had occurred, but said I had done all I could, and he would report it. The quartermaster is very unpopular. I believe they were glad I put him down. I don't wish you to name it, but thought I'd tell you to let you see I won't be imposed on. In fact I made myself popular by the act. I heard several say that he needed it sadly, but they had no right to put him down."[75]

The provisioning of a large military force in those

[75] Tompkins, "Colonel's Lady", pg. 404

mountains was an extremely difficult job. The condition of the roads was poor and the record rains that autumn had made them nearly impassable. Supplies had to be hauled in wagons from the head of river navigation to the forward areas and the trip was so long that nearly half of the transport capacity had to be reserved for food for the horses and mules pulling the loads. The wagons had to carry sufficient feed for the return trip. The quartermaster had seen this serious problem and found a solution. It was obviously easier to haul money than animal fodder and he attempted to purchase the scarce supplies on the Tompkins' farm. Ellen also had problems with animal feed and realized that her horses "couldn't eat money" during the winter and refused to sell the feed to the army. Her supporters included the Officer of the Guard on the farm at the time and the Union commander at "Camp Tompkins" who had seen his men treated with kindness. All committed themselves to Ellen's defence and it may have gone hard on the unpopular quartermaster, if he had chosen to press the issue on a return trip. Ellen felt that she had made herself even more popular with the soldiers in the area by taking a stand against the unpopular officer and several officers apparently mentioned that he deserved what he had received. She felt they had "no right to put him down"--she reserved that right for herself.

The letter went on to provide some of the news of the war in the area of the farm:

"The news is our troops have retreated safely to Meadow Bluff, near Lewisburg and are fortified there, escaped all the traps of Rosencranz and Cox, and that the secessionists are trying to cut off their wagon trains, 120 camped here last night, and fifty more wagons are here. I feel that our troops are getting on much better, but fear to trust the particulars in a letter. Don't send this letter to Anne or any one. Burn it."[76]

She had included a separate letter in the envelope

[76] Tompkins, "Colonel's Lady", pg. 404-405

which she wanted sent to Henry Wilkins:

"Send this letter to Henry."[77]

The news provided by Ellen in the letter that the Confederates had eluded the traps of the Union generals and had safely withdrawn to Meadow Bluff and were constructing field fortifications was correct. They were also receiving reinforcements from the Cheat Mountain area and General Lee would soon arrive to assume command. This could have been some of the information that Ellen may have included in the letter, if she had any confidence that the letter would have been safely delivered. With the new officers in the nearby town of Gauley Bridge who could have the same general attitude toward her that was exhibited by the quartermaster and felt by Rutherford B. Hayes, she probably feared to send significant military information in her letters for fear that they would be opened.

The two hostile armies were within sight of each other and skirmishes between pickets and patrols were beginning. Unfortunately for both sides, the Sewell Mountain region was one of the more inaccessible areas in western Virginia and the poor weather was beginning to leave the dirt roads impassable. Resupply of ammunition and food to the forward units was virtually impossible during bad weather and both sides had their lines of communication from their supply depots stretched to their limits. The combinations of bad weather, poor roads, high water at critical ferries and high levels of camp disease began to impact on the development of a major battle which was beginning to form. All of the pieces were present and what began to appear to be a decisive battle for the control of western Virginia was endangered by the tenuous supply situation. Ellen began another long letter to Sarah on October 5, 1861, but had to complete it the following day. She described the typical problems of her average day and the difficulty she was beginning to have from many of the

77 Tompkins, "Colonel's Lady", pg. 405

Union officers while another group labored to defend her and her property:

"Dear Sarah,

"I received your two letters, but wonder if mine went straight. I sent one for you to forward to Cousin H G.[78]

"I sent another with a letter for Henry. I had the pleasure of receiving a letter from Ann Tilyard. Two officers brought it and civilly informed me that they would like to remain all night. I declined the honor, but gave them their supper for the letter."[79]

Once again, Ellen is attempting to casually account for her letters to ensure they were forwarded to the right persons and remind Sarah that they should have been sent on if Sarah had not yet done it. This is a sign of a careful "bookkeeper" whose letters were going beyond casual correspondence. She continued:

"Just let me give you a description of one day and all are alike in trials to me. Yesterday first came as an officer of General Rosencranz to say that he wished three hundred horses to camp here and two artillery companies, some of General Rosencranz' staff officers. I asked him his orders. He said not to do so without my consent and General R. said, if possible, to go elsewhere. I told him very politely I hoped he would go farther. I would consider it a great favor, that I was annoyed to death, every night wagoners camping here over a hundred at a time. Well, by being civil, he went on three miles above. I thanked him and told him I was glad to speed the parting guest. But just as they

78 "H.G." was probably her cousin, Henrietta Glenn. She was probably related to Wilkins Glenn. In a previous leter, Ellen told Sarah that Henrietta was "attached to Mr. T." In order to forward the letter to Cousin Henrietta, Sarah had to send it through Union lines -- into Virginia-- and ensure that it was forwarded to Sewell Mountain. That would have been quite a feat for a family correspondence system.

79 Tompkins, "Colonel's Lady", pg. 405

were off and we were enjoying the hope of a quiet night, a party took possession of one of my fields, had six tents up before we saw them. I sent for the superior officer and asked him by whose authority he intruded on my premises. He said he did not know my property was different from other people's. I was provoked at once. I told him he'd find it was, for I was protected by General Cox and Colonel Tyler in command of Gauley Bridge. He said he hoped I'd allow them to stay all night as they were all unharnessed. He'd pay for all damages. I told him I scorned his money, I would not touch a cent if I was starving, it was the insult to my private rights. They were an awful set. They tore down the fences and were so mad that they could not do as they chose, that it was terrible to hear them cursing us, said one half of a regiment was kept to guard us while Mr. T. was killing the other half. But for an officer of the 26th Ohio, I do not know what would have happened. I ever shall remember Lieutenant Hicks. He was up nearly all night. It took two guards at the back of the house, two in front, and two at the barn, to walk all night to protect us."[80]

This was beginning to become an unpleasant ordeal for Ellen Tompkins. Her primary protector, General Cox, was farther up the turnpike preparing for combat on Sewell Mountain. His subordinate, Colonel Tyler, was in command of the post at Gauley Bridge and was instructed to provide protection for the family, but he was several miles away. He could not be constantly at the farm. Many of the Federal officers were honest, truthful soldiers and unlike the quartermaster reported on in the previous letter, they would ask permission from Ellen prior to setting up camp on her property. The latest incident was provoked by Ellen when she felt that her "private rights" had been "insulted". Provoking the Federal officers and men was becoming a dangerous game and if it were not for the loyal guard force on the farm, she may have lost the house to arson that night.

General Rosecrans was now in overall command in

---

[80] Tompkins, "Colonel's lady", pg. 405-406

the area, and while Colonel Tompkins had made the original request to protect his family in a letter to General Cox, the new commander felt required to honor it. Rosecrans accepted the responsibility as if it were his own. He had required the artillery officer to ask Ellen's permission before setting up a camp and to set up in another location, if that was possible, rather than inconvenience her. The rapid assumption of Cox's responsibility would seem to indicate some sort of relationship between Rosecrans and Tompkins had existed prior to the war.

Rosecrans -- like Tompkins -- was a graduate of West Point who finished his studies in 1842, six years after Tompkins had graduated. They did not share West Point experiences and records of an association in the pre-war regular army have not been located, but graduates of the Military Academy were generally a close group. Later, Tompkins was to write a letter to Rosecrans to thank him for the consideration shown to his family and said:

"I wish I could talk with you and many of my old friends and comrades on your side of the question. I believe we could manage affairs better than the politicians or at least differ honestly in our respective views."[81]

While there is no obvious connection between these two officers in the pre-war military, the informal style in the letter leads to the conclusion that there had been some sort of association between the two at some time before the outbreak of hostilities. This probably occurred when the two were working in the western Virginia counties to mine coal, produce coal oil, and locate markets for their products in the states to the south and west. The common experience at West Point would have given the two a reason to become closer than simply acquaintences. Ellen's letter went on:

"They were putting up a telegraph wire from Sewell

[81] Tompkins, "Colonel's Lady", pg. 412

Mountain to Gauley, and in the morning cutting down all the trees I loved to see. We have a superb grindstone where they were sharpening their axes. I remarked that it was a hard case, I had to allow them to sharpen their axes to cut my favorite trees. Willie, who is as sharp as a briar, took Chris out, and together they took the handle off and they, the enemy, were out done I assure you. They blessed us, and finally sent in Lieutenant Hicks to ask me to let them grind three axes and one hatchet and then they would cut no more of the trees, and the Captain said they would hurry the men off. I sent word I would agree to those terms, and let them have the handle."[82]

When the handle was removed and hidden, Ellen reported that the enemy "blessed us" probably in terms that only soldiers far from home and frustrated by a woman and children could give as a blessing. Ellen probably had her hands over the ears of the smaller child, Willie.

The relationship between the Tompkins' family and the Union soldiers was not necessarily an amiable one. The children were probably always trying to pull pranks or assist in "outwitting"the soldiers as Ellen explained this ability in an earlier letter. They may have been captives on their own property, but the Tompkins family was far from being defeated.

Ellen's opportunity to complete the letter was probably interrupted by some unknown aggravation, but she was able to complete the letter the following day:

"October 6: Just as I wrote this far I was interrupted and all day yesterday I was so annoyed, first one thing and then another, I quite gave up. The teamsters are the most lawless men in the army and I have the road lined with them all the time, fires extending all along the fences. Colonel Tyler, who is in command of Gauley, wrote me a note telling me I must report any trespass on my property or any complaint I had to make of ill treatment and he would see I was protected. He is a real gentleman and with all my

---

82 Tompkins, "Colonel's Lady", pg. 406

troubles there are some alleviating circumstances. The officers try to be kind to us in every way and really neglect no opportunity to do me a favor. The character and position of Mr. Tompkins secures me their civility. They assure me constantly of their sympathy and tell me I have plenty of friends in both armies. Many believe I am refused a pass because it prevents our troops from attacking Gauley, as they say our lives are held worth a regiment of ours and this place commands the fortifications at Gauley. Cannon on the lawn here would ruin them. Some officers are here at every meal and staying at night, but never without my invitation. Two of General Rosencranz' officers, sick in an ambulance, stopped and asked if I'd allow them to remain a night, as they were suffering. Well, of course, I did and they expressed themselves under great obligations. Mr. Grimme wishes me to adopt a different conduct, refuse everyone, but I am in the hands of the Philistines and have no idea of making bitter enemies, and, in truth, they are always kind to me and as a lady I must be polite. I have nothing to do with their politics *in this free country.* There are many of these officers I shall be happy to see and introduce to Mr. T. as friends to me in a dark hour of trial, when this terrible war is over."[83]

Many of the officers who came into contact with Ellen were able to imagine their families in her predicament, if the roles were reversed and the rebels had invaded Ohio. They generally went out of their way to help her and she -- like her husband -- worked to reduce some of the pain and suffering the war was causing. Tompkins had asked surprised Union infantrymen to surrender rather than shoot them down and she went out of her way to help the sick. They were people who would rapidly gain the respect of men of their class -- even though they were on opposite sides in the middle of a war. The age of chivalry was still present, but was in its' final stages. The Civil War would put an end to the previous romantic approach to warfare and families as well as combattants would become legimate

[83] Tompkins, "Colonel's Lady", pg. 406

targets of war. This was still evolving as a political and military policy at this early stage of the war. The long casualty lists had yet to totally harden the attitudes of the opposing forces, but it was not far in the future.

Because of her consistent policy of kindness, the officers began to discuss with her their suspicions that she and the family were held at the farm as hostages "because it keeps our troops from attacking Gauley." There is considerable truth in her statement. General Cox did not mention such motivation in his reports or in the book he wrote after the war, but this is not the sort of information that gentlemen warriors would want to pass on to posterity. As mentioned previously, Ellen's presence *did* reduce the probability that any Confederate army would make a serious attack against the Federal garrison at Gauley Bridge at least along the James River and Kanawha Turnpike from the Rebel positions on Sewell Mountain. She was also correct in her assessment of the strategic position of her lawn. A few artillery batteries placed there would have made the Union fortifications in the nearby town of Gauley Bridge untenable. If they were placed under a substantial artillery barrage, the Union regiments at Gauley Bridge would have been forced to retreat probably as far down the valley as Charleston, where the Elk River was a significant geographical barrier to any additional Confederate advances.

Ellen went on with the letter:

"We have had a freshet and General Cox's troops suffered for fear of not being able to get wagons across Gauley River, for General Wise burnt the bridge. Had it kept up four days longer the whole army would have had to return. But now General Rosencranz, General Cox, General Benham, General McCook, and General Schenck are on the top of Big Sewell Mountain, 32 miles above us, with 16 thousand men and our forces on the top of Little Sewell. The Big and Little Sewell are eleven miles across. The two armies are two miles apart, lying in sight of each other. The pickets have exchanged Kanawha salt for

Greenbrier beef. Our forces are under General Lee, General Floyd and Wise. Mr. Tompkins is there with his regiment. The rebels have between thirty and thirty-seven thousand men. As the officers tell me 'they have the elephant but don't know how to cage it', meaning a chance to fight but fear to risk it against such odds. General Lee's name strikes terror into these federal forces. If it was General Floyd or Wise, they would have tried to go to Lewisburg, but General Lee, they know, is so superior to their officers. The Confederate States have bound themselves to get back Western Virginia. My place is here evidently. I hope they will fall back without a battle. Some think they will."[84]

Here, again, Ellen's sources of information were exceptionally accurate. The two armies were in the positions described, the distances were exact, and Robert E. Lee was in charge of both Floyd's and Wise's troops. Significant reinforcements had moved into the area and it appeared that there would be a major battle fought in the Sewell Mountain area. She was even aware that her husband's regiment was in the fortifications on the mountain tops.

Conditions were miserable and both sides had difficulty in transporting supplies to the soldiers in the field and life for them was becoming difficult. One Rebel in Tompkins' regiment recorded the following in his diary:

"...was about 2 or 3 o'clock when we reached the first troops ... The men deployed behind logs, trees, or in open ground... and stood awaiting the attack. Continued firing among the pickets was heard -- one poor lieutenant carried along dying in a litter ... up at o'clock almost certain of attack had the men along the lines ... men worked hard and by night had made an excellent line of 3 or 4 hundred yards. Nothing still to eat. Some time in the forenoon Gen Wise sent some flour and beef -- men were sent to cook -- they used the barrel heads to cook upon, and about night some warm dough and some beef burned upon the coals

84 Tompkins, "Colonel's Lady", pg. 407

were distributed -- no salt in either the bread or on the meat. A piece of bread about the size of one's hand, and a small piece of meat were given to each man. Some received none until after night. This was the meal of the second day -- 3rd day(Thursday) about the same scenes -- food of the same character but a little more of it. I cut my dough into thin pieces, browned it thoroughly and ate it with cold water -- could eat no more beef... In a short time we were saturated. Tried to sleep but could not -- water almost running under us, and a large leak dropping in my face, and many others running upon my body..."[85]

Conditions on the Federal side were not much better. They had tents, but they had to be short of food inside their fortifications. Epidemics began to break out among the rural-origin soldiers who had not contracted many childhood diseases such as measles and in addition to the weather, exposure of the troops to the elements left them severely afflicted with colds, pneumonia, influenza and other disorders which began to fill the substandard military hospitals.

Ellen went on to explain some of the military events and explained the Federal courier system of swallowing dispatches when threatened with capture:

"But last night five couriers passed down and some passed up to General Rosencranz with sealed dispatches, papers compressed into a ball and covered with wax so the courier can swallow it if the enemy overtakes him. The supposition is within forty-eight hours there will be a change in the relations of the armies. I believe the federals will fall back to Camp Lookout, 18 miles above us at Mrs. Lewis place where I boarded two summers. There they are fortified, but the climate is so bleak they can't stand it. They have hundreds of sick men now. When a battle is expected, in both armies the hospitals get filled, but these men have severe colds and fevers."[86]

---

85 Childers, "Virginian's Dilemma", pg. 185

86 Tompkins, "Colonel's Lady", pg. 407

Once again, Ellen Tompkins proves to be a careful observer and reporter of military affairs. She was aware of the number of couriers passing down the turnpike past the farm and knew of the special technique used for transporting sensitive dispatches to prevent their capture. She predicted a change in relationships between the opposing forces and proved to be correct. Rosecrans chose to withdraw his forces back along their over-extended supply line rather than face the numerically superior Confederates under the command of Robert E. Lee.

A Confederate artilleryman wrote of the Federal retreat and Lee's disappointment:

"After remaining at Little Sewell Mountian upwards of two weeks, General Lee made preparations to attack General Rosecrans; contrary, doubtless, to General Lee's expectations, on the morning the attack was to be made, General Rosecrans had quietly evacuated Big Sewell, and only left a few broken down horses and wagons, and a few tents pitched to make it appear that he still occupied his position. This was considered a very ingenious piece of strategy, as General Lee was much disappointed when he found that General Rosecrans had so quietly and adroitly eluded him on the previous night."[87]

There was another change that would eventually have an effect on the Tompkins' family. Colonel Tompkins' commander, General Wise, had been in a constant feud with General Floyd and now Wise was being recalled to Richmond for eventual re-assignment to North Carolina. When Floyd took command as Lee moved back to the Cheat Mountain area, the rebels also became a threat to the safety of the family on the Union-occupied farm.

There was some urgency attached to the order for Wise to return to Richmond. It was delivered to him while he was under fire with some of his skirmishers:

"Sir: You are instructed to turn over all the troops

[87] Riddle, "Floyd's Operations in West Virginia", pg. 95-96

heretofore immediately under your command to General Floyd..."[88]

The order was signed by the acting Secretary of War, Judah P. Benjamin. Even though Wise was a political appointee as a General -- he had a stable relationship with Tompkins. Floyd, also a "political general", was no friend to the soldiers in the regiments and seemed to have some animosity toward the troops of his now deposed rival, Henry Wise. The 22nd Virginia Infantry Regiment was normally assigned the worst as well as the most dangerous duty in the army. "You will notice that our regiment usually is put in front on an advance and in the rear in a retreat"[89] was recorded in a Confederate officer's diary.

As a result, there was little love lost between Floyd and Tompkins. Colonel Tompkins had been a professional military officer, trained at West Point, and he was fair as he looked out for the welfare of the men in the regiment assigned to his command. Floyd continuously exhibited a dislike for the Kanawha volunteers who composed the 22nd Virginia.

Following the battle at Carnifex Ferry, Isaac Smith recorded the following comment in his diary:

"Floyd does not like Col T because he knows that Col T despises his character as a man and has no respect for his qualifications as a soldier, and it would suit Floyd's view to leave Tompkins to bear all of the blame which might attach to any mishap in the retreat.."[90]

Tompkins' regiment, of course, had been assigned the dangerous duty of rear guard during the retreat. They were able to extricate the Confederate artillery from their positions and enabled the entire army to pull out of the immediate area of the large Federal army successfully, but Floyd generally found less than desirable duties for Tompkins and the 22nd Virginia to perform. With Wise

89 Childers, "Virginian's Dilemma", pg. 184
90 *Ibid*, pg. 180

out of the picture, Floyd was completely in charge and he would eventually be able to make a major change in the Tompkins family's position and the Colonel's military career.

Ellen continued with general information :

"There is such a difficulty to have letters sent without stamps and I can't get any. Please send me some in your next letter. I hear all the eastern news from the Cincinnati papers which the officers send me. Willie is much better. He is cutting four teeth and for two months has not been well. My health is much better. Caroline says the war has cured me. I have not had a spell of nausea for two months. I am too busy and excited to be sick. I am so sorry to see Wilkins Glenn is taken up. I believe Maryland will go out of the Union in spite of Lincoln. A lieutenant-colonel of the Confederates was killed by the pickets of the federals. As officer of the day he rode between them and asked if they were Jeff Davis' men. They said, 'No!' He drew his revolver and they shot him in the side. The officers are strapped to the horses now to save their bodies. His horse galloped back to our camp, a mile. The likeness of his wife with a slip of paper fell out of his pocket. On was written, 'But for this sad war, my dear husband, we never would have been separated.' Her letters to him covered with his blood. The man was very sorry he did not let him go. He is on this place now. The wretch. What shadows we are and what shadows we pursue."[91]

She was obviously upset with the death of the Confederate officer who had carried a picture of his wife in his pocket. She could easily associate his death with that of her own husband and the slip of paper with the sad sentence "but for this sad war, my dear husband, we never would have been separated" described the Tompkins' situation exactly. She didn't have the facts this time. She described the death of Colonel Spaulding, an officer who had been drunk for several days -- perhaps loneliness for his wife and

91 Tompkins, "Colonel's Lady", pg. 407-408

that very piece of paper had produced the depression which lead to drinking -- and had lead an unauthorized attack. Nothing was accomplished except his death. Ellen was also in error about the strapping of Confederate officers to their horses to recover their bodies. Spaulding was able to cling to his saddle until he fell into the arms of his troops who were out of range of the Union pickets.

"Sunday night: The news for us is glorious. The federals had to retreat from the Sewell Mountains as the Confederates were getting too close. The South is sure to hold its own and they begin to see it now. They have fallen back nearly to Hawk's Nest and will have to go to Gauley, soon I expect to Charleston. They had to make their march at night. I feel bright and hopeful of better days, as the troops, no doubt, will go to Kentucky and Missouri, recalled from Western Virginia.

"An officer told me General Cox wrote him he was on the top of Sewell looking to the East. I told him, like Moses, he would be allowed to view the promised land but never enter it. It turned out true.

"Direct to the care of General Cox."[92]

Ellen frequently felt a compulsion to push her luck with the Union officers. Comparing the Confederacy to the promised land where the Union army would never be allowed to enter on the day the Federals had been forced to retreat seems to demonstrate a lack of good sense, but she was correct in her prediction that the Union forces would be forced to retreat from the Sewell Mountain area without a fight. She was now hoping that the same forces would be forced completely out of the state while leaving her family and farm in peace, a Confederate peace. If that were to occur, the sacrifice of the past several months would have been worth it.

Imagine, however, Ellen's nerve in telling the Union officer that Cox was like Moses: he would be allowed to look into the promised land, but he would not be permittted

[92] Tompkins, "Colonel's lady", pg. 408

to cross into Eastern Virginia. It is little wonder that the Federal officers respected the courageous, but aggravating, southern lady.

She was a good correspondent and wrote to her sister, Sarah, frequently. Ellen wrote to explain the Union army's situation following the retreat and the situation on the farm as military supplies were stockpiled in preparation for an expected Rebel offensive. This letter was written on October 10, 1861:

"This place ought to belong to the state, it has such a central, important position. Last night the road was lined with wagons and the noise such we could not sleep, the teamsters quarrelling and swearing. The barn now is filled with government property, barrels of pork, sugar, etc. If they retreat, they will burn it down no doubt, for when they fell back from Sewell Mountain they burnt tents, and the sugar, coffee, etc., was over a foot deep, mixed with mud to prevent the rebels from using it. Over a hundred wagon loads were destroyed as they had no transportation."[93]

Retreats over the steep, muddy mountain roads in the winter were nearly impossible to manage successfully. Any supplies which had been pre-positioned in forward areas normally had to be destroyed or abandoned to the enemy as there seldom was sufficient transportation to move it quickly. This was a problem for both sides, but the southern troops were affected less with this difficulty -- they simply had fewer supplies to attempt to move. Ellen continued:

"General Scott does not approve of the march up Sewell Mountain. He did not approve of the rout at Manassas. He well may be angry. It has cost Uncle Sam an immense amount of money and hundreds of sick soldiers, in fact it has demoralized and disheartened them. They return saying that the South has generals, but they have not one capable of leading thirty thousand men.

[93] Tompkins, "Colonel's Lady", pg. 409

Many talk of going home and all say they must go into winter quarters. Regiments of a thousand can't muster more than five or six hundred active men fit for service. They will be at Gauley in a week, but our troops harass them. 800 cavalry came down yesterday and drove in their pickets and as they thought possibly they were supported by infantry. The federals had three regiments out for battle, but the cavalry only galloped backwards and forwards annoying them so that they could not continue to retreat fearing an ambush. They now don't know what to anticipate as some fear the *rebels* will cut off their provision wagons from the other side of the river. They know General Lee is full of stratagems. General Scott is said to have cried when General Lee refused all of his offers and would go with Virginia."[94]

General Scott had retired from active service, but apparently spoke freely with newspaper correspondents. Ellen seemed to be supplied frequently with newspapers from Ohio and this is probably the source of her comments about General Scott, a fellow Virginian.

This was an exceptionally hard period for the Union soldiers assigned to Rosecrans' brigades. Lee's forces had been reinforced by troops under the command of Brigadier-General Loring and the Confederates were again advancing toward the Federal strongholds at Gauley Mount and Gauley Bridge.

Loring was also a well-respected officer who had served as a Major in a mounted rifleman regiment during the Mexican War. He lost his left arm at Chapultepec and had been promoted for bravery. A Confederate artilleryman explained the level of respect Loring had from his fellow southerners:

"A man thus distinguished as a Major in a war in which Robert E. Lee served as a Captain, and Thomas J. Jackson as a Lieutenant, naturally enjoyed great prestige."[95]

94 Tompkins. "Colonel's Lady", pg. 409
95 Humphries, *Military Operations 1861-1863*, pg. 12

Lee now had sufficient troops on hand and commanders who he felt could be trusted with independent commands. He planned a two-pronged advance against the Federals in the upper Kanawha valley and gave command of the "southern element" to General Floyd. The "northern element" would be commanded by General Loring and Lee, himself, would travel with Loring. Floyd was to cross New River and move into the mountains across from the main Federal bases at Gauley Mount and at Gauley Bridge. From this location, he would be in an excellent position to block all of the supplies moving up the turnpike to replenish the Union troops. Loring would push in the Union pickets and advance his regiments in the vicinity of Hawk's Nest and together, the two Confederate elements would be able to force the Federals from the upper valley without precipitating a major engagement. Lee knew as well as Rosecrans the difficulty involved in moving supplies through the mountains. After the Federals were forced out of the Upper Kanawha valley, the Confederates would have probably gone into winter quarters there.

Lee sent Floyd's command consisting of eight infantry regiments and seven hundred cavalry across New River to operate on the south side and intended to send Loring's troops along the turnpike on the North side of New River soon afterwards, but the pressing need for reinforcements in the Cheat Mountain area and in the Shenandoah Valley was so urgent that Lee had to send Loring there. Floyd was allowed to continue his operation on the south side of New River.[96]

This operation was probably intended to harass the Union camps and divert their attention from Loring's withdrawl. Floyd's force was simply too small to be able to stand against Rosecrans' regiments without Loring's support, but there was considerable protection available for Floyd from the rising water of New River. The small Confederate force could retreat to the southwest into Virginia, if pressed.

Floyd's army totalled approximately 4000 men and

96 Humphries, *Military Operations 1861-1863,* pg. 7

consisted of six infantry regiments: the 14th Georgia, the 22nd Virginia, 36th Virginia, 45th Virginia, and the 51st Virginia, as well as the 20th Mississippi. The Phillips' "Legion" from Georgia was also present and the small command had cavalry elements and artillery attached. A company of Louisana sharpshooters also accompanied Floyd's march.[97]

General Lee was indeed "full of stratagems" and would have driven the Federal army out of the upper Kanawha Valley, if Loring had been able to remain to support Floyd by maneuvering along the north bank of the river. Unfortunately for the Confederacy, Loring's troops were needed elsewhere.

Ellen, unaware of the Confederate advance that was forming,had decided to ask Rosecrans for permission to travel to Richmond for supplies and winter clothing. She explained this to Sarah:

"I intend, in about ten days, to apply to General Rosencranz for a pass to Richmond. I shall leave the children and be gone about ten days. I must see Mr. T. and attend to my house there. I want winter clothes. You perceive I am a desperate woman. Literally I never know personal fear, although I am a coward usually. Bill has not been returned. The wonder is all have not gone. They say this war is to revenge the treatment of the slaves. Live abolitionists I never saw before, for we would order them off or set the dogs on them usually. Now they enter the house. I tell them my opinions of them frankly. Please send me some stamps. We have twenty-four men on guard. General Wise had his things in the same barn."[98]

Ellen Tompkins was a southern woman who was raised around the institution of slavery and saw little wrong with it. As usual, Ellen was outspoken on this issue as she was everything else. Her slave, Bill, had been concealed by

[97] Boehm, Robert B., "The Civil War in Western Virginia: The Decisive Campaigns of 1861", Ohio State University, 1957, pg. 167

[98] Tompkins, "Colonel's lady", pg. 409

the Union troops and had not returned to his duties. She had written to General Cox about the incident and Cox promised to investigate and ordered the regimental commander, Colonel Fyffe, to have Bill returned.

A pass and orders for safe travel was issued for Ellen, her daughter, and J.H. Miller, Jr. to permit them to travel to Richmond and they soon departed for the Confederate lines and the road into the heart of the Confederacy. It is interesting that J.H. Miller, Jr. went along. He was the son of the Postmaster at Gauley Bridge, James Hodge Miller. It is obvious that Miller was a Confederate sympathizer and could have assisted Ellen with her"letters" which went through the Federal mail system and contained such interesting information.

A pair of very courteous letters were exchanged between Colonel Tompkins and General Rosecrans at the time of Ellen's departure. These are worth more than a casual review.

Rosecrans letter was carried by Ellen as she left the farm. It was written on October 14, 1861:

"My Dear Colonel,

"Your noble wife and fair daughter take this to you.

"The only condition I impose on the visit is that while giving pleasure to you the visit shall have to me and the Government of the United States no painful consequences.

"It is unnecessary to suggest to you, whose nice sense of honor I know so well and highly appreciate, that conversation on the number, condition, or position of military forces, or their equipment, discipline, supplies, or movements should be avoided. But I mention it that those of your friends and others who will probably converse with Mrs. T. and Miss Ellen may be cautioned against embarassing them by conversing on these subjects.

"I send you my warm regards. Anything I can do to contribute to your comfort or happiness I shall be happy to do.

Your Sincere Friend
W.S. Rosecrans"[99]

---

99 Tompkins, "Colonel's Lady", pg. 410

This certainly doesn't seem to be the sort of letter that a general would send to his enemy. At some point in the past, these two men of honor had known one another and had been friends. It wasn't in the Seminole Wars as Rosecrans was still a cadet at the time. There is no record of their professional lives touching. After Rosecrans graduated from the Military Academy, he served at Fortress Monroe and later went to West Point where he was assigned until 1847.[100] Christopher Tompkins resigned from the regular army while he was serving in California in 1847. How they came to know each other is not well documented.

Tompkins' return letter was written six days later from Lewisburg and shows an equal warmth for General Rosecrans:

"My dear Sir:

"Dropping the etiquette of official and more formal correspondence, I beg to thank you for your letter of the 14th instant and especially for your many manifestations of kindness to my family at Gauley farm. You will do me the justice to believe that I feel most deeply the kindness which you have bestowed upon those so dear to me, and you will find your reward in the consciousness of having exercised those Christian virtues which go so far to elevate ourselves in the estimation of all respecting people.

"Aside from truce considerations, I shall continue in all sincerity to refer briefly to the unfortunate condition of our divided country.

"It has been a source of great and momentous concern to myself and whilst I have no idea that either of us will live to see the end of the evils that now exist, I do cherish the hope that we in our respective spheres accomplish much to mitigate their atrocities.

"I wish I could talk with you and many of my old friends and comrades on your side of the question. I

---

100 Reid, Whitelaw, *Ohio in the War: Her Statesmen, Her Generals, and Soldiers*, Moore, Wilsatch & Baldwin, Cincinnati: 1868, pg. 312

believe we could manage affairs better than the politicians or at least honestly differ in our respective views.

"But this may never be.

"Once more I repeat my obligations to yourself and other officers of your Army for your kindness to my family. I only ask that they may be permitted to leave the place and return in safety within our lines, and I need hardly add that I shall be bound by every sentiment of honor to observe the strictest regard for the observance of such silence as you will require in reference to your official affairs.

"With much respect and regard I remain, dear Sir,

Very Truly,

C.Q. Tompkins"[101]

This was a very unusual pair of enemies! Tompkins' feelings about politicians were clear enough, and if he felt strongly enough to write this down in a letter to an enemy general, he must have been at the boiling point in his relationship with General Floyd, whom Isaac Smith wrote that Tompkins "despised"even at the time of the battle at Carnifex Ferry.

It was about this time that Floyd's regiments were moving along the south side of New River toward their positions opposite the Federal camps at Gauley Bridge and at Gauley Mount. The small army had crossed the river at Richmond's Ferry on October 11.

Isaac Smith recorded Colonel Tompkins' departure from the 22nd Virginia in his diary:

"Col. T met us on the way up and left us for Lewisburg to meet Mrs. Tompkins whom he had just learned was at that place. I was therefore in command of the regiment and dreaded the responsibility. Plus rode forward in great haste to tell Col Tompkins the news about his wife and the Col frequently alludes to it, says he will never forget Plus for this kindness."[102]

---

101 Tompkins, "Colonel's Lady", pg. 411-412

102 Childers, "Virginian's Dilemma", pg. 190

As mentioned previously, Christopher and Ellen Tompkins were romantically in love and had difficulty in being separated. Ellen occasionally alluded to this in her letters to Sarah, but the emotional attachment was far from being one-sided. These two people really wanted to be together.

Floyd's army occupied Cotton Hill and set up artillery positions directly across New River from Gauley Bridge and were in position to fire at the Union camp at Tompkins' farm. The artillery attack on Gauley Bridge began on November 1, 1861, and continued for nearly two weeks. Ellen was in Richmond for most of this period and did not write much about the fighting even though it was loud, intense, and long lasting. As a matter of fact, she became relatively uninterested in military affairs after being placed "on my parole of honor" by General Rosecrans. This careful observer and precise reporter of military maneuvers was no longer interested in those things.

She wrote another letter to Sarah after she returned to the farm from Richmond. The letter was written on November 16, 1861and this was during the battle of Cotton Hill, but Ellen does not refer to it in the letter:

"Dear Sarah,

"I have not heard from you for an age. Why, I cannot tell. I received your letter with stamps, for which receive my thanks. I went to Richmond on my parole of honor. General Rosencranz sent me with an escort (a squad of cavalry) from his body guard. They delivered me up to an escort General Lee sent to meet me. I had the honor of sitting in his tent on top of Sewell Mountain. I took Ellen with me and left her in Richmond. I spent some blissful days with Mr. T., but we wondered if the agony of parting under such circumstances did not outweigh the pleasure of meeting. Such is life. Why were people born with hearts at all? This *cruel, cruel war!*"

For some people, honor is far more than just a word. It involves a concept around which life is lived. Ellen and

103 Tompkins, "Colonel's lady", pg. 412-413

Christopher Tompkins were two such people and once their word was given, there was no breaking it. The Confederate military learned little from Ellen during her stay in Richmond as she given her word of honor to General Rosecrans that she wouldn't discuss his military preparations and she even began to lose interest in the conflict, itself. She, of course, was vitally interested in the political aspects of the war as its' outcome would have a serious impact on her and her family.

The letter went on:

"I found Richmond full of excitement, but the people determined to conquer or die. Knowing Southern blood, the North ought to have conciliated not invaded. Now all is lost beyond redemption. I saw General Lee, Henningsen, and Wise and talked with hundreds of officers and influential people. I must tell you I was overcome with attention from the highest in the land. I found all right at the house. I refused all invitations and sent for some of the servants and dismissed them, when I left, to their homes until I return again. Ellen is at the Reverend Mr. Peterkin's in care of Sally Tompkins. A white man has care of the house."[104]

In spite of being "overcome with attention", Ellen refused all invitations to attend social functions probably to stay at home with her husband. The servants were sent home for what were economical reasons as the Tompkins planned their uncertain future together. They had to anticipate the loss of their property at Gauley Mount and had no possibility of avoiding the financial setback of losing such a valuable investment.

Their daughter, Ellen, was to remain in Richmond at a minister's house under the care of a close relative, Sally Tompkins. It was thought to be too dangerous to return a young girl to the situation they were in at the farm. Remember that Ellen had hidden her daughter when the Federal troops first came to the farm. "Ellen is never seen"

104 Tompkins, "Colonel's Lady", pg. 413

was written in the initial letter to Sarah.

Sally Tompkins also is an unusual person who became well known in Richmond after she had opened a hospital for wounded Confederate soldiers and when the government converted all of the hospitals to military status, Jefferson Davis provided a military commission to Sally. She became the only female commissioned officer in the Confederate army.

The letter continued to explain the trip back to the farm. She was accompanied by her Brother-in-Law who soon left the farm and was accompanied by one of Ellen's sons. She planned to leave as soon as she could make arrangements for someone to take care of the farm in her absence:

"Mr. Ficklin came with me to Sewell Mountain. There we had an escort of fifteen (mostly officers) to the picket of the federal forces. They were then dismissed and Mr. Ficklin was allowed to accompany me to the farm where he has been ten days. He left today with an escort and flag of truce and took Chris with him, also Bill (who ran away), to remain until I come on which will be as soon as I can get any one who will remain at the farm. I am under great obligations to General Rosencranz. I wish all were like him and even yet, we could right. But it would startle you to see the excitement. People are mad, infuriated! They will never live with the North again. To subdue them, all must be exterminated. Richmond has taken a start. Manufactories are springing up, telegraph wires to Sewell, the railroad building to White Sulphur. The South is no longer lazy. The White Sulphur is used as a hospital. Men worth a million or more will give all they possess and their lives to the cause."[105]

Apparently, her escaped slave, Bill, had been returned to her by the Federal authorities as promised. The Union soldiers had hidden him in the woods, but Colonel Fyffe had promised to help recover Bill and had delivered him.

105 Tompkins, "Colonel's Lady", pg. 413

Bill and Ellen's son, Chris, would travel to the east with Mr. Ficklin -- probably to Charlottesville where they would remain until Ellen was able to locate a trustworthy caretaker for the property and depart.

Since Fickin left the day the letter was written -- November 16 -- and had been on the farm for ten days, Ellen returned to the farm on either November 5 or 6. This was in the middle of the battle of Cotton Hill between Cox's troops and the regiments under General Floyd which had crossed to the south side of New River that began on November 1. The initial fighting was described by General Cox:

"For the first week after the 1st, Floyd's battery on Cotton Mountain fired on very slight provocation, and caution was necesary when riding or moving about the camp. The houses of the hamlet were not purposely injured, for Floyd would naturally be unwilling to destroy the property of West Virginians, and it was a safe presumption that we had removed the government property from buildings within range of fire, as we had in fact done. Our method of forwarding supplies was to assemble the wagon trains near my lower camp during the day, and push them forward to Gauley Mount and Tompkins farm during the night."[106]

High water in New River had prevented any Federal reaction against the positions on Cotton Hill held by Floyd. The river was at a higher level than had even been seen before and Floyd was protected by a swift, rough wide stream which was dangerous to attempt to cross.

On November 10, Cox sent a scouting party across the river from the picket post at Montgomery's Ferry and once Cox was aware of the Confederate's weakness, he made plans to send assault parties across. Men from the Eleventh Ohio and First Kentucky scaled the near vertical cliffs at two points along the river and forced the Confederate cannon to withdraw. Skirmishing continued as the

106 Cox, *Military Reminiscences*, pg. 138

Confederates retreated past Fayette Court House and on toward Raleigh Court House.

Actual combat was over quickly and the only significant fight was at McCoy's Mill where the Confederate rear guard (not the 22nd Virginia, for a change) skirmished with Union soldiers and the Rebel cavalry commander, St. George Croghan, was killed. The retreat was completed by the time Ellen wrote this letter, but she certainly did not report on the military details as she had in previous letters. Either the stress of warfare within sight of her home or the"parole of honor" had caused her to shift much of her interest.

"The trial of parting with Ellen and Chris was great to me, but I rejoice they are away. I shall go very soon, so write at once. I received a letter from W.W. G. I was so glad to hear from him. Send the enclosed letter to Henry. Write no treason. Of course I have no politics, they would give me too much trouble. I enclose a letter from Anne's brother, who I met on Sewell Mountain (one of the Richmond Blues). He looked in fine health and said he liked the life very much. I brought on a number of letters and sent them North after they were examined. One to Mrs. J. Hanson Thomas. Send word to Louisa Wilkins and Anne T. if any letters come to them to forward them to me. I do not know when we will all meet, but be sure I shall ever think of you with the greatest affection and shall hope for brighter days. Give all my love to Mr. C and all the family.

Ever yours affectionately,

Ellen

"If you get an opportunity to see to my interests as you think best. Please tell Mary I received her letters and stamps. Direct to James H. Miller, Gauley Bridge, Fayette County,Virginia. Give my love to Mrs. G's family.

"It is reported Mr. T. is a General. I have no doubt it is true. John is in the Wise Legion and thought a geat deal of. He is in Richmond on a leave of absence of 30 days. Lucia Tabb is there too. He is a field surgeon.

"General Wise was ill when I was in Richmond, but

sent for me to see him in his room. He could not sit up. He is very fascinating and has a kind heart. He is devoted to Mr. T.; always says 'He is a soldier and a gentleman.'

If Anne can write at once I will forward the letter to her brother. Mr. Ficklin has placed me under the greatest obligations. I can't find the words to express his Kindness at this time. One appreciates friendship. No one needs it more than I do. You cannot tell how blest you are. God help the right for we seem cursed for our sins."[107]

Ellen thought that her husband had been promoted to General at this time. General Wise, his former commander, was trying to get him promoted and put in charge of all Confederate forces in western Virginia. The bedfast Wise obvoiusly thought well of Tompkins' ablity as a soldier and by getting him placed in overall command of his old area of operations, Wise would have revenge on his old enemy, General Floyd, who was still in the area. Tompkins had an extreme dislike for Floyd and would have probably have enjoyed having him as a subordinate. Wise probably was "politicking" to have Floyd replaced with Tompkins.

One of Ellen's final letters to Sarah was probably written on November 28. It was undated, but a short, final entry in the letter was written later as the family tutor, Mr. Grimme,was preparing to depart for "the North" was dated November 29. Mr.Grimme was probably going to handcarry the letter out of the military zone where it was less likely to be opened and mailed more securely.

The letter began:

"I had the starch taken out of me by a swollen face, but now that I am better I view the world differently. I suffered a great deal with my tooth. I am distressed to hear of the death of Colonel Croghan (shot by the federals) who travelled with me from Richmond. He was such a gallant fellow. He was the last one who shook hands with me in Lewisburg. This cruel war! How little I dreamed it was the last time I'd see him. He has a widowed mother on the

[107] Tompkins, "Colonel's Lady", pg. 413-414

Hudson River. Whoever brought on this sad war will deserve a heavy punishment. I saw enough at White Sulphur of suffering to make one weep their heart out. A poor woman arrived with her baby, two months old, just three hours after the death of her husband. How she prayed to die too! She had his body in the cars with us. Poor thing! I said all I could to console her, but indeed I knew not what to do but to weep with her. The scenes I have witnessed this summer, heart rending grief! Ah, how little you realize the horror of war. All the vile passions are aroused. Is it not curious my courage has never deserted me? Delicate and frail I certainly am, for that visit to Richmond, travelling two nights in a stage was very severe, but I am thankful my wits have been brighter and my self-possession greater than ever. Mr. Grimme leaves for the North."[108]

The cruel war had again touched close to Ellen with the death of Colonel Croghan. She had apparently visited the Confederate hospital at White Sulphur and "...saw enough ... of suffering to make one weep their heart out." She also shared the agony of the young mother who had come to the hospital to visit her injured or sick husband or help nurse him back to health only to find that he had died just before her arrival. How little, indeed, did Sarah know of war.

"I received a letter from Florence Fuller and yours came this evening. I received one with stamps, but this last one had been opened and the stamps taken out in Cincinnati, but the letter gave me pleasure. I sent it to Caroline as I had a chance by accident. I will send this letter if I can get it endorsed, but there is a new style of opening letters in Charleston. I will hope for brighter days now Mr. T. has left the army, but as the authorities wish him to be a general, I can't say what he will do except one thing is certain, he will do all he can for his state."[109]

108 Tompkins, "Colonel's Lady", pg. 415
109 *Ibid*, pg. 415

She was now aware that her husband had resigned from the Confederate army, but how she received that information is a mystery as she wrote on December 5 that she had not heard from him since leaving Lewisburg six weeks previously. Perhaps she heard about his resignation from the same source who was taking Florence Fuller's letter through the Rebel lines to Caroline in Charlottesville.

She was unsure whether her husband would accept a general's commission, if offered, but her line "...one thing is certain, he will do all he can for his state..." will be useful in determining some of his future activities. Being a Virginian meant something special to most of the state's population at the time and this factor, alone, held many of them in the war until the end.

"I expect to leave very soon and hardly hope ever to see this house again as even the majors say it ought be used as a hospital, then burned. It makes one suspicious to have a person very friendly in the house, talking, and then before they reach the gate to hear such remarks. I shall go to Richmond and no matter what happens stand my ground. I have been very busy packing, arranging things, and am filled with disgust to see this beautiful place torn to pieces by the soldiers, when I remember the cost of money and trouble to build all the houses, etc. It is a perfect desolation now. Fences are all gone. The fields set in clover as hard as roads from the encampments. There is no telling how long the man and woman and Deckert will be allowed the rooms I gave them to use, for there will be winter quarters here on this place no doubt. What a pity we ever saw the place. I cannot remain here this winter to save it, as in the spring the fighting will begin again. I have had as many cannon balls roaring round me as I wish to hear. There is no hope for peace for years. The South will not accept the terms offered by the North. The wind is roaring, rain, hail, and snow falling. I dread this journey. Think I have no way of letting Mr. T. know where to meet me. He dare not pass the lines or would go to Columbus.

"November 29: I must close as Mr. Grimme has just

concluded to leave in the carriage, starting now. Goodbye. Yours,

E"[110]

Ellen was disgusted with the damage done to the farm by the Union troops occupying it and had little patience with the officers who spoke warmly within the house, but were over heard expressing their desire to convert the mansion into a hospital and burn it after the army moved forward. She knew she was helpless to prevent the eventual destruction of the home she had worked so hard to build and understood that she must leave the area before the spring fighting season arrived.

She must have had a few close calls from the Confederate shelling of the farm from the opposite side of New River which had been ordered by General Floyd. She was not going to risk her family to any additional danger, even if it meant losing the house.

Ellen's final letter to Sarah Cooch from Gauley Mount was written in early December, 1861, just prior to her departure from the farm for safety within Confederate lines:

"You can still write to me but it is very doubtful if I can answer you. Put a letter, directed to me on the envelope, inside another envelope adressed to James H. Miller, Esq., Gauley Bridge, Fayette County, Virginia. I most likely will get it. Write any time until the spring. Say nothing of military movements, however. This place is said to be the key of Western Virginia. It is fortified and winter quarters building, all sorts of preparations being made."[111]

A special relationship must have existed between the Tompkins family and James H. Miller. Since Miller was the postmaster in the town and was probably a Confederate sympathizer, a clandestine agreement had been made between Ellen and Miller for her incoming mail from the Union states to be received in his name until it could be

110 Tompkins, "Colonel's Lady", pg. 415

111 Ibid, pg. 416

forwarded by someone he trusted who was passing through the lines. Ellen's letters would be handcarried into the Confederate lines and sent to her in Richmond. She cautioned Sarah to avoid mentioning any military subjects in her letters to protect her sister in case they were intercepted by Federal authorities and traced to Delaware.

She warned Sarah not to write after the arrival of spring as active military operations in the area would make it difficult for anyone to get through the lines, regardless of the reason. The use of the double envelopes and the cautioning of Sarah not to write about military matters were probably intended to reduce the chance that Ellen would be accused of breaking her "parole of honor" to General Rosecrans. While it was probable that she had sent military-related information to friends in the hope that it would find its' way into Confederate hands, she was going to great lengths to avoid even the slightest appearance of improper behavior at this stage. She knew that she was going to lose the farm at Gauley Mount and that there would be a huge financial loss involved. She also had property in Baltimore which was in Federal territory which could be seized, if she were openly associated with the Confederate war effort.

She continued:

"They say if they give up this all the blood and treasure expended in Western Virginia is of no account. It must and shall be held. A pretty idea, is it not? Well, I go now, I expect forever. Certainly there is no hope of my returning until peace. Altho they say they will trust me through their lines and believe me so honorable that I may come back in the spring and go to see you or stay in Baltimore, then return, but I doubt if I risk myself so far. I must tell you the Ohio newspapers of last evening gave me a touch, say that Mrs. Tompkins is again to pass the lines in a few days. How strange a woman of her accomplishments should be allowed to go through the lines and she is known to be a rebel and able to do much harm.

They give me this in a german paper. The Colonel is going to give it to me to take on. You will be surprised to hear I am so celebrated."[112]

The Ohio newspapers were beginning to develop a situation in which Ellen would be unsafe if she chose to return in the spring. The war was now being recognized for the long, bitter conflict it was to become and Ellen risked prison either by remaining or returning. Union Colonel Poschner was going to remain in her house for the winter (this was the best arrangement she could make to protect the farm from destruction) and he gave Ellen a copy of the German newspaper which was acusing her of being "able to do much harm" as a souvenir.

"When I came home I found things in a terrible condition,indeed I was much annoyed, but I have gotten the feelings towards me to be better. The fact is they were Germans and hear I said (when General Floyd fired on them below the house) that if they had been in their proper place (Ohio) they would not have been wounded. The doctor who had determined to use this house for a hospital was very angry (and so was I sure enough), finding that I said so positively he should not, reported I had refused to let a man come in while he amputated his arm. A number went to General R to know the truth, but he said all he knew was I was the bravest woman he ever saw."[113]

Ellen's difficulties were increasing. General Floyd was ordering Confederate artillery batteries to be fired at the Union camp on the farm and now there was a Union surgeon spreading camp gossip aimed at getting her forcibly removed from the house. The wounded resulted from local skirmishes, the shelling from across New River, and from the fighting as General Cox's troops crossed the river to force the Confederates from the summit of Cotton

112 Tompkins, "Colonel's Lady", pg. 416
113 *Ibid*, pg. 416

Hill.

The camp rumors increased substantially when the doctor began to tell the story that Ellen had refused to let him bring in a patient whose arm had to be amputated. An agitated delegation visited General Rosecrans to determine the truth of the accusations, but Rosecrans continued to defend Ellen. It is unlikely that she denied help for anyone. She was very aware of the constant need to maintain a good relationship with the Union soldiers and had previously gone to great lengths to help the sick and wounded and had even given them the use of the farm's vinyard house as a hospital. She had even permitted two sick Union officers to remain overnight in her home. The rumors from the doctor were probably attempts to convince the military commanders to evict her so the house could be used as a hospital.

She continued:

"They expect an attack here and are fortifying, and moreover determined, as the commanding officer told me, he would yield this place to no one but me, except with his life, and I was fortunate to own such a place. He is clearing the land, building a real village of winter quarters, and fortifying it all round, all he told me as a fine present to me. He moves in tomorrow. I will leave then certainly. He furnishes two four wagons for my servants and baggage, as general R requested it, and sent my furniture that I valued most beyond the lines for me. Indeed I like him very much as far as our acquaintance goes. I leave him plenty here to get along with. His wife is coming from Cincinnati with her two children. He is drawing me a picture of the farm as a great encampment, as it is."[114]

The commanding officer referred to by Ellen is Colonel Frederick Poschner, the commander of the garrison at Gauley Mount or "Tompkins' Farm", as it was called by the Union troops and map-makers. Poschner and his family would safeguard the farm with their presence during the

[114] Tompkins, "Colonel's lady", pg. 416-417

winter and Ellen was probably hopeful that more permanent arrangements could be made later.

She completed the final letter from the farm:

"I have not the time to write to Cousin H G's family. Will you be so kind as to write her, but not send this letter, as it is written too badly. I have sat down one dozen times to finish it. Tell Mary to direct as she did her last one to me, to James H. Miller. He will forward it. Sometimes people pass the lines. I have a quantity of letters. All have been examined, but yours will not be. Please attend to my money matters all you can. I have a private chance to send this, therefore cannot wait longer. God bless you all, if we ever meet again. The ***bliss, the bliss*** of getting out of these lines. Words cannot express my joy. Love to all."[115]

She was obviously tired of the war and the constant stress of trying to protect the farm she and her husband had worked so hard to develop. Most of their family's money was probably tied up in the property, but after trying so hard for so long, Ellen was finally giving up. "The ***bliss, the bliss*** of getting out of these lines" is a phrase that explains a great deal of the emotional stress she had been under. She had been held as a near-hostage, feared for her children's safety when the Union troops had orders to shoot anyone not in uniform, and had been fired on by cannon *from her own side*. The emotional strain must have been nearly overwhelming. In addition to all of this pressure, she had to worry about her husband and brother who were assigned to the Confederate army nearby. The relief of leaving must have been so great that it was hard to express in any other words.

She had developed a private method of sending this letter to Sarah, probably by a trusted Union officer who was travelling home on leave who would mail it outside of the military zone where the letter would not be opened for inspection. Ellen had developed a separate, secure mail system operating parallel to the regular mail service, but it

[115] Tompkins, "Colonel's Lady", pg. 416-417

utilized the services of people who could be trusted to carry the letters for her. She may have denied any activity against the interests of the Union army, but she certainly had the ability to use espionage techniques in getting her letters in and out of the Federally-occupied zone.

Ellen's final letter from the area was written on the road while she was waiting for repairs to be made to her carriage. It was written to Sarah on December 5, 1861:

"My Dear Sarah,

"I am now fourteen miles from Gauley Mount. I left this morning and Joe broke the shafts just as we got to the top of the hill and we had to send back and get the pole of the carriage and another horse and make a fresh start. The servants and baggage went on in two four horse wagons and we have a flag of truce with Captain Smith and six dragoons of General Rosencranz' body guard. They take me to the Confederate pickets, about 45 miles, then I will wait for them to send me wagons to go to Lewisburg. The trial I had today, parting from my house perhaps for years!"[116]

Unfortunately for the courageous Ellen, the house did not survive the war. It was burned, as she had predicted at an earlier time. Who did it and exactly why it was destroyed is a mystery that is not explained in the *Official Records* or in the journals of many of the officers who later served in the area. The best guess that can be made centers on the sudden Union retreat out of the area in 1862 when the Confederates again briefly occupied the Kanawha Valley. The newly replaced bridge over Gauley River was again destroyed, and the Federal magazine near the Falls of the Kanawha was exploded rather than allow it to be captured by the advancing Rebels. It is quite likely that the Union camp at Gauley Mount was put to the torch as the Federal soldiers evacuated and the house was burned at this time.

[116] Tompkins, "Colonel's Lady", pg. 417-418

"I was helped in by the Colonel, Poschner, and left him to use the house with his family. He is an honorable man and altogether it is the best arrangement possible under the circumstances, but still the trial to me! Indeed I could not help losing my self command for a few moments. But the joy of seeing my husband you cannot imagine, and Ellen and Chris will be so glad to see me, and I will be in my own house, I hope, in seven days. I intend to stop a night with Caroline; send the servants on. George drives the oxen on, and I assure you the idea of leaving home and being hired out nearly upset them. They know how to appreciate home now. Of course I shall not have Sally and Julia at home, too many children to bother us. Caroline, as usual is a trump in this move. I have gotten through wonderfully, owing to General Rosencranz, for he will see that I am treated kindly by all under his command. He is acting Major General and has all Western Virginia.

"The children are delighted at the idea of seeing their father. I brought on two puppies, two chickens, and had great difficulty in getting off from two pigs for Willie. Indeed I could not refuse them under the painful circumstances. Regrets are useless and I seldom allow such things to annoy me, but Mr.T. will be near enough to see and hear from and really I can't live separated from him. I have not heard from him since I left Lewisburg six weeks ago. You may know my anxiety. Write still and I may be so fortunate as to hear from you. Say nothing you care about being seen, for it is a military necessity to open letters now. I often think suppose you had been situated like I have been."[117]

Ellen would be in her home in Richmond in a week after writing the letter, She would finally be reunited with the husband she couldn't live separated from while she was trapped at the farm, but while her family was going to be reunited, the families of her slaves were going to be separated.

Ellen's attitude toward her "servants" reflects the

[117] Tompkins, "Colonel's lady", pg. 418

general feeling of her social set toward slaves. They were simply property which could be hired out or sold separately, if it was in the interest of the owner to do so.

The Tompkins' house in Richmond was obviously smaller than the mansion at Gauley Mount and the "three colored women, five colored children" referred to in the Union army pass [118] would be living elsewhere. The slave, George, would be hired out and probably Bill, the slave who was hidden by the Union soldiers at the farm and left with the Ficklins at Charlottesville would suffer a similar fate.

Ellen continued:

"I get a little compliment from the Ohio papers who insist I am dangerous. Well, I challenge the world to find out a dishonorable act of mine. General Rosencranz and General Cox behaved so kindly to me that no power on earth could induce me to betray them, but I take no sort of interest in military affairs and am not capable of telling anything."[119]

This letter was probably to be handcarried back to Gauley Bridge by her escorting officer, Captain Smith. Ellen was fully aware that the opening of letters was now a "military necessity"and since Smith was assigned to Rosecrans' staff, there was a possibility that this letter could be opened -- especially since the Ohio newspapers were claiming that she "was dangerous". Was this paragraph written for Rosecrans' and Cox's benefit, if the letter should be inspected? If it was inspected, she had found away to defuse much of the hostility appearing in the newspapers which could eventually result in the loss of her assets in Baltimore as well as ensuring the destruction of the farm. There is the possibility that Ellen's "challenge" to the world could have been a last defiant act -- betting the world that she was smarter than the rest and that her activities which put some significant information into the

118 Tompkins, "Colonel's Lady", pg. 417

119 *Ibid*, pg. 418

hands of the Confederate authorities would remain untraceable!

Ellen may have not had any interest in "military affairs" and did not know any military secrets, but she was a keen observer who had an excellent ability to elicit information from visitors. She reported that she took pleasure in her ability to "outwit them" and did this rather well for someone with no interest in military affairs.

"The children will go to schools now. Mr. Grimme has gone North.

"Please write to Cousin H G and give my love to W.W.G., Mary, in fact all the family and all of my friends. It is impossible to say when I will write again. I bid you all goodbye and hope you will always remember me with affection. Love to all.

Ellen

"Saturday. We are within the pickets of the Confederates and I have sent for teams to help us on. I hope to be in Richmond in a few days and to see Mr. T. and the children. The cannon was on the range of our house and fired into the meadow in front of it. Mr. T. asked General Floyd not to fire on his house as we were in it. He refused to oblige him and he resigned at once, is now in Richmond. The Confederates were on a hill in front of the house. I did not like being so near the shells. We have had delightful weather. How I wish to see you all. Heaven knows when I will. Give my love to my relations and friends, and now goodbye. With love to Mr. C, H W. and all of your children.

E"[120]

Colonel Christopher Tompkins resigned from the Confederate army when General Floyd refused to stop firing on the farm while Ellen and the children were in the house. This was the final act in a long series of disputes between the two men which came together with the harassment of Tompkins' second-in-command, Major

120 Tompkins, "Colonel's Lady", pg. 418-419

Isaac N. Smith, and the mistreatment of the men in Tompkins' regiment, the 22nd Virginia. Honor required that Tompkins resign and he left the service.

Ellen lost the farm and her beloved home on the mountain while her husband gave up his military career for the second time over incompetent "political" generals.

*Ellen Tompkins was a remarkable woman. Her husband was correct in describing her to General Wise as "thoroughly game". It would appear that her original reason for remaining behind was to safeguard the farm and the family's investment during what was thought to be a very short war which would end in a negotiated settlement. Little did they know that once the "genie was out of the bottle" that it would be so difficult to bring the hostilities to a halt.*

*Ellen's position was very difficult; her farm was occupied by unruly Union enlisted men, homes and farms in the area that belonged to Confederates were being burned by the Federal troops, and she was constantly worried about the safety of her husband, brother, and the chldren. Fortunately, the chivalry shown by General Cox in accepting responsibility for the safety of the family saved them from a disasterous situation. Another bit of good fortune was the previous relationship between Tompkins and Rosecrans which made it easier to shift the responsibility for the family's safety to a higher level of command.*

*A good deal of speculation based on circumstantial evidence could be made as to Ellen Tompkins involvement in passing information to the Confederates. In cases such as these, it is wise to evaluate the capabilities of the individual rather than to search for firm evidence. Proof is generally lacking in espionage cases -- if it were located, there would have been a trial at the time of discovery! Did Ellen Tompkins have the capability to be involved in spying?*

*She certainly had the courage, wit, and intellect to have done so. She had a well-developed ability to elicit information from her Union guests at the house and was able to determine even small details -- such as the wax-covered dispatches which would be swallowed by a captured courier and she was able to deliver the information to her sister in a system that utilized the services of the Federal postal service. This was exactly like the system used by the Confederate Secret Service Bureau in their operations.*

*Ellen was able to recruit the assistance of trusted couriers who would handcarry her letters to post offices beyond the reach of the military censor before her letters were posted. She used the services of the Union commander, General Cox, to send letters to Sarah. The letters to Sarah were the only letters preserved which could be used in this study. Ellen corresponded with persons other than her sister Sarah and may have used a duplicate system to ensure that her messages were getting through.*

*She arranged the "double envelope" delivery system with the postmaster in Gauley Bridge, James H. Miller, to prevent anyone from learning that she was being forwarded mail after she moved into the Confederate lines. Could she have used a system such as this long before she gave those instructions to Sarah on how to get letters through the lines? Could James H. Miller have been an accomplice of Ellen during the early stage of the Union occupation? Once again, Ellen had the capability to have been involved in some form of information collection and transmission and without the presence of evidence of espionage, the fact that she had the capability makes her suspect.*

*Capability can probably be used as a form of evidence if it is combined with some form of motivation-- a reason to spy. Why would Ellen Tompkins want to use such an elaborate (and potentially damning) communications system if she only wanted to pass on idle gossip about the military events in the area to her sister? She could have used the open postal system for most of what was going on and the news she was sending in her letters was generally being reported in the Ohio newspapers at the same time hardly military secrets. Why did she risk being caught sending letters outside of the postal system and when it was used, avoiding the military censors in Charleston? What was on the small slips of paper inside her letters that were to be passed to Wilkins Glenn, if not militarily significant information? What was the reason that she took these risks?*

*She was a very clever lady and may have told her sister in an early letter. There are two phrases in letters which reinforce the theory that Ellen was collecting passively, at least, information and attempting to get it to the Confederate capital. One was written as Rosecrans and Cox attempted to get their separate elements into blocking positions along the only potential routes of Floyd's army as it retreated from Carnifex Ferry:*

*"They hope to get to Dogwood Gap, 14 miles from here, and surprise our troops. Could I but have warned them..."*

*and when she wrote about the artillery fight east of the farm during which a cannoneer lost his arm and another lost a thumb:*

*"Better them than our forces should suffer".*

*Ellen had a husband, a brother,and many other relatives as well as friends in Wise's army and worried about their safety. She certainly would have warned them about the enemy's intentions, if she had the capability.*

*Ellen Tompkins had both a capability and sufficient motivation to be involved in espionage while she was held at the farm. Her perception that her presence gave the Federals some additional protection may have even provided her with additional motivation to "even things up a bit".*

*Ellen, at least in the early stages of the military campaign, probably did her best to get information through the lines. She had little reason to remain neutral and probably felt that by helping the Confederate war* effort, *she and her home would soon be back under their control.*

*This was increasingly important during the early stages of the war when most people felt that there would be a negotiated outcome. If the war was to be settled through negotiation, Ellen would have wanted to be on the Southern side of any future ceasefire line.*

*If the Confederate army forced General Cox's small brigade from their positions at Gauley Bridge, there was a good chance that the Rebels would be able to push their lines west to at least Charleston. At the time, everyone in the area hoped for a negotiated settlement -- Union as well as Confederate -- and if this had been the short-term outcome, as Ellen probably hoped, the more help she could provide, the sooner she, family, and farm would be safe. She had many excellent reasons to attempt to get information to the Rebel army and she certainly had developed excellent mechanisms to do so.*

*As time went by and the reality of a long war began to be recognized by Ellen Tompkins, she had also begun to appreciate the friendship and protection afforded the family by both Cox and Rosecrans. When she applied for a pass to go to Richmond temporarily and was placed on her "parole of honor", Ellen's willingness to collect and pass information -- outwitting them -- to the Confederate army came to an end. She knew that a long war was coming, that her husband had left the army shortly after she returned from Richmond, and that the friendship of Cox, Rosecrans, and several of the other Union officers had saved her and her family from several potential dangers. They were certainly more concerned about her welfare than was General Floyd when he ordered the shelling of her farm! The gratitude was becoming so strong that she was serious when she wrote that "no power on earth could induce me to betray them".*

*During this period of history, honor was far more than simply a word to be spoken, it was a way to live, a code that both gentlemen and ladies lived by. Their social standing, prestige and general acceptance by their peers was closely linked to this "code of honor". Giving one's word required that promises be kept. Ellen and Christopher Tompkins did have a well-developed personal sense of honor and once they had given their word to Rosecrans that Ellen would not under any circumstances discuss "the number, condition, or position of military forces, or their equipment, discipline, supplies, or movements...", the matter was settled.*

*Ellen adopted the attitude "...I take no interest in military affairs and am not capable of telling anything." This continued for the rest of her life. Her granddaughter and namesake said that Ellen often spoke of the beauty of the farm, but never talked about her experiences during the fighting. She told her grandchildren the same thing she wrote to Sarah in 1861: "But, really, I knew nothing about the war. I was interested only in the safety of Colonel Tompkins."*[121]

*Ellen Wilkins Tompkins was a remarkable woman.*

---

121 Tompkins, "Colonel's lady", pg. 390

# The Rest of the War

*If luckey is our doom Brave Boys*
*in old Abe lincoln hall*
*On our next Independent day*
*We will take a Sothern Ball* [1]

The year of our Lord One Thousand Eight Hundred and Sixty-one saw the beginning of a sad time for the entire nation, but it began an especially difficult period for the inhabitants of the upper Kanawha valley. The early expectations of jaunty uniforms, sabres, military banners snapping in the wind, and martial music faded into a reality of sick-to-death soldiers, amputations, sudden death, horribly slow death, rape, burnings and the murder of modern warfare in which there really are no real non-combattants. The illusion of southern military superiority over the North was also fading into a saddened dream as everyone quickly discovered the dedication and tenacity of the typical Union soldier.

This was one of the problems that Christopher Tompkins had with his political commanders -- he was simply too frank about the fighting ability of his former comrades-in-arms with whom he had served in the pre-war National Army. The political generals didn't want to hear any dissenting voices in the ranks. One of the Confederate enlisted men who had been drafted into the Confederate 22nd Virginia, Frederick W.B. Hassler, claimed after the war that Tompkins "had assumed his command with reluctance in obedience to a mistaken view of the rights of his native state; but retired into private life, as soon as he could do so consistently with soldierly honor."[2]

Hassler wrote about some of the events which followed the fighting on Cotton Hill and the retreat:

1 Howe, *Rebellion in the West*, pg. 48

2 Hassler, Frederick W.B., "A Military View of Passing Events From Inside the Confederacy", *The West Virginia Historical Magazine*, Vol. 5, No.1, January, 1905, pg. 305

"...Floyd received orders to go to Bowling-green, Kentucky, and thence to Tennessee, with all his command, except my Regiment, the Twenty-second Virginia. It appears that my Colonel, Christopher Q. Tompkins, had a quarrel with Floyd, at Cotton Hill-mountain. Rosecrans occupied the Colonel's house, at Gauley-bridge, and sent the family through the lines, to Richmond. When Colonel Tompkins asked General Floyd for a leave to go and see his family, the latter accused the Colonel of being a disloyal man, on account of his intimacy with Rosecrans.

"It appears that Tompkins had either served with Rosecrans or was friendly with him. I knew Tompkins well; for he was a Cadet when my grandfather, F.R. Hassler, was a Professor at West Point. We often talked together; and the Colonel said that he did not believe in the Re'bellion. He always told the rebels that 'the Yankees would fight as well as they would. They disliked him for this; and so he resigned, and never would have anything more to do with the War."[3]

Hassler's story of Tompkins' treatment by Floyd closely parallels the general's actions toward Isaac Smith when the unfortunate major attempted to resign from the Confederate army. Smith and Tompkins were exceptionally close friends and with the history of animosity between the colonel and the general, it is not surprising to locate the information recorded by Hassler. Floyd was an exceptionally bitter, if not mentally ill, person and was probably simply waiting for an opportunity to sink his vindictive hooks into the colonel. It is fortunate for Floyd that Tompkins was an even-tempered man and that the colonel's family was not harmed when the Confederate artillery opened fire on the colonel's farm. One command problem facing the Confederacy would probably have been settled on the spot by an angry colonel!

The talk about Tompkins and his loyalty to the Confederacy persisted for some time after his resignation. General Floyd, had been a powerful and popular political

3 Hassler, "Military View of Events From the Confederacy", pg. 304

figure in pre-war Virginia and had a considerable following. The Colonel wasn't one to let any accusation reaching his ears go unanswered. Soon after he left the army he began to hear rumors of accusations being made against him and wrote to the Confederate army's Adjutant General to determine the sources:

"General

"Intimations from several sources have reached me lattely that communications to my prejudice either officially or personnally have been made to the War Department.

"You will admit that I cannot disregard such statements, & I beg leave to inquire (if such have been made) the names of the authors & the specific character of the inputations against me."[4]

The rumors and local gossip probably continued for some time in war-time Richmond, but it apparently had no substantial effect on Tompkins. No other references to this type of malicious gossip was located in the remainder of the literature examined. All of his problems centered on his truthfulness -- he was quite frank about his feelings about Floyd and the fighting ability of the Union soldiers at a time when no one wanted to hear the truth.

But as for the average Union soldier who Tompkins respected as a fighting man, he had enlisted with the intention of saving his country from disintegration as the southern states pulled away from the Union which had been won from the British by their grandfathers at such a great cost. He was hearing that even some of the northern areas such as New York City were pondering the advantages that independence from the Union might bring them and holding the Union together became the goal as Unionist neighbors met to discuss their reasons for volunteering to serve.

[4] This letter was written to the Confederate Adjutant General, S. Cooper, on January 30, 1862. There is a copy in the Virginia Historical Society.

This was especially true in the non-slave states west of the Ohio River. These people had more recent experience with warfare against both the British and their indian allies during which an army under the "Star-spangled Banner" had saved the country from defeat. Stories told to children and grandchildren around fireplaces over the years had been of soldiers, flags, glory, and warfare against a savage, merciless, and murderous foe, had helped form a national outlook which held the western regiments to their duty during some of the worst campaigns of the war. Additionally, many of the settlers of the western areas were poor farmers who had been able to build lives only under a system such as which had been developed by the founding fathers of the nation. They were ambitious, free men who felt that slavery robbed men of any hope of advancement through hard work and were determined to resist the spread of that inhibiting institution to any other areas other than the ones where slavery was common and legal. They had made many personal gains under the freedom guaranteed by the National government and were determined to save it. This firm foundation of the average Union soldier helped hold him to both his duty and his goal as the war began to harden attitudes on both sides and the fighting began to become even more deadly than ever before.

Against this, the southerner had his loyalty to his state --especially true in Virginia -- and pride held the soldier to his military unit. They felt they were defending their way of life against hostile invaders who intended to incite the region's slaves into armed rebellion against their homes and families. This was a major concern for Virginians in 1861 as they had both the largest slave population in the country and had experienced the slave revolt incited and lead by John Brown at Harper's Ferry as well as the slave rebellion which had been lead by Nat Tyler. As the war progressed, many of the small farmers from southern fields began to ask one another why this seemed to be a "rich man's war and a poor man's fight" and desertion started to be considered by many, but most of them stayed for the duration of the war, even though it was only a poor man's fight. There are probably as many reasons for their individual actions as there were men in the ranks, but one of the most commom reasons that most of the men remained in the ranks when desertion to the Yankees and the taking of the "Oath" would have taken them out of the war for good: they were fighting a defensive war and they were the ones who had been invaded. They remained in the Confederate army to protect their homes and families from occupation by a hostile military force.

While the western Virginians were also "defending their way of life", many of them paused to reflect on a troubling thought: *Was their way of life worth preserving?*

With the history of political and economic domination from the eastern counties of the state, why should they fight and die for more of the same at the hands of the Confederate government which promised exactly that -- more of the same! This line of reasoning became more common after Wise began his retreat from the Kanawha valley. As the men in the ragged regiments realized that their poorly commanded regiments would be unable to hold the Union army at bay, they began to voice the familar complaint: West Virginia is sold out! But it was still expected that these Virginia volunteers would remain in Confederate service to defend the homes and the families of the easterners from invasion such as had happened to their homes -- under the command of the easterners. Many of the men didn't like this situation, but there were few options available. Commissioned officers could resign their commissions, but they would then face a double threat. They risked potential reprisals from the Federal government or a strong liklihood of being drafted back into the Rebel army again -- as privates. Enlisted men could only desert, but this act held some harsh penalties if the deserters were ever to come under the control of the army in the future. Many simply chose to remain in the army until the end and fought on without hope of recovering their homes from Union control. These homeless soldiers didn't receive the recognition afforded to the Kentuckians under similar circumstances, Breckinridge's Brigade came to be known as the "Orphan Brigade" because of their homelessness. Nothing like this came to the western Virginians who remained true to the Confederacy, regardless of their reasons. They simply remained in the ranks as "Virginians" until the war ended for them -- one way or another! This lack of recognition has remained true into modern times as history has been simplified to show only that West Virginia became a separate state during the Civil War in order to remain in the Union. The many dedicated men who remained true to the cause they had chosen to support and stayed with their regiments until the bitter end have been forgotten, but they were loyal to both the southern cause and their friends and they served to the last.

The Confederates from Virginia's western counties, primarily the 22nd, the 36th, and the 60th Virginia Infantry Regiments -- the former 1st, 2nd, and fledgling 3rd Kanawha Regiments organized under the command of Christopher Tompkins -- continued their retreat from the Cotton Hill area. They remained under the command of General John B. Floyd and their officers as they crossed the New River at Narrows, Virginia, into the relative safety of southwestern Virginia. They were reorganized and several of the regiments were marched off toward Tennessee with General Floyd to a place known as Fort Donelson.

The 22nd Virginia, Tompkins regiment, was in sad condition following the retreat from the Kanawha valley region and the misuse of General Floyd. They had been literally trapped between the two antagonistic personalities, Wise and Floyd. Nothing illustrates the feelings of their commander, Colonel Tompkins, better than a letter sent to General Wise from White Sulphur Springs on August 19, 1861:

"Yours of yesterday was duly received. I had previously received a characteristic letter from Gen Floyd which has been referred to Genl Lee. As I am about marching with the remains of these two regiments I have barely time to refer to one or two matters in your letter. You say 'I hear your men prefer his command I shall ask him to detatch them from mine & attach them to his.' I do not know who it is that communicates so much camp gossip, nor do I think it worthy of attention.

"Nevertheless I protest against these volunteers being transferred like so many coach-horses, & submit that it is entirely unnecessary to request until their preference is ascertained, or even then..."[5]

Tompkins wasn't the type of man who would sit idly by and let the men under his command be misused. He certainly wasn't intimidated by the loud, overbearing Henry Wise and told him quickly enough that it was improper to march the Kanawha volunteers back and forth like "coach-horses." He also didn't hesitate to refer the "characteristic letter from Floyd" directly to General Lee for review. It is little wonder that General Floyd and Colonel Tompkins didn't get along. Tompkins was a "no nonsense" commander who was stuck with two arrogant amateurs as generals. Wise probably came to rely on Tompkins' judgement and gradually developed considerable respect for the abilities of the West Pointer and later tried to persuade the Confederate War Department to commission Tompkins a general and place him in command of the entire western Virginia theater. Tompkins was, however, thoroughly disillusioned by that time and probably wouldn't have served an active military role for Lee's stars.

His men had suffered greatly at the hands of his bungling superiors and the senior commander, Lee, had done nothing to correct the command problem that was as obvious to Tompkins as it was to the average private in the ranks. The long-suffering men of the Kanawha regiments had been seriously depleted during the retreat from the valley the first time around. Tompkins wasn't understating the strength of his two regiments in the letter to Wise when he referred to the "remains of these two regiments". They had started into the war with normal strength, but by the time they began their march back to the valley with Floyd,

[5] Tompkins' letter to Wise is in the National Archives, Record Group 109. The coversheet is titled "Protesting against 22nd and 36th Regts being transferred to Floyd's Brigade.

there were far fewer of them on the morning report. The entire 22nd was understrength and the individual companies strength is surprising. Both the 22nd and the 36th were so understaffed that they were organized under Tompkins as a "brigade" by combining them on August 13, 1861. The strength report at the time:

Company A.......Barbee.......86
" B.......Tyree........35
" C.......Shelton......39
" D.......Swann........67
" E.......illegible....53
" F.......Liscomb......56
" G.......Watts........52
" H.......Duncan.......49
" I.......Ruffner......57
" K.......Huddleston...53 [6]

The 36th Virginia under Colonel McCausland had fared about the same on the retreat. Two of his companies, however, Company D and Company I were at 28 and 27 men, respectively. In many respects, the long retreat out of the vally and away from their homes had been a tempering experience for the regiments as the less-than-fully-committed dropped by the way and returned to their homes for the remainder of the war. Those who chose to stay in the ranks generally remained in their regiments until the end of the war, left as invalids, or died in service.

The march from Cotton Hill had been another of those "tempering" experiences for the Kanawha volunteers. They were even required to finally endure the speech Floyd had so greatly desired to give during the middle of the night while they were fleeing from General Rosecrans, but had been over-ruled by *Colonel* Henry Heth.

Whether the men liked to hear Floyd or not, they had their final opportunity to hear him at his finest. The speech was made on December 26, the day after Christmas and Floyd probably felt that he had given them a gift they would treasure:

---

6 Special Orders dated August 13, 1863. Coversheet title states "Order forming Va. regmts into a separate Brigade". National Archives Record Group 109

"*Soldiers of the Army of the Kanawha:* The campaign in the western portion of this state is now, as far as you are concerned, ended. At its close you can review it with pride and satisfaction. You first encountered the enemy, five months since, on his unobstructed march into the interior of the State. From that time until recalled from the field, you were engaged in perpetual warfare with him. Hard contested battles and skirmishes were matters of almost daily occurrence. Nor is it to be forgotten that laborious and arduous marches, by day and by night, were necessary, not only as furnishing you the opportunity of fighting there, but of baffling the foe at different points upon the march of invasion. And it is a fact which entitles you to the warm congradulations of your General, and to the thanks and gratitude of your country, that in the midst of the trying scenes through which you have passed, you have proved yourselves men and patriots, who, undaunted by superior numbers, have engaged the foe, beaten him in the field, and baffled and frustrated him in his plans to surprise you.

"On all occasions, under all circumstances, your patriotism and courage have never faltered nor forsaken you. With inadequate transportation, often illy clad, and with less than a full allowance of provisions, no private has ever uttered a complaint to his General. This fact was grateful to his feelings; and if your hardships have not been removed or alleviated by him, it has been because of his inability to do so. But your exemplary and patriotic conduct has not passed unobserved nor unappreciated by the Government in whose cause we are all enlisted. It is an acknowledged fact that you have made fewer claims, and imposed less trouble upon it, than any army in the field, content to dare and do, and become true soldiers and patriots.

"Now, at the close of your laborious and eventful campaign, when you may have looked forward to a season of rest, your country has bestowed upon you the distinguished compliment of calling you to another field of action. That you will freely respond to this call your past services, so cheerfully rendered, furnish the amplest assurance. Kentucky, in her hour of peril, appeals to Virginia, her mother, and to her sisters for succor. This appeal is not unheeded by their gallant sons. The foot of the oppressor is upon her. Trusting in the cause of justice, we go to her relief, and, with the help of Him who is its author, we will do our part in hurling back and chastising the oppressor whois desecrating her soil.

"Soldiers! your country, your friends whom you leave behind you, will expect you, in your new field of labor, to do your duty.

"Remember that the eyes of the country are upon you, and that upon your action, in part, depends the result of the greatest struggle the world ever saw, involving not only your freedom, your property, and your lives, but the fate of political liberty everywhere.

"Remember this, and, relying on Him who controls the destinies of nations, as of individuals, you need not fear the result."[7]

Most of the men were probably as impressed as was William Clark Reynolds, the private from the 22nd Virginia who had written a short phrase in his diary at the end of the retreat from Cotton Hill which told of his feelings about General Floyd:

"The old Governor killed his hogs and scalded them in hot water and hung them up to dry, he did."[8]

The five months of campaigning under the command of General Floyd had left the Virginia volunteers from the Kanawha valley feeling as if they had been butchered, scalded and hung out to dry. Little worse could have happened to them. Many of the men must have cringed in the ranks to hear that they were being sent to Kentucky to conduct a winter campaign under Floyd. It would be interesting to review the brigade morning report the roll-call after the speech was made -- many of the tired

7 Moore, *Rebellion Record*, Vol.3, pg. 511-512

8 Reynolds, *Diary of William Clark Reynolds*, pg. 20

soldiers probably packed their bags and walked away from the Confederacy after hearing that speech which described the end of their fighting in the mountains of western Virginia as -- they were "recalled," indeed. How many of them really believed that after the deadly winter retreat which Floyd, himself, described to Henry Heth as nearly a "rout!"

Some evidence of the feelings of the men in the ranks is available from an inspection of Floyd's brigade by the Confederate Inspector General's office following the retreat. The report mentioned a strength of raw and undisciplined troops numbering about 5000 and 1,500 sick and absent.[9] The "distinguished compliment" of being called to another field by the government and serving there under Floyd was more than many of them could take.

The command problem which had plagued the Confederate regiments operating in western Virginia was finally solved when Jefferson Davis decided not to "hang" Wise and sent him with his Legion to defend the Outer Banks of North Carolina. He was to lose the fight there with a Federal amphibious landing and lose a son as well.

Captain O. Jennings Wise, commander of the Richmond Light Infantry Blues, died defending the Confederacy's coast. Wise remained a general through the war and was near Lee when the end came at Appomatox Court House. During one campaign, he was still cursing as strongly as before in spite of being cautioned on his language by Lee. Wise reportedly responded to the mild chastisement by saying:

"General Lee, you certainly play Washington to perfection, and your whole life is a reproach to me. Now I am perfectly willing that Jackson and yourself shall do the praying for the whole of the Army of Northern Virginia, but in Heaven's name, let me do the *cussin'* for one small brigade."[10]

9 Husley, "Men of Virginia - Men of Kanawha - To Arms", pg. 224

10 ____, *Battles and Leaders*, Vol. II, edited by Robert U. Johnson and Clarence C. Buel, The Century Co., N.Y.: 1887, pg. 277

Floyd took his troops to Kentucky from where he was quickly assigned to Fort Donelson in Tennesse at about the time it was completely surrounded by the Federal army under a new type of general the Rebels hadn't encountered before in the field...Grant!

It was cold along the Cumberland River and in the fortifications at Fort Donelson in February. The Virginians moved into the trenches and on February 14, 1862, they concentrated and sallied from their fortifications in an attempt to break the seige of the Federals. They pressed the Union lines back for nearly two miles, but were halted by the order of General Pillow. They were then forced back into the fortifications as the Federal noose tightened and General Floyd and the other commanders in the beseiged fort had to consider Grant's "unconditional surrender" terms.

Floyd had the usual problem -- he was scared to death of being taken prisoner by the Union army. He was convinced (and was probably right) that he would be placed in that "iron cage" if he ever fell into their hands. During the surrender conference with the other two Confederate generals at Fort Donelson, Pillow and Buckner, he told them "We will have to capitulate; but, gentlemen, you know my position with the Federals; it wouldn't do; it wouldn't do."[11]

Floyd was able to escape once again from the potential wrath of the Federals he feared so much on Sunday, February 16, when two small steamers arrived at Fort Donelson. He and most of his Virginians managed to escape from Grant's seige and another future Confederate notable, Colonel Nathan Bedford Forrest, also escaped with his cavalry by riding over a flooded road to safety beyond the Union lines.

Floyd may have escaped from the wrath of the Federals, but he was soon in the hands of a very angry Jefferson Davis and the Confederate War Department. He and Pillow had left General Simon Bolivar Buckner in Fort

[11] Brown, James E., "Life of Brigadier General John McCausland", *West Virginia History*, Vol. IV, No.4, July 1943, pg. 247-248

Donelson to surrender the rest of the garrison. The questions were difficult to answer: why didn't they evacuate earlier? Why was the rest of the command abandoned? How did they escape and the others were left? Why were only certain troops selected to escape from the doomed fort?

This time Floyd may have had an excuse for losing to the Union army. He tried to explain his decision to leave the fort by explaining several unknowns to the Confederate High Command: first, he was faced by 119 enemy regiments. His men were not in condition to continue the resistance or attempt to escape -- they had been in constant combat for eighty-four hours and were totally exhausted. He refused to surrender the entire army and Floyd felt he had taken the dangerous duty by personally leading the escape. The reason given for the escape of the Virginians -- his troops were the nearest to the boats and were taken out.[12] He may have felt some pride in the fact that five thousand soldiers had escaped from the surrounded fort, but President Davis was less than impressed. Floyd was relieved from his duties and he returned to his home until given a minor command of Virginia "State Line" troops, a militia-like unit which accomplished little. Floyd sickened and died before the end of the war and finally escaped from that "iron cage" that had plagued all of his military planning from the beginning of the war.

The men from the Virginia regiments were returned to Virginia from Tennessee and continued to fight throughout the war. Many of them fought in campaigns in the Shenandoah Valley and were with General Early when they threatened Washington, D.C. with capture and some of these men from the valley camped in Bethesda, Maryland -- within sight of the Capitol dome. The survivors were released from Confederate service by General Echols shortly after the news of Appomattox reached them and they finally went home to the Kanawha valley and surrounding areas.

The men of the 22nd Virginia, however, had been

---

12 Brown, "Life of McCausland", pg. 248-249

contaminated by the presence of Colonel Tompkins and Isaac Smith and were equally infected by having been under the command of Floyd's hated rival, Wise, and the entire regiment was excused from making the fateful trip to Fort Donelson with the others who listened to Floyd's rousing speech on the day after Christmas, 1861. They hadn't been a formal part of Wise's Legion -- they were simply shuttled back and forth between the two brigades like Tompkins' "coach-horses" and they missed the defeat on Roanoke Island and the Outer Banks as well as the seige and defeat at Fort Donelson.

The 22nd Virginia was put under the command of Henry Heth, the officer who served as the military advisor to Floyd during the previous western Virginia campaigns and they went back into the mountains to try again. The strategic targets in the area were on the approaches to the Virginia and Tennessee Railroad and Heth attempted to guard it from Federal attack by spreading his available force into a wide defensive screen across the region and their patrolling was probably quite aggressive. By May, Heth was sufficiently confident to order an offensive against the Federals at Giles Court House and pushed them back to their New River defensive line. Having seized the initiative, the confident Heth pushed northeast toward Lewisburg, the Greenbrier county seat which had been occupied by Union troops.

Lewisburg was defended by Union General George Crook with a force approximately equal to that of the attackers and the Confederate attackers didn't do well. William Bahlmann, of the Fayetteville Rifles, wrote about the attack:

"At the battle of Lewisburg, May 23, 1862, we got the surprise of our lives. We had not lost a fight in 1861, but in 1862 'we caught a Tartar.' Our company lost 21 men out of 36. William Sandige was killed, Miles Johnson was mortally wounded, and Warren Jones has been missing ever since. Nine of us were captured and spent part of the summer in Camp Chase. When we got back some of us were married..."[13]

Bahlmann later expanded his narrative of the battle and explained how the defeat had occurred:

"We reached Greenbrier bridge, 3 miles east of Lewisburg, in the evening and our co. was sent on a picket. I had put on my oldest clothes, thinking we would soon drive the enemy out of Lewisburg and then return and take breakfast with the girls in the town. But wasn't I disappointed. Col. afterwards Maj. Gen'l., Geo. Crook, a very efficient officer, had command of two good regiments, the 36th and 44th Ohio Inf. and instead of retreating, advanced to meet us. It so happened that as B and K left flank companies were on the right and owing to the fact that one of our regts. on the left flickered on as four companies of us became exposed to the fire from two regts. I won't name the regts. although I remember its number distinctly. For a year afterwards our regt. and it could not march together because the men would fight. But at the battle of Dry Creek, Aug. 26, '63, the regt. in question repulsed 11 charges of the enemy and the 22nd cheered them and the feud was settled."[14]

The remaining men of Heth's regiments moved into safer areas to rest and refit. They spent the summer conducting raids into Union-controlled territory and during one of these, the 22nd Virginia captured Summersville and its entire Federal garrison -- 200 men from the Ninth West Virginia Infantry.[15] The Confederates began to gather strength and momentum as the Rebel successes in the

13 Bahlmann, William F., *History of Fayette County, West Virginia*, Cardin and Peters, editors, pg. 219

14 Bahlmann, William F., "Down in the Ranks", *Journal of the Greenbrier Historical Society*, Vol. II, No.1, October, 1969, pg. 61. The unnamed regiment was Edgar's Battalion which was in its first battle. The new and untrained conscripts simply weren't prepared for the fighting they were thrust into. Later, at Dry Creek, they were to redeem themselves with the 22nd Virginia.

15 *Official Records*, Vol. XII, Part 3, pg. 430-431

Shenandoah valley and eastern Virginia caused the Federals to shift their troops to adjust to the strengthened Confederates. In early August, General Cox was ordered to move his "Kanawha Brigade" to join General Pope and the Army of the Potomac. Cox was to leave a force of 5000 men in western Virginia to hold it against any Confederate threat. Cox was more than willing to move his command to a larger theater of operations and larger forces where promotion would be more likely to occur.

Unfortunately for the Federal planners, the copies of General Pope's offficial correspondence, his "letter book", was captured by the rebels and sent to Lee.

The following letter to General Loring was probably a welcome surprise to the Confederates and the jubilant Secretary of War wrote the news:

"Pope's letter-book has been captured. On August 11 Cox was ordered to retain 5,000 men in Western Virginia and to send the remainder by river and railroad to Pope. On August 16 Cox telegraphed from Gauley Bridge that his command would be at Parkersburg on the evening of the 20th, and asked for railroad transportation. Clear the valley of the Kanawha, and operate northwardly to a junction with our army in the valley. Keep us advised of your movements."[16]

The Confederates had managed to pull off what today would be called an "intelligence coup." They had copies of all of the official correspondence of General Pope and replies from his subordinates in their hands. This was the equivalent of reading the General's mail and he may not have realized that they had captured the courier who had custody of this precious letter-book.

Lee quickly saw that the undermanned Kanawha valley was ripe for Confederate picking and ordered Rebel regiments to prepare for their invasion.

One of the participants on the Confederate side wrote:

---

16 *Official Records*, Vol. XII, Pt. 3, pg. 946

"On August 29 the Secretary of War wired Loring that Pope's letter-book, captured, revealed the fact that Cox had orders to retain 5000 men in West Virginia, and to send the rest to Pope, and added: 'Clear the Valley of the Kanawha and operate northwardly to a junction with our army in the valley.' Loring sent Jenkins on a raid through the region lying north of the Kanawha Valley and concentrated the main force or greater part of it near Giles Court House (Pearisburg) just above the narrows of New River. On September 6 he marched down the south side of the river with all the infantry except Echols' brigade, and all the artillery, about 16 pieces. He says he marched with 5000 men, but it is not clear whether this number includes Echols' brigade which he says pursued a much longer route."[17]

The Confederate regiments marched quickly through the mountains and were back in their home territory in only a few days. Loring had been in the area the previous year when he reinforced Lee on Sewell Mountain, but he didn't cross New River when Floyd marched to Cotton Hill, but many of the men in the ranks had been with Floyd and knew the area very well. For the men of the Fayetteville Rifles, they were coming home after a long absence. The town had been fortified and the Rebels maneuvered carefully. Joel Abbot was from the area and was sent on a patrol by General Loring:

"I was ordered to pilot a detatchment of cavalry through the woods to Cotton Hill, cut the wires, and hold the road until forced away. We got axes from David Harshbarger and cut the poles and wires to the top of Cotton Hill, then went up the road to the red bank on George Tyree's place where we could see the road leading down to Miller's Ferry. All day they went down the Hawks Nest road, crossed the river at Miller's Ferry, and went down the other side of the river to Gauley Bridge. Cox's men made no

---

17 Humphries, "Military Operations in Fayette County, West Virginia", *The Fayette Tribune*, Fayetteville, West Virginia. Undated copy in the West Virginia Archives.

effort to dislodge us. And all day the battle at Fayetteville raged."[18]

The Federal Regiments in the area were under the command of a boyhood friend of "Stonewall"Jackson, Colonel Joseph Andrew Jackson Lightburn, who began to pull his troops back into a relatively close perimeter. Lightburn was concerned by the imminent approach of the Confederates under General Loring, but he had to consider the threat to his north created by the presence of Albert Gallatin Jenkins and the Confederate cavalry. The Union commander at Gauley Bridge had no idea of the numbers of cavalrymen he could potentially face as he fought Loring's advance. He pulled back the regiment under Colonel Siber which was posted at Raleigh Courthouse to Fayetteville and ordered the Federal troops positioned up New River to return to Tompkins' farm. There was a Union force at Summersville and Lightburn was sufficiently concerned over the Jenkins' threat that he sent six companies from the Forty-seventh Ohio to reinforce that potential hot spot. He then ordered the quartermaster and commissary stores for the entire army which were in the large depot at Gauley Bridge to be shipped to Charleston to keep them from the hands of the Confederates, if they should prove victorious in the upcoming fight.[19]

There had been a minor miracle in bridge-building since the Confederates on Cotton Hill had been repulsed by Cox and Rosecrans during the previous winter. The original Bridge had been burned by Wise during the first Confederate retreat from the valley the previous summer. Gauley River had been crossed on the ferry constructed by Captain Lane until early in 1862 when a new bridge was erected. A correspondent from the *Cincinnati Commercial* wrote on February 17, 1862:

18 Abbott, Joel H., "A Civil War Narrative", *History of Fayette County, West Virginia*, edited by Peters and Cardin, pg. 216

19 Kincaid, Mary E., "Fayetteville, West Virginia, During the Civil War", *West Virginia History*, Vol. XIV, No.4, July, 1953, pg. 353-354

"The Gauley Bridge, burnt by the rebel General Wise, has been rebuilt by Captain E.P. Fitch, the brigade quartermaster, attached to the staff of Gen. Cox.

"It was constructed in twenty-three working days from the date of making the contract, and was open for travel on the first day of this month. This bridge is about five hundred and eighty-five feet long, ten feet in width, divided into three spans. The main sustaining parts are one and one quarter wire ropes.

"The roadway is of wood and so ingeniously braced that detatchments of cavalry ride over it at a charge, producing no more, or in fact not as much vibration as is induced under similar circumstances on a thorough truss-bridge. The Twenty-eighth regiment, Ohio volunteers, Col. Moor, Capt. Simmons's battery, and Capt. Schonberg's cavalry, marched and counter-marched across it some days since, for the purpose of trying its stability. The entire Twenty-eighth regiment was closely packed on one span and a half, two sections of Capt. Simmons's battery occupying another span at the same time.

"This immense load upon the bridge was borne at a halt and in motion, portions of it marching to the music of the band at a cadence step, without producing the slightest weakness. The entire work was executed by Messrs. Stone, Quigly & Burton, bridge-builders of Philadelphia."[20]

This excellent new bridge was lying across the bottle-neck in the supply lines of the Union forces operating to the east of Gauley River. The lack of bridge had been a serious concern for General Rosecrans during the campaign against Lee on Sewell Mountain late in the previous year. Now the bridge was more likely to end up in Confederate service as Loring's men moved closer. The Federal garrison at Gauley Bridge began planning for a general evacuation as the Confederates fought to get control of Fayetteville, only a short distance across Cotton Hill from the town.

Floyd had accomplished one thing when he occupied

20 Moore, Frank, *The Rebellion Record*, Vol.4, 1862, pg. 46

Cotton Hill and spent nearly two weeks shelling the Federal camp at Gauley Bridge. He had demonstrated the strategic value of that mountain to the Federals. They probably considered fortifying the summit, but supplying it during the winter was probably sufficient deterrent to cause them to re-think that option. They settled on constructing fortifications on the approaches ot Cotton Hill and began to construct breastworks and other field fortifications in the town of Fayetteville, now about to come under Confederate attack.

The chief engineer of the Confederate Army of western Virginia described the Federal fortifications in the town:

"First, an irregular work of three faces, each of 40 yards'development, 8 feet in command, and 7 in relief; barbettes in each salient, covering well the ground in front; located on admirable selected position, enfilading the surrounding open plains. Second, a similar work, constructed as a musketry defense, flanked by felled timber, rifle-pits. Third, a formidable, well-constructed, and inclosed lunette, connecting, by covert way, with flanking redan on commanding ground, barbettes in each salient, commanding each of the advance works, with development sufficient for a regiment."[21]

Union Colonel Siber fell back from Raleigh Court House and moved into the strong, fortified positions which had been prepared the previous year. This set of fortifications would prevent the Confederate army from occupying the slopes of Cotton Hill as Floyd had done the previous year during the seige of Gauley Bridge and the Rebel regements were compelled to attack it. They couldn't afford to by-pass the Federals and move on -- their lines of both communication and retreat would be threatened, if the Federal garrison sallied from their trenches. The Confederates couldn't spare the men to beseige the Fayetteville fortifications; they simply had too few men to be able to contain the Federals while continuing

[21] Kincaid, "Fayetteville, West Virginia", pg. 354

the offensive. They had to attack.

Colonel Siber had some advance warning that the Confederates were in the area when he sent his entire cavalry force, six orderlies and a sergeant, to pick up a secessionist civilian living in the area who had announced that he would need his rifle the following morning. The small cavalry force reached the Confederate sympathizer's house, but were pursued by thirty Confederate cavalry. This incident alerted Siber that the Rebels were in the immediate area and he assembled a six company force from two regiments and sent them forward on the Raleigh Pike Road in an attempt to locate the Confederate main force and determine its size. These Union companies were more successful than they had planned as they had marched only three miles from the Courthouse when they made contact with the advance elements of General John S. Williams' Second Brigade. The Federals were forced into a position in a nearby field and began to fight off the Confederates.

A second Confederate force composed of regiments under Colonel Gabriel C. Wharton, Colonel George S. Patton, and Lieutenant-Colonel Augustus Forsburg and accompanied by the Thirtieth Battalion Virginia Sharpshooters under the command of Lieutenant-Colonel J.L.Clarke was sent forward in an attempt to get into the rear of the main Federal position in the town.[22]

Milton W. Humphries was assigned to an artillery battery assigned to Lorings' small army and later wrote about the battle for the town beginning with the movement of the Confederate force attempting to get into the rear of the Federal position:

"This force was guided by Mr. Benjamin Jones, the father of Beuring H. Jones, Colonel of the Sixtieth Virginia Infantry. The distance around and the obstacles to rapid movement were so great that it was about 2:15 p.m., when Wharton took position near, but not extending across, the road to Cotton Hill, and about 1000 yards from the Federal

[22] Humphries, *Military Operations in Fayette County*, pg. 13

works fronting on that side. While the Confederates were taking position to begin action, the Federals made a vigorous attack upon them with 6 companies of the Thirty-fourth Ohio, 4 of which were led personally by Colonel J.T. Toland and 2 by Captain H.C. Hatfield on the Cotton Hill road on Toland's right. They made three attacks, but were repulsed each time and retired to their works. Similar attacks of the Confederates upon the Federal works were likewise repulsed. In this fight both sides used artillery, the guns of the Confederates being rifled, but how many and of what battery is not stated in the reports. The Federals used 4 mountain howitzers under Lieutenant H.H. Anderson at the main redoubt. At length both sides became inactive."[23]

The Federal positions were strong and well-defended against the repeated Confederate attempts against them. Once the Rebel force got into the rear of the Union positions they discovered that the Federal artillery batteries were on either side of the road to Gauley Bridge and were in positions where they were mutually supporting. Major Augustus Bailey, from the 22nd Virginia, was able to clear the Federals from the battery on the right, but couldn't hold it since it was fully covered by the other battery.

Colonel Siber had been ordered to clear the Confederates from the woods to his rear and the two companies under Captain Hatfield attempted to drive them from the Gauley Road. These Union companies fought for three hours but were unable to get past the Confederate troops. Union reinforcements arrived from Gauley Bridge and were thought to be of regimental size by General Loring and the fighting slowed at sunset. With the perceived arrival of additional Federal troops, Loring waited for the arrival of the Confederate brigade under General Echols before bringing on a general engagement on the following morning. When the Federals learned of the arrival of Echols they wisely withdrew form their fortifications and retreated to Gauley Bridge.

[23] Humphries, *Military Operations in Fayette County*, pg. 14

Milton Humphries had a great deal of admiration for the Federal commander who managed this feat while under fire, but was far less kind to the Confederate commander who allowed the Union soldiers to escape:

"The day's fighting of this small force -- 1 regiment and six companies of another with 4 mountain howitzers and two 6-pounder smoothbores -- against 2 brigades and 16 pieces of artillery, some of them heavy calibre, constitutes either one of the most brilliant feats of the war or one of the most dismal failures and instances of inefficiency on the part of the Confederates. In any case Colonel Siber merits the highest praise. There was a report current in the Confederate army that Loring ordered Wharton to leave the way open for the Federals to escape, but there is no hint of this in the Official Records. Loring says there were so many roads leading from Fayetteville that it was not possible to guard all of them; but he left unguarded the very one the Federals were sure to take. Siber speaks of it simply as his line of retreat and ascribes its being left open to the 'considerable loss' (which was really very light) that Wharton had sustained in trying to block it. It looks very much as if Loring thought it best to get what he then supposed to be 5 regiments out of their stronghold by any means that might offer, and so disposed his forces that the Federals could march out; but whether intentional or not, *he let them escape.*"[24]

The relieving force from Gauley Bridge had given Siber the idea of marching out of the trap in which he had supposed they were caught. Colonel John L. Vance was the commander of the Fourth West Virginia Infantry Regiment, the unit that marched over the mountain and into Fayetteville. He wrote about the march and the retreat from the town:

"About 2 o'clock in the afternoon of the 10th of September, I was ordered to report to Colonel Lightburn

24 Humphries, *Military Operations in Fayette County*, pg. 16

with three companies of my regiment, (4th W.Va. Inf.) in light marching order and with a double supply of ammunition. No time was lost in making ready and moving to headquarters near the Ferry. On reporting, verbal orders were given me by Colonel Lightburn to 'cross the ferry and move at once by forced march, to the relief of Colonel Siber at Fayetteville,' with the statement that 'the enemy had attacked him.'

"It was a few minutes after three o'clock in the afternoon when the three companies under my command crossed the Kanawha at the ferry below the Falls and started for Fayetteville, a distance of thirteen miles. The march was by the only road -- that over Cotton Mountain -- which began at the ferry.

"The men were in good condition and moved rapidly. Before the top of the mountain was reached, we met a number of civilians who gave information that Fayetteville was surrounded; that Siber's force was cut to pieces; that when they last saw the town, it was burning, and in truth, all the stories that would naturally be told at such a time and under such circumstances. As we continued to advance, the number of refugees, seeking shelter at Gauley, increased, and the stories grew in horror.

"When near to Fayetteville, we saw evidences of conflict and in the woods to the right of the road, within short rifle range, several bodies of troops were plainly seen, supposed to belong to the enemy and such afterward proved to be the case.

"It was after sundown, but not dark, when my command entered Fayetteville. I reported at once to Colonel Siber. He received me cordially, thanking me for coming to his aid, asked the number of men and a few other questions of like character. In response to his inquiry, I said we had not been fired upon. He expressed surprise, saying 'We are surrounded.' After instructions in regard to the disposition of my command, he gave an outline of the procedings of the day.

"There is no doubt that the contest that day at Fayetteville had been a severe one, waged against heavy odds. The Union troops had displayed great courage under the leadership of Colonel Siber and the officers of the two regiments.

"After the interview with Colonel Siber I returned to my command; but a few minutes only passed when I was asked to report at headquarters. Upon doing so I found several officers assembled, and a council was held, at which the question was discussed as to the best way to get out of the town and to Gauley. A proposition was made to move troops to New River about three miles away, and thence down that river to Gauley. This was abandoned when the fact was made known that only a devious and difficult foot-path led to the river, and that there was no causeway practicable down the left bank of the stream to Gauley, and no boats or pontoons by which to cross to the right bank. The council dispersed, leaving undecided the matter of the evacuation of the town.

"It is proper to say that during the discussion at the conference or council, no reference was made to orders from Lightburn to retreat. On the contrary, the question of holding the town was canvassed and opinions offered pro and con. It was the distinct understanding, however, that retreat be decided upon, it was to be made to Gauley, from which place, to give the unamious verdict of those present, it would be impossible to dislodge or seriously disturb the troops.

"After leaving headquarters I again returned to my men. After the lapse of perhaps half an hour I was for the second time summoned to the presence of Colonel Siber, who informed me that he had decided to fall back to Gauley; the he would move by the road over Cotton Mountain, the one by which I had reached him; that the troops would begin the movement about two o'clock the next morning, and that my command would constitute the rear guard.

"When the hour arrived, however, Colonel Siber changed the order of march. He said to me: 'You will open the way for me out of this town; you will not fire unless you are fired upon, and then you will return the fire and cut your way to the big white house (referring to a dwelling about two miles from Fayetteville standing by the side of the road) and there you will wait for me.'

"I marched to the point indicated without molestation. As the command moved forward, the advance deployed, disturbed and dislodged a number of the enemy, who were posted at points along and at the side of the road; but they retired, without firing, to the main line stationed in the edge of the woods and plainly visible.

"The entire body of Colonel Siber's command followed and was unmolested until nearly all had passed, when a small detatchment of the enemy opened fire, wounding a few men.

"I may say here that some years ago, perhaps in 1880, when in Florida I met General Loring, the commander of the Confederate forces invading the Kanawha. The above incident was related and he explained that we were permitted to get out of Fayetteville unmolested because his men, stationed along the road leading to Cotton Mountain were without ammunition; that they had exhausted their supply during the fight on the 10th and the train carrying it did not reach the ground until we had passed.

"The detachment of the Fourth West Virginia was placed in the rear after leaving the 'big white house,' and the entire command was moved to a point near the top of Cotton Mountain. A halt being made here the enemy was discovered drawn up in line of battle and soon opened up combat. They were driven back to the foot of the mountain without trouble, and the retreat was resumed. It was interrupted several times by the enemy, attacks being made upon the rear guard.

"The descent of the mountain toward Gauley Bridge was made in a comparatively leisurely manner by the rear guard. This guard would halt at an available point when pressed by the enemy, check his advance, then move forward. By this course it was believed sufficient time would be given for the ferriage across the river of the troops in advance, preparation for doing which, in a speedy maner, it was also believed, had been made.

"When near the foot of the mountain, but not yet in sight

of the river and the ferry, I was ordered to hold the enemy in check as long as could be done, in my judgement, without risking destruction or capture; in the event of either contingency arisin, to fall back. The foe did not make his appearance for some little time, and when he did appear, was not as keen for conflict as at points preceding. Not much thought was given to this until it was discovered that an attempt was in progress to flank us. This discovery was known to the enemy as quickly as it was to us, and a brisk onslaught was made, which was futile, by reason of the narrow roadway, and we fell back rapidly to the mountain. Here great was the surprise that no attempt had been made to cross the ferry, and concentrate at Gauley. The command of Colonel Siber was moving down the left or south bank of the Kanawha. The government buildings at the foot of the mountain and stretching along the bank of the Kanawha, had been set on fire and were burning briskly. The houses were long and low, built on both sides of a narrow road, and by the time we reached them the passage was rendered hazardous by reason of the flames.

"Fortunatly, a great number of blankets were scattered around on the ground. These were caught up by the men, and mainly through the protection thereby afforded they were able to run the gauntlet of the fire.

"The fire, growing in intensity, proved a check to the enemy and we were enabled to overtake the main body under Colonel Siber. The retreat was continued. with frequent interruptions of the rear by the enemy, until Armstrong's Creek was reached. At this point, a determined attack, made on the rear by the enemy, was repulsed."[25]

The Federal retreat from Fayetteville was successful, thanks to the arival and efforts of Colonel Vance and the Fourth West Virginia Infantry. They had marched into Fayetteville after a forched march over Cotton Hill and had

[25] Vance, John L., "Lightburn's Retreat Before Loring At Fayetteville Sept. 10-11, 1862, *The Fayette Tribune*; an undated copy is in the West Virginia Archives.

soon been ordered to take the most dangerous duty during the retreat. Colonel Siber had ordered the West Virginia troops to lead the breakout from the encircled town and ordered them to rally at the nearby house. While there, he switched the units in order that the West Virginia companies were forming the rear-guard for the remainder of the retreat. Colonel Siber had managed to put Vance's men at the most dangerous positions during both stages of the retreat -- they were the lead element during the break through and they formed the rear-guard after the column had escaped from the town.

This was similar to the practice of General Floyd with the 22nd Virginia during their marches. Both Colonel Tompkins and Major Smith constantly complained about the regiment being in the lead during advances and forming a rear-guard during a retreat. Colonel Siber, however, had managed to elevate this misuse of a unit to an art form -- he used Vance's men in both roles during a single march.

The motivation of Floyd and Siber is simple to understand. The men of their regiments were recruited from the same communities and were generally composed of the friends and neighbors of the commanders. Floyd's brigade was composed of men he had recruited and organized from his home region of Virginia and Siber's men were from Ohio. It was in their political and emotional interest to safeguard their men whenever they could; so the western Virginians -- strangers to each commander -- were obviously more expendable than the men of their home areas. The western Virginians saw rough duty under commanders from other states during the war and this factor also helps to account for the fairly high desertion rates, especially from the Confederate army. Fairly led and serving under their own commanders, their steadfastness could become legendary. Many of the men in several of the regiments of General Jackson's unit, the "Stonewall Brigade", were from the counties of western Virginia -- as was Jackson, himself.

The loss of Fayetteville wasn't the only problem facing Colonel Lightburn, the commander of the Federal forces in the Kanawha valley. He was faced with a situation which was filled with unknowns. The total number of the Confederate regiments attacking over Cotton Hill after taking Fayetteville were among the unknown factors, but the presence of the large Confederate cavalry force operating to the north of the valley and their general intentions were the biggest problem he faced when trying to make plans for his defence. That large Confederate force could easily swing to the south to support an attack on Gauley Bridge as the regiments under General Loring crossed the river at several points to assault the Federals at once. Lightburn was faced with such a large number of unknown variables that he realized that a miscalculation could have lead to a disaster and he ordered a general retreat.

The quartermasters had been preparing wagon trains for their supplies and ammunition for several days and moved the trains swiftly down river toward Charleston. There were several matters needing attention to prevent the large ammunition stores from falling into the hands of the Confederates and a final detail had to be completed , if the Rebel pursuit was to be stalled -- the new bridge across Gauley River which had been constructed so quickly had to be destroyed. The men were quick to make their preparations as the Confederate threat came closer.

There were men in the Confederate advance who recalled the artillery positions of General Floyd during the earlier campaign and they suggested this same tactic to General Loring who agreed that this was an excellent plan. They soon prepared to move several cannon to the summit of Cotton Hill to fire on the retreating Federals, but they were not interested in destroying the Union supplies or facilities -- they intended to capture them intact for their own use. The story was later told by Captain Joel H. Abbott, who because of advanced age or simply story-telling exaggeration related some questionable material:

"On the morning of the 11th, The Federals made a

determined stand on Cotton Hill, but Colonel Wharton and General Echols managed to flank them, while General Williams attacked them in front, driving them out. I realized at once they were escaping down the Miller's Ferry road, and that we might head some of them off at the mouth of Gauley, and so reported to General Loring. Through Major King, a twelve pound howitzer, a five-pound brass cannon, and detachment of men, was assigned, which I lead down a long ridge to the top of the cliffs overlooking Gauley Bridge. The artillery being placed, we made several clean hits and sections of the bridge could be seen in flames. We then opened on the magazine in the mouth of Zull's hollow, which soon blew up.

"Our attention was then called to the Confederate forces under Williams going down the lower river side, and we left one of the guns in a ravine, and soon joined the forces moving down the valley. At Montgomery or Riggs Ferry...we saw the ferry barge was on fire...The surgeon, Joseph Watkins, declared he could put out the fire, secure the barge and get us over the river. He was joined by some six or seven men, who swam over, holding on to their hats and caps, which they used to dip water out of the river. The barge was saved and as fast as we could cross we followed the Federals..."[26]

The situation for the Federals was getting to the point where they felt themselves in serious danger of being trapped in the fortifications at Gauley Bridge -- without a relieving force to get them out before they would have to surrender. Colonel Lightburn was fully aware that General Cox had been ordered to retain only 5000 troops in western Virginia when he was ordered to join the Army of the Potomac. It didn't require much addditional pressure from the attacking Confederates to cause Lightburn to order a general retreat.

Milton W. Humphries was an eyewitness:

"On the morning of the 11th it was discovered that the

26 Cook, "The Destruction of Gauley Bridge", pg. 25

Federals were gone. General Williams pursued instantly and reports having found the road 'strewn with guns, knapsacks, blankets, overcoats, wagons, hospital and sutler's stores, horses and men.' Whether these men, strewn on the road, were dead, wounded or asleep, he does not say. Wharton and Echols immediately followed Williams. At Cotton Hill Siber made a brief stand. Williams attacked in front, while Wharton and Echols moved to turn the right flank, whereupon Siber retreated to the Kanawha River and moved down the left side, burning magazines as he went.

"On the 10th at 3 p.m., when Lightburn heard of the battle going on in Fayetteville, he ordered Gilbert to bring his force, stationed on the Lewisburg pike, down to Gauley, which he promptly did, reporting in person to Lightburn near the falls at 8 p.m. On the 11th, when the Confederates pursuing Siber descended the mountain, some sharp fighting took place between them and Gilbert with the river between the opposing forces. Soon Gilbert, having burned such stores as had not been removed and having blown up a large magazine in the mouth of a hollow near the falls, retreated down the pike on the right side of the river. It has been pointed out that Loring's report is ambiguous as to whether Federals or Confederates blew up this magazine, but the ambiguity is only grammatical, and besides there is no conceiveable reason why the Confederates should have destroyed ammunition virtually in their grasp. As to the destruction of the bridge over Gauley River, about which there has been much discussion, it would be useless to add anything to what others have written except that it may be worth while to give assurance that the Sixtieth Virginia Regiment was certainly with Loring and there was a Sergeant in it named Andrew Summers. Those interested in the discussion will see why this statement is made."[27]

There has been considerable confusion regarding the destruction of the bridge at the town of Gauley Bridge during the Federal retreat in 1862. Joel Abbott claims to

27 Humphries, *Military Operations in Fayette County*, pg. 16-17

have seen the bridge in flames as the shells from his battery struck it, but there was no reason for the Confederates to destroy that which they were soon to capture intact. Loring had no conceivable reason to order the destruction of the bridge; Lightburn had many. The Federals could slow the Confederate pursuit and deny them the use of the bridge in supplying their own column and this was certainly enough to order it burned.

How the bridge was destroyed is still in question, but the local residents later reported that the Federal troops tried to burn it, but even oil poured on the green timbers failed to ignite the wood. The ends of the cables had to be hacked at with axes until the bridge deck fell into the current and was swept away.

This story has considerable merit. The bridge had been constructed in a very short time by a firm from Philadelphia and it was apparently a "pre-fabricated" design. The cables and metal pieces had to be hauled in by wagon, but it would have been quite uneconomical to haul the wood as well -- especially when the hills around the town were filled with timber. The wood in the ill-fated bridge was obviously still green when the Union soldiers tried to burn it.

The soldiers in the squad ordered to destroy the bridge were from the same regiment that had helped the Ohio troops escape from Fayetteville by serving as both advance and rear-guard, the most dangerous positions. This dangerous detail was left to some of the men of the 4th West Virginia as the Ohio regiments retreated down the turnpike toward Charleston.

A very interesting story was reported in *The Republican* of Middleport, Ohio, on July 15, 1915:

"Sergeant McDonald, detail twelve men, and go back and burn Gauley Bridge, after our wagon train from Fayetteville has passed over it.' This order was issued by Lieutenant Colonel Dayton, of the Federal forces, on September 11, 1862, to first duty Sergeant Donald McDonald, a member of Company A, 4th West Virginia Infantry. The Federals were then fleeing down the great Kanawha Valley, and at that moment were at Kanawha

Falls, closely pursued by the 60th Virginians, Confederates, in Command of General Loring.

"With a military salute, Sergeant McDonald wheeled on his heels, picked up his twelve men, and turned back on the double-quick for the bridge that spanned the mouth of the historic and picturesque Gauley Bridge.

"The Federal wagon train rumbled across and then McDonald and his twelve men applied the torch to the wooden structure. But he was too late to make his escape with his squad. In a moment the bridge was a roaring flame, but one company had crossed in boats and headed off the firing squad. McDonald and his men fled up the side of the steep mountain to the northward, and hid in the thick woods until the next morning when they attempted to find their way out.

"Shortly afterward, breaking cover, they ran into a squad of Confederates, headed by Sergeant Summers, of Company A, 60th Virginians, and were captured. From there McDonald and his comrades were taken to Dublin Depot, and from there to Libby Prison, where he remained three months. Being paroled, he was taken to Annapolis. There he broke guard, walked to Pittsburg by way of Baltimore, being three weeks on the way, long detours being necessary to dodge General Lee in Pennsylvania. Later he joined his command at Charleston, went through the campaign of the south, veteranized at Larkinsville, Alabama, and later headed toward Cedar Creek. The fight at Piedmont, twelve miles below Staunton, followed soon. There, by a trick of fate, Sergeant McDonald captured Sergeant Summers, who two years before had captured the bridge burner."[28]

Except for the part of the story which covered the bridge in flames, this story is probably accurate. The wood of the suspension bridge was probably green -- as reported by the residents of the town -- and would not have burned. It was probably chopped down, but this doesn't have the same impact in the press later in history as a bridge in

[28] Cook, "The Destruction of Gauley Bridge", pg. 7

flames. "Journalistic license" is probably responsible for this small inconsistency in the story.

Milton Humphries says that there was an Andrew Summers in the 60th Virginia and that that regiment was assigned to Loring's invading army. Humphries should know -- he was with the Confederate artillery battery that remained at Gauley Bridge as the rest of the Confederates pursued the Federals toward Charleston. The part of the story about the capture of Summers at Piedmont also has the ring of truth to it. The 60th Virginia was at the battle of Piedmont and its commander, Beuhring Jones, was captured while trying to rally the *rear-guard*, a common duty among the western Virginians. The 4th West Virginia was also at the battle of Piedmont where the Confederates suffered a disaster at the hands of the Federal troops.[29]

The Federals had been cleared from the town of Gauley Bridge at last and the victorious Confederates were busy chasing them out of the rest of the valley as well. There were several Confederate units which remained as a garrison for the town and this group included the men of Bryan's Battery, the unit that included Milton Humphries. He was put in charge of a small group of prisoners -- which could have included the men who destroyed the bridge -- and they were ordered to march the captives to Lewisburg. Humphries tells an unusual story:

"An order came for those of Bryan's men who were armed with muskets to guard the prisoners and the ordinance train to Lewisburg and there 'await the head of the column.' This order amazed everybody. On the 10th the ordinance train arrived and on the next day a lieutenant with most of the men took charge of it, while a corporal with a guard of about 12 men was placed in charge of the prisoners, the latter in front started for Lewisburg on the 11th.

---

[29] Fitzgerald, Gertrude B., "Colonel Beuhring Hampden Jones: Descendent of Christopher Jones" *The United Daughters of the Confederacy Magazine*, Vol. XX, No.1, January, 1957, pg. 28; Cook, "The Destruction of Gauley Bridge", *The West Virginia Review*, October, 1925, pg. 7

"On the march the prisoners got considerably ahead of the train, there being no order to keep them near each other. This led to a little episode which it seems admissible to narrate as it occurred at the best known spot in Fayette county. Early on the morning of the 12th when the prisoners and their escort approached a place where a path leads a short distance out to Hawks Nest, the prisoners begged earnestly to be conducted out to look down from the crest of that famous vertical solid rock cliff 650 feet high. The corporal in charge very reluctantly granted the request, and the prisoners were required to go in front of the whole guard. When the former reached the crest, the latter were formed into a curved line behind them. When the prisoners were huddled together on the brink and conversing in a low tone, it occurrred to the corporal, especially since the prisoners had been so insistent, that they, outnumbering the guard nearly or quite three to one, might have formed a plot to seize the guard and hurl them over. So to be ready for such an attempt, he very imprudently, in the usual sharp military tone gave the command:'*Fix bayonets!'* The effect on the prisoners was like an electric shock. Certainly some, possibly all of them for a moment expected instantly to be shoved over. Of course it quickly occurred to most of them that such an act on the part of the guard was out of the question, but action on the first impulse might have precipitated a horrible tragedy, and certainly all, guards and prisoners alike, breathed easier when they got away from that place. Especially was this true of the corporal,who is today the writer of this narrative."[30]

Loring continued down the Kanawha River on the heels of the retreating Federals. Colonel Siber arrived at the town of Brownstown with the 37th Ohio on the morning of September 12 and he crossed to the north side of the river to Camp Piatt where his troops joined the other Union elements under Colonel Lightburn. Other Union troops under Colonel Gilbert had marched down the north side of

30 Humphries, *Military Operations in Fayette County*, pg. 18-19

the Kanawha River and also arrived at Camp Piatt during the afternoon of the 12th. As a standard practice of both sides, the expendable rear-guard composed of western Virginians was left -- this time at Witcher's Creek -- to help screen Siber's river crossing while holding back the Confederate advance force.[31]

Early in the morning of the 13th, a Federal brigade moved through Charleston, crossed the Elk River, and took up defensive positions along the shore. Some of the rear-guard was pushed back from positions above the town and engaged in a small battle near the present location of the state capitol building. The Rebel western Virginians had finally returned home. The attackers were the men of the 22nd Virginia who were from the Kanawha valley. George Patton's Kanawha Riflemen had been organized here, their homes and families were still in the town. The exiles who had been so misused by their early commanders were home again, as victors for a change.

The Federals were far from finished, however, and they began to make a serious attempt to defend the west bank of the Elk River where it flowed into the Kanawha. It was an ideal defensive position and by holding here, the Federal wagon train evacuating large amounts of war supplies could escape toward the Ohio River. The men of another West Virginia infantry regiment, the 9th, moved into position along Elk River and began to throw up log breastworks for additional protection in the coming battle. The 34th Ohio moved into positions on the opposite side of the turnpike where it crossed the Elk on a suspension bridge and made threir preparations to receive an attack. The 4th West Virginia Infantry, fresh from the evacuation of Fayetteville, was also involved in this holding action at Charleston. Colonel Vance used his companies to protect the remaining Union troops until they could cross the suspension bridge to the relative safety of the new Federal defensive line. The Ohio regiment from the Gauley Bridge

31 Cook, Roy B., "Joseph Andrew Jackson Lightburn", *West Virginia History,* Vol. XV, No. 1, October, 1953, pg. 16. Brownstown is the current town of Marmet and Camp Piatt was located at the present site of Belle.

garrison, the 47th, and the 37th Ohio under Colonel Siber -- the officer who had defended Fayetteville -- crossed and took up their positions. The cables on the western approach of the suspension bridge were cut after the Federals had crossed and the bridge decking fell into the river and the men in the Union regiments waited for the approach of the Confederates as their valuable wagon train continued to wind along the valley toward safety.[32]

A young Charleston resident, Thomas E. Jeffries, witnessed the fighting in Charleston and much later wrote his story for a local newspaper:

"Time passed without any excitement until September, 1862, when it became known that there was heavy fighting near Fayetteville, and the Federal troops were getting the worst of it. The people had been warned to get out of town as it was to be set on fire and shelled by the retreating Federals. One of my brothers was only a week old so my father, one sister, and a younger brother stayed at home with my mother, and two of my sisters and I were to follow the crowds up to the cemetary for safety. The next morning I heard some firing and set off back toward town to investigate. The Kanawha hotel, the Bank of Virginia, the Southern Methodist church, the Mercer Academy and a large warehouse were burning.

"The first I saw of the Confederate army was a small-gun pulled by a large mule. While we were watching the small-gun, a squad of Confederate skirmishers appeared, coming up the hill. There were two or three of us boys wearing blue flannel shirts and caps, and were mistaken for Federal troopers. The soldiers fired on us but missed us, but we started up the hill in high and never stopped until we were behind some women.

"The Confederates fired on the retreating Federal army from the hill and a battery on the south side joined in. In the meantime the Federal forces had crossed the old suspension bridge across Lovell (now Washington) street and after setting fire to the floor, set to cutting the cables.

32 Cook, "Joseph Andrew Jackson Lightburn", pg. 17

The Federals returned fire from their cannons long enough to hold the Confederates in check so that their army might retreat safely.

"When I started homeward and ran into some Confederate soldiers resting. One of them offered me a half-dollar for my cap, but I refused to part with it, so he took the cap away from me. When I reached home I found that part of both armies had gone through our yard and had knocked down the fences on both sides of the house. Some dead soldiers were lying within a short distance from our house and were later buried where they had fallen."[33]

The Unionist residents of Charleston were terrified of retribution from the Confederates as the town was occupied. Some of this fear was fed by rumors that the town was to be burned by one side or the other and shelled by the departing Federals. The residents evacuated to the vicinity of the cemetary on Cox's Hill, but were in serious danger as the Confederates occupied a higher level on the hill and fired on the retreating Union soldiers from there.

Others decided to take advantage of the river and left town in boats, rafts, and nearly anything else that would float. A young girl, Victoria Hansford recorded the civilian evacuation:

"...I was quite sure it was cannonading afar off. Oh, they were coming! They were coming. And I set to work to put my house in order. About ten o'clock, Aunt Lucy, an old colored woman, came up from the mouth of Coal and said, 'Mrs. Thenie says if you want to see a sight, to come to the Kanawha, that everything from Charleston was on the retreat.'

"I was there in a few minutes, father and the negroes coming on behind. Such a sight about me I never saw nor ever expect to see again. The river as far as the eye could reach up and down was covered with boats of all kinds, large flat boats, jerry boats, jolly boats, skiffs and canoes.

---

[33] Jeffries, Thomas E., "City Occupied by Both Sides", *Charleston Daily Mail*, June 4, 1939, pg..4F

In these were all kinds of people and all kinds of things.

"My aunt, Mrs. Wilson, who lived at the mouth of Coal, and on the Kanawha, said it had been going on this way since a little after daylight. When I say the river was covered with boats I mean just what I say, and a person could almost have crossed the river by jumping from one boat to the other. They had been looking for the retreat and had boats prepared. Not the soldiers I mean, but citizens who wished to retreat with the Union army. Or those who had acted so shabbily towards the southern people whose friends and relatives were off with the Rebs they were afraid to stay when the country fell into the Rebel's hands.

"Several families were on gunwales lashed together, and I will never forget a woman and man were on two short pieces of gunwales lashed together. A tub sat at one end of it containing their property. The woman sat in a rocking chair at the other end, while the man stood in the middle and paddled them on as best as he could. The woman was wet to her waist from the water washing over the planks, the man seemed to be wet all over from the pushing and pulling. I felt so sorry for them and said, 'Poor fools, the Rebels won't hurt you.' But on they went."[34]

The fighting began in earnest as the Confederates began to shell the Federal positions across the Elk River. Artillery on both sides kept up a fierce bombardment while the infantry on both sides fired continually. The engagement continued until darkness fell and Lightburn continued his retreat from the valley. Colonel Lightburn had managed a significant retreat while in what was essentially one continual skirmish with the rapidly advancing Confederates. He had moved his troops safely over one hundred miles and saved approximately one million dollars in supplies from destruction or capture by Loring's regiments.

Lightburn wrote his report of the short campaign when he arrived at Point Pleasant on the Ohio River. Lightburn

[34] Turner, Mary E., "Charleston's Dunkirk", *The West Virginia Review*, December 1941 -- February 1942, pg. 106

was a western Virginian and he submited the report to the Union governor in Wheeling, Francis H. Pierpont:

"I have the honor to submit the following report of what has transpired since I assumed command of the District of the Kanawha, pursuant to Genl. J.D. Cox's order of August 17, 1862, I assumed command of that district -- The troops composing that command were the 34th, 37th, & 47 O.V.I., the 4th & 9th Va.V.I., and 2nd Va. Cav., together with (8) Eight Mountain Howitzers, 3 rifles & three smooth bore field pieces of artillery manned by a detail from infantry regiments. These forces were stationed as follows -- the 34th &37th Regts. O.V.I., with four Mountain Howitzers and two smooth bore field pieces under command of command of E. Siber of the 37th O.V.I. at Raleigh C.H. with two companies of infantry, as a guard for trains at Fayette C.H. The 44th and 47th O.V.I. with 2 companies, 2nd Va. Cav. at Camp Ewing a distance of ten miles from Gauley on the Lewisburg road under command of Col. S.A. Gilbert, 4th O.V.I. Two companies 9th Va. Infantry, and two companies, 2nd Va. Cav., under command of Major Curtis was stationed at Summersville. The remainder of the 9th and 4th Va. Infantry, and 2nd Va. Cav. were stationed at different points from Gauley Bridge to Charleston, including an outpost at Coal River in Boone county, with my Head Quarters at Gauley. Soon after assuming command I became satisfied that the enemy was massing troops at the narrows of New River, Union and other points for a demonstration upon the Kan. Valley, finding it impossible to obtain reinforcements and my flanks and rear being unprotected, I ordered Col. Siber at Raleigh to fall back to Fayette C.H., and Col. Gilbert also to fall back to Gauley Mountain or Tompkins' farm. A day or two before I gave the order to Col. Gilbert I learned that Jenkins with a heavy force of cavalry had left Union, Monroe County, and fearing he would attack Summersville, I ordered Col. Gilbert to send six Co's. of the 47th O.V.I., under command of Col. Elliot to reinforce that point.

"Finding these positions untenable against the reported

force of the enemy, and Jenkins already in my rear, I ordered Col. Paxton with six co's. 2nd Va. Cav., to look after him and if possible keep open communications with the Ohio River by way of the Kanawha River. I at the same time ordered the Q.M. and Commissary stores, of which there was a large quantity, to be shipped to Charleston, directing that the most valuable be shipped first which had to be transported by land to Camp Piatt and Charleston but before much could be done in moving the stores, except the clothing, which was mostly got away. My outpost at Fayette C.H., under command of Col. Siber, was attacked by an overwhelming force of the enemy. Learning that his communication with me was cut off, I immediately ordered three Companies of the 4th Regt, Va. V.I. to reinforce him with orders to fall back to Gauley if he thought he could not hold his position. I also ordered Lieut. Col Parry with five companies of the 47th O.V.I. to Cotton Hill to meet the retreating force of Col. Siber who fell back, skirmishing the entire road from Cotton Hill to the Kanawha River. I also, upon learning that Fayette was attacked, ordered Gilbert with his command to Gauley, also Col. Elliot's command from Summersville, which command did not reach until the enemy got possession of the opposite side of the river, and consequently was compelled to destroy their waggons and cross the mountains, joining the command near Cannelton. Col. Gilbert's command with his artillery was stationed in a position commanding the road, leading from Fayette, and did good execution in covering the retreat of Col. Siber's column. I also ordered all the waggons at Gauley to be loaded with the most valuable commissary stores and to push forward without stopping until they crossed the Elk River below Charleston. This order however was not obeyed from some cause, the waggons and teams being found in and above Charleston. which no doubt caused the confusion among the Quarter Masters referred to in Col. Gilbert's report. After Col. Siber's command had passed and the enemy somewhat dispersed, Col. Gilbert retired skirmishing, which was kept up almost the entire road until we reached Charleston, September 12, where I thought to make a stand. I accordingly ordered the waggons, that had been stopped in town, across the Elk River which had hardly been done when the enemy made an attack on the 47th O.V.I. which had been ordered by Col. Gilbert to take a position above town, feel the enemy, and bring on the engagement, which was done in a spirited manner, as seen by Col. Gilbert's report. At three o'clock P.M., the 47th O.V.I. not being able to hold the enemy in check fell back below Elk River, and the engagement became general, both with artillery and infantry and lasted until dark.

"Finding the enemy at least two to our one in front, with Jenkin's force, twelve to fifteen hundred strong, on our right flank and rear, and owing to our immense train of waggons -- over seven hundred in number -- I ordered the command to fall back under the cover of night and took up the line of retreat on the Riply road from this point where we arrived on the 16th Inst., bringing off all of our train except some few waggons and one or two ambulances that broke down. All our artillery, including five extra pieces that were not manned.

"I am sorry to have to report the destruction by fire of a large amount of stores which was done to prevent their falling into the hands of the enemy. During the march from Gauley and during the engagement at Charleston the officers and men behaved nobly, everyone seeming to perform his duty as though upon him alone depended success.

"I do not wish to speak disparingly of any officer, all did their duty, but in addition to what is said in the respective reports, I wish to say that Colonels Siber, Gilbert and Tolland deserve particular mention for their excellent council, gallantry and promptness in the discharge of their respective duties. They are officers who have heretofore won the confidence of their officers and men and in our late engagement their conduct has merited the confidence and esteem of all Union loving citizens.

"The 2nd Va. Cav., under Col. Paxton, did good service in keeping Jenkins' force at bay preventing an attack in our rear.

"Col. Paxton with three hundred men attacked Jenkins' whole force of from twelve to fifteen hundred , driving him from Barboursville which no doubt kept him from harassing our retreat.

"Our loss is twenty-five killed, ninety-five wounded, and one hundred and ninety missing. It is supposed that a number of the missing will come in as some have already reported. The loss of the enemy is not known but from the best information we can get their loss is heavy.

"My command is at this point and will be ready for a move again in a few days."[35]

The Confederates had finally succeeded in forcing the Union regiments out of the entire Kanawha valley. The Federals had chased Wise out of the area the previous summer and even with the reinforcements of Floyd and Loring under the command of Lee, they had been unable to manage this in the earlier fall and winter campaign from Sewell Mountain. The capture of Pope's letter-book had shown the Confederates that the Federals had lowered their strength to a level that an attack would be successful.

The brilliant campaign had involved a march through mountains over very long distances and casualties had been light. The Confederates had reported 18 killed and 89 wounded. They had forced the Federal commander to abandon his supply bases and much of their contents which Loring estimated to be worth about $1,000,000 and the South now had possession of the vital salt works located in the valley.

Now that the valley was held firmly by the Confederacy, General Loring lost no time in issuing a proclamation to the population:

"The army of the Confederate States has come among you to expell the enemy, to rescue the people from the despotism of the counterfeit State government imposed on you by Northern bayonets, and to restore the country once more to its natural allegiance to the State. We fight for

[35] Cook, "Joseph Andrew Jackson Lightburn", pg. 20-22

peace and for the possession of our own territory. We do not intend to punish those who remain at home as quiet citizens in obedience to the laws of the land, and to all such, clemency and amnesty are declared; but those who persist in adhering to the cause of the public enemy and the pretended State government he has erected at Wheeling, will be dealt with as their obstinate treachery deserves."[36]

The Rebels occupied Charleston for a short time and while Lee had plans to operate out of the Kanawha valley against the Baltimore and Ohio Railroad, Loring misunderstood or ignored his orders and lost the valley a second time. He had received orders directing him to move toward Winchester, but to leave a detachment in the valley to assist General Floyd and his new "State Line" troops in holding the Kanawha valley. He marched his regiments rapidly from western Virginia, was relieved, and General John Echols was placed in command and ordered to re-occupy Charleston. Echols had little chance of moving back into the Kanawha valley. The Federals were returning in strength and were under the command of a general who was familar with mountain operations -- Jacob Cox. The senior commanders of the Federal Army had realized that the situation in western Virginia required the presence of an officer who was familar with the problems of operating in the difficult terrain. They ordered General Cox to Washington, promoted him, gave him control of his original regiments, and sent all of them back to the Kanawha valley to counter the recent Confederate successes.

Cox wrote:

"...bits of news began to arrive, with rumors that Loring was retreating. The truth was that he in fact withdrew his infantry, leaving Jenkins with the cavalry and irregular forces to hold the valley for a time, and then to make a circuit northward by way of Bulltown, Sutton, etc., gaining the Beverly turnpike near the mountains and

36 White, "West Virginia", pg. 67-68

rejoining the infantry, which would march to join Lee by roads intersecting that highway at Monterey. Such at least was the purpose Loring communicated to the Confederate War Department; but he was not allowed to attempt it. His instructions had been to march his whole command by the route Jenkins was taking and at least hold the valley stubbornly as far as Charleston. On receipt of the news that he was retreating, orders were sent to him to turn over the command to Brigadier-General John Echols, the next in rank, and to report in person at Richmond. Echols was ordered immediately to resume the positions which had been abandoned, and did so as rapidly as possible. Loring had in fact begun his retreat on the 11th, three days before I reached Galliopolis, but the first information of it was got after the scouting had been begun which is mentioned above. By the 18th I was able to give General Wright confirmation of the news and a correct outline of Loring's plan, though we had not learned that Echols was marching back to Charleston. We heard of his return two or three days later. As evidence of the rapidity with which information reached the enemy, it is noteworthy that Lee knew my command had left the Army of the Potomac for West Virginia on the 11th October, three days after Crook marched from camp in Pleasant Valley. He reported to Richmond that four brigades had gone to that region, which was accurate as to the number, though only half right as to identification to the brigades. On the 13th he sent further information that I had been promoted and assigned to command the district."[37]

Lee was generally well-informed as to the intentions and movements of the Union army. He is reported to have disliked the use of spies and agents, but was usually telling the Confederate War Department about the latest plans of the Federals.

Cox carefully moved his men back into the Kanawha valley and began to clear roads which had been obstructed. This was all familar territory -- Cox and his men had

37 Cox, *Military Reminiscences*, pg. 408-409

cleared the area of Wise's Confederates the previous year. Cox continued to explain his plans:

"My purpose was to concentrate the force at Pocataligo, assume command in person, and attack the enemy in the positions in front of Charleston, in which Wise had resisted me in the previous year. I should have been glad to make the expected movement of a column from Clarksburg under Crook and Milroy co-operate directly with my own, but circumstances made it impracticable. The operations of the Confederate cavalry under Jenkins were keeping the country north of the Kanawha in a turmoil, and reports had become rife that he would work his way out toward Beverly. The country was also full of rumors of a new invasion from East Virginia. Milroy's forces were not yet fully assembled at Clarksburg on the 20th, but he was ordered to operate toward Beverly, whilst Crook, with the old Kanawha division, should move on to Summersville and Gauley Bridge. Both had to depend on hiring wagons for transportation of supplies. Separated as they were, they would necessarily be cautious in their movements, making the suppression of guerillas, the driving out of raiders, and the general quieting of the country their principal task. Their role was thus, of course, made subordinate to the movement of my own column, which must force its way without waiting for the results of other operations... Reconnoissances showed nothing but cavalry in our immediate front, and it afterwards appeared that Echols began a rapid retreat from Charleston on that day. He had called to him Jenkins with the greater part of the cavalry, and entrusted the latter the duty of holding us back as much as possible. Suspecting this from evidence collected at Pocataligo, I determined to put Siber's brigade and a battery, all in light marching order, on the south side of the river, accompanied by a light-draught steamboat, which the rise in the river after the storm enabled us to use as far as Charleston. This brigade could turn the strong position at Tyler Mountain, and passing beyond this promotory on the opposite side of the river, could command with artillery fire the river road on the other bank behind the enemy in our front. The steamboat would enable them to make a rapid retreat if the belief that no great force was on that side should prove to be a mistake. Siber was also furnished with a battery of four mountain howitzers, which could be carried to the edge of the water or anywhere that men could march...All moved forward simultaneously on the morning of the 29th. The dispositions thus made rendered it vain for the enemy's cavalry to offer any stubborn resistance, and Jenkins abandoned Tyler Mountain on our approach, thus giving us certain knowledge that he was not closely supported by the infantry. Our advance-guard reached the Elk River opposite Charleston in the afternoon, and I made personal reconnoissance of the means of crossing. The suspension bridge had been destroyed in Lightburn's retreat, and the enemy had depended upon a bridge of boats for communication with their troops in the lower valley. These boats had been taken to the further bank of the river and partly destroyed, but as the enemy had continued his retreat, we soon had a party over collecting those that could be used, and other flatboats used in the coal trade, and a practicable bridge was reconstructed before night of the 30th. Meanwhile I entered the town with the advance-guard as soon as we had a boat to use for a ferry, and spent the night of the 29th there. We had friends enough in the place to put us quickly in possession of all the news, and I was soon satisfied that Echols had no thought of trying to remain on the western side of the mountains."[38]

Cox was correct in this assumption. Echols was far from his bases and supply depots while the Federals could at least use river transportation to move supplies as far as Charleston. Neither side had missed the lessons of the previous year when active operations were gradually forced to grind to a halt because of the difficulty of supplying the men in the field. Cox ordered some of his regiments

---

38 Cox, *Military Reminiscences*, pg. 411-413

forward to Gauley Bridge, but was not planning to recommend that the Federals begin offensive operations into the mountains beyond:

"I did not conceal the opinion which all my experience had confirmed, that no military advantage could be secured by trying to extend operation by this route across the mountains into the James River valley...On the 8th of November Halleck telegraphed to General Wright that no posts need be established beyond Gauley Bridge, and that about half of my command should be sent to Tennessee and the Mississippi valley...It was thus definitively settled that my task for the winter would be to restore the condition of affairs in West Virginia which had existed before Loring's invasion, and organize my district with a view to prompt and easy supply of my posts, the suppression of lawlessness and bushwhacking, the support of the State authorities, and the instruction and discipline of officers and men."[39]

The Confederate invasion of the Kanawha valley was at an end and the region remained under Union control for the remainder of the war. Loring had made a mistake by ignoring his orders, but the end result would have been the same regardless of his actions. Most of western Virginia was lying adjacent to Union territory and far from any possibility of Confederate reinforcement. Supplies were easily transported on Union steamboats up the wide rivers, but Confederate resupply was far more difficult. There were mountains to cross and the roads were normally in poor condition at any time of year, but were normally impassable during the winter. It was an area where the Union forces could be rapidly reinforced -- even a trip from the headquarters of the Army of the Potomac could be made quickly over the Baltimore and Ohio Railroad. The small Confederate army had no chance of achieving any long-term successes in the Kanawha valley.

The Confederate invasion did have one long-term effect -- it hardened the ill feelings each side had for the other for

39 Cox, *Military Reminiscences*, pg. 414-416

a very long time into the future. Cox discussed the developing bitterness:

"The invasion of the Kanawha valley by Loring had stirred up much bitter feeling again between Union men and Confederates, and was followed by the usual quarrels and recriminations among neighbors. The Secessionists were stimulated to drop the prudent reserve they had practised before, and some of them, in the hope that the Confederate occupation would be permanent, persecuted loyal men who were in their power. The retreat of the enemy brought its day of reckoning, and was accompanied by a fresh migration to eastern Virginia of a considerable number of the more pronounced Secessionists. I have said that Mr. George Summers, formerly the leading man of the valley, had studiously avoided political activity after the war began; but this did not save him from the hostility of his disloyal neighbors. Very shortly after my re-occupation of Charleston he called upon me one evening and asked for a private interview. He had gone through a painful experience, he said, and as it would pretty surely come to my ears, he preferred I should hear it from himself, before enemies or tale-bearers should present it with such coloring as they might choose. During the Confederate occupation he had maintained his secluded life and kept aloof from contact with the military authorities. Their officers, however, summoned him before them, charged him with treason to Virginia and to the Confederate States, and demanded of him that he take the oath of allegiance to the Southern government. He demurred to this, and urged that as he had scrupulously avoided public activity, it would be harsh and unjust to force him to take a test which he could not conscientiously take. They were in no mood to listen to argument, and charged that his acquiescence in the rule of the new state government of West Virginia was, in his case, more injurious to the Confederate cause than many another man's Unionism. Finding Mr. Summers disposed to be firm, they held him in arrest; and as he still refused to yield, he was told that he should be tied by a rope to the tail of a wagon and forced to march in that condition, as a prisoner, over the mountains to Richmond.

"He was an elderly man, used to a refined and easy life, somewhat portly in person, and, as he said, he fully believed such treatment would kill him. The fierceness of their manner convinced him that they meant to execute the threat, and looking upon it as a sentence of death, he yielded and took the oath. He said that being in duress of such sort, and himself a lawyer, he considered that he had a moral right to escape from his captors in this way, though he would not have yielded to anything short of what seemed to him an imminent danger of his life. The obligation, he declared, was utterly odious to him and was not binding upon his conscience; but he had lost no time in putting himself into my hands, and would submit to whatever I should decide in the matter. It would be humiliating and subject him to misconstruction by others if he took conflicting oaths, but he was willing to abjure the obligation he had taken, if I demanded it, and would voluntarily renew his allegiance to the United States with full purpose to keep it.

"He was deeply agitated, and I thoroughly pitied him. My acquaintance with him in my former campaign gave me entire confidence in his sincerity, and made me wish to spare him any fresh embarassment or pain. After a moment's reflection, I replied that I did not doubt anything he had told me of the facts or of his own sentiments in regard to them. His experience only confirmed my distrust of test oaths. Either his conscience already bound him to the National government, or it did not. In either case I could not make his loyalty more sure by a fresh oath, and believing that the one he had taken under duress was void in fact as well as in his own conscience, I would leave the matter there and ask nothing more of him. He was greatly relieved by my decision, but bore himself with dignity. I never saw any reason to be sorry for the course I took, and believe he was always afterward consistent and steady in his loyalty to the United States."[40]

[40] Cox, *Military reminiscences*, pg. 417-419

The Confederates weren't the only people dealing harshly with the non-combattants of the other side. The Union army normally burned homes of Southern sympathizers after forcing the families out. Men were left destitute during winter months and deaths from exposure and disease were common. They forced more people to take the "oath" than the Rebels and the practice so common and useless that when Union soldiers captured a snake, the normal comments made were something like "Swear'em and let him go!" Guerilla band members captured were administered the "oath" and released only to be captured in fighting again in the future. The ordinary soldiers quickly tired of this and the ratio of killed-to-captured guerillas shifted dramatically as the attitude toward the prosecution of the war began to produce harsh acts on both sides.

The Union occupiers dealt harshly with Confederate sympathizers -- especially those who were outspoken. A good example was the episode of Jake Pinson, a resident of one of the remote valleys located to the northwest of Gauley Bridge. The story is best told in the original words of Forrest Hull:

"It is difficult after a lapse of so many years, to make a clear estimate of the character of Jake Pinson. He was bearded, rough, quick-tempered, and regarded by his neighbors as being a bad man to cross. Legend says that his dark, moody spells made him a terror to his family. He was a strong pro-Confederate sympathizer, outspoken, courageous to a point of rashness, and the added fact that he possessed a rough wit, gives a fairly clear picture of the man.

"The war between the states broke in the spring of 1861. Its real causes were vague to the hill people. They paid little attention to politics until a strange invading army of Ohio soldiers came marching up the Kanawha valley and began to fortify the village of Gauley Bridge. Soon scouts, detachments, and foraging parties in blue uniforms were patrolling the creeks and hollows. These Federal soldiers, according to published diaries of their officers, regarded the mountain people with contempt. On the other hand, the natives began to compare the soldiers with the indians their fathers had fought -- a set of 'thieving furriners.'

"...all of these strange goings-on worried Mrs. Pinson. She came from a family that 'leaned' toward the Yankees. One of her sons had already left home and joined the Union army, and Pinson had sworn to kill him on sight. A daughter, Morning Pinson, had married one of the Yankees. Her father and brothers on Blue Creek were Union men.

"On a Saturday, in the fall of the year 1861, Pinson took his customary trip to Cannelton, across the mountains in Kanawha valley. He was in a genial mood. He accosted Mr. Macananny, the merchant, with the request for some '*Yankee bait.*' Yankee bait, of course, meant powder and caps...But there was one man who did not laugh, and when Pinson had made his purchases and had departed, this man set out for Gauley Bridge to report his disloyal remark to the Federal authorities... Anyhow, the commanding officer, who already had a report on the movements of these mountain men, ordered a large detail (some say that it was 40 soldiers) to go at once to the Pinson farm and arrest the ring-leader, Jake Pinson...It set out on Sunday morning, going up Bell Creek and crossing the ridge to the Pinson farm.

"...He was getting his noon dinner, eyed by his frightened family, when a Grandma Wills, a neighbor, arrived and stood in the doorway talking to Mrs. Pinson. Suddenly Mrs. Wills cried out: 'Oh, Mr. Pinson, look at the Yankees coming down the ridge!' Pinson leaped to his feet, took one look at the advancing troops, and grabbed his two muskets. In a second the horrible tragedy was under way.

"From the window Pinson took dead aim at the officer leading the Federal force. At the crack of his gun the officer fell dead with a bullet in his brain. The startled soldiers stopped in surprise, then deployed and took cover behind barn, pig-pen, and trees, and opened a heavy fire upon the house. In the house at the time were, besides Pinson and his wife, Grandma Wills and five Pinson children. Pinson was firing through the open doorway and window. Smoke filled the cabin. The soldiers crept closer, firing hundreds of bullets into the log walls. The door was shot to pieces and the window glass crashed to bits. A minie ball came through the wall, pierced a stone above the fireplace, and off the skull of young Phil Pinson. As the boy fell, covered with blood, another ball killed his sister, little Blythe Pinson. Mrs. Pinson took the younger children into the upper story and began to cry out, 'I am a Union woman! I am a Yankee!' But the battle went on. Pinson continued firing, cooly and carefully, just as his ancestors had in an indian raid years before. An hour went by. The firing went on.

"At last the soldiers paid attention to the cries of the women and children. They began to parley. Mrs. Wills called out, 'Mr. Pinson, they say they will not hurt you if you give up.'

"They are damn liars,' said Pinson. But he finally agreed to talk with the soldiers. He opened the door and stepped outside. A bullet struck him. He reeled. Another entered his breast. Inside the doorway he sank down, his beard sank on his breast. His gun fell from his grasp. In his own cabin, his humble castle, he died. The soldiers ran up and pinned his body to the log wall with their bayonets. His blood crept along the hewn floor boards, mingling with that of his two children...The Federal soldiers searched the house...without giving aid to the stricken family, they departed, taking the dead body of their officer with them on a horse from the Pinson barn."[41]

There was cruelty enough on both sides to fairly divide the blame for atrocities. The major problem, however, with the increasing cruelty of the war was the hatred that it would generate which would carry far into the future. The strength of arms was with the Federals and their Unionist allies, the Home Guards, and with each house burning or arbitrary arrest for comments such as Jake Pinson made at the country store, there was an increasing anger among the

[41] Hull, Forrest, "Hillbilly Saga", *The West Virginia Review,* Vol. 17, No. 9, June, 1938, pg. 239-241

Southern sympathizers. Since they were weaker militarily, they had to choose safer methods of retaliation and many helped in the murder of their most prominent and out-spoken Unionist neighbors and solitary Federal sentries. They frequently joined Confederate guerrilla companies and participated on raids against small Union outposts and acted as auxillaries to the regular Confederate cavalry when it was operating in their home regions. Unfortunately, one outrage by one side against the other produced another outrage in retaliation for the first. It was a cycle of violence which was difficult to stop and in many areas it continued in the form of "bushwhacking" far after the end of the war.

The celebrated Hatfield and McCoy feud had its origins in the hatred of the Civil War. "Devil Anse" Hatfield had been a Confederate and the McCoys were an outspoken Unionist family living across the river in Kentucky from the Hatfield territory. Undoubtedly, there were additional factors which produced the hatred that lasted for so long, but much of it began when the blue uniforms of the "thieving furriners" first appeared in the hollows claimed by these proud mountain people and some of it remains to the present day.

The primary subjects of this study had all departed from the Kanawha valley. Christopher Tompkins was in Richmond with his wife, Ellen, and Isaac Smith was finally a civilian again. General Cox was soon to leave the region with his best regiments to fight until the end of the war.

The activities of Cox for the rest of the war are probably the easiest to follow as these are a matter of public record. The others are more difficult to ascertain and there may be more than simply time associated with their attempts to remain relatively anonymous. There is circumstantial evidence that they were involved in activities which would not have endeared them to the reconstruction authorities, if their actions became a matter of public record -- as had Cox's.

Cox left his duties in western Virginia just prior to the entry of the new state of West Virginia into the Union. He was ordered to report to Colombus in late March, 1863, and he was assigned to field command in the Union's Middle Department where he was the commander of the Ohio military district. He commanded a division in the Twenty-third Corps during the Atlanta campaign and afterwards commanded the entire corps. He served in the battle of Nashville and was sent into North Carolina in early 1865 to meet up with General Sherman.[42] He served through the entire Civil War and had served the country with an honest effort. He had done much in an attempt to reduce the horror of the war and had continually behaved as a gentleman at a time when lesser men looked more toward retribution. All of this was not without pain, however, as he had some levels of personal tragedy affect him as the war went on. He told of one event which took its' toll on him:

"The period of my separate responsibility and of struggle against great odds was not to close without a private grief which was the more poignant because the condition of the campaign forbade my leaving the post of duty. On the day I visited General Rosecrans at Carnifex Ferry I got news of the critical illness of my youngest child, a babe of eight months old, whom I had seen but a single day after his birth, for I had been ordered into camp from the legislature without time to make another visit to my family. The warning dispatch was quickly followed by another announcing the end, and I had to swallow my sorrows as well as I could and face the public enemy before us, leaving my wife uncomforted in her bereavement and all the more burdened with care because she knew we were resuming active operations in the field."[43]

Cox was an unusual man who has not had the recognition that he deserved from historians.

The other three are more difficult to trace, but there was a close association among them for the remainder of the

42 Bailes, "Cox in West Virginia", pg. 6-7

43 Cox, *Military Reminiscences*, pg. 103-104

war. Christopher Tompkins returned to his pre-war trade, the iron and steel manufacturing business at the South's primary armaments factory, the Tredegar Works, with his former West Point classmate, Joseph R. Anderson. He apparently managed the mines that supplied coal to the iron foundry located near Richmond. He and the family resided in their residence in the city and he maintained a home near the coal pits.

Ellen Tompkins owned property in Baltimore and later was to travel there to manage the property or arrange for sales. She travelled there at least one time during the war and played a role in transmiting information from Isaac Smith to her husband, probably through the Confederate message delivery system that relied heavily on the services of the Federal mail system. She had managed to obtain a pass through the lines from both the Confederate and Union authorities before she left for Baltimore.

Christopher Tompkins and his wife, Ellen, were doing well as civilians far from the front, but Isaac Smith was a man with a problem. He had resigned from the Confederate army, but still had to remain in areas under Rebel control. His wife had remained in Charleston and if he were to attempt to visit her, he faced arrest by the Union authorities on potential charges that ranged from sedition to open treason. He could have been as unfortunate as his acquaintance, Major Parks, had been. Parks had been imprisoned even though General Cox had provided a safe conduct pass. Smith had a good idea of his prospects if he were to stray into any area under the control of the Federal forces.

He also faced potential problems by remaining under Confederate control. He was a young, able-bodied civilian and was now subject to conscription by Confederate authorities. He had recently been a major, but a quick encounter with the Provost Marshall would make him a private in a Rebel infantry regiment. After his experiences with Rebel commanders as a field officer, he was extremely reluctant to re-enter the military as an enlisted man.

As was previously mentioned, Smith had some problems

with General Floyd over the subject of resignation and the young Major was fortunate to get away when he did. He was writing a letter to Tompkins on November 17, 1861 -- explaining that he had to cut the letter short as he was explaining McCausland's poor choice of a camp (which was shelled by Union guns from the opposite side of New River). He completed the letter from Lewisburg on November 24:

"...was interrupted when writing the above by Col Jackson's return from Headquarters, he handed me a paper which I supposed was some order about building huts etc., & to my great joy and surprise, found it to be the acceptance of my resignation. I believe the paper had been retained some days in Floyd's hands. It was dated November 6th, & I received it Nov 17th. I commenced my preparations at once, & left next day at about 9 o'clock A.M. -- Thence by Union,Monroe county to this place."[44]

Smith wrote to Tompkins again on November 29 from Arbuckle's, the farm near Lewisburg where Smith had found lodgings. He was concerned about the small sums of money owed one another within the group of officers in the regiment -- even the one dollar he felt he owed Tompkins "for sardines". Aside from the accounting, Smith explained that he had made a decision:

"...The unfortunate position in which I am placed here leaves me as I think, no alternative but a return home if such a step is practicable -- I cannot participate in any possible way with the government that seeks my father's life, & out of the army and its dependencies, see no prospect of earning a livelihood. I am exposed at every moment here, to overhear remarks of a most unpleasant character, & am forced to shun society where every member is not my personal acquaintance and friend. I am not regarded as overmuch [illigible] myself -- The idea of

[44] Smith wrote this letter to Tompkins on 17 November, 1861. A copy of the letter is in the Virginia Historical Society collection.

John Clarkson hunting my poor father & mother from their homes (for they have gone I know not where) is beyond endurance. My desire is to unite all the family, & seek some place where we may as far as possible from these civil commotions, live in peace, until the status of the country is settled. It is folly to bring my wife here, we should starve, and more that if I cannot side with my father I will never be his enemy. What is necessary to accomplish my purpose honorably, I scarcely know; it has been a subject of conversation between Mr. Matthews and myself, & I write letters by this mail. If you thought proper to give it, your advice & assistance to my friends would be of great service to me & would make me very greatful. There is difficulty in ascertaining how I should be treated by the enemy upon my return -- With Genl Rosecrans I should not fear, feeling assured, he would permit me to return if no [illigible] could be made for my stay -- I have no confidence in any of the other officers. I would prefer to stay on this side of the line, but my father's position renders that impossible so far as my views are concerned; my wish is to occupy as far as practicable, a position of neutrality, & bring him to the same platform.

"What I have written upon this subject, it is best should be confidential, except to those friends who have or may hereafter undertake to aid me -- In truth I have not yet abandoned the expectation expressed to you just before Floyd arrested me, of finding lodgings in a prison.

"...I know that I am taxing you unreasonably in pressing my difficulties upon you; but the suspense, anxiety & painful character of my present situation emboldens me...

"...P.S. This day is the first anniversary of my marriage -- What unhappy changes this short period has wrought in my life"[45]

Smith had made the crucial decision to risk a visit to his

[45] Smith to Tompkins dated 29 November 1861. This letter was completed the same day as Smith's last diary entry prior to its being sent back into the Kanawha valley where it was captured by General Cox's forces. A copy of the letter is in the Virginia Historical Society.

family in Union-controlled territory. He had written Tompkins that he had no fear of General Rosecrans and soon decided to visit the General to test his theory. He apparently wrote to the general for permission and received a reply in the form of a pass.

The Office of the Provost Marshall, Headquarters, Department of Western Virginia, issued the following pass in Wheeling, Virginia, in February, 1862:

"Commanders of Posts, Lines, and Stations

Will pass safely into our lines Isaac N. Smith, late a major in the Confederate army, who will report in person immediately to these Headquarters to Brigadier W.S. Rosecrans, Comdr Dept. West. Va."[46]

There is no evidence that Isaac Smith kept the scheduled appointment with General Rosecrans in Wheeling. He may have had an interview with the general and after recalling the experience of Major Parks -- held hostage to guarantee the safety of a Union prisoner under a death sentence in Richmond -- he may well have decided not to take the risk. General Rosecrans wasn't the ultimate authority as there were several military commanders of greater rank in the region and Smith was aware that he was also answerable to the civil authorities. His prospects of being imprisoned were great if he returned to Federally-controlled territory. As strong as his desire was to visit his wife and family, he was more afraid of the Union authorities.

He wrote again from Arbuckle's farm in Greenbrier county on March 19, 1862. He had either returned there from Wheeling or had declined to make the journey. Smith wrote about one of his least favorite subjects, General John B. Floyd, and the general's latest retreat to escape from the threat of Federal justice. Smith was fully aware of Tompkins' feelings on the subject of the evacuation of Fort Donelson:

---

46 A copy of this pass is in the National Archives with a few other records regarding the brief military career of Isaac N. Smith. These are in Record Group 109.

"I know how heartily you concur in the action of the President relative to Floyd & Pillow -- Floyd's report, garbled as it is, makes but a poor apology for his most remarkable course -- How plainly the miserable spirit of the politician appears when contrasted with the chivalry of the soldier, who remained to perform the most painful duty the soldier is ever called to perform, & to shoulder the heavy responsibility, thrust upon him contrary to all rule or decency, by the man who dared not undertake it; How much more pitiful still, the course of Pillow? When he undertakes by forestalling public opinion, in the unauthorized publication of his report, to tarnish the reputation of the officer in captivity, whom he had ordered into captivity that he and Pillow might escape. I regard this passing of command from officer to officer, as nothing less than an order (which it probably was in terms) to an inferior officer. It passed through two politicians, the soldier received it & obeyed; he would have scorned to follow the base example."[47]

Smith and Tompkins could certainly understand how Floyd and the other political general, Pillow, could have maneuvered to place the blame of surrender at Fort Donelson on the unfortunate General Buckner. Smith could probably recall quite vividly the rear guard duty the previous summer during the retreat from Carnifex Ferry. Smith had recorded in his diary that he felt it would suit Floyd's purpose to blame the defeat on both Tompkins and the Virginia volunteers under his command. Both of the former Confederate officers could fully identify with the plight of the captured general, Simon Bolivar Buckner.

There was a bright side to all of the recent war news. A man Smith admired greatly was soon to take command of the Confederate army. Jefferson Davis had made two key personnel moves which greatly pleased Isaac Smith; Davis had removed Floyd from command and had elevated Robert E. Lee to the command of the Army of Northern

[47] Smith wrote this letter to Tompkins on 19 March 1862. A copy of the letter is in the Virginia Historical Society collection.

Virginia.

He wrote Tompkins:

"I rejoice over the appointment of Genl Lee, as the vindication of a great man from the miserable criticism & political sycophancy, but I am alarmed for him. Had he been early in control, I should have no fear, but it is a Herculean task to bring order & success out of this confusion & the late overwhelming reverses. The license of the press will prove a sore annoyance to him -- Sir, what we call "Liberty of the Press' is a nuisance --

"These two acts of President Davis exhibit great firmness & resolution, & augur better for his government than anything I have yet seen."[48]

Lee has been under some severe criticism from the Southern press for his managing of the western Virginia campaign in which Smith and Tompkins had served. They both understood the reality of the military situation Lee had faced and the impact that the two feuding subordinate commanders had on the conduct of the campaign. It appears the Smith took exception to the press labelling the new commander "Evacuating Lee." The much maligned soldier's general was soon to redeem himself in the eyes of the press and the Confederate public, however.

This letter contained information for Colonel Tompkins regarding the solution to the dual threat faced by Smith and two other former members of the 22nd Virginia -- Union prison or being drafted into the Confederate military. They had made plans to leave the country:

"I have therefore determined to leave for Europe as early as possible, & the original object of this letter was to enquire whether we could not exchange money here, for your drafts upon your agents in Baltimore. Mrs. T -- & you both have spoken in my presence of means in Baltimore, & your desire to withdraw them. There can hardly be any confiscation of Mrs. T --'s property & if you would at all

48 Smith to Tompkins, 19 March 1862. Virginia Historical Society.

be benefited by such an exchange, I think it would be better for us to take your drafts, & collect from Europe. We have a number of schemes on hand to procure funds at as low a rate as possible: this is one, & we would all be much obliged if you will write Dr. J.P. Hale (care of James Hunter) Hanover Junction -- whether such an exchange is available and whether it would suit you to make it. Dr. Hale is to consider the different methods & to choose that which he thinks most certain. Stirling exchange is preferred, but it will probably be very high. Please write Dr. Hale at your first convenience, for if success attends our efforts we hope to get off as early as April 1st. I apprehend great difficulty in getting passports from the Confederate government. Hale and Q -- r rely confidenly on Mr. James Hunter's efforts through RMT Hunter. We have all three spoken of the pleasure it would afford for you to accompany us, but I can hardly hope you would be willing to leave your family."[49]

The Kanawha Riflemen had been formed from the young, well-educated aristocrats of the Charleston area. Many were lawyers and several were physicians, but most served outside of their chosen profession. "Hale" was John P. Hale, a physician from Charleston who commanded the "Kanawha Artillery", one of the original companies of the 22nd Virginia. Dr. Hale was a wealthy area resident who became the principle financier of the artillery battery which came to be called "Hale's Battery".

Q -- r probably was William A. Quarrier, one of the lieutenants of Hale's Battery. Both Hale and Quarrier had been original Kanawha Riflemen and had closely associated with Isaac Smith since the time of the Riflemen's formation. Both of these officers had resigned their commissions on the same day, August 21, 1861 and were in a situation similar to that of Isaac Smith.

Some of the bitterness of Smith and these men toward the actions of Floyd and Pillow at Fort Donelson was due to the fact that the some men of Hale's Battery were

49 Smith to Tompkins, 19 March 1862. Virginia Historical Society

captured when the fort fell to General Grant.

Since these young men had come from the best of society in western Virginia, they had excellent contacts amoung the aristocrats in the eastern counties. The man they looked to for assistance was James Hunter, obviously closely-related to R.M.T. Hunter, one of Virginia's most prominent politicians and no admirer of either Floyd or Wise. Hunter would have retained sufficient Confederate government contacts to be able to help in the acquisition of the passports needed by the three former officers in their plan to escape to Europe.

Smith completed the letter with a paragraph which illustrates the admiration he had for the military ability of both Colonel Tompkins and General Lee:

"I am confidentially expecting to hear of you being under or with General Lee in some capacity, which you can honorably accept, & which will be worthy of you -- I know you can serve under General Lee --"[50]

It is probably sufficient to understand from this section that the two men were close friends who had not been able to perform to their personal satisfaction while serving under Floyd or Wise. Smith obviously believed that Tompkins cound perform well while serving under the command of a soldier, not a politician.

Smith wrote again to Tompkins on March 21, 1862. He was writing to advise Tompkins that he was preparing to move. There was an great probability that Union troops would soon move into Greenbrier county and occupy Lewisburg and he was travelling to southwestern Virginia with Quarrier. They had made so many plans together that they couldn't afford to become separated at this point in their planning:

"In order that we may not become separated so far as previous arrangements would have required, I have determined to accompany Quarrier to the southwest, where

[50] Smith to Tompkins, 19 March 1862. Virginia Historical Society.

he expects to visit his brother, & we will there await advice from Dr. Hale."[51]

Smith could feel the Union or Confederate nets drawing closer and closer to all of them. With the threat of the Federal troops moving east along the turnpike they had previously fought to defend and rumors of another Confederate "retrograde movement", he began to worry that he would not be able to escape. He included this in his letter:

"I am much afraid of being entrapped in our efforts to get out -- If Va. is abandoned & I am caught in Cottondom unable to get out by land or sea, my misery will be complete."[52]

There is some significance to this paragraph beyond the obvious concern Smith has of being caught. Two major issues now appear for the first time in his letters. First, there is the concern that Virginia could be abandoned to the Northern forces as western Virginia had been -- the men of the 22nd Virginia had said it best: "West Virginia is sold out!" There had to be some level of concern that Virginia would be sold out as well. Second, Smith refers to the Confederacy as "Cottondom". This name is significant since it is shared between Smith and Tompkins and shows the relatively low esteem these former soldiers had for the Southern politicians who were busily losing the war through their meddling and mismanagement. Smith had been a luke-warm Rebel at best; referring to the United States flag he wrote: "In spite of my position, I love it still."

Tompkins had many of the same feelings and their previous duty under the two bungling generals, Floyd and Wise, had only served to reinforce their cynicism toward the Confederacy.

Smith heard from his friend, Dr. Hale, in early April, 1862, and wrote of his disappointment to Tompkins from

---

51 Smith to Tompkins, 21 March 1862. Virginia Historical Society.

52 *Ibid*

Marion, Virginia, on April 12:

"Dr. Hale having accepted a special commission for a special purpose, from the government, our trip has been postponed, & I regard it abandoned, although the Dr. still has it in view. The change on his part was very unexpected, & somewhat singular under the circumstances, but perfectly innocent on his part, and though it had been a great disappointment to me, I should be unwilling to have him know that the result of his trip to Richmond was so contrary to all my expectations. I am still anxious to go, & would do so if an agreeable companion could be had. There is said to be no difficulty in leaving from Matamoros. I should be delighted if you were at liberty to go, but presume you are not ... at present and have no definite plans or purposes."[53]

Hale had accepted a special commission from the Confederate government for a "special purpose" and this commission was obviously confidential as no specifics were mentioned in the letter. This "special purpose" is not clearly defined, but additional sketchy details point to clandestine activity. This is extremely difficult to conclusively prove and only circumstantial evidence remains, but there is a strong possibility that the "special purpose" involved espionage.

The western Virginians were well-suited for that purpose. Their accents more closely resembled those of the residents of the mid-west rather than the South and many of them were familar with Union territory from pre-war travelling. Hale and his small party seeking to avoid conscription into the Confederate army may have been offered an unusual option -- non-military and "special purpose" service.

It would require a great deal of either persuasion or coercion to force Isaac Smith into the service of the Confederacy a second time. He felt that he had been misused, abused, and then insulted. He had no intention of

---

53 Smith to Tompkins, 12 April 1862. Virginia Historical Society.

returning to military life and was very frank about his views in a letter to Tompkins that was handcarried by a mutual friend rather than trust it to the Confederate mail:

"Mr. Dryden's visit to Richmond affords me an opportunity of writing more freely than I care to do by mail ... but for the prevalence of martial law, I should probably return to Greenbriar & enjoy the comfortable home I had formed there -- when located again (& all thought of the European trip abandoned) I shall not retreat from the enemy's approach, my comfort and purse but illy afford such flights. Located near the center of the state if the government abandons it, I shall not feel it my duty to go further. It is impossible for me to remain much longer in uncertainty about my wife. All communication is cut off, & at this moment I cannot tell whether she is dead or alive. A great difficulty stares me in the face, in the conscription law. My determination as to entering the service is fixed -- like yourself I feel acquitted of further obligations to my state. I have given up everything man holds dear, & in return have met with insult and brutality from an officer whose authority I never intended to acknowledge, when I entered the service, & whose private and public character has always commanded my strong contempt. My state could give me no redress -- I would not ask it from any other source. In this feeling, there was much that influenced me in refusing to demand a court of inquiry. I have never said so much to you before -- If pressed by the conscription law I am in hopes with what money & property I have here & can command, exemption may be purchased by substitution, but if forced to extremities, unless some other mode of escape can be secured, I shall frankly state my views & go to prison. I am full to overflowing on the subject of the war, the government & matters generally, but will say nothing more ... & looking upon political matters with more or less distrust I do my utmost to keep my tongue still, lest my speech offend others or put myself into difficulty -- the same feelings made me shun society in Richmond."[54]

Here were expressions of very strong emotions in a man to whom honor meant so very much. Smith had decided to go to prison before returning to the Confederate army and he didn't bother to hide this fact from Colonel Tompkins. He had recently made a trip to Richmond where Tompkins had probably confided in a conversation that he "felt acquitted of further obligations" rather than risk such a statement in a personal letter. Tompkins obviously had detractors in Richmond -- there was a letter to the Confederate army's Adjutant General demanding the name of one of them -- and these personal enemies would use such a statement against him. Tompkins was far too intelligent to risk such a statement in the mail and following the visit, Smith felt safe in confiding his true feelings -- but only in a handcarried letter. Smith knew he could trust Tompkins with the knowledge that he planned to remain in Lewisburg when it was next occupied by the Federal troops since he was now aware that Tompkins had similar feelings. Both had served their state, had done their best, and had been betrayed by their "political general".

This distrust of the Confederate army had now extended to cover the entire system. They had little idea that the other side was behaving in similar ways. The democracy that they had known before the war was significantly changed on both sides since the war came.

While both were totally disillusioned about their former cause, they had to survive under the system of government where they were living. An offer of assistance was soon to arrive from an unlikely source -- their former comrade-in-arms in the early "Kanawha Brigade", John McCausland, had a suggestion for them.

The young, agressive McCausland wasn't a likely source of either advice or assistance. He had remained with Floyd's Brigade when it was ordered to Tennessee and his regiment, the 36th Virginia, was one of those evacuated

[54] Smith wrote this letter to Tompkins on 14 April 1862 and marked the letter "private". A copy of the letter is in the Virginia Historical Society collection.

from Fort Donelson when Floyd made his last escape from Yankee justice. Isaac Smith had recorded in the diary he kept for his wife that McCausland had been drunk during the rear-guard preparations that followed Floyd's retreat from Cotton Hill and neither Smith nor Tompkins appear especially close to McCausland and a sugestion from him for Smith to follow to reduce his "problem" was an unexpected discovery in Smith's letters. McCausland probably had a purpose in mind -- he was not prone to being overly sympathetic, later fully obeyed an order to burn Chambersburg, Pennsylvania, and died of old age after describing himself "an unreconstructed Rebel". McCausland was not thinking of Smith's welfare -- whatever the suggestion actually recommended.

The first mention of "McCausland's idea" came in a letter written by Smith to Tompkins on May 1, 1862. Smith had departed southwest Virginia and had moved in with a relative who lived about five miles south of Staunton, Virginia. He had received three letters from Tompkins which had been written on April 18, 20, and 22. This flurry of letters indicate a fast developing situation to which Smith would have to respond, if he were to be part of it. Two of the letters had been routed to Marion, Virginia, and a third had been delivered to Lewisburg. Tompkins was trying to contact Smith in the shortest time possible.

Smith's reply included additional information on his desire to get information about the welfare of his family in Charleston. He had not seen them in approximately ten months, but he had recently received a letter from his minister, who was at the time in Lewisburg, and expressed a desire to see Smith -- saying it was of great importance. Smith was becoming increasingly anxious to return home.

He read the proposal in Tompkins' letters and wrote:

"Under these circumstances it is impossible for me to discuss fully the propositions of your letter relative to the journey -- McCausland's idea at present best suits my fancy, but if successful I should stop in Canada."[55]

55 Smith to Tompkins, 1May 1862. Virginia Historical Society.

It is obvious that part of McCausland's suggestion involved a "journey" and that there was an element of potential failure implied -- "but if successful..."-- is a clear indication that there was some risk associated with the proposal. It was also into Union territory since the northern states would have to be transitted in order to get to Canada.

All of the new "ideas" had been proposed in the three letters recently received from Tompkins. The former Colonel was apparently considering a return to active Confederate service and had mentioned the possibility of Smith's return as well -- under Tompkins' command, of course. Smith wrote:

"I am deeply sensible of your great kindness in the proposition you made when expecting to enter the service. I am very grateful for all your goodness & assure you that if by any possibility I could be persuaded to enter the service it would be under your command -- But my dear sir, my duty to my family & especially my dear wife, appeal more strongly than aught beside; and it is not probable I shall enter the service at all -- indeed I can scarcely act conscientionably & do so."[56]

Isaac Smith had been attempting to travel from Staunton to Lewisburg to meet with his minister from Charleston. This was the only possible source of news regarding the welfare of his wife and family. The distance was not great, but the perils of such a journey forced Smith to cancel his travel plans. He explained some of his reasons in a letter to Tompkins on May 5, 1862:

"My hope of seeing Dr. Broun has been frustrated, & I have been obliged to abandon the trip to Lewisburg.

"The imprudence of my coming to Richmond is more evident than ever -- In this part of the country there is no safety for travellers, even along neighborhood roads -- Men travel about & arrest any citizen they meet without regard to law, and carry the prisoners to the army. You of course

[56] Smith to Tompkins, 1 May 1862. Virginia Historical Society.

would be subject to no such danger, but a quiet retinacy is my only safety. Until a few days since, the country from Staunton to Lewisburg offered every facility for the test of McCausland's idea -- It is not much changed now. Could you run up to Staunton & consult on the subject of your letters to me?"[57]

Once again, Smith refers to "McCausland's idea" and his willingness to test it. He and Tompkins do not discuss this suggestion in letters sent through the Confederate mail system since these could be opened by military censors. The fact that there was no obvious explaining of the "idea" in the letters is also a good indication that this involved clandestine activity.

It is also obvious that a great erosion of constitutional protection had occurrred in the area of Staunton and Smith was afraid of impressment into the Confederate army if he attempted to travel to Richmond to discuss plans in person with Tompkins. Smith completed the letter by informing Tompkins that he had received information

"that an event which was looked for in March, has resulted in giving me a son. I have no direct & no other intelligence -- my letters have not been sent to me. I have some suspicion that they had been detained by military authority, but I hope that this is a mistake. The condition of my wife & child I know nothing of & am in great anxiety -- Don't mention my suspicions -- it may be & I earnestly hope is erroneous."[58]

Additional letters sent by Smith discussed the progress of the war, especially the Southern defeat at Lewisburg where the 22nd Virginia suffered such heavy casualties. An additional topic was their agreed lack of faith in the newspaper reporting on both sides. They felt that the newspaper articles were generally misleading and were intended to "fire the soldier's zeal", in Isaac Smith's

57 Smith to Tompkins, 5 May 1862. Virginia Historical Society.
58 *Ibid*

opinion. Smith was also concerned about the possible invasion of northern territory and the reaction of the Northern soldiers when they eventually re-entered Virginia:

"...I believe the time to carry out the purpose spoken of more favorable now than ever heretofore; & that after the movement now contemplated by the army assembling here, the difficulties & dangers will be greatly increased -- The government heeding the cry for invasion of the enemy's country evidently intended to push a column into Pennsylvania or Maryland, most probably the former -- In my opinion the time for this movement has passed; the column will be too far advanced beyond the base of defense & from re-inforcements -- it could be attacked in flank and rear at any point from Harrisonburg northward; it will have to draw its supplies from too distant a point; & whilst Jackson may make a foray & a successful one, he must be forced to fall back very rapidly. The consequences of such an incursion I can scarcely conceive; you who have witnessed the temper & spirit of the soldiery in the western campaigns, & from the character of the army (Texans, Mississippians &c) now serving here, can form an appropriate idea of the course they would adopt in the enemy's country -- the North will be aroused & exasperated to an extent hitherto unknown, & the war from that time forward will become a war of savage barbarity on both sides. At an earlier period, the South might possibly have been perfectly willing the war should assume such a character, but with the enemy controlling & occupying seven states, & enough of the remaining six to make one large state, the experiment is at least hazardous if not fatal -- The occupying and invading Yankee armies will not only commit such excesses as they have already committed, but they will exceed if possible the outrages attributed to them so freely by the papers, for the purpose of firing the soldier's zeal in the Southern cause. The temper of the people & the army now is to respect nothing in the enemy's country neither property, age or sex -- Devastation & fires will mark their course. The country expects and demands this of them, & they will not be slow to gratify the country in their wish. I have no idea that a Southern army can occupy Northern territory;they can only enter it & retire after inflicting all the injury they possibly can. Occupying the advanced position Jackson will have to do, retreat is inevitable -- His last advance shows that fact -- his army was strong enough to check Fremont & Shields together, but he was forced to retreat to Port Republic before he could fight. Until he reached that place his flanks and rear were not secure.

"Under all circumstances I fear the course I have determined to pursue will be too unsafe. There are other causes too operating very strongly to make it necessary I should make some change. I have always believed in the feasibility of McCausland's suggestions, but should choose a different direction, in which its accomplishment would be very easy. I am very much concerned & unhappy & would give a great deal for a short interview with you, but cannot meet you. I have no definite plan in view & ask if you adopt any course relative to these matters, I beg you to give me an opportunity to join you.

"The suggestions I have made in regard to affairs here, have first presented themselves to me. I believe Jackson will invade Pennsylvania & I equally believe he will be compelled to retreat & I'm further south than he now is -- Then wo betide the individuals who fall into the enemy's hands -- If anything is done therefore I believe it should be done now."[59]

The suggestion McCausland made to Smith -- through Tompkins -- may have involved a plan to have Smith and his associates remain within Union lines once the Federal army was able to permanently occupy the territory where they were residing. They could ask for sanctuary since they were resigned Confederate officers originally from Unionist areas of Virginia and were also seeking to avoid the Confederate draft. This "cover story" would probably hold up under close Federal scrutiny, especially since

59 Smith to Tompkins, 17 July 1862. Virginia Historical Society.

Smith's father was one of the more prominent Unionists in the state. The acceptance of their story would allow them to return to their homes in Charleston where they could assume more covert duties for the South.

Smith argued that the timing of the operation was critical. It was one thing to be a Confederate draft resister caught up in a Union advance, but would be another matter entirely to be captured after a devastating Confederate invasion into Pennsylvania. The resulting death and destruction would make their potential captors far less understanding under those circumstances and as Smith wrote "...wo betide the individuals who fall into the enemy's hands." He definitely preferred to begin implementation of the plan as soon as possible, rather than wait until the probable advance was repulsed.

Dr. Hale was apparently able to travel -- possibly as a result of his special commission from the government for that "special purpose" -- and he met with Tompkins in Richmond. Tompkins reviewed the letters that Smith had sent to Hale and agreed with the general plan they had outlined. Interestingly, some portion of the plan involved Tompkins' family. Whether the family was part of a contingency plan to move to Staunton where they would be safer than in Richmond, if the Confederate capitol came under direct attack, or Tompkins had planned to move them there to be safe during his absence is unclear. The letter from Smith written on July 2, 1862 clearly indicated that the family was involved in the plan:

"Dr. H -- tells me you saw my recent letters to him, & are much disposed to pursue the same course, if at all admissible by the situation of your family. I can only hope both you and he will at once consider to adopt that course... If I had known your views, arrangements could have been made surely would have been satisfactory. My relative has a good, large substantial, but plain brick house, with all the necessary out houses, stables, &c, within 3/4 of a mile of this our residence, which until a week since was vacant -- It was furnished with everything necessary doubtless for comfortable living, having been occupied by a granddaughter's family, & left recently because her husband has been taken to the wars. I could have rented house, furniture, pasturage, cows, & everything of that sort for you at a reasonable rate..."[60]

The relationship that began as the Kanawha valley regiments were organized developed into a bond of trust and confidence. Both Smith and Tompkins confided in one another on subjects that could have resulted in condemnation by many of their acquaintances, if these came to the attention of the Confederate authorities. At this stage of the war, Confederate censors would not want to read in opened mail that Smith would "frankly state his views and go to prison."

But at the same time, Smith was apparently willing to go along with "McCausland's idea", a plan that could have resulted with Smith completing a journey in Canada. McCausland wasn't explaining the proposal directly to Smith, he was going through Tompkins. Was this because McCausland knew that he had little influence over the former major and was also fully aware that Smith greatly admired Tompkins and would respond to nearly any suggestion made by the former colonel? This remains unclear, but it is obvious from Smith's letters that he would be willing to help Colonel Tompkins in any endeavor in which his help was requested. If Tompkins was developing agents who would loyally follow his orders while they were in Union territory, Smith was going to be a loyal one.

Smith wrote again on July 23. It would appear that Tompkins was on his way to Staunton or Charlottesville to initiate the first stages of 'McCausland's plan". Smith was concerned that he would pass Tompkins on the road and miss the initial contact. He felt that neither Tompkins nor Hale fully understood the difficulty he had in moving around safely:

"I meet difficulty upon the first increment. The

60 Smith to Tompkins, 2 July 1862. Virginia Historical Society.

Provost-marshall here gives a pass to every one who goes on the cars & examines them as to liability to service &c before the pass is given. The private and public roads are scoured by the provost guard who question and arrest every man in the county liable to service. I see waggon loads of men, taken by the door here everyday or two, many of them I learn tied and handcuffed. These difficulties of mine neither you nor the Dr. seem to appreciate. If you could be with me, the application for passports might be made by you in my absence and my title (defunct as it is) might save me. I will telegraph you also -- Shall I come down or can you come up & help me off -- telegraph your reply to James G Cochran -- Staunton who goes to town for me & attends to this matter.

"I most earnestly entreat you not to act without me. Had I received your letter at the proper time I should have been at Charlottesville at the appointed time. I should most heartily & bitterly deplore any action on your part which I could not be permitted to share."[61]

Things were beginning to come together for the plotters. Hale and Tompkins were preparing to travel and were making arrangements for passports for their trip. They were either planning to go to another country or were going to complete their journey in a foreign country, possibly Canada, as Smith had previously mentioned. One thing is certain -- whether Tompkins was going to safety or into mortal danger -- Isaac Smith wanted to be there to share either with his former commander and close friend.

Smith wrote to Tompkins again of September 1, 1862, and most of the letter centered on Smith's need for a pair of "pantaloons". He asked Tompkins to obtain a pair in black or mulberry -- anything other than grey. He appeared to be rather tired of this particular color. The most informative section of the letter was in the postscript.

Smith had been unable to get the letter to the post office and wrote the postscript on the following day, September 2:

---

61 Smith to Tompkins, 23 July 1862. Virginia Historical Society.

"Have just received three letters from home, of Aug 19 & 20th. All well -- They say that they have every comfort & luxury.

"Have also learned that Loring's force had received orders -- the cavalry to go to Cumberland Gap -- If so I shall expect to see you at once --"[62]

Smith was correct in his assessment of Loring's potential troop movement. The Confederates had been waiting for an opportunity to move against the Union troops in the Kanawha valley and with the capture of the official correspondence in Pope's letter book, Lee learned that Cox had been ordered to transfer the bulk of his troops out of western Virginia. Lee wrote to the Secretary of War advising that he had ordered Loring to move west. Lee first informed the War Department of his plans on August 23.

Lee wrote later that Cox was departing for duty with the Army of the Potomac and that:

"I deem it important that General Loring should be informed of the force opposed to him and directed to clear the valley of the Kanawha and then operate northwardly, so as to join me in the valley of Virginia."[63]

Now that Cox and his Federal regiments were on the move -- toward Washington, D.C. -- Lee was quick to order the Confederates under the command of W.W. Loring to move back into western Virginia. Lee felt that their large force would quickly roll over the 5000 men in the garrisons under the Union commander. A well-planned diversionary attack was also planned.

Confederate cavalrymen under the command of Albert Gallatin Jenkins moved into western Virginia to the north of the Kanawha valley on August 24. This was probably the cavalry movement mentioned by Smith, but the most interesting part of the letter is the phrase "... I shall see you

62 Smith to Tompkins, 1 September 1862. Virginia Historical Society.

63 Lee to George Randolph, *Official Records*, Vol. XII, Part III, pg. 943

at once". It would appear that the movement of the Confederate troops toward the Kanawha valley was a signal to initiate the first phase of "McCausland's idea".

There is very little information available to support this conclusion, but it appears the Isaac Smith and Dr.Hale followed the invading troops of General Loring into the Kanawha valley and rejoined their families in Charleston. The occupation of the valley was quite short and the Union army soon forced the Confederates to once again evacuate the strategic valley. Cox had returned and Smith was now faced with a final decision -- he could evacuate with the retreating Rebels and risk the forced conscription awaiting him or he could remain in Charleston (possibly according to their plan) and risk Federal justice.

He wrote again to the Colonel on October 9, 1862 to advise him that the mare and saddle lent by Tompkins for the trip were being returned to Matthew Arbuckle's farm for Tompkins' eventual recovery. Smith would not be coming. The text of the letter seems to indicate that he was dropping out of their plan to remain with his family. He explained:

"I write you in a state of great distress. It is probable that no trial has been presented to me which has borne so hardly upon me as my present position. My decision which is perhaps fully made is one of the most important of my life, & will affect my interests & happiness for years to come --

"In accordance with views & opinions hitherto expressed I have determined to remain at home, but I have never conceived the struggle & pain it would cost me to carry out that determination. I seem to be cutting off forever from the friends & companions of youth & manhood & from all the gratifying associations of life. If I could have found any means to transport my family & could have forseen any means of support for them in the east, my purpose could not have withstood promptings which impel me to a different course. But although reproach & vituperation will surely fall upon me I have too long considered & concluded upon the propriety of this course to abandon it from fear of public opinion. A calm consideration of the whole matter when tranquility shall have been restored will with my true friends acquit me of errors & at any rate accuse my judgement only. My sympathies for the success of the Southern arms & also my aversion of the leading spirit of this revolution in the Northern states -- the cause cannot precisely indicate, but I seem to feel it sensibly. Enough of this however -- the alternative to leave my wife & child & take my place in the Southern Army perhaps never to see or hear from them again, or to remain, meet with my father whom I have been so anxious to see & submit to Yankee mercy -- I cannot hesitate. I will dare almost anything than undergo another separation from those I love, more especially when I can find no objection to that course which reason suggests. Prejudice and excessive enthusiasm will find many which calm reflection would condemn."[64]

The Yankees and Smith's father returned soon after the last Confederate cavalrymen abandoned the area near Charleston. Cox crossed Elk River and entered the city during the evening of October 29, 1862. Smith relied on the "Yankee mercy" which was mentioned in the letter to Tompkins and he was interviewed by the Federal authorities. He was apparently found to be suitably reformed from his Confederate background to be able to reside within Federally-occupied territory. He was apparently not required to take an oath of allegience to the United States -- Cox felt that "test oaths" were useless -- but his father and father-in-law posted a bond for him. The bond permitted him to "reside within the lines of the Federal army" and was signed by General Cox.[65]

Smith now had managed to get his wish. He was with his wife and family, could attempt to persuade his father to a "position of neutrality", and was far from the

64 Smith to Tompkins, 9 October 1862. Virginia Historical Society.

65 A copy of the bond is located in the National Archives, Record Group 109.

impressment gangs of the Confederate Provost Marshall that were constantly scouring the area for new Confederate "recruits". He was finally safe, but there was a single factor which he had not taken into consideration -- his loyalty to Christopher Tompkins.

No letters between these two during this period were preserved, but there must have been some correspondence. Letters could have been sent to Smith through the Federal postal system much like Ellen Tompkins used with her sister in Delaware and his letters could have reached Tompkins. There were also frequent visits into the area by Confederate scouts and partisans who could have been used to deliver messages between the two. One thing is certain -- Smith and Tompkins continued to correspond. A letter was sent to Tompkins from Charleston which was written on February 18, 1863 which is filled with interesting information:

"Dear Col -- I wrote to you about three weeks since,& hope you received my letter."[66]

Tompkins had received the letter. Tompkins kept a diary throughout 1863 and recorded on January 3, 1863 that he had received a letter from "Mjr Smith." It mentioned others people of interest to Tompkins:

"Richmond. Weather perfectly beautiful. A letter this morning from Mjr Smith ...from Meehan to the [three illigible words] begging his interpretation for his release from the Yankees. So much for overzealous friendship..."[67]

The "overzealous friendship" comment probably referred to their mutual acquaintence, Meehan. From the remainder of Smith's letter, it is obvious that they were having problems with this man.

66 Smith to Tompkins, 18 February 1863. Virginia Historical Society.

67 Tompkins, Christopher Q., *Personal Diary for 1863*, Virginia Historical Society.

Smith continued his letter with information about Ellen Tompkins -- she was back in Baltimore, again, and may have served as the conduit of letters between the two friends. Smith wrote:

"Since then I have heard again from Mrs. T--, & my letter had not reached her. I wrote again, & shall still write another letter. She spoke somewhat of trying this route, but gave no positive indication of what course she would take in reference to her return. A passport by Fortress Monroe had been refused, but I presume some other way was open, for she spoke of remaining but two weeks at No. 7 Cathedral Street. It has been a great disappointment not to hear from Mrs. T more directly since my own letters were written. I have felt a great disposition to go to see her -- but it is not convenient to my diminished funds. Dr. H hopes to meet her, he has gone to the western states & will visit New York before his return, & Baltimore also if Mrs. T is there when he is in east."[68]

This letter reveals a great deal of information. Ellen Tompkins was in Baltimore and Smith was able to get (at least) letters to Tompkins -- who remained in Richmond. The letters had to get through the Union lines and this again implies a formal mechanism such as would be operated by an intelligence organization.

It is also interesting that Dr. Hale had also come to Charleston with Smith, just as they had probably planned when discussing "McCausland's idea". Hale was not only there, he was travelling all over the North. He was in the "western states", was going the New York, and had the freedom to go to Baltimore, if he chose. He was an especially mobile former Confederate officer who probably on a "bond" similar to that of Smith with the Federal authorities. The original planners were together in Union-controlled territory and they were corresponding with Christopher Tompkins -- possibly through Ellen Tompkins, now conveniently placed at No. 7 Cathedral

[68] Smith to Tompkins, 18 February 1863. Virginia Historical Society.

Street in Baltimore, a very curious arrangement!

Smith now explained some of the difficulty he was having with one of the others in his former Confederate group, a man named Meehan. This was the same individual referred to by Tompkins in his January 3, 1863, diary entry. Smith wrote:

"Meehan is here & is well but fretting of course -- his great difficulty lies I think in his excitable temperament. I have heard that a passport was promised him (during my absence from this state) & Meehan talked so much on the subject that it was deemed imprudent to permit him to go, lest his want of caution rather than want of integrity, might prove prejudicial. This was told me by Meehan's friends & my own since my return. It may, or may not be correct. Meehan's only difficulty is his inability to get to Richmond, he is under no other restraint, but is much annoyed. You recollect a trip he made to the country & its results; he is eager to continue so successful a beginning, & it is grieving him to know he can't. Dr. H and I think this weighs more heavily on his mind than anything else."[69]

Smith had been out of the state and Meehan was to be issued a passport for a trip. More interesting details emerge on the relationship among the conspirators involved in "McCausland's idea". Dr. Hale was present in a leadership role, possibly since he had accepted that special commission from the Confederate government for a "special purpose". Smith was also in a position of trust and respect within the group composed of both Smith's and Meehan's friends.

More curious is the fact that Meehan had made a very succesful initial trip for the group and *Tompkins was aware* of both the trip and the results.

Here was a very unusual situation. Travellers from Union-held territory who moved about as they chose -- Dr. Hale had travelled to the "western states", New York, and would have travelled to Baltimore, if there was an

[69] Smith to Tompkins, 18 February 1863. Virginia Historical Society.

opportunity to meet with Ellen Tompkins. Smith had made a trip out of the state and Meehan had made a very successful journey into the "country".

It still appears that they were either collecting information for the Confederacy or were serving as couriers to areas where there was a great deal of pro-Confederate sentiment. There was a very active "Copperhead movement" in many of the Northern states and Smith could have been involved in coordinating with them.

If this was true, however, why did Smith frequently finish his letters with anti-war statements or at a minimum, appear to be at odds with the Confederate government's policies? He could always be expected to write something to indicate that he was not in favor with the rebel government or he would remind Tompkins of the way he was abused while an officer. He wrote in the February 18 letter:

"I am satisfied our sentiments on the subject of the war are coincident, as they have always been hitherto, events since we separated, have affected my views in the same manner, they have for ours. By events I mean government policy not battles. Battles test strength, not opinions -- Satisfied that I have been & shall be roundly abused by many, my conscience finds nothing to accuse. I have been thoroughly & entirely consistent from beginning to end & will remain so."[70]

Smith was not a stupid man. He had learned when he had his initial encounter with General Floyd back on Cotton Hill that he had to be careful about what he wrote in his diary. He began to tailor his entries to be able to defend his account of events, if ever brought under charges by the general and the diary used against him. It is quite likely that Smith's habit of entering such paragraphs in his letters to Tompkins, while avoiding writing any incriminating information, could be used in his defense if the letters were ever intercepted by Federal authorities. Espionage was a

[70] Smith to Tompkins, 18 February 1863. Virginia Historical Society.

serious crime at the time and Smith, an attorney, was well aware of the punishment. He was probably keeping a viable alibi option open in his letters -- just in case it was ever needed. The alibi could mean the difference between a short period of incarceration rather than execution, if he were ever exposed.

Unfortunately, the remaining letters from Isaac Smith to Colonel Tompkins which were located were written after the war. They dealt primarily with business matters -- at one time Tompkins was trying to purchase the cables salvaged from the destroyed bridge over Gauley River, but Smith reported that the cable had been cut into small pieces to transport more easily and the deal was cancelled. There had to be more letters exchanged between these two, but nothing has been discovered which would help open the story further. There was only one additional entry in a story by Tompkins which indicates that these people involved in "McCausland's idea" were active until the end of the war.

Tompkins wrote a short narrative in which he described the fall of Richmond and in it he pointed out some unusual events that point to additional clandestine activities on his part.

First, he wrote that:

"About sunrise whilst standing in my front porch I spied three horsemen coming up the road. They proved to be Gov. Smith, his son Bell & boy George. They were from Richmond since 1 A.M. There was a sad expression about the Gov's face & evidence enough of fatigue & exposure ... A good breakfast, warm room & cordial greeting, combined to give him a nap which no doubt proved very refreshing. Everything ready they left about 11 o'clock for Lynchburg."[71]

The Governor of Virginia came to Tompkins when he

[71] Tompkins, Christopher Q., "The Occupation of Richmond, April 1865," edited by William M.E. Rachal, *The Virginia Magazine of History and Biography*, Vol. 73, 1965, pg. 191

was forced to leave Richmond as it fell to the Federal army. That alone would not be suspicious, but this was not the first visit by the Governor's son, Bell.

Tompkins mentioned the governor's son in a diary entry on February 14, 1863. The younger Smith had come to Tompkins and the diary entry told about it:

"Peter Bell Smith arrived & left a package & also $100 in gold from Balt--"[72]

Why would the son and personal aide of the Confederate governor visit the former Colonel and leave behind both a package and $100 in gold, possibly both from Baltimore -- Union territory? Why was Tompkins the recipient and what was he supposed to do with these items? No other clues were discovered in the remainder of the diary. Tompkins, like Isaac Smith, was not a fool and he avoided keeping any records that could later incriminate him in a Federal court.

One other event recorded by Tompkins in his story of the fall of Richmond is even more interesting. He was visited by another Virginia official needing help. Tompkins wrote:

"I had not the heart to send him away on foot, but gave him a mule & put a boy upon another to carry him to the R. Road. The boy came back the next day, minus the mules. Mr. Baxter took him to Flat Rock & the boy started back & got two miles when he met a soldier who dismounted him & in a pencil note politely informed me the Yankees were close upon his track & he regretted the necessity of pressing my mules, but must do it, signing himself, naively enough Jas. N. Snead, singularly enough the initials Issac N. Smith."[73]

Several questions quickly develop after reading this paragraph. First, why would a soldier fleeing from the

72 Tompkins, *Personal Diary for 1863*

73 Tompkins, "Occupation of Richmond," pg. 192

Union army stop to write a note to Tompkins to apologise? Second, Why did he bother to sign the note, if he were not already known to the colonel? Third, why was Tompkins concerned that the soldier had naively used a name which were the initials of Isaac N. Smith?

One likely answer to these questions -- Tompkins was irritated that Smith had chosen to travel in an alias which so closely resembled his true name! Smith probably became even more active in his travels for the Colonel as the war went on and one reason for the lack of correspondence between the two until after the war may have resulted from the fact that all letters had to be destroyed since they contained so much incriminating evidence from their activities as they carried out "McCausland's idea".

## EPILOG

As the creaking of harness, swearing of teamsters, and the thunderous crashing of both cannon and musketry faded away, the solitary eagle returned to repeat its periodic patrols over the mountain valleys and ridges. It had witnessed a great deal of violence -- particularily during the initial phases of the war. Lately, however, the blue-clothed men had been able to dominate the area and only small, ragged bands of the brown or gray men would be seen occasionally as they slipped quietly through the mountains. Lately, the eagle had experienced some peace and quiet.

Now that the flashing noises and hurried movements of large groups of men had stopped, the large bird was able to range freely throughout the area and observe the changes that had occurred. There had been several major differences.

The large farm on the mountain top was completely ruined. The large house on the farm which had been occupied by the lovely woman and her children was missing. Only ashes and a ruined foundation remained. The small town at the junction of the two rivers was missing its' bridge and even the small church on the hill was missing. Like the house on the mountain, all that remained were ashes and blackened timbers. There were piles of coiled wire rope piled on the riverbank -- all that remained of the replacement bridge which met the same fate as its predecessor when it was also destroyed by a retreating army. A few men wandered about quietly reviewing their past and probable future in the devastated region.

Small groups of the ragged gray or brown men could be seen returning, but not in the numbers who so proudly marched away with their friends. Where the others were located was a mystery to the eagle, but Beuhring Jones remembered:

"...And the 'Dixie Rifles'; where are they now? Alas!

some are sleeping beneath the magnolias of the south; some on the hills of Fredericksburg; some at Mechanicsville, Cold Harbour, and Frazier's farm; some at Piney, Princeton and the Narrows; some at Cloyd's farm; some at Piedmont, Winchester, Kernstown, Cedar creek, Fisher's hill, and on the banks of the Opequon; some at the White Sulphur, Richmond, and Lynchburg; some at Camps Morgan and Chase; some at Point Lookout and Elmira; some have gone home with broken constitutions; some maimed and almost helpless for life. With their gallant comrades of the glorious 'old 60th,' they everywhere bore their full share of suffering, and danger, and death; and, when at the close of the war, they, with streaming eyes and aching hearts, turned away from the 'Conquered Banner'... In that sad hour, not more than a dozen of the original Dixie Rifles answered at roll-call."[1]

The war was over and the area could begin to repair the damage, but the human losses could never be replaced. The area lost some of its finest men to the war and even among the survivors there were the "broken constitutions" and maimed bodies which had to begin new lives.

The Civil War was a national tragedy and strongly impacted on the people of the Kanawha Valley. Rebuilding was difficult in an area where there was little capital to invest and few reasons to invest, even if money were available. The ferry left in place at Gauley Bridge by the victorious Federal troops was to serve passengers for a long time. It wasn't replaced with a modern bridge until 1925. The area was without a highway bridge for sixty-three years after the Union army's suspension bridge was destroyed during Lightburn's retreat in 1862 and the economic growth that generally accompanies excellent transportation was denied the area. The Civil War had a long-term effect on the region -- an effect which was felt well into this century.

[1] Jones, Beuhring H., "The Dixie Rifles", *History of Fayette County, West Virginia*, edited by J.T. Peters and H.B. Carden, Jarrett Printing Company, Charleston: 1926, pg. 241- 242

## Bibliography

Ambler, Charles H. *West Virginia: Stories and Biographies.* Chicago: Rand-McNally 1942

Ambler, Charles H. *West Virginia: The Mountain State.* New York: Prentice-Hall 1946

Andrews, J. Cutler. *The South Reports the Civil War.* Princeton: University Press 1970

Atkinson, George W. *Bench and Bar of West Virginia.* Charleston: Virginia Law Book Co. 1919

Bahlmann, William E. *The Journal of the Greenbrier Historical Society.* Lewisburg: October 1969

Bailes, Clarice L. *West Virginia History.* Charleston: West Virginia Historical Society. October, 1944

Blackwell, Lyle M. *Gauley Bridge: The Town and its First Church.* Parsons: McClain 1980

Boehm, Robert B. "The Civil War in Western Virginia: The Decisive Campaigns of 1861"(Thesis) Colombus: Ohio State University 1957

Brown, James B. *West Virginia History.* Charleston: West Virginia Historical Society July, 1943

Burton, Pierre. *Flames Across the Border: The Canadian-American Tragedy -- 1813-1814.* Boston: Atlantic Monthly Press 1981

Childers, William. *West Virginia History.* Charleston: April, 1966

Clark, W.C. *The West Virginia Review.* Charleston: November 1930

Cook, Roy B. *The West Virginia Review.* Charleston: October, 1925

Cook, Roy B. *The West Virginia Review.* Charleston: October, 1931

Cox, Jacob D. *Battles and Leaders.* Secaucus, N.J.: Castle

Cox, Jacob D. *Military Reminiscences of the Civil War.* New York: Charles Scribners 1900

Cohen, Stan. *Kanawha County Images: A Bicentenial History 1788-1988.* Charleston: Pictorial Histories 1988

Cohen, Stan. *West Virginia History.* Charleston: April, 1965

Cullum, George W. *Biographical Register of Officers and Graduates of the U.S. Military Academy at West Point, N.Y.* New York: D. Van Nostrand

Davis, James A. *51st Virginia Infantry.* Lynchburg: H.E. Howard 1984

Dickinson, Jack L. *8th Virginia Cavalry.* Lynchburg: H.E. Howard 1986

Estvan, Bela. *War Pictures From the South.* Freeport, New York: Books for Libraries Press 1971

Fitzgerald, Gertrude B. *United Daughters of the Confederacy Magazine.* January, 1957

Hassler, Frederick W.B. *The West Virginia Historical Magazine.* Charleston: West Virginia Historical Society January 1905

Hayes, Rutherford B. *Diary and Letters of Rutherford Birchard Hayes.* Ohio State Archaeological Society: 1922

Hazelton, Joseph F. *Spies, Scouts, and Heroes of the Great Civil War.* Jersey City: Star Publishing 1892

Heth, Henry. *Civil War History.* 1962
Hodges, M.S. *West Virginia Legislative Handbook and Manual and Official Register.* Charleston: 1929
Horton,Joshua and Teverbaugh, Solomon. *A History of the Eleventh Regiment, Ohio Volunteer Regiment.* Dayton: W.J. Shuey 1866
Hotchkiss, Jed. *Confederate Military History.* Dayton: Morningside 1975
Howe, Henry. *The Times of the Rebellion in the West.* Cincinnati: Howe's Subscription Book Service 1867
Hull, Forrest. *The West Virginia Review.* Charleston: October 1926
Hull, Forrest. *The West Virginia Review.* Charleston: West Virginia Historical Society June, 1938
Humphries, Milton W. *Military Operations in Fayette County, West Virginia.* (Privately Printed) 1920
Husley, Val. *West Virginia History.* Charleston: West Virginia Historical Society
Jones, Beuhring H. *The Sunny Land.* Baltimore: Innes Co. 1868
Kincaid, Mary E. *West Virginia History.* Charleston: West Virginia Historical Society July, 1953
Kelley, Donald B. *West Virginia History.* Charleston: West Virginia Historical Society
Klement, Frank. *West Virginia History.* Charleston: West Virginia Historical Society April, 1947
Laidley, W.S. *History of Charleston and Kanawha County and Representative Citizens.* Chicago: Richmond-Arnold Publishing
Lyle, W.W. *Lights and Shadows of Army Life.* Cincinnati: 1865
McKinney, Tim. *Fayette County in the Civil War.* Charleston: Pictorial Histories 1988
McPherson, James M. *Battle Cry of Freedom.* New York: Oxford University Press 1988
Mahone, John K. *History of the Second Seminole War: 1835-1842.* Gainsville, Florida: University of Florida Press 1967
Moore, Frank. *The Rebellion Record.* New York: G.P. Putnam 1862
Official Records. *The War of the Rebellion: A Compilation of the Official Records of the Union and Confederate Armies,* Series 1, Vol. V.
Peters, J.T. and Carden, H.B. *History of Fayette County, West Virginia.* Charleston: Jarrett Printing 1926
Reid, Whitelaw. *Ohio in the War: Her Statesmen, Her Generals and Soldiers.* Colombus: 1868
Reynolds, William C. *Diary of William Clark Reynolds.* (Unpublished) West Virginia Archives
Riddle, Thomas J. *Southern Historical Society Papers.* Jan-Dec 1883
Roler, A.B. *The Diary of A.B. Roler.* (Unpublished) Virginia Historical Society
Scott, J.L. *36th Virginia Infantry.* Lynchburg: H.E. Howard 1987
Scott, William F. *Philander P. Lane: Colonel of Volunteers in the Civil War.* (Privately printed) 1920

Sedinger, James. *Border Rangers.* (Unpublished) West Virginia Archives
Smith, Isaac N. Personal correspondence. Virginia Historical Society
Sprague, John T. *The Origin, Progress, and Conclusion of the Florida War.* Gainsville, Florida: University of Florida Press 1964
Stutler, Boyd B. *The West Virginia Review.* Charleston: January 1934
Stutler, Boyd B. *West Virginia in the Civil War.* Charleston: Education Foundation 1966
Time-Life Series. *Spies, Scouts, and Raiders -- Irregular Operations.* Alexandria: 1985
Tompkins, Christopher Q. *Personal Diary for 1863.* Virginia Historical Society
Tompkins, Christopher Q. *The Virginia Magazine of History and Biography.* Richmond: Virginia Historical Society 1965
Tompkins, Ellen W. *The Virginia Magazine of History and Biography.* Richmond: Virginia Historical Society October 1961
Turner, Mary E. *The West Virginia Review.* Charleston: West Virginia Historical Society December, 1941- February, 1942
Vance, John L. "Lightburn's Retreat." Fayetteville, W.Va.: *The Fayette Tribune.* (Undated copy in the West Virginia Archives)
Wallace, Lee A., Jr. *A Guide to Virginia Military Organizations*: 1861-1865. Lynchburg: H.E. Howard 1986
White, Robert. *Confederate Military History.* Dayton: Morningside 1975
Williams, Harry T. *Hayes of the Twenty-third: The Civil War Officer.* New York: Alfred A. Knopf 1965
Wilmot, David. *America, Great Crises in our History as told by its Makers.* Chicago: Veterans of Foreign Wars 1925

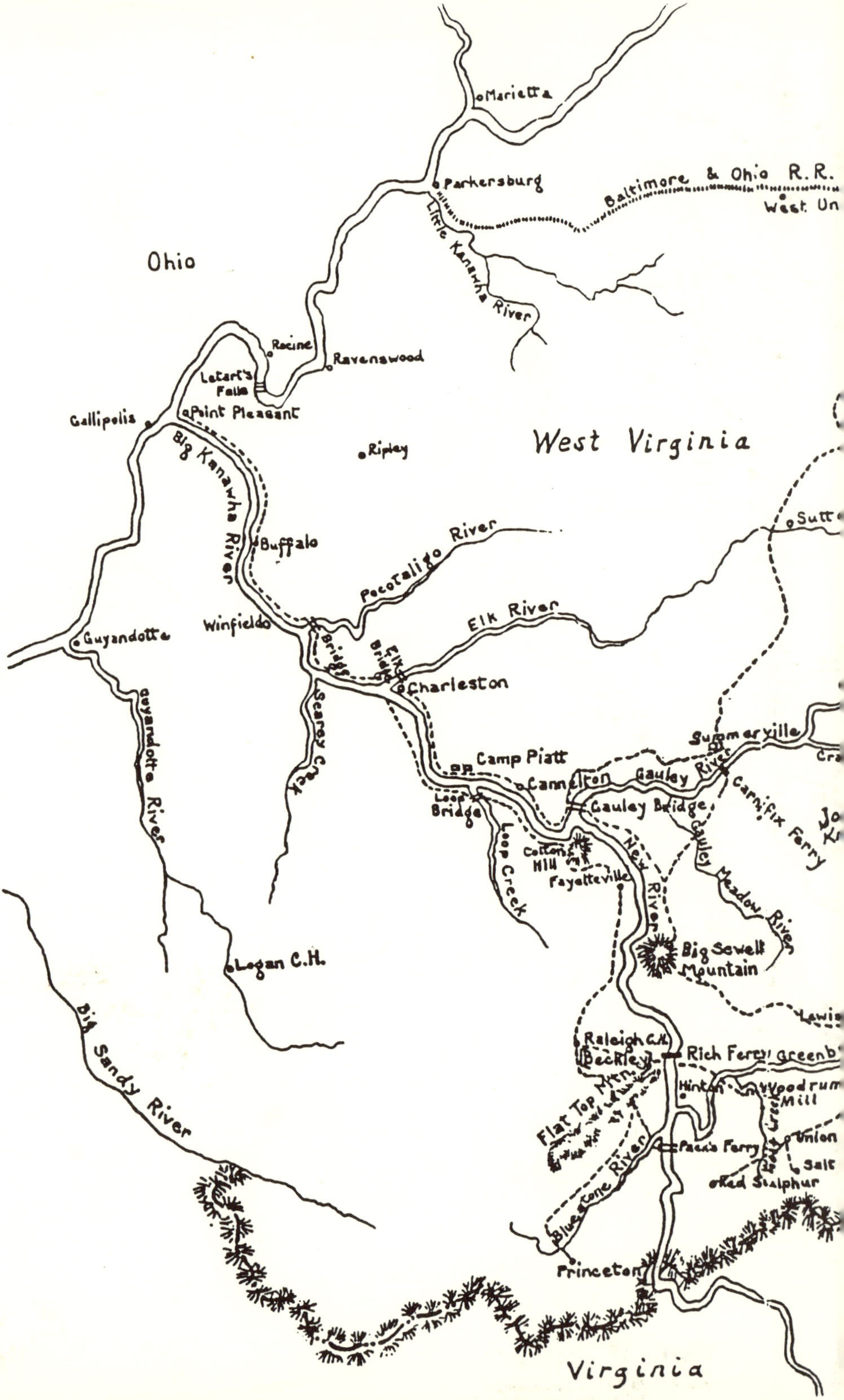
Marietta
Parkersburg
Baltimore & Ohio R.R.
West Un
Little Kanawha River
Ohio
Racine
Ravenswood
Letart's Falls
Point Pleasant
Gallipolis
Ripley
West Virginia
Big Kanawha River
Buffalo
Pocotaligo River
Elk River
Winfield
Guyandotte
Bridge
Elk Bridge
Charleston
Searey Creek
Guyandotte River
Camp Piatt
Cannelton
Gauley River
Summerville
Carnifix Ferry
Loop Bridge
Gauley Bridge
Gauley
Cotton Hill
Loop Creek
Fayetteville
New River
Meadow River
Big Sewell Mountain
Logan C.H.
Big Sandy River
Raleigh C.H.
[Beckley]
Rich Ferry
Hinton
Woodrum Mill
Flat Top Mtn.
Pack's Ferry
Union
Salt
Red Sulphur
Bluestone River
Princeton
Virginia